Networked Reenactments

July 2021

NETWORKED REENACTMENTS

Stories Transdisciplinary Knowledges Tell

KATIE KING

Foreword by
Donna Haraway

DUKE UNIVERSITY PRESS
Durham & London 2011

© 2011 Duke University Press
All rights reserved
Printed in the United States of America on acid-free paper ∞

Designed by Jennifer Hill
Typeset in Chaparral Pro by Keystone Typesetting, Inc.

Library of Congress Cataloging-in-Publication Data appear
on the last printed page of this book.

In memory of days spent with my mother—Jean Anderson King—at her nursing home, where, huddling over my laptop together, we watched downloaded episodes of Boston Legal *and laughed out loud—sharing ironies and contradictions of same-sex silliness.*

CONTENTS

CAT'S CRADLE IS A GAME of relaying patterns, of one hand, or a pair of hands, holding still to receive something from another, and then relaying by adding something new, by proposing another knot, another web. Or better, it is not the hands that give and receive exactly, but the patterns, the patterning. Cat's cradle can be played by many, on all sorts of limbs, as long as the rhythm of accepting and giving is sustained. Scholarship is like that too; it is passing on in twists and skeins that require passion and action, holding still and moving, anchoring and launching. Maybe that is why Katie King is such a good partner in worlding. Over three decades, she has been that kind of partner for me, and *Networked Reenactments* is an invitation to readers to join in thick, collaborative patterning. Networked reenactments is her practice for sf worlding, for speculative fabulations and speculative feminisms in the big, generous knottings that open up ways to think, play, connect, distinguish, work, and live.

Recently, King named "epistemologies" as "stories knowledges tell."[1] That is what *Networked Reenactments* does; this important book performs "stories knowledges tell" with great skill, in different material and conceptual grains of detail and resolution. She shows her readers how to ask what "grain of detail" might mean in situated inquiries. She writes about "epistemological melodramas" with verve and appreciation, and she is herself a master weaver of these grainy stories. A geometrician at heart, King thinks about whether a pattern is linearly layered or nodally networked and how that makes a difference. She appreciates, practices, and theorizes both "intensive" scholarship, with its demands for considerable focused and exclusive expertise, and "extensive" scholarship, with its powers of linking, speculating, and attaching unexpected agencies and territories to each other. This kind of appreciation entails understanding the mechanisms and affects of inclusion and exclusion in communities of practice, including sustained pain and suffering from mutual incomprehensions and angers in unavoidably heterogeneous knowledge worlds and unevenly distributed power. Tuned to scalar grains of detail in both authoritative membership and peripheral participation in knowledge-making communities of practice, King makes palpable the important and often unacknowledged suffering, as well as pleasures, in networked reenactments inside and outside the academy.

In its own terms, this book "scopes and scales," focusing in and out, up and down, inside and outside, and side to side in the dimensionally manifold weave of knowledge worlds that are at stake in science displays; science-styled television documentaries; serial TV fabulations like *Xena: Warrior Princess* and *Highlander* with their rambunctious nationalities and sexualities; and emergent transdisciplinary scholarship enmeshed with nonacademic communities of practice with their unsettling ranges of expertise. King rethinks and re-feels what counts as genres of reenactment and how that matters. Attuned to the painfully unchosen, but also not-yet-closed and still-to-be-shaped "urgencies of global academic restructuring" and academic capitalism, King explores potent agencies, materialities, and effectivities in realizing knowledge stories. This book examines and makes available a rich range of "sensations of agency" and epistemological affects. In the diverse projects that King calls networked reenactments, the fibers of transnational and transmedia commercial and production apparatuses interweave with the tendrils of scientific and artisanal crafting and the myceliar hyphae of cross-linked generations of transdisciplinary scholars. Another term for King's sort of mycelium might be a vibrant, livable, feminist transdisciplinary posthumanities.

King contributes to the important insights in current humanities and social science scholarship about the limits of critique, even while re-disciplinizations, often called interdisciplines, continue to extract acts of debunking critique as their exorbitant and exclusionary price of admission.[2] But best of all, King shows me how to do something else, even inside both my guilty pleasures in popular television or Internet media and also my self-righteous pleasures in my favorite politics, analyses, and theories. She does not even make me forswear the pleasures of debunking the unenlightened as a knowledge practice, or at least not all the time. Quite the opposite, she is as unafraid of the heterodox tastes of intellectual and political pleasures as she is resolute about their limits and coercions when they get fixed, obligatory, and self certain. She provides a feast of reading pleasures in this book, asking only that the reader learn to taste from a menu that ranges out of the gustatory comfort zone of many disciplined eaters.

King thinks and writes inside a polyskilled, polyracial, polysexual web of testy friends—of companion species, living and dead, in the text and in the flesh—who tell knowledge stories that she needs—that we need, however that object of desire, non-innocence, and craft called "we" is re-enacted. Her web holds in its silk threads Gregory Bateson, Susan Leigh Star, Bruno Latour, Lucy Suchman, Chela Sandoval, Gloria Anzaldúa, Eva Hayward, Kara Keeling, and many more. Bateson is in King's ancestry, in the sticky threads of her DNA, with extraordinary results; he was her undergraduate teacher and friend at the University of California, Santa Cruz (UCSC). Would that scholarly generations could always play out like this! It would change the meaning of heritage culture, to say the least. Earning her doctorate in 1987, King was also a graduate student in the History of Consciousness program at UCSC, and she met me at the airport for my Santa Cruz feminist theory job talk in the winter of 1980. From that time on, she and I have played a sometimes uncomfortable but more often joyful game of cat's cradle, teaching and learning with and from each other about the craft of speculative feminism and speculative fabulation.

In the beginning, King taught me about just plain sf, science fiction of the sort written by one of her favorites, Robert Heinlein, and especially about the thick weave of feminist science fiction. She told me what to read, and it changed my life. Inhabiting the worlds of writers like Joanna Russ, John Varley, Octavia Butler, and Samuel R. Delany does that to one, making a femaleman out of less promising gender material. I think that such reading gave both King and me our primary meanings for "world-ing," and her sotto voce working of that vein is deep in the tissues of Networked Reenactments. When I turned 66 on September 6, 2010, and the dog of my heart Cayenne turned 11 the same month, divisible 6 times into my time on earth, I wrote a riff for friends on 666, the mark of the beast in the Christian book of the Apocalypse; Octavia Butler's space-virus-infected quadrupedal, beast-marked humans in her Clay's Ark; the Greek word for six (hex), and the tempting but unfortunately false etymology to northern European hexes, hags, hedges, and all the untamed dames with their wer-lighted unruly hair proper to old earth powers. I have never been deterred by false etymologies, and I need a little eschatology along with witches, woods, and hexes of the kind Ursula Le Guin would plant in Earth Sea, seasoned with a bit of number play from the Greek brainwomb of the West.

King entered into my reenactment, and she inflected it in the ways that readers of this book are about to experience; she thickened the knots and then relayed a mutated and resituated pattern for the next play. She remembered Heinlein's novel, *The Number of the Beast*, in which the biblical number of the beast turns out to be, not 666, but $(6^6)^6$, or 10,314,424,798,490,535,546,171,949,056—the number of parallel universes accessible through the continua device, Heinlein's sf mechanism for traveling through time and between universes. Heinlein thus gets a natural number (if a huge one) from 6 to the 6th raised to the 6th because he imagines parallel universes. What happens, King asks, when the universes are not parallel but entangled and networked? Ah, there the hags and hexes exceed the 6s; natural numbers go trans; and King entices her reader into the serious play of scoping and scaling, intensive and extensive scholarly pleasures and tasks, and collaborative critical reenactments without the seductions of Critique Itself.

In a much-quoted passage from *Specters of Marx*, Jacques Derrida wrote, "Inheritance is never a given; it is always a task. It remains before us."[3] I love that quote; it helps me to "stay with the trouble," which is the motto that sustains me in my current work with and on animal-human-technical agroecological practices, in companion species and transmodal ways. Derrida's words help me think in many kinds of time, flesh, vulnerability, and ways to learn to inherit in order to go on in the face of deep and urgent trouble. *Networked Reenactments* stays with the trouble. Katie King—in her cat's cradling thinking, feeling, speaking, teaching, and writing for restructuring and dangerous placetimes, whenwhere responsive and responsible inheritance can and must be woven from networked re-enactments—gives me similar sorts of wisdom and subtlety that Derrida does. But King's are tied into different and, I think, more generous skeins of conversations that are dearer to my mindheart. Her pastpresents seem richer to me than Derrida's generatively refigured temporalities. I live haunted by King's specters, who also owe Marx a ghostly and ongoing debt. The conversations that King knots her readers into are most practiced in feminisms, science studies, science fiction, arts, media apparatuses, and the quotidian of heterogeneous and disparate sorts of expertise nurtured by and in knowledge-making communities in layers and nodes of locals and globals, in and out of the academy.

King's approach teaches us about "befriending transdisciplinarity under the urgencies of global academic restructuring."[4] Friendship is a big theme and a demanding practice in this book. These pages are full of richly needed and sometimes prickly friends for taking consequential, worldly knowledge-making seriously. *Networked Reenactments* is an extraordinary book that explores how to inhabit with seriousness and pleasure the many discomforts that we experience when trying to do work that matters to us and maybe to others. This is work and play that must "address actively diverging audiences simultaneously and [must] author knowledges as merely one of multiple agencies with very limited control." Because any serious person is obliged to "traverse knowledge worlds in terms not of our own making," King shows her readers how to "befriend transdisciplinary movements" with all of our vulnerability and power, capacity and incapacity, hope and worry.[5] It is all about learning to play, or, as King writes, "learning to be affected."

Inhabiting this book rearranges my insides, redoes my reading habits, reintroduces me to intellectual pleasures and political possibilities that I have been in danger of forgetting, brings me into worlds I do not know how to enter without her, and inculcates practices of attention to how consequential worlding gets done—in fact and fiction, in speculative fabulation, in networked reenactments. Perhaps, in the threads of King's cat's cradle relays, the much-quoted passage to come might read, "Networked reenactment is never a given; it is always a task; it is always in play. It remains before us."

WHAT ARE REENACTMENTS IN THIS BOOK?

I repeat here words from the middle of chapter 4, at which point all these elements of reenactment will have been networked over the nineties among layers of transnational infrastructure and systems described in the preceding chapters. But for those longing to hear that their intensive definitions of reenactment are honored in this book, even as they are also extensively positioned promiscuously with other ways of thinking about reenactment, I offer these words in both places: both here at the very beginning of this exploration, then later, nearer to my conclusions, just after I recall the realisms of Cold War military gaming, and just before I reflect on the emergent academic study of reenactment. Consider this a kind of hyperlink that allows these words to exist simultaneously at two differing points in these arguments, first to invite engagement and later to demonstrate an accumulation of accretions and associations.

Why does this book not pivot around what many would consider this properly pure type of reenactment? Because it is my argument that reenactors mean both what they mean to themselves and also mean things beyond and differently from that to many others. And that understanding this and other doubled workings of reenaction has wide implications for a whole range of kinds of knowledge work today. This book is all about these implications.

WHAT ARE REENACTMENTS IN THIS BOOK?

UNDERSTANDABLY DIFFERING communities of practice work to center their own fabrication, conventions, and explanations of reenactment, and there are more and more such communities and practices. Each in itself properly understands its version of reenactment as the most significant, real, or central. And, each of these communities of practice (both scholarly ones studying reenactment, and reenactors producing reenactments) has a history or taxonomy through which their *intensive* version of reenactment is vitally produced. Each may feel that reenactments are objects that they, perhaps alone, are uniquely qualified to address. "Reenactment" may or may not even be the term they prefer for all the things I enumerate as reenactments; in fact, it may even be a term *against* which some define their own special and significant activities. Nonetheless there are some continuities that network among all these, and overlapping concerns can be understood to animate them; indeed the strange histories of militarized gaming offer nodes for attachment. Let us unknot some of these entangled and *extensive* associations.

For most, as intensively used within their own communities to describe their own activities or those of others, the term "reenactment" centers on those *hobbyists meeting together on the battlefields* of, say, Manassas, recreating in their persons and material objects and actions an American Civil War confrontation. These reenactments are usually military in focus, although they also include important concerns about the material culture and place-shaped character of everyday life during the time periods depicted, even more especially as they come to or do include women playing a variety of parts. And somewhat similar reenactments, partly or wholly shorn of military associations, instead focus especially on artful and pleasurable elements of everyday life in historical periods—food, music, crafts, stories, and games—and are recreated for *festivals, fairs, and other celebrations*. Usually separately or even competitively, but sometimes together, these two strains of reenactment produce their own hobby cultures in which research into historical events and objects, community building in person and on the Internet, and volunteer or semiprofessional work for living history sites may be generated. Heritage interests or nationalisms can be represented in these, although some explicitly intend to refuse such associations. "Authenticity" may be used to distinguish between these, or to rank some practices among these over others. This form for reenactment stands for many as its "pure type," what one ought to mean by the term. My own use is often disappointingly diffuse to those who long to address this form of reenactment most carefully and in enough satisfying detail.[1] I hope however that this book will successfully even work with that sort of fulfillment and frustration of expectation, the very stuff all kinds of gaming depend upon, and at the right moment offer its deferred reward, a vista very much worth working through levels of analysis to come out upon.

So, to continue with such goals in mind, for some the term "reenactment" might range among such hobby recreations not only in person, but extending out also to *war game simulations* of varying degrees of impersonation: from board games with dice and cards reenacting a specific military battle, to graphically sophisticated computer simulations also with military-style objectives and movements, to the newly under construction war games simulations produced by Hollywood for the US military for training purposes. And to this mix might also be added other similarly constructed simulations with less or without obvious "military" significance. These are often *multimedia fantasy games* modeled upon versions of *Dungeons & Dragons*, which over time have come to include sometimes more or sometimes less media, telescoping, or collapsing among multisensory, kinesthetic, and proprioceptive creativities, from drawing, playacting, game board making, costuming, event celebration, and so on, as well as including, or limited to, sophisticated computer graphic versions.[2] And explicit fantasy elements may be more appreciated in this mix, as groups such as the Society for Creative Anachronism may play deliberatively with issues of realism and authenticity in savvy, joking forms. In some ranges, any "military" elements may shift intensively and alternatively into various styles of contestation or fighting, from individual combat to street-style gang encounters to apprehending criminals and beyond these, merging with other *tournament games*, like baseball or golf. Despite my way of explaining these here, exactly how these are all materially and historically intertwined with war gaming is reasonably open to question, although emphasizing the intertwined cocreation of military-based and culture-based reenactments might be important. Gender, race, nationality, and nationalism are all evaluative elements in differentially emphasizing some kinds of reenactments over others across a wide range of communities of practice.

More extensively—and this is the level at which my explorations of the work of reenaction are positioned in this book—there are new television versions of reenactments, some of them included within the scope of so-called *reality TV*, others are variations on *documentary TV* techniques. They range from historical documentaries with intensively defined mini-reenactments positioned to illustrate historical points to documentary TV in which the whole show is somehow a reenactment. Sometimes they actually include hobbyist reenactors, sometimes they also mix in an alternatively intensive range of *professionals, semiprofessionals and volunteers, doing first- or second-person impersonations or role-playing* as for living history sites. Other times, inside the reality TV rubric, people chosen in a contest of admission are engaged to "time travel" to another period and try to take up life within material and physically difficult constraints that interactively count as "authenticity" for that program.

Of course film and television might also be understood as always having been kinds of (extensively defined) reenactments anyway, as, for example, when situating TV's historic roots in vaudeville or film's in Lumière-style fantasy.[3] And indeed some gaming analysts detail other fictions of many varieties as simulated worlds in literary products.[4] This most extensive, fully telescoped meaning of reenactment, *modeling "reality" in simultaneous media,* is culturally powerful: the play between realities and things clearly not whatever that thing "reality" is, and things only too closely like "reality," are pivotally entertaining with varying degrees of cultural value and neurological and hormonal pleasure.[5] Which differences between these make a difference—sharply drawn differences or only too shaded transitional meanings, all embracing and even ritualizing constraints or rule-governed systems—these matter enormously in knowledge work. Validity, objectivity, rigor, standardization, explanation, modeling—all these and other essentials of knowledge in production, transmission, and pleasure are at stake when we extensively interconnect reenactment, entertainment, and scholarly production.

ACKNOWLEDGMENTS

THIS BOOK'S CREATION has involved a long and complicated journey, one full of people to whom I am indebted as well as with whom I have had wonderful fun, intellectual companionship, and humbling experiences. All the networks involved matter to me, and if I have left some out mistakenly, I offer my heartfelt apologies for an aging memory. From the beginning Chrys Sparks was my companion through *Trek*, *Highlander*, and media fandoms, while Kit Mason, HIGHLA-L, the PWFC, and a great many *Highlander* and *Xena* folk, fans, and production people widened this particular thread through reenactments. As projects morphed and interconnected, Debby Rosenfelt, Donna Landry, Gerald MacLean, Jonathan Lamb, Bill Sherman, Helen Weinstein, Judy Hallett, Chris Kelly, Nancy Linde, Arthur Molella, and Jim Bono each stepped in at some extraordinary moment to open a new door into reenactments and their knowledge worlds or to supply help, information, or resources.

Mark Engel, Nora Bateson, Eric Vatikiotis-Bateson, Lois Bateson, and the Bateson Archives Board have been sustaining points for transdisciplinary connection as well as beloved anchors in my universe. The Trans Knowledges that have taught me so much about what a feminist transdisciplinary posthumanities might become are now crossing together from many angles: with special thanks to Bailey Kier, Eva Hayward, Lindsay Kelley, Wendy Pearson, Laura Mamo, JV Sapinoso, Christina Hanhardt, Helen Merrick, and a range of feminist folks queering transnational ecologies among science fictions, animal studies, technicity, embodiments, racializations, infrastructures, and genomics.

I am continually inspired by networks circulating around, through, and allied with folks from the History of Consciousness and elsewhere at the University of California, Santa Cruz. They keep entering and reentering my life when I really need hope, when I need science and cultural studies—anthropology, inspiration, a new connection—companions to that sort of thinking just at the edge of apprehension. Folks such as: Sharon Traweek, Ulrika Dahl, Lisa Bloom, Megan Boler, Ron Eglash, Deborah Gordon, Chela Sandoval, Shelly Errington, Zoë Sofoulis, TV Reed, Noël Sturgeon, Bill Pietz, Astrid Schrader, Helene Moglen, Christine Rose, Harry Berger, Eben Kirksey, Caren Kaplan, Tilly Shaw, Thyrza Goodeve, Hayden White, Billie Harris, Kami Chisholm, Elizabeth Bird, Sharon Ghamari-Tabrizi, James Clifford, Natalie Loveless, Mischa Adams, Valerie Hartouni, Anna Tsing, Adele Clarke, Malin Rönnblom, Nobby Brown, Chris Connery, Carole McCann, Sheila Peuse, and others much appreciated over many years.

And these networks come to intertwine with many more—of students, colleagues, and friends at my home institution, the University of Maryland, College Park—through social media such as Facebook and even the virtual world Second Life (SL). So I also thank the SL Feminist Reading Group and its members on Facebook, among them Julie Enszer, Maria Velazquez, Barbara Ley, Scout Calvert, Karen DeVries, Jere Alexander, Kimberly TallBear, Laura Brunner, Red Washburn, Ryan Shanahan, Ramona Fernandez, Sharon Collingwood, and others.

I thank the students, former students, colleagues, and friends at the University of Maryland who have supported me over many years now, especially Martha Nell Smith, founding director of the Maryland Institute for Technology in the Humanities, and Marilee Lindemann, director of LGBT Studies. Others include Lee Badget, Max Grossman, Christopher Perez, Elizabeth Hagovsky, Ellen Moll, Robyn Epstein, Kari Krauss, Matt Kirschenbaum, Kimberlee Staking, Kimberly Williams, Damion Clark, Ana Perez, Sabrina Baron, Donald Synder, David Silver, Sarah Tillery, Vrushali Patil, Bettina Judd, and others inside and outside LGBT and women's studies as they have each shared their work or given me courage while working on this book. I thank them all for research support and listening ears and hearts: Evi Beck, Jeffrey McCune, Lynn Bolles, Michelle Rowley, Claire Moses, Bonnie Dill, Elsa Barkley Brown, Ruth Zambrana, Debby Rosenfelt, and Seung-kyung Kim, together with Laura Nichols, Cliffornia Howard, and Annie Carter.

Life happened, quite a lot of it, as I tried to complete this book. I am humbled by it all. I can never thank enough my family—a large, extended field of love over an international geography—and especially my brother, Ed, my sister-in-law, Paula, and my aunt, Lois, who have cheered every final benchmark as it has been accomplished. Loving friends and intellectual buddies have made this work and my life possible, from taking up watching *Highlander* so they could discuss it with me, to visiting *Science in American Life* with me—or photographing it, or helping with technologies of illustration—to introducing me to principles in a range of reenactment practices, to helping me out so I could care for my mother, take care of my own health, and get work done too, to opening new doors to other worlds, to making the overwhelming manageable in tiny pieces or in compassionate perspective: Rusten Hogness, Alicia Maris, Lillian Doherty, Barry Schwartz, Gretchen Dunn, Stephen Ordway, Peter Bothel, Bindu Bambah, Chandrasekher Mukk, Eleanor Shevlin, Marcia Reecer, Kathleen Biddick, Michael Moon, Vikki DuRee, Carter Wilson, Cynthia Nordstrom, Carole Farber, Siobhan Somerville, Kris Halstead, Johan Linderholm, Lisa Lowe, Michele Mason, Geoffrey Schramm, Susan Meehan, Barbara Nnoka, Patti Lather, Claudia Rector, Josephine Withers, Kathleen Earle, Angel Nieves, Mary Sies, Katherine Broadway, Lucy Kemnitzer, Suzanne Bost, Mel Lewis, and many others I cannot name here but hold in my heart.

I thank those responsible for getting this book to press: Ken Wissoker; Leigh Barnwell; the publication board; all the production people at Duke, among them Rebecca Fowler and Alex Wolfe; and all the anonymous reviewers of this manuscript.

Research support of various kinds, formal and informal, I received from: the Mellon Foundation and Women's Studies at Cornell University; Cornell's Society for the Humanities; the Folger Institute; the University of California Humanities Research Institute; the University of California, Santa Cruz's Center for Cultural Studies; two University of Maryland Curriculum Transformation Summer Institutes; the Maryland Institute for Technology in the Humanities; DC Queer Studies; and Women's Studies at the University of Maryland.

For listening and responding to presentations that eventually became parts of this book, I thank audiences at: Wright State University; the University of Notre Dame; the Corcoran Art Gallery; the Georgia Institute of Technology; the University of California, Santa Cruz; Vanderbilt University; the DC Print Culture Area group; Colby College; the University of California, Los Angeles; the University of Western Ontario; DC Queer

Studies Symposia; the Nordic Research School; and Gender Studies and Science and Values at Umeå University. At the University of Maryland, College Park, I thank audiences in Classics, the Art Gallery, the Maryland Institute for Technology in the Humanities, and my own Women's Studies Department. And a special thanks to the Cedar Island community in the virtual world *Second Life* for reading and discussing my work.

Parts of chapter 1 were previously published as "Globalization, TV Technologies, and the Re-production of Sexual Identities" in *Encompassing Gender: Integrating International Studies and Women's Studies*, edited by M. M. Lay, J. Monk, and D. S. Rosenfelt, pp. 101–24, copyright © 2002. They appear here with the permission of the Feminist Press at the City University of New York, www.feministpress.org. Parts of the introduction were previously published as "Networked Reenactments: A Thick Description amid Authorships, Audiences, and Agencies in the Nineties" in the journal *Writing Technologies* 2, no. 1 (2008), full text available for free online at www.ntu.ac.uk/writing_technologies. And parts of chapters 3 and 4 were previously published as "Historiography as Reenactment: Metaphors and Literalizations of TV Documentaries" in "Extreme and Sentimental History," a special issue of the journal *Criticism* 46, no. 3 (2004): 459–75, wsupress.wayne.edu/journals/criticism.

Donna Haraway's name could be in almost every section of these acknowledgments. Her work has inspired me since I first read it in *Signs*, as has her person since that day Mischa and I picked her up at the airport for her job talk at Santa Cruz. Thinking with Donna Haraway has mattered enormously to this book and to my life. May we all flourish in the kindly care and the daring analysis she and those networked together here share, labor for, and dream—in worldly forms of becoming with.

Networked Reenactments

A THICK DESCRIPTION AMID AUTHORSHIPS, AUDIENCES, AND AGENCIES IN THE NINETIES

WHAT NINETIES, WHAT REENACTMENTS, WHY?

THIS BOOK GREW out of, through, and back into the nineties. Something, or rather, some many things, happened in the nineties, things that set us up for *now*, whenever that is. This book keeps trying to work among some *things* of the nineties, work among them and as them, glimpsing our "other-globalizations" mixed in among the ways and places at work in, around, and transporting through culture industries, cultural studies, and feminist analysis.[1] Among these *things* of the nineties are reenactments, both the focus and theme of this book.

Reenactments, you might say, *what do you mean?* Well, I do mean those reenactments we might most immediately think of, hobbyists reenacting battles of the War of the Roses for example or interpreters at Colonial Williamsburg showing visitors how to make candles, but I am also working with a notion of reenactment that has other layers of meaning and scope too. Some of these other layers, more inclusive and perhaps less obvious, connect additional activities, venues, objects, skills, people, and circumstances together with such *living history* reenactments.

Saying "additional" and "together with" is in order to emphasize an extensive and overlapping *range*. Such an emphasis recognizes all these nodes among the cobbled together *ranging infrastructures* we are engaging today. Infrastructures are piled-upon assemblages within which there are many discontinuities but also connections, some deliberative, some inadvertent. These infrastructural connections or *flexible knowledges* make up a networked and emergent reorganization of knowledge making and using that those of us linked together by the publication apparatus of this book are likely a part of, probably even agents within. Investigating reenactments helps us to perceive together many of these transdisciplinary connections and helps us to contemplate and participate in what something perhaps called a "posthumanities" will become.

"Things" is a useful word here: its etymology stresses that things are processes as well as subjects and objects, that they are simultaneously the location for dispute and the subjects of dispute as well as the outcomes of dispute. At some points in this feminist book, women are centered, at some points social processes of power such as racialization are centered, at some points issues of sex, gender, and sexuality in flux are centered. But these are not the only fields, forces, and objects of power engaged, and recentering is not the only feminist practice demonstrated here. Transdisciplinary movement among knowledge worlds is unsettling, something feminist analysis sometimes celebrates and other times experiences unhappily. Specific chapters take up these and other power-knowledge concerns, all connected together through this fascinating thing or things, reenactments.

The book works among levels of perspective in which three large social domains scale in and through its analysis. Roughly focused on a "long" decade, actually ranging through the mid-nineties to the middle of two thousand, it moves around even there, onto more edges as well, onto the beginning of the nineties all the way to that *now* no publication can ever pin down. So I call this range "the nineties" for simplicity's sake, and, while addressing some of its specifics, I do not claim they are unique to this timeframe, just very interesting within it.

This introduction centers reenactments in *a particular kind of science-styled documentary TV*—think the Discovery Channel and PBS. Demonstrating reenactments at work sets up a practical point of departure and provides a bit of detail to share immediately, as well as setting up themes and groundwork for the rest of the book. Beginning here is intended to offer an immediate enumeration and extension of possible kinds of reenactment as well as to display reenactments as experiments in communication emerging from the nineties.

All this goes to show that while some communities of practice might consider themselves "intensively" (within their own communities of reference) to own or define the term "reenactments," "extensive" displays such as this thick description do a very different kind of important work, and can do so without throwing away or displacing the intensive work specific communities of practice do too. Investigating communities of practice and their various definitions and commitments, "extensive" investigations work perpendicularly to analyze the relative and relational shifts across authoritative and alternative knowledges that processes of definition entail. Attending to such extensive explorations among intensive meanings is one of the practices of transdisciplinarity.

Some appropriate differences here are ones of scope and scale, and an attention to scope, scale, membership, and grain of analysis allows one to participate actively, maybe even pleasurably, and move among knowledge worlds. Movement among knowledge worlds requires understanding authorships, audiences, and agencies in ways that keep redrawing forms of inclusion and exclusion, virtually moment to moment.

This introduction also initiates a reading practice that emerges from the nineties, a practice we might call something like "web action." The specific forms web action takes beyond the moment of this writing or at the moments described in the book, into moments over the book's production, and at many moments in which the book comes to be used, these are unknowable as these words are written. This set of undecidabilities is something to note explicitly, not something from which to try to deflect attention. Such undecidability traces possible worlds, and the *tense*, that is to say, the time grammar of transdisciplinary practice, means that this *now* and other timeframes are worth indexing and analyzing in their dislocations.

SCOPING AND SCALING

Being inside and moved around literally by the very material and conceptual structures you are analyzing and writing about is a kind of self-consciousness only partially available for explicit discussion. In practicing such research, writing obliquely is sometimes a necessity, not an obstinate refusal to be specific or propose something in particular. Thus at times the writing in this introduction and in the rest of the book is necessarily performative rather than deductively argumentative or inductively hypothetical. At other times it is descriptive, thickly or narratively, in order to share materials among communities of practice, or to set out tools, things,

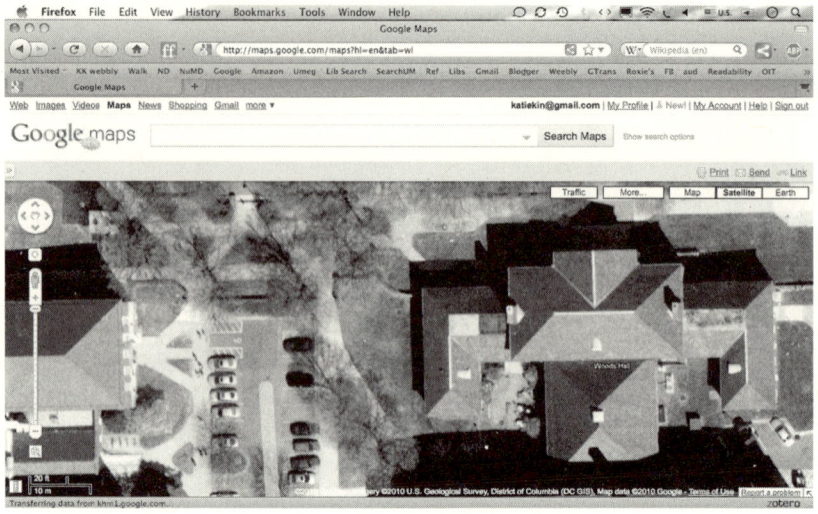

Scale in for a close view on Google Maps of Woods Hall at the University of Maryland.

and contexts to think with. Transdisciplinary work befriends and experiences a range of academic and other genres of writing, entailment, and analysis, together with their consequent and diverging values.

So, imagine the term "reenactments" referring to a Google Earth map's departure point, a concrete venue also coming to include a lot of conceptual territory around it.

To see the whole territory we pan out and up for a satellite view, or we come in closer and closer to see the very particular street patterns, maybe even to detail the backyard of a specific house, the parking lot of a particular building. We move the orientation point around with our mouse, cursor, finger, or whatever, to shift *scope and scale*.

Notice how such web action can take place—say, in the delivery system of a paper book—as a thought experiment or in supplementation, in one tense of *now*. It is possible *now*, in my moment of writing this, to curl up with one's book and one's iPod Touch, reading about Google Maps, searching them and altering them simultaneously. For some other *now*, web action has other experimental forms and supplements. The ideas of scoping and scaling include these *other* possibilities of tense as well.

How are scoping and scaling both realities *and* simulations of activities of reenactment, and in ways emerging out of the nineties? Well, three large social domains of power-knowledge relations are pertinent to

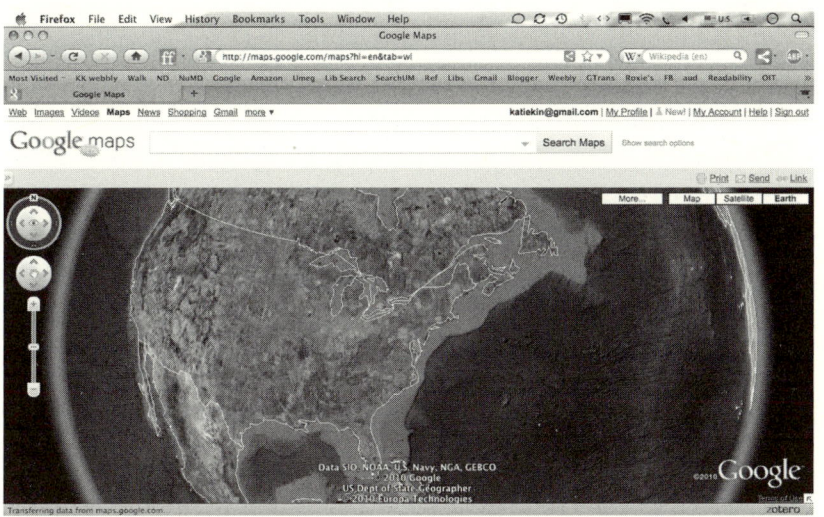

Scope out, pulling back for a Google Earth planetary view that still centers Woods Hall.

locating these literally metaphoric networked reenactments as flexible knowledges under globalization. Examining each of these domains requires good faith investigations into the foundations and assumptions undergirding knowledge worlds and communities of practice; it requires engaging them critically but also without immediately debunking them. For example, backgrounding uncertainties and ambivalences, material and political, embodied by, say, Google itself, are its multiply cultural academic founders in the US dotcom boom of the nineties; its new media writing technologies including but not limited to inscription; its technological and political optimisms and intentions among naive necessities (an informal company slogan is or was once "don't be evil");[2] and its taking on (and perhaps becoming another) such a giant as Microsoft, very much to its own benefit. Such points are references for continuing evaluation as well as for provisional judgments, in the example of Google, and also in these three domains.[3] In other words, being for or against, say, Google, is an evaluation that might properly have to be deferred at moments in the writing of this book, indexed rather than essentialized in a critique. But in the *now* of some readings such deferral may well have ceased to be appropriate. Such *tense* of analysis also matters, and an explicit attention to tense is invaluable in transdisciplinary communication, a sensitivity that critique sometimes elides prematurely.

And Google, not coincidentally, maps among all three domains in ways that matter to reenactments. This is how I describe these three domains:

— **knowledge work,** that is to say, work cultures centering knowledge and information systems and technologies as economies themselves and as forces in various economies.

— **culture crafts, publics, and industries,** or public culture sewn up with economic development amid shifts in cultural value, all displaying in varying proportions among old and new technologies of entertainment. (Think of the culture, history, science, and image wars impacted by so-called heritage culture and enterprise culture.)

— **academic capitalism,** where is displayed recombinations of national interests, global economies, and ideological shifts in the nineties that develop across the Anglophone academies, evident in various forms of privatized education and technology transfer and favored by both (US-described) neoliberals and neoconservatives.[4]

Imagine tracing these domains using Google's trademark hybrid maps in several kinds of view, say, "satellite" or "terrain" view marked up with names from "street" view, with the "traffic" view button pushed.

In Google hybrid view these three ways of tracking the nineties can be overlaid upon each other in particular venues, and, as with Google Earth, we can pan in and out or move our point of reference around a bit to work with the specifics of any particular view, dynamically scaling and scoping.

Although roughly the same area keeps coming up—this extensive ranging infrastructure the term "reenactment" creates connections within—each view—as in Google Earth now, say, history, camera, weather, sky—actually emphasizes different features amid quite specific forms of relationality. Each chapter in this book works to scope and scale among these three domains differently in order to emphasize another variant set of relationalities among reenactments and communities of practice.

Scoping and scaling action in these domains, as in reenactment, necessarily operates amid a pastiche of timeframes, what I call in the book *pastpresents*, all too similar to a Google Map's so-called real time of traffic flows in color, its montage effects of time and place and national security served up as *history* in satellite or, differently, as street view, and its longer more fundamental features offered as terrain. Duration, political meanings, and myriad embodiments and materialities are at stake in what might at first seem like a god's eye view, but quickly we refresh in history

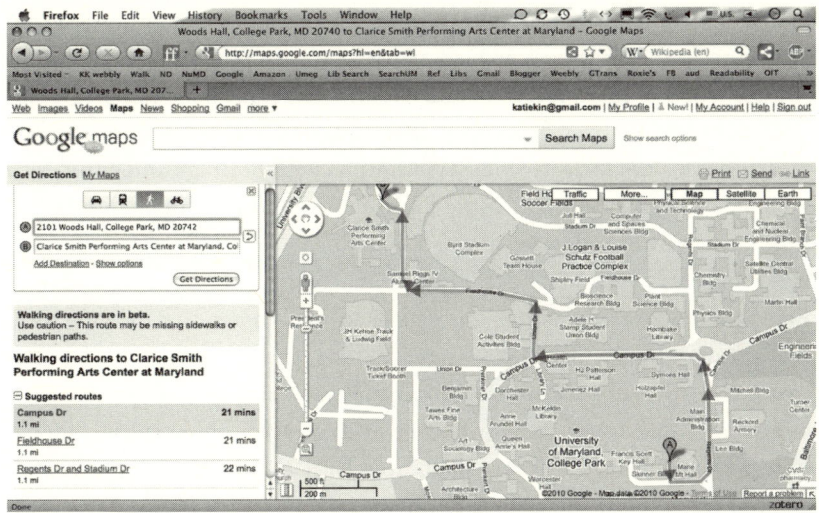

The *cognitive sensation* of walking through Google Mapped spaces, refreshing our distributed embodiments, we *feel inside* rather than outside Google's mappings.

view, seeing and being its more material and assembled embodiments ourselves. ("Whose car is that next to my office building there, and check out that landscaping and weather; let's see how many months ago on some weekend that was?")

Locating us inside Google mappings rather than outside, denaturalizing and *feeling* our own movements among knowledge worlds and distributed memberships, among authoritative and alternative knowledges and politics, we find ourselves drawing on a wide culturally altering sensorium and an individual and collectively cultivated set of affects. *Feelings* are ways of perceiving ourselves under satellite view, not in the god's eye or only under surveillance, but in a humbling inclusion as agencies ourselves, only too partial and uncertain among political opportunities and exigencies in various knowledge worlds. Some of these specific *feelings*, as created and as studied, mark out some of the terrain and ethics of a posthumanities.

Chapter 1 takes off from the point in which, in the nineties, transnational image and media wars refigure the multiple-racial, multiple-cultural European Union amid globalizing connections and competitions, those with the United States and those with cultural industrial districts around the world. These are some contexts for the reenactment heavy, science-styled television documentaries of this introduction, unpacked more closely in chapter 3, as well as for the action adventure television shows chapter 1 examines in detail. Around this same time period globalizing culture industries obviously come to include more and more academies and museums in refreshed associations with heritage and enterprise "culture," as described in chapter 2 and later elaborated in chapter 4. Of course, including academies means I include myself amid shifts in knowledge workings and global academic restructuring. These inclusions and their productive complexities and televisual genres are especially focused in chapter 4. And while "we"—that is to say, those agencies distributed among the culture industries materially networked by this very book as an object—may well traffic in knowledge worlds, indeed broker culture shock, we experience it ourselves, are dislocated by it all, and work, whether we like it or not, among our own experiments.

Thus across all the chapters of the book I describe how, in the nineties, science-styled television documentary forms, internet repurposings, museum exhibitions, and academic historiographies worked hard to shape an array of cognitive sensations accessed, skilled, and displayed by new technologies. These emergent embodiments became experiments in communication and offered epistemological melodramas of identity, national interests, and global restructuring. The term "cognitive sensation" names what we were just experiencing, literally and figuratively, as we felt ourselves moving around in Google hybrid view within and articulating one sort of embodiment. But what does it mean to call reenactments *experiments in communication* and also *epistemological melodramas*? Well, let us turn to one of these documentaries, scaling closely to consider how such reenactments work, as well as scaling and scoping out to make explicit a particular set of knowledge worlds and the work reenactments do to travel among them.

KNOWLEDGES AS "SCIENCE"

In 2003 a two-part documentary titled *Leonardo's Dream Machines* was broadcast in the United States on PBS. Written and directed by Paul Sapin, it was produced by ITN Factual, a TV production company in the UK that creates content for European and UK broadcasters and for such US television venues as PBS, the National Geographic Channel, the Discovery Channel and A&E.[5] In one *now*, trailers for the show have been loaded on

YouTube and Paul Sapin's own website, and consequent web action allows for scoping and scaling, that is to say, reading about this show and watching a piece of it, virtually simultaneously.[6]

The show centers around two devices visualized from sets of drawings made by Leonardo da Vinci, each device chosen for building and explanation by specialists in overlapping but different knowledge worlds. One drawing becomes pivotal and animated as a single element in a disparate set of famous Leonardo flying-machine conceptions, this one a very tiny detail of *pilot control* that may be intended to elaborate previous Leonardo flying drawings.

The other plan is for a war machine, a giant crossbow. In two collaborative teams, design and structural engineers, aircraft restorers, skilled carpenters, art and science historians, and a world-record breaking pilot labor to make full-scale and part-scale working models from these drawings. They are aided by other art, science, military, and church historians, a practicing and teaching artist, and skilled craftspeople in carpentry, metal work, and restoration, as well as a bioengineer, a cardiac surgeon, and a robotic engineer; all specialists themselves who offer expertise and imagination in interpretation of skills, devices, natural processes, people, and infrastructures. While the two teams are not exactly in game show competition, still we and they are encouraged to explicitly compare their effort and each project's success. And the timeframes are conspicuously limited by the materialities of expense and the availabilities of materials, specialists, venues, devices, and film crew in ways shaped by the filmmakers to create suspense, tension, and dramatic conflict.

Each team is composed of two engineers of various sorts, a historian, either of art or science, and a person concerned with safety issues as part of the operation of the device; on the crossbow team it is the lead carpenter, and on the glider team the pilot. In part one we see the present day specialists of the crossbow team fixing what they consider Leonardo's mistakes so as to ensure that their team's machine will work. We watch the glider team worrying how to ensure the safety of their pilot while adhering to Leonardo's own knowledges. When the crossbow team discovers at the end of part one that their alterations have failed to produce a properly working model, they realize just how far away they have gotten from Leonardo's design. What we could call the *epistemological melodrama* of this particular series gets clearer at this point. The contest it turns out is not between two present day teams but rather across time with Leonardo. That

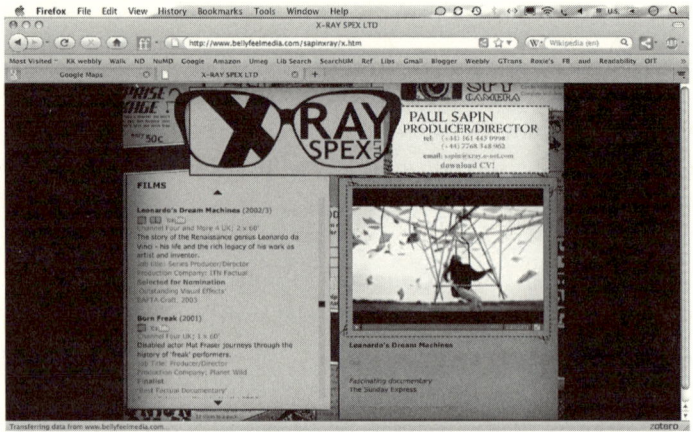

Paul Sapin's website with its embedded video trailer of *Leonardo's Dream Machines* acts as a model for *web action*.

Pivotal *detail* of A-frame operation from Leonardo's notebooks in *Leonardo's Dream Machines*.

means that in the second part each model actually works only when team experts do it "Leonardo's way." Yet, if it is Leonardo who wins this contest, it is folks in our time who make it all happen; those who reinterpret the drawings against their own errors, with the knowledge of what they know must also be the case; together with those who film, shape, use, and show to us many and more agencies involved; together with, finally, a range of additional *reenactments* offered to contextualize the multiple histories and present day forms of Leonardo's expertise necessary to the series.

Many kinds of reenactment are part of the show in addition to this playful historical investigation of model making from Leonardo's drawings, which in or across some communities of practice might be called *experimental archaeology*. Some of the other kinds of reenactment include not only the *costumed recreations* of actors—Leonardo is played in the series in fictional flashbacks by Paul Arliss, for example—but also the hobbyist *reenactors* or *historical interpreters*. The Woodvilles reenactment group is hired for this series in particular; like other reenactors they describe themselves as practicing *living history* for their own entertainment and education, to people sites for historical preservation agencies and various charities, and for such film and television work.[7]

Interconnected with such costumed recreations are also several kinds of material and computer *simulation* and computer and film *animation* used in the series; these derive from both film special effects and gaming environments. When so connected, living history recreations become available to be re-understood or *refreshed* also as similar simulations for action adventure and trial and error understanding.

Add to all these more and different simulation effects, for example the now taken for granted *televisual movement* across objects accompanied by *narration* of historical meaning, what iPhoto for example calls "the Ken Burns effect." And another, now common, documentary device, in which narration by expert *talking heads* of past events and activities is overlaid upon pictures of those same *venues* in the present, where past and present are seen and listened for simultaneously. One such sequence in the series, created together with a computer simulation, visually represents for us speculations about the innovative scaffolding used by Leonardo to finish off Brunelleschi's dome in Florence. Similarly narration by *actors* voicing the words of Leonardo can be laid over present day venues or over *fictional* scenes. Finally, there are *repeating sequences* of reenactor battles, of flying papers animations, and of a surreal Mona Lisa door opening upon reenactments, all used to connect edited sections in stirring montage effects.

The range of reenactments, example piled upon example, used in this one documentary spans hobby, semiprofessional, and professional historical interpretation; computer gaming, animation, and film effects; battles and contests; and material culture displays such as in museum and national trust sites. Less obvious to connect as reenactments perhaps are the medical, biomechanical, and aviation development sites and uses described in the series. For example, in layer upon layer of simulation, the robotic engineer Mark Rosheim's own robots are inspired as reenactments of Leonardo da Vinci's automata designs and indebted to da Vinci's modeling of the human wrist. Add now, as more trial and error simulations, all the scholarly and fictional narratives of the series, conflated in various ways, that shift the centrality of authoritative knowledges without deauthorizing them, and open onto alternative knowledges, without valorizing them. These too are reanimated as additional versions of research and development.

All these, not at all exempting the traditional scholarship essential to the series or research such as Leonardo's own, contribute to ranging affects and sensations displayed and available for vicarious experience by viewers as reenactment.

The epistemological or knowledge maker melodrama enacted in this series emphasizes what we could call *pastpresents*, run together all in one word, in which pasts and presents very literally mutually construct each other.[8] They do so before our eyes in multiple and concrete forms of reenactment, forms in which it is impossible—and undesirable—to keep some singular and differential past and present apart. Nor is it just new (and old) knowledge about Leonardo that is displayed in the documentary but also scientific and technical knowledges coming into being today as part of interactive relationships with Leonardo objects crossing time.

Thus the sense of the documentary is that today these interactive pastpresents are actually necessary for important forms of knowledge *making*, not limited to teaching knowledges in entertaining ways. Such making and sharing of knowledges are not properly separated; in *use* they are brought together.

IT'S AN EXPERIMENT

It is in these multiple versions of reenactment added among the show's formats of comparison that we also perceive how this television series is an explicit experiment in communication across knowledge worlds. Please note that the word "experiment" in this context does not mean something cutting-edge new, something original and novel at this historical moment. The reference is not to "experimental" art, as in electronic literature, or to special effects startling and experientially intense on some movie screens or computer environments. While these experiments charted here do indeed play with sensation and affect in multiple modes in the very traditions of melodrama, it is not with the purpose of shifting, say, physiological thresholds of intensity; and while they also do embody historical specificities, these specificities are not offered as radical disjunctures from pasts. Connection and continuity are important here.

In other words, these are not descriptions of experiments that jump out and yell "I am a novel experience!" although, sometimes quite subtly, they may be a bit novel. Rather, the better these experiments work, the more possible it is that they can be taken for granted, even forgotten, as they are added to workable infrastructure, material and conceptual, already in place.[9] That said, some are new, some require new media amid technologies of cognition and sensation. But such newness can be valued and valuable in quite incremental variations. And some of these "newnesses" are worth questioning and devaluing, critiquing *and* appreciating. Experimental does not mean good, or better, or successful or progressive. What it does mean is trial and error learning and making taking place in multiple layers and units of interaction and articulation.

The very sense of Leonardo's "genius" in the series is that many of his conceptions might now be completed or, even better, *used*, once they become understood among contributing elements of present day material and conceptual infrastructure. Reframed epistemologies, those between ideas of Leonardo as artist and those of Leonardo as engineer, contrast his conceptions: from the artist as fantasy machines, and from the engineer as potential working models for devices of use. Although Leonardo as artist is not displaced, still the cardiac surgeon, the robotic and bioengineers do not look to Leonardo for one-off artistic successes, for single objects passing through time as unique and unmatched, in other words, for the Mona Lisa. Rather, opening up an initially surreal Mona Lisa door into reenactment (one of the arresting repeating sequences in the documentary[10]), instead they look to Leonardo for experimental, interactive, and recontextualizing ways of viewing always interconnecting bits of the world, ways that open onto devices that enhance and play with those views.

These devices are thus themselves agents among agencies and can be used in ways both conceived by Leonardo and not remotely conceivable by him, the results of trial and error learning and making for which gaming and other current interactivities can be considered epistemological shorthand.[11] Thus, as a kind of reenactment, the work of collaborative teams

The Mona Lisa door into reenactment from *Leonardo's Dream Machines*.

creating models today for a television series from drawings among pasts, can be connected to other experiments in learning and communication as well as to other practices involved in knowledge making; experiments conjured up by phrases such as "experimental archaeology" or "living history" or "gaming simulations." Some of these animate too inside whatever it might turn out we mean by such a term as "posthumanities."

AFFECTS AND SENSATIONS AS COGNITION AND EVALUATION

All these terms and activities, as included within or apart from the term and activities of "reenactment," themselves excite different *affects* and *sensations* taken together with a range of *judgments* by specialists of various sorts with specific interested ways of understanding: scholars, curators, historians, television producers, authors, journalists, hobbyists, craftspeople, and more. These exemplify a range of *knowledge worlds* in that cocreation we could call "transdisciplinary."

For example, when someone asks me what my current book is about and I say "reenactments," sometimes the immediate response is "we don't do reenactments." That usually signals the end of any conversation. For the purposes of more conversation the more promising response is "what do you mean by reenactments?" In either case, though, people may well have strong *feelings* that go together with strong *evaluations* of what THEY mean by the term "reenactment." These are the sorts of managing definitions I call "intensive" definitions, definitions that mark out specific communities of practice amid knowledge economies and culture crafts, publics, and industries. Such intensive definitions may be part of elaborate taxonomies of this large *extensive* area I am referring to by the term "reenactment." Some folks may be strongly declarative in explanation of such taxonomies and in their careful differentiation of various forms they would not use the term "reenactment" to name, differentiations specific to their forms of expertise and evaluation. Pleasure or animosity may mark these careful differentiations, and I have had some great conversations with this focus and some very difficult ones.[12] Intensively experienced affect is what signals movement across knowledge worlds, as well as what indicates cognitive and affiliative shifts across what counts as authoritative.

So, with all that in mind, let us cast these intensities in terms of *Leonardo's Dream Machines* in one interested staging of its various forms of reenactment. The TV contest between teams and with Leonardo is intended to create drama and pleasure in understanding quite *detailed* points of expertise ordinarily of interest, perhaps quite passionate interest, only to a limited membership of folks in specific communities of practice. *Grain of detail* is the signal of and for membership in particular communities of practice. Notice that these communications are not about referring to some general sort of knowledge that everyone already shares or even should share. Rather it is about teaching folks with alternative expertise to take a lively interest in and journey among knowledge worlds, even to invest in knowledges they do not have or value, yet. But this grain of detail is carefully limited and dynamically interconnected, via reenactment, to a *range* of possible interactive, or "playful" contexts, not all salient or available to every viewer, but presumably each salient and available to various sets of some of those viewing. This is an element of that scoping and scaling activity that reenactments produce, and of an ability to address simultaneously audiences actively and temporally diverging.

Such transmission skills were especially honed in the nineties, when they became experiments amid the ideological complexities of the so-called culture wars, themselves elements in the turmoil of knowledge, culture, and entertainment economies restructuring and intertwining under globalization. Privatization and public financing are important pivot points in various dynamics of any such stories, and they are discussed in greater detail in chapter 2. Notions of what count as authors and audiences are pivotal as well. Having to address many actively diverging audiences simultaneously and having to author knowledges as merely one of multiple agencies with very limited control are both circumstances that become more and more intrusive as well as intensively affective for various communities of practice. I understand *Leonardo's Dream Machines* and similar science-style television documentaries to be, quite inadvertently and yet necessarily, themselves reenactments of these very shifts in authorship and audience as they wade among and exemplify products of knowledge, culture, and entertainment industries as these altered in the nineties. I understand my own work in this way as well.

That the male engineers, the male and female art historians, and the woman pilot—all of them different sorts of white Europeans or Anglo-Europeans on, and at the side of, the stage of a new multiple-racial, multiple-cultural European Union—that they disagree on what technologies of control the pilot will be able to have in the working model of Leonardo's glider dramatizes a kind of culture shock. It is the culture shock of those who, on encountering different knowledge worlds, at first think they are all talking about the same things and sharing conventional ways of evaluating them. But they discover quickly, in various gradations of surprise and salience, that nothing of the kind is the case, and that all these knowledges and this reaction are going to have pivotal consequences.

THE SENSATION OF AGENCY BEYOND INDIVIDUAL CONTROL

A claim by knowledge engineers that the twenty disciplines that came into being in 1900, have today fractured into eight thousand specialized topics in science alone probably better reflects this sense of culture shock than it does a precise history of knowledges and their specificities.[13] Intensities and degrees of experience, and assortments and ranges of affects individuals have and desire amid such clashing knowledge worlds, are also specific to their forms of specialization, while their skills in working with, resolving, polarizing, overriding, or describing these clashes precisely vary with such experience among these specializations too. In chapter 4 it becomes even clearer that the policy, intellectual, and economic trajectories of the term "transdisciplinary" signal some of this complexity and risk as well.

Making all of this relatively explicit and highly interactive, indeed play-ful, adds another layer of sensation and affect to the epistemological melodrama of *Leonardo's Dream Machines*. With viewers vicariously par-ticipating, the show creates their pleasure with experiences made simul-taneously exotic and familiar; these just frustratingly alien enough to actually be nodes in trial and error learning, yet satisfying and success-ful enough to keep viewers hooked on their own sensations of shifting cognition and intensities of affect, however plain or subtle, hooked on sensations of their own possible agencies in groupings beyond individual control.

The narration of the show presents it simultaneously as many events that have happened across pasts, all to be filmed in a variety of forms of reenactment, but which can be experienced as if happening in the *now* of viewing. Costumed actors play characters in various reenacted incidents in Leonardo's life as well as in subsequent ones, involving in particular his notebooks, art works, or devices—these objects, knowledges, and peo-ple that outlive him. Graphic bits of animation frame patterns produced within these various kinds of reenactment, sometimes blurring them to-gether, sometimes separating them out, recombining them and literaliz-ing the difficulties of that one word "pastpresents." These are all experi-ments in various kinds of inclusion and connection:

— some in movement across *authoritative* knowledges, watching the center of authority shift
— some in displays of *alternative* knowledges, where a contrast of knowledge against knowledges alters their value

In other words, to create viewing communities where folks feel *included*, the *exclusions* of authoritative knowledge need to be repositioned. Knowl-edges cannot be just separate territories with their unchallenged experts where viewers enter as strangers. Instead viewers are encouraged to com-pare and value new knowledges, encouraged as both strangers and com-panions to take up some steps in journeys among knowledges we discover already exist but are not yet finished. These kinds of learning do not simply consume knowledges but rather *use* them, use them in ways that both remake and newly make them. *Not knowing* some knowledges even offers a valued venue from which substantive contributions become pos-sible; peripheral participation signals insights into *using* that full member-ship in carefully bounded and authoritative communities of practice actually hides. In travel, knowledges look newer and older accordingly. Viewers and other peripheral participants become users as learning and making knowledges are interconnected and valued quite literally in demonstration. Such characterizations of learning are not original ones, but they have their novelties staged in the particular venues of these television genres where, amid televisual technologies, they generate excitement as experiments in melodrama and reenactment.[14]

Therefore, it is especially important that reenactments are not a way to keep pasts and presents apart—or a way to keep authorities and alternative knowledges, metaphors and referents, materialities and abstractions, forms of academic expertise and cultural entertainment, or affects and cognitions separated, managed, or delimited by membership. Flexible knowledges, transdisciplinarities, new media, all plunge us into uncertainties, risk, collusion, and collaboration; all conditions that—as with responsibilities to multiple audiences from painfully limited authorships—we do not control and in which we are elemental "bits" in emergent reorganizations of knowledge economies and among altering evaluations.

"But what if," as a friend worriedly, wistfully, earnestly asked me recently, "you *love* your discipline?" Is the assumption behind her question that a transdisciplinary practice requires giving up all that "discipline" registers? Of course *we love our discipline*, even while registering "discipline" in still widening associations of scholarly and political meaning, all of which makes its evaluation an uncomfortably ambiguous "good." After all, within and engaging disciplining communities of practice, we become cocreations of and among our own and others' cognitive, hormonal, and sensory pleasures and distastes—some of the very elements that make up cognitive sensation and complex personhood.[15]

So we might consider that one way to explore what this question and its caring even means is precisely taken up but structured alternatively in each chapter of this book, each time within another varying range of *disciplines* or *case studies*. This very variety intends to honor the work I call reenaction and the many ways disciplines might care about or instantiate agencies I index as reenactors. Entities for examination and modes of analysis are promiscuously multiplied here, but not in some insensitivity to the pleasures and powers that disciplines instantiate. Their exquisite parsimonies of explanation and validity, those (sometimes terrorized or terrorizing) delights in greater and greater detail honed and scaled within communities of practice among respective knowledge worlds is not debunked here but is revalued. Working out in a multiverse of articulating disciplines, interdisciplines, and multidisciplinarities, such transdisciplinary inspection actually *enjoys* the many flavors of details, offerings, passions, languages, things, even while also demonstrating that its own forms of validity are not entailed only within those elegant but divergent parsimonies of explanation. Instead, one index for the evaluation of transdisciplinary work is in how well it learns and models *how to be affected* or moved, how well it *opens up* unexpected elements of one's own embodiments in lively and re-sensitizing worlds.[16]

So in the spirit of scoping and scaling Google-style, chapter 1 explores how nationalities, sexualities, and global TV intertwine at the beginning of the nineties, as the European Union comes into being and as political economies of media and images shift. The TV shows *Highlander* and *Xena* are occasions for an analysis of globally interactive cultural economies and the agencies of niche producers, fans, and industries, while their reenactments are examples of pan-European identities and politics.

Then, chapter 2 works to recall the various "wars" of the nineties: the culture, history, image, and science wars, by examining reenactment technologies of diorama and political meaning instantiated in the exhibition *Science in American Life* at the Smithsonian's National Museum of American History. It explores the uses and limits of debunking critique as they powered these culture wars and some of the many historical roles commerce plays in strategies of education, entertainment, and nationalism, as exemplified in this particular museum reenactment.

The transmedia convergences of TV and the web are explored in chapter 3, as PBS science-styled television reenactments of various sorts are invented and displayed, becoming the settings for experimental histories and cascading communications among knowledge worlds. Reenactors and the work of reenaction animate the complex boundary objects that allow for collaboration across unevenly distributed knowledges, as seen in the example of time traveling DNA technologies moving among unstable meanings of gender and race.

All along the nineties then, as described in chapter 4, scholars start mobilizing reenactments in new roles as intellectual entrepreneurs, intensively engaging a globally restructuring academic capitalism that becomes newly explicit and more and more intrusive over the nineties and after. Reenactment studies itself comes into being as a version of these trends as international academics and creative industry workers collaborate in both

TV experiences and in critical reaction, attempting to sensitize national priorities for knowledge transfer.

And my conclusion tries to put all this fervent variety of reenactment into some sort of transmedia story for knowledge work emerging out of the nineties and into some *now* farther on, wondering about the possibilities of a feminist transdisciplinary posthumanities as it contemplates what an engagement with reenactment, reenaction, and reenactors might sensitize us to, in lively worldly ways, scoping and scaling among agencies.

Indeed, scoping and scaling keeps relocating the agencies we have even as we discover that agency and control are rarely at the same scale of analysis. And awareness at the levels of infrastructure, variation, inclusion, and undecidability means we are "bits" *of* complex transdisciplinizing "consciousness," not a Leonardo-like "Man" or even "Hu-man" at its center.[17] Laboring to participate in a universe in which we are only some of the objects, devices, things, processes, and trial and error reassemblages in self-organizing "learning" is one work of reenactment. Engaging cognition as sensation and affect is another.

A NOTE ON CITATIONS AND LITERATURES IN A TRANSDISCIPLINIZING POSTHUMANITIES

A transdisciplinizing posthumanities networks across many knowledge worlds. These do not all share the same practices of citation or the same sets of core and cutting-edge literatures. Indeed some ranges of these knowledge worlds are not located in academies. This book labors to demonstrate one version of the work of a transdisciplinizing posthumanities without intensively promoting a set of new standardizing practices. It is, of course, impossible to satisfy equally the evidentiary standards for all these knowledge worlds or to account for all their possible literatures, objects, issues, and intentions. This means that some forms of affiliation are deliberately or inadvertently demoted. Other literatures and communities of practice are centered here in a play of contingent affiliation, a proper possibility among highly distributed conditions of production, display, and reception.

ONE

NATIONALITIES, SEXUALITIES, AND GLOBAL TV

Highlander, *Xena*, and Meanings of European Union

COUNTDOWN, 1992: TRAVELING IMAGES

THE YEAR 1992 was the countdown year for the formation of the European single market, the regional economic entity—utopian for some, dystopian for others—now intended to recenter Europe in a global politics fragmented in the wake of the breakup of the Soviet Union (even given that earlier plans for "European Community" considerably predated "the fall of Communism"). It was this new "European Union" that would necessarily refigure what counted as Europe—literally which countries now would be in this redesigned entity "Europe" and which not—and that now would also reconceive the telescoping meanings of nationalisms, regionalisms, and localisms backdropped by the global economy. The year 1992 also marked the five hundredth anniversary of the so-called discovery of the new world: the invasion of the Americas by European conquerors.[1] The contest to represent that moment in this one was part of a new "war" of "image superpowers":[2] engaging national desires to valorize old colonialisms in the face of new ones, and oppositional political movements attempting to address the face of new racisms in Europe and elsewhere only too often traveling as national and ethnic identities.

The year 1992 was also when the action adventure TV series *Highlander* first premiered—"the first European co-produced weekly hour to be sold into the US syndication market."[3] Based on a fantasy world of immortal sword fighters similar to the worlds created in comics and computer games, *Highlander* might well be historically positioned among conventions refined in hobby communities such as the Society for Creative Anachronism. Today *Highlander* communities are managed on the web, often by commercial interests. It is here with *Highlander* we begin looking for and at *reenactments* networked under globalization.

And in this chapter *Highlander* is paired with its mid-nineties US counterpart, *Xena: Warrior Princess*, as a complementary but differently centered response to changing conditions in media making, one in a trajectory of off-shoring production at other ranges of globalization. This chapter takes as its case study of globalization processes the political economies of images within and beyond the European Union generated by those making, using, selling, and showing off the action adventure TV shows *Highlander* and *Xena*. It introduces thick descriptions of globalization processes that in later chapters work to narrate and demonstrate interconnecting televisual infrastructures.

So this chapter starts off with noting how sexual and national identities inhabit strangely shifting geographies, literal sets on which to stage productions of European Union. Commercial powers named in cultural studies by David Morley and Kevin Robins, "enterprise culture" and "heritage culture," showcase a particular kind of "global citizenship." Freddie Mercury of the mega-international rock group *Queen* displays such citizenship in a range of sexualized masculinities, before and together with the *Highlander* films and TV series. Sexual and national identities are intertwined as forbidden topics in interactive *Highlander* Internet communities of practice. Such communities literally construct a map of the niche markets for consuming the reenactments of *Highlander* and *Xena*, while their interactive dynamics animate image maps of European Union. All together these shiftings, stagings, and mappings exemplify forms of consciousness cultivated, sometimes celebrated, and necessarily inhabited by those of us altered and altering under globalization.

GLOBAL GAY FORMATIONS AND LOCAL HOMOSEXUALITIES

My own pleasure in *Highlander* began with the principal actor Adrian Paul's eroticized image. I immediately (and somewhat idiosyncratically) "recognized" it as gay (the image, not necessarily the main story character Duncan MacLeod, or the actor Adrian Paul). It was in this "recognition" that I discovered my pleasure in the show. As a lesbian I was surprised: this was really the first TV show since my adolescence in which an eroticized male image seemed so powerfully attractive to me. Perhaps that is why I

assumed it was somehow gay. Other signs appeared to heighten my pleasure in what seemed to me to be a circulation of gay meanings. First was
the use of Paris's *Shakespeare and Company* as a location and story site—
this bookstore that in the twenties on the Rue de l'Odéon had been run
and made famous by lesbian lovers Sylvia Beach and Adrienne Monnier
was now known on the show simply as "the American bookstore."[4] Second was the powerful emotional engagement of the show's theme music,
"Princes of the Universe," composed and performed by *Queen* and originally sung by the late Freddie Mercury. Mercury had died of AIDS in
November 1991, the year before the TV series *Highlander* began.[5]

It was not that I assumed that there was a latent homosexual subtext, a
topic repeatedly raised in the mid-nineties on the international Internet
newsgroup alt.tv.highlander but usually treated with scorn by those fans;
no, I assumed it was something else. I puzzled over it. On impulse at the
supermarket I picked up a special issue of *Entertainment Weekly*. This issue
shouted on its cover "The Gay '90s: Entertainment Comes Out of the
Closet." In the cover article by Jess Cagle, "America Sees Shades of Gay," I
found words to describe the impression I had received from the show:
"mutual inclusiveness—the *give* and *take back*—of gay and straight audiences. Its sex appeal bids for the attention of all sexual persuasions; so
do its jokes, and the screen winks broadly in all directions." Or, "the most
striking and omnipresent outgrowth of that awakening has been in the
mass marketing of erotic male images." "They're all things to all persuasions." Or, "not gay per se but *something*. 'It's all become one bright pop
blur.'" And finally, "in short, this revolution is the only kind Hollywood
can trust—one driven by the marketplace."[6]

WHAT SORTS OF QUEERS?

Entertainment Weekly's political angle differs markedly from the cautionary analysis narrated in Marxist terms by the feminist theorist Rosemary
Hennessy when she discusses "Queer Visibility in Commodity Culture";
she says,

> capitalism's need for expanding markets has in its own way promoted
> the integration of art and life . . . continuously working and reworking
> desires by inviting them to take the forms dictated by the commodity
> market. . . . The aestheticization of daily life encourages the pursuit

of new tastes and sensations as pleasures in themselves while concealing or backgrounding the labor that has gone into making them possible. . . . We need a way of understanding [queer] visibility that acknowledges both the local situations in which sexuality is made intelligible as well as the ties that bind knowledge and power to commodity production, consumption, and exchange.[7]

It was in 1995 that I first encountered *Highlander* and read Cagle's essay. Two years later I could watch the final episodes of the US TV comedy *Ellen*, after being both captivated and depressed by the "Ellen Watch," the countdown to its coming out episode.[8] I recall with a similar ambivalent mixture my interested speculations concerning the commercial success of "*Xena* feminism," and the politics of the producers of the globally successful action show of the late nineties, *Xena*. I and others especially speculated about their playful encouragement of multiple readings of the sexual lives of main characters Xena and Gabrielle, who adventured through a postmodern world vaguely modeled on ancient Greece.[9]

These TV events are examples, in telescoping layers of locals and globals, of what I call *global gay formations and local homosexualities*, intersecting with what David Morley and Kevin Robins have titled *Spaces of Identity: Global Media, Electronic Landscapes and Cultural Boundaries*. Large political and ideological issues are played out in concrete terms clearly economic in the Canadian and French TV show *Highlander* and also in the US show shot in New Zealand, *Xena*. *Xena* here is a counterpoint to *Highlander*, each with a ranging Internet media fandom, a subculture of fans that is largely female and was, once upon a time at the beginning of my research in the early to mid-nineties, a rare site of women's concentration on the World Wide Web. While importantly international, these media fandoms still tend to be dominated by English speaking fans from all over the world and by fans within the TV shows' principal market, the United States. Australia, however, is increasingly a new center for *Highlander* fandom.[10] Part of my aim in this chapter is, using the science journalist and semiotician Steven Johnson's vocabulary, to "probe" the complex "telescoping" patternings of globals and locals in layers that constitute the processes of globalization in "spaces of identity," that is to say, in intersections of nationality, sexuality, and gender.

The point of all this is not to celebrate female media fandoms, TV shows, identity politics, or globalization. With other feminists I am complexly critical of and influenced by (and sometimes take necessary pleasures in) all, indeed, I am inextricably embedded in all, on the one hand in ways deliberate, political, perhaps even visionary, but also in other ways structural and inevitable, in unintended but certainly not innocent complicity. Fandoms, TV, identity politics, and transnationalisms are sites of and for political contestation, and the many cognitive styles that register such contestation are at stake as examples here. Single-hearted stances of negative critique are only partial registers for our accountabilities among dynamically altering regimes of globalized capital. Mindful of the Chicana theorist Chela Sandoval's vision and analysis of "differential movement," potentially liberatory but ever dangerous, tools from technoscience studies prove helpful for working with these locals and globals in layers.[11] For example, using Donna Haraway's non-innocent historical "naturecultures," or invoking Bruno Latour's "parliament of things," facilitates an alternate feminist and progressive politics about *technology cultures* under globalization.[12]

PLAY AMONG LAYERS OF LOCALS AND GLOBALS

Steven Johnson's vocabulary of popular culture cognitions is also a great resource, especially for considering the technology cultures of media fandoms and other users.[13] He describes skills cultivated in gaming and extended to television, computer use, and to film: "probing" (learning the rules of a game by trial and error, while necessarily also checking out its edges, limits and unexpected artifacts or patterns; in queer contexts you may add many sexualized jokes here as well) and "telescoping" (apprehending simultaneously all the structures of nested hierarchy and mobilizing them in various sequences; once you attend to the phallic imagery it is impossible to escape it but highly possible to joke about it!).

This chapter will also point "flashing arrows" (signposts to help readers entangle themselves properly into the book) to such practices as "filling in" (tentatively trying out possible materials in spaces left empty in production, sometimes deliberately, sometimes inadvertently), "multiple threading" (keeping track of many *story arcs* and a range of narrative frames, noting which ones are currently *active* and which ones are *latent* but potentially significant), "texture" (noting which details are irrelevant but added tacitly for the pleasure of a heightened realism), as well as significant layered jokes (rich associations built up humorously over long time frames that animate a complex intermedia intertextuality).

My intentions are similar to Johnson's, that is, to point to cognitive skills used in these global television technology cultures. Very occasionally this book itself might perform such practices, subtly and not so subtly asking readers to work together on these intellectual engagements, or to examine and care about jokes and play, as they might in games, television shows, and Internet sites. While it is asking a lot to be so cognitively nimble, how else could users *probe* (yes, do laugh, while continuing to notice how appropriate this imagery is) the sensations and affects of these globalized products and processes, or index global economic knowledges across narrative, anxiety, and play?

STRANGE AND WONDERFULLY TEXTURED ECONOMIC GEOGRAPHIES

Let us start with the economic arrangements surrounding the coming-into-being of the TV show *Highlander* concretized in 1992, this year of formation of the European single market. Gaumont, the French firm that has been called "the world's oldest film company," was *Highlander*'s principal production partner.[14] That first year financing was a money mix from France, Germany, Italy, and Japan, but in the second year Gaumont found another partner, Canadian Filmline International.[15] *Highlander* thus became a coproduction filmed entirely in France and Canada and shot in English for a world market. It has been seen in seventy countries in Europe, North and South America, Asia, Africa, and Australia, where it has competed with syndicated series produced in the United States.[16] In distinctly French and Canadian cultural strategies *Highlander* has been another of those culture products intended to combat US media hegemony. Its quotas on European content were insured during several seasons by shooting half the time each season in Vancouver and half the time in Paris under a Franco-Canadian agreement in which "segments shot in Canada qualify as European, and segments shot in Europe qualify as Canadian."[17] Note these European single market's strategically shifting economic geographies!

The year 1997 was *Highlander*'s last broadcast season; indeed, the US distributor ordered only thirteen episodes (rather than the usual twenty-two), all of which were shot in Paris. A TV spinoff series lasted one season —*Highlander: The Raven*.[18] It starred the principal female recurring character and was clearly intended to capitalize on *Xena*'s commercial success and demographic appeal, thus attempting, if unsuccessfully, to mobilize the interests of female media fandoms among others. So far two, not very good, feature films starring the TV series actors have been released, *Highlander: Endgame* (2000) and *Highlander: The Source* (2007).[19] Contrasting with the previous three feature films from the late eighties, early nineties, the cast of each of these combines actors and premises from both previous films and from the TV series.[20]

Looking back, in 1991 Gaumont had just opened its new television division. This marked a shift in economic strategies by the company that pioneered massive vertical integration as the winning strategy among global media corporations. Gaumont's empire, begun in 1895 with manufacturing and selling photographic equipment, quickly became first "the world's largest film studio" with the first woman producer, director, editor and soon after "the world's largest movie theater."[21] Today media corporations are a complicated mix of parent companies and subsidiaries with multinational lineages. For example, the US company, MCA, the principal partner with Sam Raimi's Renaissance Pictures first creating the TV show *Xena*, became a private subsidiary of the Canadian multinational Seagram, who bought it in 1995 from the Japanese multinational Matsushita. MCA in the mid-nineties had divisions and subsidiaries involved in movies, TV, videotapes, publishing, music, concerts, audio tapes, cable TV, and more.[22] Seagram renamed the company Universal Studios, but it was sold in 2000 to Vivendi in France becoming Vivendi Universal.[23] In 2004 NBC combined with Vivendi Universal Entertainment to form NBC Universal, 80 percent owned by General Electric and 20 percent owned by Vivendi. The television stations division was built from NBC and Telemundo stations, while networks distribution oversaw properties, including, in addition to NBC, Bravo, Sci Fi, and the History Channel, while TiVo is managed by Digital Distribution.[24]

This kind of massive vertical integration is about being altogether in control of production sites, materials, and talent, distribution, sales, and promotion, and places of exhibition and retailing or technologies of delivery. National boundaries may only get in the way of such decentralized but interconnected systems, and in their turn, they require new forms of coordination and servicing, now often centralized in so-called global cities.[25]

As Gaumont's president Nicolas Seydoux said in 1994: "Gaumont began life as an integrated company. . . . A screen has no reason to exist without a movie to show on it, and a movie doesn't exist without a screen to show it on."[26] But although Gaumont may have pioneered integration, it had ceased being a winning player in the global market: its attempts to parley its many decades long management of film production, distribution, and theatrical exhibition into new chains of theaters throughout Europe in the eighties had failed. Entering into economic retrenchment Gaumont had become very vocal about French film culture, announced its plans to concentrate on making films in French only, and clearly intended now to take advantage of state protection of culture industries. Supporting limits on US films and TV programs abroad, Seydoux insisted: "This is not a trade war. It is an identity statement. All we want is to preserve a world in which grandchildren have the same national identity as their grandparents."[27]

On the one hand, that is. Film would be Gaumont's site of cultural nationalism. But TV would be Gaumont's entry into global media. At the end of the first three years of its existence Gaumont's TV division accounted for one fifth of its profits.[28] Gaumont's first French production partner in this *Highlander* venture, channel TF1, had had to end its partnership after the first year, because it was no longer allowed to count English-language TV products, like *Highlander*, as "French." French channel M6, however, "had the right to produce non-French European programs," but was a smaller channel, with less money to invest.[29] So, in order to continue production on this English-language TV show, Gaumont had to find its Canadian partner, Filmline.

THE SETS ON WHICH TO STAGE PRODUCTIONS OF EUROPEAN UNION

As a joint venture between Canada and France, *Highlander*'s production elements were carefully quota-ed. Indeed, the quotas on European content are the reason that for several seasons *Highlander* was shot on location in both Canada and France. *Highlander*'s narrative elements are a clever "recombinant subgenre" as well: part traditionally masculine martial arts action adventure, part traditionally feminine historical romance costume melodrama.[30] These elements have traveled well and widely, engaging multiple global audiences. The audiences for *Highlander* were "split pretty equally between men and women, which is something kind of unique for an action show," said Ira Bernstein, head of domestic syndication for Rysher, *Highlander*'s distributor, which meant more women viewers than usual.[31]

Each episode contains both highly ritualized sword fights between Immortals and historical flashbacks recreating past events in their long lives and loves; thus each episode depends upon both *reenactments* and their corollary *pastpresents* (interacting and relational engagements among pasts and presents, neither of which is meaningful without or separable from the other). Narrative action takes place in both historical time and apparent contemporary time in specific spots on a clearly colonized globe; this global map has literally been drawn and chronologized by fans, activating an embodied sensitivity to *telescoping spacetimes* among these historical geographies. Fancily reproduced it has been sold in the US and Canada out of the *Highlander* catalogue along with other merchandise.[32] The map (and some of the other merchandise) emerges from and is itself a resource for fan writing, criticism, and culture. As with other media fandoms, *Highlander* fandom in the nineties was largely female, white, and middle-aged.[33] I use both the present and past tenses here because *Highlander* and *Xena* fandom continues even after each TV show's cancellation; and the shows themselves are still seen on old videotapes, new DVDs, and iTunes downloads. Although the immediacy of a series in production is over, the pleasure in synchronic engagement with each entire series' oeuvre is even heightened for fans; pastpresents are simultaneously palpable and virtual.

In fact the web facilitates communities of practice among *Highlander* fandoms. They are, in Steven Johnson's terms, "participatory," creating new and reembodied forms of *social interaction*, and depend upon and probe shifting *interfaces*, literal and liminal (and eroticized). Once any season was over, it could be repeatedly recaptured in libraried collections built from shows taped, perhaps transmitted off satellites, and discussed online, in order to probe and fill in gaps and withheld information, and—as when some fans actually visited locations of production—such resources of librarying, downloading, discussing, and visiting could be shared in neighborhood viewing groups. Once a series is over, fans are free to move among its *timescales*, heightening the interconnections already built among story characters, actors, production people, viewers, and fandoms; these are opened and refreshed, first in video and then on DVD, at cons (fan conventions) and cruises, in catalogue gear and commodities, and especially in the layered jokes and other intertexualities of fan fictions.

SYSTEMS AND INFRASTRUCTURES MATTER

Both *Highlander* and *Xena* paradoxically depended and still depend on both the wide global currency of genre elements and an appeal to gendered interests in the niche markets of media and electronic fandoms, on both broad narratives that do not rely on dialog and on complex systems of self-referentiality that layer audiences, markets, styles, and forms of viewing and consumption locally as well as globally. Both *Highlander* and *Xena* are examples of and created by and for economic strategies responsive to new global conditions of accumulation. *Xena*'s executive producers, Sam Raimi and Robert Tapert, known for "chic-horror" movies like *Darkman*, or postmodern "pop-apocalyptic" Westerns (like *The Quick and the Dead*),[34] "off-shored" their twin TV shows *Hercules* and *Xena*; indeed preemptively mobilizing New Zealand's own film and TV resources into an elaborate localized "cultural industrial district." *Highlander*'s previous Canadian location, Vancouver, is also a similar cultural industrial district, where Hollywood products like *The X-Files* have also been made.

Speaking of the first season of *Hercules* but true of its offshoot *Xena* too, as reported in the Auckland *Sunday News*: "Contributing to its appeal here will be the local locations and actors. Shooting in Auckland not only kept the budget low but provided the heroics with an exotic backdrop that hasn't been seen on US television." And the Wellington *Dominion* said: "The series has a distinctly New Zealand flavor with Kiwi slang creeping into the dialogue." MCA enthusiastically boasted of the sudden spurt of international markets *Xena* was sold into for its second season, a surprise they said, having been "developed almost exclusively with the domestic market in mind." (They meant the US market.[35]) In sum, *Highlander* represents European attempts during the nineties to counter Hollywood in joint ventures with other beleaguered cultural sites, while *Xena* on the other hand represents Hollywood's attempts then to "externalize" its economic risks and to "maximize a variety of creative resources."[36]

In the movements of globals and locals among "image superpowers," *Highlander* and *Xena* complexly combine ideological strategies, economic and representational, that media theorists David Morley and Kevin Robins have explicated as "enterprise culture" and "heritage culture."[37] These terms, originating in a specifically British context, refer on the one hand, with enterprise culture, to Thatcher-like political promotions of national capital and local labor in pursuit of strategic alliances and joint ventures, the price of admission to a global club of flexible transnationals; and on the other hand, heritage culture refers to Prince Charles–like exploitations of nostalgia and invented traditions intended to make places attractive locations for global investment and tourism. Enterprise and heritage cultures have intertwined but also sometimes competing ideological mandates. *Highlander*'s dual locations have been entirely resonant with both these notions: Vancouver as enterprise culture, an up-and-coming newly reglobalized city in the nineties, re-created by shifting capital and repeatedly lampooned in economic racist terms as Hong-couver, the inheritor of fleeing capital from a decolonized Hong Kong. Or Paris as heritage culture, long a global city but concentrating "larger shares of most financial sectors than it did ten years ago" (that is to say, over the course of the nineties) with its "place-specific differences" parleyed as "tools in competition over positional advantages."[38]

Such linked cities in global networks are the subject of extensive analysis by the feminist economist Saskia Sassen.[39] Although some are built upon and within the sites of cities historically powerful, such as Paris, they are nevertheless "new" in "formation of [a] new urban economic core of financial and service activities that comes to replace the older . . . core. . . . The growth of producer service firms based in New York or London or Paris can be fed by manufacturing [here read "production"] located anywhere in the world as long as it is part of a multinational corporate network."[40] The "off-shoring" of media industries, like the economic arrangements creating *Xena*, requires these producer service firms' expertise, as they are capable of managing the complex network that such dispersal of labor processes is embedded within. Sassen points to the ambiguous "locations" of production—decentralized—paradoxically requiring highly localized "centers" of services in these new global cities. In such concrete networked infrastructures are locals and globals, pluralized, layered, made relative and relational in nested hierarchies of structure and power. Concentrating only on "centers" or only on "distribution" would be misleading; it is this nested and telescoping layering of locals and globals in nodal networks that is significant.

Alternatively, consider such location shots in *Highlander* as Vancouver cityscapes, which stand in for cities all over "America" (in quotes). Location in Vancouver is not only important to *Highlander* but to Hollywood products as well. As a cultural industrial district for film and TV industries, Vancouver's cityscapes are recognized all over the world as various and nonspecific North American cities. Thus *Highlander* fans, writing stories that took off from and went beyond the TV show, called the Vancouver location "Seacouver" (combining Seattle and Vancouver) as they delighted in the ambiguous national possession of pivotal sites in *Highlander* narratives. Influenced by fans, the writers and directors of *Highlander* also came to use the term "Seacouver" themselves in their screenplays to refer to the virtual city in which contemporary *Highlander* stories take place.

Now consider the location shots from Paris. The barge the main character Duncan MacLeod lives on when in Paris is parked conveniently along the Seine: right behind the Cathedral of Notre Dame. Almost every shot of Duncan and the barge is backgrounded by a rear view of Notre Dame. When, during the fourth season, for one episode the producers were unable to rent that exact, now taken for granted site, their alternative dock for the barge was backgrounded by the Eiffel Tower instead. The "place-specific" is being sold as heritage culture Paris, not the "place-ambiguous."

In these terms Seacouver becomes an emblem for that very US cultural hegemony that the show's economic arrangements are intended to foil. Is *Highlander* really a kind of US cultural economic off-shoring like *Xena*, but in disguise? Suddenly the fact that British citizen, also half-Italian, principal actor Adrian Paul made his home in Hollywood makes a particular kind of professional sense. Or rather does this mean something more complicated about the meanings of globalization? Seacouver mingles locals, in a fictional regional entity that simultaneously crosses and repositions na-tional, economic, and cultural boundaries. Both relational and relative, it simultaneously exploits similarities *and* differences.

SCALE, SCOPE, AND TELESCOPING

Seacover is a "glocalization," where globally mapped venues are remapped by users and by local use for small-scale power realignments, available for appropriation by alternative-scale users too. Glocalizing practices share with gaming practices a textured awareness of multiple threads among layers of locals and globals, an ability to find holes to fill in within an only seemingly determinative story arc, thus a joking layering and probing of determinative meanings. *Highlander* fans practicing glocalization and writing fan fiction might remark with Johnson, describing gamer plea-sures: "there's something strangely satisfying about defining the edges of a simulation, learning what it's capable of and where it breaks down."[41] Manipulating scale and scope matter in gamers' strategies of play among nested hierarchies. Johnson stipulates:

> I call the mental labor of managing all these simultaneous objectives "telescoping" because of the way the objectives nest inside one another like a collapsed telescope. I like the term as well because part of this skill lies in focusing on immediate problems while still maintaining a long-distance view. You can't progress far in a game if you simply deal with the puzzles you stumble across; you have to coordinate them with the ultimate objectives on the horizon. Talented gamers have *the ability to keep all these varied objectives in their heads simultaneously.*[42]

Consider the term "American" (in quotes). In general usage all over the world, "America," which describes almost half a hemisphere, northern and southern continents together, is used as a synonym specifically for the United States. American-in-quotes is one of those specious generics that are emblems of unequal power relations, like the word "Man" or the word "White." Yet in Mexico the term "North America" might name an English-language historically colonized but now colonizing cultural power, in which Canada and the United States are seen as a linguistic and cultural unity, and thus might also obfuscate the "Canadian experience of subservience" to US cultural interests.[43] Richard Collins refers to the

"Canadianisation of European television," by which he means a Europe-wide extension of the experience Canada has suffered in relation to the United States. Such "Canadianisation" undergirds the economic alliance between Canada and France that *Highlander* embodies and the fear of one kind of future into which it attempts to intervene. Yet to be "North American" or indeed "American" and be incorporated by the body of the United States is not always to Canada's disadvantage; the unity imagined from Mexico also emphasizes Canada's relative economic and cultural advantages vis-à-vis Mexico.

"From where do you see what?" Such a telescoping question is perhaps even more appropriate under the terms of globalized power than another question such specious generics also suggest, one often centered by US feminist identity politics, the question, "Am I included?" Scoping and scaling powers of inclusion and marginalization are reworked and ameliorated by glocalizations of varying liveliness. From British Columbia, Canada, where the *Highlander* locations are distinctively Vancouver—from there it is no place-ambiguous city. It is full of city landmarks and neighborhoods, distinctive buildings, sky- and sea lines, mountain backdrops. Internet fans of *Highlander* learned from Canadian counterparts and touring US friends that Duncan's dojo was located in Vancouver's Gastown district. Walking tours were provided online, and neighborhood viewing groups huddled over someone's vacation photos personalizing such tours.

However, although folks from Vancouver could see their own city quite recognizably the location of *Highlander*, still the set was dressed with US postal workers' uniforms and US car license plates. But even these can be read ambiguously: US cars are certainly to be found in Vancouver and postal workers are similarly capable of travel. Glocalization can work with and against globalization's dependence upon *a new kind of horizontal integration*; that is, markets identified as demographic groups beyond rather than within geographical boundaries, as Morley and Robins suggest. This explains too how sexuality can "globalize" as ethnicity, naming and exploiting an international "gay" market, especially one traveling, migrating, and moved around.[44] We practice such "demography" by engaging with online materials that create niche commercial and political identities, but also morphed identities like that of "the fan." Morley and Robins emphatically emphasize that under regimes of globalization, the local—or better, locals—are always both "relational and relative."[45] So is the global—or globals.

The mega-international rock group *Queen*, which composed and performed the music for the first *Highlander* movie, offers another concrete example, here of the kinds of shifts in social and personal identities produced under globalization. *Queen*'s lead singer Freddie Mercury embodies the global market's physical, cultural, and economic migrations—for some possible, for others compulsory. Born in Zanzibar of Zoroastrian parents of Persian descent, Mercury was educated in Bombay, India, from ages ten through sixteen. Following the Zanzibar Revolution in 1964 he and his family fled to Britain where he studied art and in 1970 hooked up with the other folks who made up the "British" group *Queen*, which he named. Over the twenty years of Mercury's association with *Queen* before his death, his image morphed in self-consciously parodic shifts of cultural association, at times accentuating and at times deaccentuating his own multiple-cultural travels, always parodying and exploiting contemporary images of masculinity.[46] As he died of AIDS, Mercury denied that he was homosexual, although every element of *Queen*'s self-presentation in each decade parodied the then-current subcultural image of the gay or bisexual man.[47] Indeed, bisexuality, in both international rock image and cultural manifestations, and as a morphed and remixed global sexuality, was exploited by *Queen* and particularly by Mercury.

The music for the first *Highlander* movie appeared in *Queen*'s album *A Kind of Magic*, the lead song of which was number one on the charts of thirty-five countries in 1986.[48] Mercury's song "Princes of the Universe" is heard in the opening and closing sequences of every episode of the TV series *Highlander*. In the music video of "Princes of the Universe" Mercury struts through the song with Christopher Lambert (star of the first *Highlander* film) on a concert stage built to echo and monumentalize the site of the climax of the movie, the final sword fight.[49] The homoerotic energy of the rock music and staged and parodied dance between Mercury and Lambert has explicit undercurrents in both movie and TV show. (Cuts from the movie darkly flash by in swift succession, many of them surreally "historical.")

Fans pointedly pronounce the name "Lambert" as "Lam-BEAR," intended as a mark of familiarity with Lambert's national origins, which are Belgian, and fans tell stories that his language coach for the film *Greystoke* attempted to create for him an accented English that would be recognized as "European" generally, but would be impossible to pin down as belonging to a particular European nation; a very *literalization* of European union. Lambert's, Mercury's, and half-British, half-Italian TV show star Adrian Paul's images all can be read as multiethnic: as locally "like us" in a large number of markets globally. They are profoundly attractive in a global market that also creates images like the infamous Benneton ads' computer-morphed ethnics, parodied in gay political posters.[50] Thus the generic and the particular are *telescoped* back and forth in layers of locals and globals under globalization; ethnic and also sexual mixtures— morphed or remixed—have special salience, necessarily both relative and relational.

Despite Seydoux's avowed desire to preserve and even generationally stabilize national identity in the era of European Union, *Highlander* culture demonstrates "how the cultural construction of national identity, as articulated in both official policies and informal popular practices, is a precarious project that can never be isolated from the global, transnational relations in which it takes shape."[51] *Highlander* and *Xena* participate in remixed identities of various intentions and commercial realities, sometimes ambi-sexual, sometimes ambi-cultural, sometimes ambi-ethnic, and always ambi-local.

FORBIDDEN TOPICS

When I first subscribed to the listserv that is one site of *Highlander* international media fandom, I found to my dismay that homosexuality was a "forbidden topic." After all, my own attraction to *Highlander* was very much founded in my "recognition" of a circulation of gay images. Indeed I had sought out *Highlander* fandom in order to make community with others I thought must have similar attractions. On the list, though, homosexuality as a topic had been forbidden as "flamebait," that is, as a topic that was assumed to inevitably incite "flame wars," or long, exhausting vituperative attacks. Still, I also soon discovered that some fans occasionally made fun of and attempted to subvert the ban by posing mock questions using a blank instead of words like gay, homosexual, and so on. For example, someone might say, "Surely we know that Duncan isn't *BLANK*." If reprimanded by another post, the trickster might claim, "Oh, I wasn't raising a forbidden topic, I was referring to CANADIANS." This became the joking equation, the word "Canadian" was invoked instead of the word "gay," to the delight of some Canadians on the list and to the horror of others. Placing the word "Canadian" in this context, always cute, a bit trivializing, and always edged with connotations of abnormality or subordination, was only too close to "colonizing" assumptions on the parts of US fans about Canada anyway, and also very close to complacencies on the part of "tolerant" fans in what was also a running joke about homosexuality. Many pleasures, some sadistic, some campy, some subversive, some smug were encapsulated in this running *layered joke*, which also did allow for some very limited encouragement to those of us who wanted to discuss things gay and possibly gay on *Highlander*. Here the sexual and the national stood in for each other, highlighting and trivializing the relations of power that made such a substitution possible.

Somewhat later a new character was introduced to the series, the oldest known "immie" (what fans call Immortals), the five-thousand-year-old Methos, who was hiding out as a Watcher, one of the mortals who keeps track of immies. He was an immediate hit: list members went crazy over the character and the actor, who shortly thereafter came to the *Highlander* convention in Denver in October 1995. The actor, Peter Wingfield, told us during his question-and-answer session how he had heard about his success with the fans from the production people, who got reports from their creative consultants on the reactions of fans on the various Internet sites. He bubbled over with excitement about getting such immediate feedback on his performance and about how it had encouraged the producers to use the new character in a series of *story arcs* (the term used by writers, actors, directors, and fans). It was his appearance in the next story arc that initiated a final refusal by list members to continue the homosexuality-as-forbidden-topic policy.

Many fans found provocative a brief on-screen exchange between Methos and Duncan, in which, while helping him renovate a house, Methos teased Duncan in a playful, flirting kind of way and then was painted on the nose in retaliation. The exchange charmed even those who were in principle against changing the forbidden topics policy.[52] Many could not resist speculatively *filling in* possible story elements working with the charismatic charge generated between the two characters: Was it erotic? And if so, who was doing it? Who was the object? Who was the subject? Almost no one was willing to allow the principal character to have such erotic interests; but this new character, without a series history—him, they were willing to speculate about. In an unbroken discussion, marathoned by fans and about forty-eight hours long, the gay as forbidden topic policy became moot. The list owner did not intervene into this nonstop discussion, which was almost entirely flame free. Although from then on homosexuality was no longer a forbidden topic, it became instead a "marked" topic: one had to include in the subject line of posts with homosexual content the header: "Same Sex Sex." This would permit those who found the topic offensive to delete these posts unread, without banning the subject altogether. While later in that fourth season Methos briefly acquired a mortal woman lover, some fans had begun to write fan fiction in which instead Methos and Duncan were lovers, *filling in* this *thread* in the narrative space now virtually opened.[53]

SLASHING INTERACTIVITY

Such fiction is known in the media fan world as "slash." Slash has a long and varied history originating in the female fandom surrounding the TV show *Star Trek*.[54] The slash is a typographic cue to an eroticized relationship between characters of the same sex, usually men; in the original *Star Trek*, between Kirk and Spock (Kirk/["slash"]Spock); in *Highlander* fandom, between, say, Methos and Duncan (Methos/Duncan). It is a kind of pornography written most often by heterosexual women. Slash is thus not equivalent to gay fiction, although as time goes on the two genres may be overlapping more, and writers and characters may be self-consciously bisexual, lesbian, or gay. I speculate myself that slash is a site for the production of new bisexualities, of both characters and fan writers. It is one cultural site in which the constructions that produce heterosexuality and homosexuality as mutually exclusive are denied, eroded, refused, or simply ignored.

One might argue that slash moved into mainstream TV by 2007 in David E. Kelley's ABC show *Boston Legal*, where legendary science fiction (SF) actors William Shatner (*Star Trek*) and James Spader (*Stargate*) ended each episode teasing each other in double entendre terms of affection and friendship, arranging, say, dates for heterosexual men's "sleepovers."[55] Indeed the final episodes of *Boston Legal* played out an ongoing erotic ambiguity by marrying Shatner's and Spader's characters Denny and Alan to each other, an event difficult to extract from this mixture, neither strictly heterosexual or homosexual even while clearly "same sex" and teasingly, maybe, politically progressive. This term "same sex" has several registers of currency today, and same sex sex separates, or maybe better, refuses to conflate behaviors and sexual identities. It is a useful term in global AIDS education and increasingly in AIDS activism, as well as in the anthropology of sexuality. It has been used less often in, say, the history of sexuality.

Slash is one site for popular performance of this wording same sex sex, and, as in Mercury's denial of homosexuality, usually refuses social, cultural, and political meanings of homosexual identities. Early slash explicitly depicted the eroticized relation between Kirk (played in *Star Trek* by William Shatner—and thus recalled and joked about continually in *Boston Legal* for example) and Spock (played by Leonard Nimoy) as *situational, not homosexual*, and as *conflicted but romantic* within narrative structures and pleasures stereotypically "female."[56] Contemporary slash is more varied, sometimes utopian, sometimes romantic, sometimes brutal, and always intended to be erotic to someone. Slash once was privately circulated in circles of female fans who were both writers and readers of it (in the United States and probably also in Britain, Canada, and Australia). Today slash is still sometimes shared in the fanzines (xerox anthologies) that emerged from such private circulation and that were sold at cons or through mail order, or now most widely displayed and exchanged on the web and through e-mail, with what international distribution one has to imagine.[57] (I know of no studies or direct information about international reception of slash on the web, and I have only seen or heard of slash in English myself.) Although personally I encountered early forms of slash from women Trek friends, my understanding of it today is in this web displayed form and subculture.

How *Xena* fan fiction fits into the world of slash is perhaps more ambiguous; whether lesbian stories about Xena and Gabrielle are slash, enlarge the practice of slash, or are something else is perhaps part of some morphing and shifting, not as easily framed within its jokes as the broadcast slash of *Boston Legal* became later.[58] The press made much of the lesbian following among *Xena* fans in the nineties. The producers of *Xena* and Lucy Lawless, the actress who played Xena, said during its run that they were "aware and not afraid of" their lesbian audience, as the *Xena: Warrior Princess FAQ* proudly proclaimed at the time in the website section entitled "The Sapphic Subtext."[59] And indeed actress Lucy Lawless had appeared before *Xena* in a short film, *Peach*, in which she played the part of a bisexual woman.[60] Nonetheless, media stories also made much of her public relationship and now marriage with her producer Tapert.[61] On the fan list called the XenaVerse, talk about lesbian narratives concerning Xena and her sidekick Gabrielle was a taken for granted thread of discussion in the late nineties.[62] Yet both characters Xena and Gabrielle on TV had had conspicuous male lovers; in the episode "Destiny," which I will discuss below, Xena is famously paired with Julius Caesar, for example. The *Xena* FAQ makes its explanation: "[The writers] have done a great job of making it so viewers can see whatever they want in the show. *XWP* is a fantasy/action series with a riveting relationship between the two main characters, and so appeals to many people in many different ways."[63]

My impression is that, in contrast, *Highlander* producers were never at all sure exactly how they wanted to play any of the meanings possible within their own circulation of sexually ambiguous images, and answers from Adrian Paul at fan conventions suggested he was not so blasé as Lucy Lawless about such sexual readings, nor were questions directed at him so open either. But fans with contacts with crew members always claimed that such interpretations were the stuff of jokes and talk on the *Highlander* set, while fans with contact with Peter Wingfield claimed that he got a kick out of hearing about the fan fiction that links Methos and Duncan. Fandom is filled with folks claiming insider information, and such seeming authority does subvert official and authorized readings. *Xena* producers apparently decided to milk their ambiguities for all they were worth: and indeed multiple, complicatedly contradictory and noncontradictory stories, associations, and allusions are the stuff out of which *Xena* was made. Such telescoping and probing processes of fill in storytelling also mark the pleasures of fan writing in general and of slash in particular. You can see now why the phallic imagery of probing and telescoping is especially pertinent as well as funny for this kind of analysis, and also why it is not strictly "male" or not "feminist."

SOCIAL WORLDS, TECHNOLOGY CULTURES, AND WOMEN'S STUDIES CLASSROOMS

Having anything to do with *Highlander* or *Xena* means coming right up against divergent values of multiple and sometimes telescoping social worlds. Although entertainment and popular culture are in social and economic terms increasingly *valuable* forms of knowledge, academically they are unevenly *valued*, appreciated most when serving as forms for knowledge *transmission* particularly. Working on, or even reading about, *Highlander* and *Xena* means encountering in the academy, often bewilderingly, presuppositions from a range of social worlds, only some of them mutually intelligible and all of them ever only partially "academic."

Angry or trivializing reactions are a normal upshot of moving with, at the margins of, or outside an admittedly quite large and international but nevertheless still very specific and thus rather local set of knowledge worlds. These are the ranging communities of practice that make up academic cultural studies in the English-speaking academies of the UK, Australia, the United States, and Canada. From either, say, local campus SF fans who hate slash or from US conservative national talk-radio jocks that ridicule as frivolous and "politically correct" academic projects about TV (both circumstances I have unhappily endured), the in-your-face difference of values among knowledge worlds and their instantiation in specific objects can be only too confrontational. Judgments, affect, and cognition are all in play as feelings escalate. Anyone's *membership* in communities of practice or social worlds happens over time. It requires developing expertise and building on relationships to objects that identify such knowledge worlds and anchor their practices. Evaluations of and relationships to television may work to distinguish particular groups from one another. The horizontal integration made possible under globalization creates "local" television identities, including, say, fandoms, or alternatively, media scholars, shared across a country or across many countries. TV communities of practice educate or train their members to distinguish those TV objects that matter, how and why, each in their own versions of authoritative knowledge. And, of course, everyone lives in and among *many* communities of practice, some of them TV specific, compartmentalizing and negotiating differences between communities. Thus, presumptions about TV can be quite contradictory, especially when passionately held.

Members of many communities of practice, students arrive in my classroom with a set of authoritative knowledges they have gained elsewhere. It is my job at times to displace some knowledges with others, or to revise, at least locally, which sets get to count as authoritative and which alternative. Many, maybe most, teachers take drawing lines around authoritative knowledge to be a pivotal mission, especially today, especially to undergraduates, whether or not teachers or students are progressive, conservative, or politically unaligned. Education is certainly politicized today and media ecologies are uncertainly shifting. To specify some knowledges as authoritative and some not, or to position the authoritative and alternative against each other or in some other relationship, one has to consciously or unconsciously center a set of knowledge worlds, maybe just tentatively in the classroom at that moment or maybe very strongly as elements of one's training, experience, and alliances. All this happens in a context in which popular culture and its commerce are often marshaled in useful things, like ads or reality TV, made newly open for reanalysis and critique in media and women's studies classrooms. Indeed the "ah-ha" moments of debunking media mark some of the first forms in which many college students are taught to engage critical thinking.

Students' values about TV and about TV fandoms, meanings and activity, come from their families, other courses, popular culture itself along with other media, their own experiences, and from experiences vicariously practiced with important others. As a teacher I am often dismayed too by my own presuppositions about what students think, know, and expect. My assumptions are constantly violated, sometimes in ways that are exciting, often in ways that leave me trembling in anxiety. And of course, over time, generational specificities mean that my student audiences are always shifting and altering, and practices that have worked well for years suddenly cease to work.

When I first started teaching material on transnational cultural products, media fandoms, *Highlander* and *Xena*, I assumed that my women's studies students themselves would often be fans, and if not, they would have friends who were and have experiences with fandoms, even if as outsiders. I found instead that many, even those simultaneously taking courses on TV or film, had rigid investments in the authority of high culture, were sometimes frankly frightened of fans because they had strong stereotypes about them, and were mostly dismissive of fan activities as alternative forms of intellectual work. Student investments in university education as intellectual capital eclipsed any alternative experiences they engaged in themselves, for example as fans of music genres or performers. To my dismay, when I wore fan paraphernalia and brought in objects from cons for students to examine and analyze, I found discussion paralyzed, only later to learn from course evaluations that students had from that time marked me as one of "them"—a fan—a stigmatized category I had not anticipated. As an out lesbian teaching in women's studies classes, I was, rather foolishly, astonished.

Such students were usually convinced that fans must be from moneyed groups, with lots of time and cash spent on fan activities, equipment, and paraphernalia. And they were also simultaneously and somewhat contradictorily convinced that fans were not cultured in the proper bourgeois use of such resources, not spending them properly in the pursuit of "higher" education and products of "high" culture. "Watching television" was an activity that middle-class students especially had had "rationed" growing up at home, and such promiscuous viewing of TV was grasped with some alarm. Women's studies students were also convinced that media fan feminisms were not "real feminism," unwilling to recognize anything other than their own forms of identity politics cultivated in women's studies classrooms as feminist.

Women's studies classes are an especially volatile brew as everyone including the teacher works with knowledges politicized, both affective and intellectually challenging, and which all together have implications for interactions with others from roommates to partners to family to other teachers to groups demanding and requiring social justice. Just ask any women's studies student how many times a day they have to justify to someone taking a class or pursuing a major in women's studies. Being a "good" person matters enormously in women's studies. How many different knowledge worlds one can be "good" in underlies some of the anxieties women's studies can generate. Teaching this material in a local political microenvironment alerts me to my own unintended complicity with such academic values and continually literalizes the work of making explicit the discomforts of moving among authoritative and alternative knowledges in and between knowledge worlds. It also literalizes how invested, in myriad locals and globals, we all are in televisual infrastructures and images, how these come to mean so much and to evoke so many individual and collective feelings.

RECUPERATED HISTORIES AND THEIR "AUTHENTICITIES"

So with volatile feelings and meanings in mind, let me return here to Morley and Robins's notion of heritage culture. They point out that in a new economic regionalism characterized by a "war of images," the question, "Where will the pictures come from?" is crucial; this fuels some of the heat surrounding such issues as European content quotas on TV.[64] These concerns are seen by some as issues of national identity, as in Seydoux's remarks on grandchildren having the same identity as their grandparents. Particular pictures of the past are conflated with current national identities—under the pressures of heritage culture such past-presents are essentializing and yet also simultaneously and unavoidably shifting. Although a European single market may have been a directing motive for the EU since the fifties at least, the range of historic entities that have pillared or shadowed the EU has intertwined enterprise and heritage cultures. From 1992 to 2009—and perhaps even into whatever *now* of your reading of this—the entity the EU, in its range of treaties, communities, and unions, can be seen simultaneously as an attempt to *conserve* such current national identities while protecting European identity and as a *threat* to the national identities of some of the states that are located on the geographical entity, continental Europe, and within the ideological entity usually called European or the West. For example, US news reports in the first part of the twenty-first century on the politics of immigration in Europe and on who will be admitted to the union especially play on fears of Islamic minorities after 9/11; the admission of Turkey to the EU remains contentious at the time of this writing in precisely these terms. Heritage culture continues to be a symptom of and to exploit these and other anxieties, as well as being the site of new forms of pleasure and invented traditions. Historical dramas and reenactment today cannot help but be co-opted by the painful pleasures of heritage culture, and recuperated histories are mixes—real, hyperreal, imagined, and pastiche.

Highlander and *Xena* represented, beginning in the nineties and continuing after, two approaches to being such mixtures: *Highlander*, on the one hand, thought of itself as committed to real history, that is, real history within low budgets. Some might consider *Highlander* "real" history thus as reenactment history in a restricted sense—using an intensive definition of reenactment—indeed, as that kind of history that war games folks put together in epic battle reenactments, and in the production of which they mobilize the term "authenticity" carefully.[65] *Xena*, on the other hand, was always in "meta" or joking mode: preferring to self-consciously refer to its own mix, to make jokes about the contradictions produced, to focus on the simultaneous, the synchronic; thus playfully postmodern in remixing globalized cultures, and yet somehow also newly, differently "authentic" or perhaps refusing the very term "authenticity."

"Authenticity" is particularistic in the reenactments of specific communities of practice, even as the abstracting term creates the appearance that something larger and more common is understood by it. Authenticity is localized by and within the resources amassed for the production of any reenactment, characterizing its set of infrastructures. Such resources are comprised not only of the objects, skills, and historical information upon which they depend, but also the people chosen to act, the venues of performance, and a range of ideologies. Those ideologies include assumptions about what reenactment is, as well as ideologies of heritage culture under globalization, of national and other identities required and produced, of political powers mobilized and threatened, and so on. More than one local meaning of authenticity can clash in, say especially, public histories. Restricting the scope of what the abstraction "authenticity" could mean by centering particular communities of practice is always the most effective way to ensure that the local notion of authenticity is directly addressed and not questioned. By "local" here one might mean even an entity understanding itself to represent the global as much as, say, the US Congress might. Or this meaning of "local" might properly designate an entire academic disciplinary formation, one that assumes that reenactments are primarily "historical" and are thus inadvertently essentialized as memory and commemoration, such as, say, literary historians might.

FRAMED AND NESTED MULTIPLE THREADS

The reenactments of both *Highlander* and *Xena* take pleasure in a conflation of the mythic and the historic, the chronological and the anachronistic, thus, in *pastpresents*. The episodes of each I will turn to now are such elaborate fusions. Both *Highlander* and *Xena* depend on the use of multiple frames, the most conspicuous of which are flashbacks. Historically multiple frames in TV specifically are the legacy of product placement, as the TV historian Lynn Spigel points out. In early television the stage-within-a-stage structure, a "quagmire of meta-realities," was found in domestic comedies with heritages from vaudeville, shows like *Burns & Allen* or *I Love Lucy*. The stage frame contained the domestic space; and the stage space that viewers inhabited, the strangely more real space, was also inhabited by the product being sold. Such early TV framing conventions achieved the effect of making "the advertiser's discourse appear to be in a world closer to the viewer's real life," a kind of virtuality easily naturalized.[66]

In *Xena* the final credits, which flash by more quickly than one can read and which share the screen with upcoming episode trailers, are followed by disclaimers, one legal, one humorous. In the episode "Destiny," the production credits end with the following humorous disclaimer: "Julius Caesar was not harmed during the production of this motion picture. However, the Producers deny any responsibility for any unfortunate acts of betrayal causing some discomfort."[67] Rather than the product occupying the stage/frame space, we have the campy production comments, which parody the "legal" disclaimers. Unlike the early product placement, meant to be the clearest communication if also often humorous, these comic disclaimers on broadcast were so embedded as to be hidden: I never could read them off the TV myself, and only could barely see them on "pause" or "slow" with a two-headed VCR when I videotaped episodes. To get this one I raided the store of such carefully, even compulsively visioned sightings produced by fans at the Logomancy fan site on the web.[68] But new DVD libraried versions are a different commercial case now, and when I downloaded a first season episode "Altared States" from iTunes, the campy comments were now fully and easily readable.[69] "Real" and "virtual" spaces are in shifting play among historical materialities, embodied in new devices and altering sensory assembly.

Most of these humorous disclaimers use the same format: something was not harmed in the making of this motion picture. The play between TV episode and "this motion picture" reminds us that this was *Xena* producers Raimi and Tapert's first TV venture in careers of movie production. Like the *Highlander* producers Peter Davis and Bill Panzer, Raimi and Tapert moved from low budget independent movies to independent, limited budget, syndicated TV at a particular economic moment.

What was not harmed here was "Julius Caesar," the chronologically specific character in a play of anachronism, the emblem of Western culture who parodies himself for us as he mentions conversationally "Gaul is divided into three parts." In first season episodes other such Western authorities mocked in disclaimer but not harmed were "Unrelenting or Severely Punishing Deities," "Fathers, Spiritual or Biological," or "Males, Centaurs or Amazons," each of these poking fun at the kind of feminism displayed both subversively and often commercially in *Xena*.[70] I call this exuberantly commercial feminism "*Xena* feminism."

It is not just that the producers make fun of possible objections to the violence of this episode of *Xena* when, after saying Caesar was not harmed, they also "deny any responsibility for any unfortunate acts of betrayal causing some discomfort."[71] Here they also make fun of any fussy concerns about their recycled versions of myths, cultural traditions, and national histories, some of the sources of their many layered jokes. As the early TV framing devices included the advertiser's product (with embodied viewers) in the spectacle, so the humorous disclaimer on *Xena* includes as *pleasures of reception* the conditions of production, the credits and legalities (and other materialities of viewing) inside this spectacle.

Indeed the obvious joke of this episode's disclaimer is that Julius Caesar is never hurt in the story—only Xena is hurt, in fact killed. It is all about his betrayals of her, and these are both emotional and violently physical. Whoosh!, the wonderful Xena fan site that parodies itself as the "Birthplace of the International Association of Xena Studies," archives the original *TV Guide* promo: "After being critically injured in a fight, Xena lets her mind flash back to the time that Julius Caesar taught her a valuable lesson about destiny. Part 1 of two. / A fierce battle with Sitacles and his men leaves Xena lying near death and dreaming of the past encounters that have shaped her into a warrior princess, including her adventures with Julius Caesar and her relationship with a mysterious girl."[72] This episode provides additional backstory for the series, explaining the passion behind Xena's mission.

So, Caesar woos her and then kills her. And Caesar's mode of killing Xena is to crucify her: the Western cultural betrayal by the producers then being to elevate Xena to Christlike status, and indeed to construct a story in which she is resurrected not just once, but twice, once in the frame story and once in the flashback story. Note how the ironies and humors accustom and habituate viewers to casual movements from one level of abstraction to another, to sorting out easily those telescoping relative and relational shifts among levels of locals and globals involved in getting all the jokes and negotiating flashbacks, frames, and spectacle, in playing one's proper market roles in a highly embedded globalized economy.[73]

TELESCOPING POLITICS ON TV, VIDEO, AND VIDEOCAM

Let me formally compare "Destiny" to an episode of *Highlander*, "The Valkyrie."[74] I want to point to the multiple framings that include the flashback, story-within-a-story structuring in this episode in telescoping layers of political and historical association. In the opening teaser we first see a picture of St. Basil's in the Kremlin, the architectural element that stands for "Moscow," captioned in case we do not get it. (*Highlander* eschews subtleties.) We are cut immediately to a TV picture, revealed to be so as the camera pulls back, then revealed to be a video tape as the viewer within the story reverses the tape momentarily and replays the speech we hear. (This is an especially pointed allusion within *Highlander* fan culture, since in many viewing areas *Highlander* was shown during the "fringe" viewing hours, say, late at night, and even when it was shown in prime time, fans were likely to videotape episodes. So in either case, videotape is an important element of *Highlander* fan worlds. In the opening sequence of *Highlander* a Watcher is shown cut next to a shot of a videocam, thus conflating the group who investigates Immortals with the TV show viewers "watching" the show.) The first lines of dialog then set the terms of the narrative throughout this episode: the character Igor Stephenovitch, obviously modeled on the Russian ultra-nationalist politician Vladimir Zhirinovsky, says: "Do they not love me? Of course they love me. I fill their empty bellies with something more than food. I fill them with someone to hate. Someone to blame for their wretched lives. Jews, Muslims, Chetchnians, it really doesn't matter. There are glorious days ahead, Dimitri. Lousy TV, that's the first thing we'll have to fix." (Such TV watching allusions make viewers complicit in the morally dangerous world depicted in the episode.)

This episode is explicitly about pan-European racism in its neo-Nazi forms, but at every point this theme becomes explicit, it is quickly shifted, and then reembedded, as also references to specific nationalities are raised and then delimited. It begins in Europe, or one might say, the EU's "margins," that is Russia, *not* in, say, Strasbourg, France, where shortly after this episode first aired in 1997 demonstrations against the racism of the French ultra-nationalist politician Jean-Marie Le Pen's National Front occurred.[75] Although in this highly colored and even stereotyped version the possible French allusions are displaced, in addition the episode quickly moves to its American-in-quotes location, to focus on another rather cartoon-style racist, the figure Wilkinson, about whom we are told, "At sixteen he and his friends beat two gay men to death, at twenty burned three black churches in the south. . . . Now all he does is give a speech and other people go out and burn churches for him." Of course, within the flashback, all these allusions are grafted onto the figure of archevil, Hitler himself. In such cultural shifts of register and allusions to chronological event, history is left behind and reframed as morality play. Historical event, present and past, is *contained* as morality play, indeed contained, as are all episodes of *Highlander*, within battles between good and evil, battles that take place in individual psyches, then also externalized in single combat. Methos and Duncan offer two versions of history in their interchanges throughout this episode, one a simplified and parodied version of Marxist determinism, as when Methos paraphrases Marx, saying: "History makes men, MacLeod. Men don't make history"; and the other a simplified heroic capitalist-equals-democratic version, Duncan's emphasis on pivotal actions by specific individuals. But even these highly simplified versions of possible European political ideologies are trumped by the Interpol inspector's banal moralisms: "when I was a little boy everything was black and white, good and evil you see, then I grew up and discovered there was only gray."

History becomes morality play is an effective method of defusing but also strangely including actual political content, and certainly any current politics in this episode is immediately defused, although also played up in a scattered pattern of allusions relevant to multiple audiences and markets. Thus they are similar to the commodified forms of queer visibility Hennessy talks about, or very much like exuberant "*Xena* feminism," already depoliticized and only democratized within encrustations of capitalist commodity formations and individualism.

Yet, one cannot help but notice that some of the betrayals on the part of the producers have some, though quite limited, subversive effects. On the one hand, the Interpol inspector's banalities are only too reminiscent of the only kinds of resistance imaginable amid the apathy and deeply paralyzing depression that are understandable responses to economic shifts of catastrophic proportions. The inspector's references to a life in Romania are an allusion to these responses to history and politics in especially East European countries in the wake of the break up of the Soviet Union. Nor on the other hand is an explicit if rather opportunistic stance against European racism unimportant. Its very defusion indicates how volatile such contemporary politics are.

In fact concerns about racism infuse *Highlander* as a series, being a recurrent if also always redirected theme. Antiracisms in *Highlander* are almost always projected onto the screen of the history of slavery or segregation in the United States, and Duncan is almost always a heroic figure helping slaves to freedom on the underground railroad or supporting

African Americans in desegregation. He always exacts a price, however: he lectures them on the meanings of freedom and tells them how to be good democratic citizens.[76]

The propaganda value of such lectures and liberal encouragements, visions and simplified histories, are the didactic heart of *Highlander*. The creative consultant and head writer David Abramowitz refers to the show as "a kind of romantic Talmudic discussion with action," while the principal actor Adrian Paul refuses a fan club unless it is directed toward charity and peaceful community building.[77] In the US fan context and convention culture these obviously liberal American-in-quotes undertakings are substitutions for an occasionally almost-mentioned British labor agenda.

Morley and Robins point out that heritage culture, in the context of the European collectivist dreams for 1992 and the European Union, has possible racist implications, that national identities may be in a process of transformation into a "white continentalism."[78] *Highlander* itself—within its recurrent interests in racism—is also conspicuously white, despite the inclusion of prominent and striking Immortals of color, for example, Roland Gift of the British rock group *Fine Young Cannibals*.[79] Vancouver and Paris sets are also conspicuously white, despite these cities' own multicultural complexities. Heritage culture is based on these catered to and contradictory visions, while European Union in 1992 was the result of uneasy bargains struck despite contradictory visions. For example, the bargain struck up among principals Germany and France, in which Germany pledged to eschew past imperial dreams while undergoing reunification by reinforcing commitments to a federal Europe and pushing for political integration, while France pushed for monetary union giving it some degree of control over Germany.[80] Such tensions over and economic and political attempts at resolution of Germany's past are even another level of allusion in "The Valkyrie" episode of *Highlander* and another appropriation by heritage culture.

AUDIENCE POLYPHONY

A few years ago my mother persuaded me to take her to see the movie *Disclosure*, the film version of Michael Crichton's novel, starring Michael Douglas and Demi Moore.[81] I was already sure, by its reputation without having seen it, that this was an "antifeminist" film belittling sexual harassment in the workplace. I was unsurprised that Michael Douglas played the leading character after his work in the notorious film *Fatal Attraction*.[82] But I took all that back when I was bowled over by the film; I even loved it. It addressed me as a feminist in its construction of sexual harassment as about power, in its sympathetic portrayals of women numerous enough to be victims and heroes and villains and just cast and in its amazing gender reversal in which Douglas's authority to voice his sexual experience is questioned in double-bind terms. One could view it as a feminist, as I pleasurably experienced it on that first screening, but even then I could uneasily see how one could also view it as an antifeminist, simultaneously and multiply. Each audience watching the same set of images on the screen was given simultaneously parallel or alternate or complex characters and words and elements of plot that together could produce a consistent narrative supporting very divergent political positions. I was stunned by the film and by its *complex address of multiple audiences*, but it was to be only the first one like this I came across. Indeed, such audience polyphony is more and more common in commercial narratives today, from ads to film dramas to TV comedies to genre literature and so on.

The term "niche markets" is usually used to describe commercial products made for specific local audiences, like rainbow jewelry for gay folks. But what we see in the film *Disclosure* and in the TV show *Xena* is something similar but also taken to the next level of complexity in layers of locals and globals: a single global product intended for a *contradictory nest of niche markets*, some of which may derive their cultural pleasures from this very "contradictory nesting." Despite the common wisdom of Hollywood that valorizes the simplicity of genre formula as globally attractive, this complexity of address may also be attractive to specific audiences.

Indeed such complexity of address in telescoping forms may be the form of "consciousness" cultivated by such cultural products, a consciousness appropriate in a globalized world not only of worldwide divisions of labor and production, but also of migrating populations, of cultural mixings in a range of media, of newly invented traditionalisms, such as religious fundamentalism and ethnic identities, and of sexual and family arrangements altered by the shape of global capitalism. Individual producers and advertisers are not in control of, indeed barely grasp, the commercial implications of these tastes and forms of consciousness. Nor do cultural critics know what they will come to mean in the future, what their political effects will be however much we might suspect terrors, or however much we might long for possibilities.

As I suggested, some of the effects of global production itself are pleasurable: the backdrops of New Zealand and Kiwi slang enlivening the other anachronistic postmodernisms of *Xena*'s appropriations of many cultures' mythologies and histories. Global production itself becomes a spectacle bundled with the TV show. Actors as "stars" have always been part of this bundled package sold along with the film or TV product, and "behind the scenes" elements of production that exploit the actors further have long been the stuff of fan interest. But today there exists an intensified interest that is also focused on box office sales, the buying and selling of multinational corporations and stories about their owners and CEOs, the quoting of producers and writers about their intentions with the product, speculations about the political effects of the contents of stories, and so on; all these are now "bundled" with the product as items to be sold, in TV venues like *Entertainment Tonight* or supermarket magazines like *Entertainment Weekly*. Nowadays, this is especially obvious in the packaging of DVDs with their "extra features." Some such concerns were narrowly professional ones in the past, of importance largely to folks in the industry and not as consistently commodified and sold as they are today. Consider DVDs with soundtracks by the directors and producers describing their production shot by shot as you watch the film.

And the fact that multinationals now encompass many forms of media makes for multiple *Xena* products: tie-in novels and paraphernalia like dolls, calendars, CDs, screensavers, and t-shirts, and alternate venues like websites and conventions, and coffee table and companion documentary books telling the stories of production, listing episodes and their writers, and offering critical discussions, from fans, from journalists, and from academics.[83] One might call such a proliferation of commercial products, especially those with an emphasis on the pleasures of commercial production itself "commercially exuberant."

The cyberculture theorists Jay Bolter and Richard Grusin point to this proliferation as "repurposing":

The entertainment industry defines repurposing as pouring a familiar content into another media form; a comic book series is repurposed as a live-action movie, a televised cartoon, a video game, and a set of action toys. The goal is not to replace the earlier forms, to which the company may own the rights, but rather to spread the content over as many markets as possible. Each of those forms takes part of its meaning from the other products in a process of honorific remediation and at the same time makes a tacit claim to offer an experience that the other forms cannot. Together these products constitute a hypermediated environment in which the repurposed content is available to all the senses at once, a kind of mock *Gesamtkunstwerk*. For the repurposing of blockbuster movies such as the Batman series, the goal is to have the child watching a Batman video while wearing a Batman cape, eating a fast-food meal with a Batman promotional wrapper, and playing with a Batman toy. The goal is literally to engage all of the child's senses.[84]

The *Highlander* and *Xena* online catalogues, both of which are produced by Davis Anderson Merchandizing Corporation, are other examples of such *immersive experiences*, with their forums and news all centered around and instantiated by their merchandise.[85] If you had gone to the *Xena* online store in 2005 you could have signed up then for "The *Xena* Circle." There you could register for what looked at first like a fan club but turned out to be "M80," "online grassroots micro-marketing teams, community outreach, online publicity and promotion, and a traditional street marketing campaign."[86]

For example, when the then new *Highlander* movie, *The Source*, began filming I got in my e-mail an "exact-target" message from the "Official *Highlander* Store" with up-to-date information. Declaring that this new movie began another *Highlander* "trilogy" celebrating the (then) twentieth anniversary of *Highlander*, Davis-Panzer Productions (together with Sequence Films and Grosvenor Park) were set to film it that October in Lithuania. With the announcement that it was to be directed by Brett Leonard of *Lawnmower Man* fame, the style and special effects of the film were positioned and communicated. The movie would "be distributed in North America through Lions Gate Films and in forty foreign territories through the top independent distributors." That announcement also pointed to other media forms continuing the *Highlander* franchise: "an anime feature film in partnership with Imagi and Madhouse of Japan and a video game with SCI Games Ltd. of London."[87] Below all this hype directed at fans were images of stuff to buy connected to the new film, such as *The Source* director's chair, while clinking the link entitled "The

Source" carried the browser to another commodity-saturated web page where the image of a jacket was captioned: "Crew members are already clamoring for one of these."

This announcement and its mirror on the website Sci Fi Wire (now rebranded as Blastr) caused a small flurry of e-mails on the *Highlander* listserv. Fans speculated whether the title *The Source* would be retained or was copyrighted by an earlier possible production company, what should be the content of the film and its connection to other *Highlander* venues, and if it would bomb and go direct to video. They produced commentary about seeing friends made at the first *Highlander* con in 1994, compared how many times one had watched the last *Highlander* movie, and talked about how it measured up against other movies.[88] All this multisensoria of commercial products and fan conversation create a strangely immersive experience, one that associates commercial exuberance with *reenactment* in multisensory simulation.

FILLING IN AMONG MULTIPLE THREADS

Female friendship was the most valued theme in the TV show *Xena*, and it is visually complicated and narratively explored in most episodes. Ways of expressing female friendship, love, and the possibilities of sexuality among women are parallel threads of imagery, narrative, symbolism, and humor, even while both Xena and her female companion Gabrielle have explicit male lovers in various episodes. Audience polyphony allows for such multiple interpretations of specific moments in pivotal episodes, described in "The Sapphic Subtext" on the Whoosh! fansite.[89] "Commercial exuberance" allows fans that explicitly see audience polyphony in production intentions to be empowered to argue for their audience interests with producers and writers, in web venues they all share. From the XenaVerse fans argued with writers and producers to make "the subtext" more explicit. In the episode that follows "Destiny," called "The Quest," Xena and Gabrielle share a much-hyped kiss, but one that simultaneously melds both the image of Xena and Gabrielle kissing and the image of Gabrielle and the man in whose body Xena's spirit has been sheltered kissing.[90] We see both possibilities on the TV screen, in swift parallel. Notice how this shapes new "bisexualities" and alters ways of "reading" the TV screen, now assimilated to a computer screen (where fans may play this shift over and over again).

My favorite episode of *Xena* is elaborately allusive, even referring to this episode. Some of the most complexly edited episodes of *Xena* are what are called "bottle episodes." Bottle episodes created out of clips of previous shows, were originally intended to conserve production time and thus costs. *Xena* is now famous for its bottle episodes and for using this highly allusive episode form even in more expensive production intentions. My favorite episode is entitled "The Bitter Suite."[91] The trailer for this episode calls it "the most talked about episode of the season . . . an all musical adventure." And indeed many musical genres, most with TV versions, are sewn together and parodied in this show. *Musically* alluded to are both specific productions and generic forms; for example, there are several specific allusions to the Judy Garland film version of *The Wizard of Oz*, while there are also more general allusions to Gilbert and Sullivan, to nursery rhyme songs, to Broadway musicals, to classic films in the Ziegfeld Follies tradition, to old episodes of *I Love Lucy* making fun of operas, to country music, and so on. In addition there are striking *visual* allusions to productions of Wagner's Ring cycle to Busby Berkeley movies and to Las Vegas show productions.

Xena's recurrent enemy Callisto is both a figure and narrator in the complex dreamy tarot game show structure of the episode, which is both very funny and surprisingly poignant and touching. A climax episode in a long story arc with complex multiple threading, Xena and Gabrielle have become enemies in the course of Callisto's manipulations. Each one has had a child, and Callisto has manipulated their children's deaths in such a way that each is in some way responsible for the death of the other's child. In the previous episode Xena and Gabrielle's friendship and love have become murderous hatred, hatred that is reviewed at the beginning of this episode when Xena brutally attempts to kill Gabrielle. Both plunge into a waterfall and the swirling visuals suggest naked bodies undulating in the waters. Xena is awakened by Callisto's kiss, which recalls the moment of her climactic kiss with Gabrielle in the past. Callisto's mocking voiceover ironizes both the kiss and episode title when she sings, "You taste it, how evil and good coexist; the bitter and sweet of it, all on the lips that you kissed." The episode elaborates upon Xena and Gabrielle's painful reconciliation, on memory, betrayal, and forgiveness in friendship, and on friendship's alterations of the self.

Multiple ironies make it possible to interpret the episode emotionally, pop-psychologically, humorously, politically, mockingly, or in recombinant variations on all of these. The emotional climax fades to a final scene of Xena and Gabrielle lying in each other's arms, engulfed by waves on a beach, in a momentary allusion to the famous erotic cinematic moment in the film *From Here to Eternity*—an allusion that is immediately defused by Xena and Gabrielle leaning back into the sand in hilarious laughter.[92] Journalist interviews of actors, writers, and producers always emphasize this comic element of *Xena* and paint a picture of a production company having a great time making fun of it all. This "commercial exuberance" might be understood as the keynote of *Xena*, bundled together with its varying products, always creating and coloring its "*Xena* feminism" as well as its many forms of same sex friendship shared with its female fandom.

FORMS OF CONSCIOUSNESS, OR HOW DO WE KNOW IT WHEN WE SEE IT?

Think again of the kind of consciousness and embodiment cultivated by such global products, created out of commercial intentions but also out of conditions of global production, which hone new skills from such altering pleasures, tastes, and sensations. I call ideologically shaped allusions to the conditions in which production, distribution, and consumption become overlayered, sometimes collapsing in on each other and recentered and sometimes extending out and distributing telescopically, the "spectacle of production." Such global products bundled with this "spectacle of production" engage world historical subjects now properly addressed in these telescopic layerings of locals and globals. Such layerings distributively structure that globe of worldwide divisions of labor and production among many migrating populations I pointed to before, requiring all these new cultural mixings and newly invented traditionalisms, as well as working to proliferate such various forms of sexuality as those I have discussed, shaped inside global capitalism for its own purposes but hardly exhausted by them. The feminisms created among layers of locals and globals are also structural as well as intentional, are necessarily extraordinarily various when properly transnational, and their political futures are yet to be actualized.[93] A posthumanities now emerges to account for the possibilities of agency and embodiment among such dynamic networks, transdisciplinary in practice and description.

I take seriously the implication that it is within globalization processes themselves, and our intra-action with them, as them, out of which we must wring liberatory possibility. How do we recognize the areas of fruitful possibility, even as we clearly analyze the very circumstances of heightened oppression they also implicate? The *forms of embodied consciousness* traced throughout my analysis of the technology ecologies of the global TV shows *Highlander* and *Xena* offer venues for understanding who we are becoming, what we can make of ourselves and the ecologies of which we are a part—that is to say, our actual conditions of agency—as well as how we intervene into globalization processes for social justice projects. Critique is crucial but far from sufficient here. What forms of engagement with and beyond critique do we need? How does the notion of "telescoping layers of locals and globals" help? Where do reenactments take us next?

TWO

SCIENCE IN AMERICAN LIFE
Among the Culture Warriors

PART 1. TRUST, DEBUNKING, AND THE MUSEUM IN THE EXHIBIT

ON THE MALL: SMITHSONIAN HISTORY
WARS OF THE NINETIES

IT IS SPRING 2007, and the block-long security lines into the Smithsonian Institution's National Museum of American History (NMAH) are missing now while it is closed for renovation. The once controversial and "technically superb" exhibition *Science in American Life* is due to be phased out. The hot new museum exhibit is at the National Museum of Natural History's (NMNH) Kenneth E. Behring Hall of Mammals. There, entering this multimedia, multisensory immersive installation, we are invited to a "Mammal Family Reunion—Come meet your relatives!"—in a savvy response to antievolution religious activism.[1]

Headlines blare that the Smithsonian's former secretary, Lawrence Small, has resigned. Interim leadership of the institution falls to the acting secretary, Cristián Samper, a biologist and the director of the NMNH.[2] "Castle in Disrepair" shouts the *Washington Post* in an article that begins: "The Smithsonian has just awakened from a leadership nightmare. On this groggy morning after, it finds itself soiled by commercialism, Disneyfication and politicization, and sorely in need of a meticulous scrubbing."[3]

Another spring, April 1994, more than a decade before and after more than five years of planning and research for this "permanent" installation, the exhibition *Science in American Life* (SAL) opened at the NMAH. Its chief curator was Arthur P. Molella, later also the director of the Lemelson

Center for the Study of Invention and Innovation.[4] The funding author-ship of the American Chemical Society (ACS) had its modest but signifi-cant recognition near the beginning of the exhibit's narrative trajectory. There, in an interactive display of the chemical derivatives of coal tar was referenced the World War I era "chemists' crusade," the move in which the ACS had been a leading professional player in popularizing US industrial "big" science, courting government support for the American dye indus-try, and thus countering Germany's chemical embargo.[5]

The interlocking "culture wars," "science wars," "history wars," and "image wars" overtaking the Smithsonian in the nineties became, partly intentionally, partly inadvertently, some of the "stuff" of *SAL*. The Smith-sonian version of these so-called wars began in particular with the highly controversial 1991 exhibit installed at the National Museum of American Art, *The West as America: Reinterpreting Images of the Frontier, 1820–1920.* That exhibition's critique of nationalist images of Manifest Destiny, al-though current at the time among art historians, culture critics, cultural historians, and anthropologists, came itself under critique by conserva-tives and others in polarizing popular media, as at best sanctimonious and prosecutorial, and at worst as radical, anti-American revisionism.[6]

Following *SAL*, in June 1995 the *Enola Gay* went on display at the Smithsonian's National Air and Space Museum, its exhibition dramatically narrowed in scope after preemptive complaints by the Air Force Associa-tion, the American Legion, and veterans' groups that the exhibit was not going to express the view that the bombing of Japan had saved American lives.[7] The Air and Space Museum Director Martin Harwit, forced to re-sign because of the controversy, had rather pointed out that *it was not possible to know* what would have happened without the bombing.[8]

Congressional surveillance of US heritage sites, national museum ex-hibitions, funding of artists and art works, and other culture processes and products increased in the nineties, requiring that such "displays of power" conform to popular expectations and national pride or be denied funding.[9] For example, with the installation of a Republican majority in Congress in 1995, in the fiscal year of 1996 the budget for the National Endowment for the Arts went from $162 million to $99 million.[10]

Criticism of *SAL* was spearheaded by Robert Park, a physicist at the University of Maryland who was the director of the Washington office of the American Physical Society. He claimed that the exhibit fueled an "antiscience sentiment" "growing since the Vietnam War," an effect quite contrary to the American Chemical Society's funding intentions to counter "public misunderstanding of science" by illustrating "how science has changed life on our planet in the course of a few generations." Park characterized the exhibit as "technically superb" but unbalanced, painting science as "a servant of the power structure." Instead, "What people need to know, and are not told, is that we live in a rational universe governed by physical laws. It is possible to discover those laws and use them for the benefit of humankind."[11]

A decade later, this pro-science conservatism stood in stark contrast to forthright mistrust of science in fundamentalist revivals of creationism and apocalyptic Christianity, all too politically evident and powerful, yet maybe waning with the fortunes of the Bush administration. Such pro-science conservatism even supplied significant support against neoconservative manipulations of science for policy and corporate interests, as in denials of data on global warming or the manipulations of data to allow environmentally fragile sites to be opened up for development. That Park's scientism might be recontextualized a decade later is one indicator of how successful assaults on science from the Right became, how much they were collapsed together with concerns from the Left, which Park and others understood earlier as perilous attacks to be countered. In the untrusting climate under the Bush administration clearly it was creationism that must be invitingly countered in the NMNH's Kenneth E. Behring Hall of Mammals by our invitation in 2007 to our mammal family reunion.

Interrelations between trust and epistemology are the context for the *reenactments* of this chapter, as I extensively define them. (In museum worlds "reenactments" have particular intensive meanings, usually referring to the actions of semiprofessional costumed interpreters.) The so-called culture wars and its variants, science wars, history wars, and image wars, are addressed here by looking at what I would call the reenactment-styled Smithsonian exhibit *SAL* and its telescoping, contexualizing, and controversial layers of locals and globals. This chapter probes the limits of debunking as a critical practice in reflections on scale making, scale shifting, and rescaling in these reenactments under globalization.

The chapter also reenacts encounters in and with *SAL* in layered *past-presents*. Indeed, the exhibit itself was scheduled to be dismantled over the course of the year 2009, but as of this writing still continues, albeit in a stripped-down form. Further, the chapter works to animate interactively several wings of academic science studies, using Donna Haraway's insights and tools as anchors for the point of view she calls "feminist technoscience," and Bruno Latour's auto-analysis of constructivism as a node for working with critique. Apparatus for understanding how knowledge is produced and communicated among unsettled communities of practice is pulled together in the classification theories of Geof Bowker and Leigh Star, and these structure much of the argument of the chapter as a whole. For how science is made to appear as a discrete area of expertise in forms of public "boundary work," the chapter's arguments are assisted with reenacting narratives across knowledge worlds by the sociologists of science Tom Gieryn and Lynn Mulkey, and their colleague the network management theorist William Dougan. In the second half of the chapter the historian of public communication about science Bruce Lewenstein, the anthropologist and feminist analyst of science and technology Lucy Suchman, and the philosopher and knowledge manager Sue Stafford, all most directly discuss issues of trust that authorize or deauthorize knowledge produced by and among commercial interests as they crisscross knowledge worlds.

These "wings" of science studies also work to model divergent communities of practice within a current and capacious academic "interdiscipline," as well as their sometimes smooth, sometimes fraught, movements beyond, together with, outside of, and intertwined with academic knowledges and their relative and relational systems of "authority." (In this spirit we might remember that "science" etymologically refers to "knowledge" broadly understood.) This chapter works with quotations of greater than normal length in order to preserve and value, or, if you will, reenact, some of the characteristic technical terminology or jargon of particular communities of practice, and thus to encourage cognitive *feeling* of their use of metaphor and the rhetorics of persuasion they depend upon. I deliberately do not simply paraphrase and substitute my voice for theirs, although my thick descriptions are also comments upon voices, rhetorics, and purposes, among them my own. The effect intended here is an experience of many voices speaking within communities and to others outside their communities. Enabling the second, members of particular communities of practice must perform some of the *metacommunications* they value as they work to present their own worlds to others within and outside them. In this way members demonstrate the forms in which they reflect upon and understand their own and others' knowledge worlds. Readers properly will read or skip over these quotations, rather like opening and closing hyperlinks, as they desire more detail or less. And choosing *grain of detail* itself becomes a topic within the chapter, toward its end, and is unpacked in greater and more interactive detail itself in chapter 3.

Swirling all around *SAL* on the National Mall were and are the Smithsonian controversies that preceded and postdated it, generating the "iconoclash"—Bruno Latour's term for those misrecognitions and analyses very much not shared—that characterize culture wars.[12] A chapter pastiche simulates a collective "walk-through" of the someday-to-be-missing exhibit. This walk-through is useful as we engage other scales of reenactment involved in the exhibition, among them the shadowing and witnessing that visitors were once invited into through the use of "dummy scientists" —large-scale photo figures of actual scientists. Time claims, structures of scale, and contradictory nesting receptions are all elements in the simulation experiences of visitors and analysts.

In sum, *SAL* receptions were critical—that is, essential, combative, and overfull. How "selling epistemology" was involved, in whose interests and within what much broader systems of science communication, *matters*— to academic interests, to public histories, and to various nationalisms. Finally, the chapter asks questions about strategies needed to reclaim publics and appreciates the roles of reenactment for witnessing science knowledges.

GOOD FAITH?

To the extent that Park and various critics of the Smithsonian in Congress acted in good faith, their angry reaction was to what they perceived as dangerously calling into question vitally essential truths, but such critiques were also challenges to their cultural power. Evidence of social breakdown or even "unreason" was how they understood the debunking forms of critique that characterized some of these exhibits, or characterized parts of their implicit and explicit arguments about how we come to know what we know.

Debunking critique depends upon upsetting a range of processes that assist the "things" that affiliate members within and across communities of practice, assist these things seemingly to appear as natural, obvious, normal, even vitally essential. "Naturalization" is one name for the trajectory of such processes. These crucial things work to create, authorize, and empower these very communities of practice. Following the science studies scholar Bruno Latour, we can argue that such "things" are no longer "'objects' which had been conceived as wholly exterior to the social and political realm." Instead, considering a range of etymologies, they "have become 'things' again, that is, in the sense of the mixture of assemblies, issues, causes for concerns, data, law suits, controversies which the words *res*, *causa*, *chose*, *aitia*, *ding* have designated in all the European languages."[13]

Both *things* and the *ways we understand things* are dynamically moving and interacting, as are we. Reenactments bundle together both things and some ways of grasping things, bundle together the making of knowledge with demonstrations of how to use and understand it.

In parts of *The West as America* exhibit, for example, the notion of Manifest Destiny was debunked as well as examined as just such a "thing" vital to a distinctive version of American identity. "Manifest Destiny" and "American triumphalism," for example, were displayed in the exhibit as actual materials created within and used for a set of specific interests, carefully not assumed in the exhibit to be unmediated expressions of some great animating truth. The intentions of those creating and using, say, the notion of Manifest Destiny, were also dissected for racist assumptions about who should have power, as were its uses to justify generalized racisms. Thus Manifest Destiny themes, as instantiations of distinctive versions of progress favoring a particular elite, were debunked.

In other words, all these elements were *displayed* as already saturated with political intentions—thus *denaturalized*—rather than unquestioningly understood as plain expressions of profound truths or essential natures. That such a form of critique was presented in a major national institution also marked a change of cultural power among intellectual generations nationwide despite then recent conservative political ascendancies in Washington.

"Things," such as exhibits, are *literalized* bits of the worldviews of particular communities of practice. One confirms one's membership in a community of practice over time as one learns and demonstrates the naturalization of these pivotal things, as the science studies scholars Geof Bowker and Susan Leigh Star argue in *Sorting Things Out*. Even the very practice of debunking critique is in some communities a similarly naturalized thing, the practice of which confirms one's membership.[14]

Consider quotation marks around the word "things." Such *metacommunication* assumes that the word at this level of context justifies commentary; it does not just express itself; in this telescoped or *meta* setting it is not transparent or obvious. When people make fun of this use of quotation marks (and not just of an excessive or pretentious display of typographical play), part of this joking may contain an anxiety about or discomfort with metacommunication itself, perhaps with the possibility of a denaturalization of an important "thing." On the part of teachers or exhibit makers, or by cultural critics or analysts of any kind, talking *about* something may appear to others confusingly to require *denying* that something, or making talking *about* it more important than the thing itself. And, of course, many of these critical folks precisely *are* enacting denials, refusals, and reevaluations.

Nevertheless, all such examinations may not be such debunkings: other critical engagements might either *not* refuse or deny these things even as they examine them and the values they embody, or *defer*, briefly, or perhaps forever, such refusals. They might reflect on *how little we know* about, say, what else might have happened in the past, what is going on in the present, or what is still possible to happen in the future, rather than assume that each is already predictable on the basis of core assumptions.

ON ALLIANCE MAKING AND NOT
ALWAYS DEAUTHORIZING

Debunking is a reflection of and intensifies polarizations. Culture critics who understand the practice of debunking critique as their primary political and moral obligation also value these intensities as guarantors of political alliance and ethical affiliation, as do those who loudly object to being victims of such debunking and who may practice their own debunkings in turn. On either end of debunking, the crucial initial "double take" immediately renaturalizes alliances. Debunking makes alliance making so salient and so emotionally imminent that other practices existing simultaneously with it, near it, or even differently from it, are hard to register.

Hearing (whether it was said or not) that one's dearest "things" are not natural may appear to mean (and sometimes does mean) that others are contending that these things are not "real," not deeply "true," or not pivotally important. In other words, "things" *could be some other way.* Such apparent deauthorizing of one's things may threaten one's assumption of membership in communities of practice, since ease in naturalizing these things, of taking them for granted, is itself evidence of such belonging.

Bruno Latour points out the significance of wanting to practice and to communicate the possibility of *denaturalizing without deauthorizing.*[15] He examines the term "construction" with these concerns in mind: "At first glance though, the notion of construction does not seem very compelling, since it suffers from one of modernism's major faults: it is usually associated with social construction and with the vocabulary of criticism. When we say that nature is 'constructed,' that God must be 'produced,' that the person must be 'fabricated,' it is immediately assumed that we are attacking, undermining, criticizing their supposed solidity."[16] Latour uses the metaphor of diplomacy to imagine communication across communities of practice about their pivotal "things": "The relevant question for the diplomats would no longer be, 'Is it or isn't it constructed?' but rather: 'How do you manufacture them?' And, above all, 'How do you verify that they are well constructed?' Here is where the negotiations could begin: with the question of the right ways to build."[17]

Latour is vivid in describing the limitations of human instrumentalism:

If there is one thing toward which 'making' does not lead, it is to the concept of a human actor fully in command. This is the great paradox of the use of the word construction . . . as soon as this metaphor of 'making,' 'creating,' or 'constructing' barely begins to shine, then the maker, the creator, the constructor has to *share its agency* with *a sea of actants* over which they have neither control nor mastery . . . there is no maker, no master, no creator that could be said to dominate materials, or, at the very least, a new uncertainty is introduced as to what is to be built as well as to who is responsible for the emergence of the virtualities of the materials at hand.[18]

Communities of practice are overlayered, range over different scales tele-scoping layers of time, place, and abstraction, and are constituted by multiply allied persons, things, and other worldly elements. Drawing a single unit, the "community of practice," is done with difficulty: the cura-tor and other institutional staff and the advisory board attending to creat-ing ("constructing") the SAL exhibit worked together as *a vulnerably emer-gent community of practice*, incorporating its members and naturalizing its things over the trajectory of the four or five odd years of the advisory board's meeting. Always and already at the same time its persons were also members of other, indeed multiple, knowledge worlds: subgroups drawn from particular ranges of the museum and particular museum practices, from particular disciplines inside and outside the museum, from particu-lar industries, and across particular political affiliations.

Thomas Gieryn animates these abstractions about things, construc-tion, negotiation, and membership in communities of practice, and all the scale making involved, with his reflections on the board's *flexible knowl-edges* and his place among them:

> Our Advisory Board meetings provided the occasion to display not just the distinctive expertise that each member brought to the planning table, but also the professional and even political interests that divided us. About half the members of the board were appointed by the Ameri-can Chemical Society, which had provided the $5.3 million needed to muster the exhibit—most were chemists. The rest of us were appointed by Smithsonian curators, and came mainly from history of science (I was the only sociologist). As we sat down to negotiate what did and did not belong in science in American life, I recall my struggles in trying to decide whether the sociology I uniquely embodied was a systematic body of knowledge and perspective that could be *used* effectively to choose themes and objects for display—or that *was itself one of the objects to be displayed*. Early on in our deliberations, the board was forced to *decide the boundaries of "science" for purposes of demarcating the outer limits of the exhibit*. Several chemists were quite certain that they knew what science consists of: the investigation of natural or physical phenomena, with reliable tools such as experiment and math-ematical laws.

It was ironic for me of all people—having studied for a decade just this kind of *"boundary-work"* as others did it—to hear myself offering up principled arguments for why social science belonged inside SAL. In making those arguments, the distinction between my *professional expertise* as sociologist and my *professional interests* became cloudy. As a dispassionate and detached analyst of science-in-society, I tried to convince recalcitrant chemists that one historical thread simply must be presented: the gradual expansion of scientific methods and scientific authority outward from the study of bugs and rocks to the study of people's practices, politics, and beliefs. Wasn't the emergence and increasing legitimacy of social science an objectively unignorable feature of "American Life"? Or was I, in my boundary-work, the *engaged and calculating professional* well aware that the exhibit offered an opportunity to display *our discipline's* salutary contributions to American life—and in a way that surrounded our efforts and accomplishments with the authority and credibility of science? Had I become as *instrumentalist* and self-interested as the American Chemical Society surely was in their decision to invest millions in an exhibit that would undeniably *educate* and *entertain*, but also (if properly executed) *sweeten* the public's image when they see or hear the word "chemical?"[19]

Gieryn's reflections back on the constructive process here take place in the midst of the worst of the controversies, in and around 1995, with the scaling back of the *Enola Gay* exhibit and the removal of the Air and Space Museum director. Indeed it appeared possible then that the pressure on the Smithsonian to remove portions of the exhibit that were deemed "nonscience" or worse, "antiscience" by critics might be successful. And even that the controversy itself might be maneuvered, in its turn, additionally to deauthorize the work of researchers in the field and the communities of practice of science and technology studies (STS). It is in the middle of all these struggles that Gieryn with difficulty and vulnerability both examines and defends his interests in SAL:

The American Chemical Society has (at this writing) asked the Smithsonian to remove some displays and alter others, presumably to leave visitors with a more upbeat feeling about what science has done for American life. Curiously, the ACS has asked specifically for the removal of "Big Social Science" and its discussion of the American Soldier studies. Or not so curiously. Critics have linked SAL's negative slant to broader intellectual currents of anti-science and unreason—postmodernism, (de)constructivism, relativism—which have taken hold in some quarters of the social sciences.[20]

Gieryn wonders himself whether sociology is positioned or should be positioned in these discussions as an object or a metacommunication upon objects. That is to say: *where*, in telescoping layers of locals and globals, he and others need to engage; as well as *how*, simultaneously or by making priorities or what other scale making to perform; not to mention, *which* critical "double takes" to highlight. His expertise examines so-called boundary work: how boundaries such as "science" and "nonscience" are constructed by and in specific scientific-cultural debates and events. Thus he is sensitive to the decisions the board makes about what to include in the exhibit because they carry implicit and explicit judgments about a boundary between "science" and "nonscience." He notices and is both curious and defensive about how difficult it is in practice to separate his use of his professional expertise from his professional interests in instrumentally calculating the effects of disciplinary display. He notes the complexities of many motivations for the exhibit—some of its flexible knowledges, such as education and entertainment and proselytizing for the chemical industry.

ICONOCLASH

In the midst of such controversy any fragile stabilities produced in the negotiations within and around the board as tentative and emergent community of practice are disrupted by other alliances and memberships. Under these circumstances it is virtually impossible to simultaneously display one's political and professional commitments while at the same time "foreswearing claims to absolute epistemological authority" in Leigh Star's description of what others might decry as "relativism."[21] Epistemological authority, the power to claim to know, in this context is held to be virtually identical with one's political and professional commitments and knowledges. Any alternate scale making, that is, modestly seeking perspective on the range and scope of one's knowledges, then marking their edges via metacommunications, may appear only too beside the point, or even appear debilitating to fragile alliances and their crucial naturalizations and authorities. Latour describes such situations, with an eye to museum events among them: "Thus, we can define an icono*clash* as what happens when there is an *uncertainty* about the exact role of the hand at work in the production of some mediator: is it a hand with a hammer ready to expose, to denounce, to debunk, to show up, to disappoint, to disenchant, to dispel one's illusions, to let the air out? Or is it, on the contrary, a cautious and careful hand, palm turned as if to catch, to elicit, to educe, to welcome, to generate, to entertain, to upkeep, to collect truth and sanctity?"[22] Of course, as Latour points out, it may likely be all of these, simultaneously, both within persons and together with others. It is only too easy to misrecognize one's own and others' efforts in the midst of such uncertainties: "a new reverence for the images of science is taken to be their destruction."[23]

WHEN YOU ARRIVE: SOME LAYERED REENACTMENTS OF *SCIENCE IN AMERICAN LIFE*

Let us position a reenactment here of my many actual and your, perhaps virtual, visit to *SAL*, as from a previous time but using the present tense. (Since apparently, soon none of us may return there, this reenactment is what we have to share.) I want to give here most a sense of how it feels to move through these spaces, the proprioceptive sensations, and how they match up with the content in possible narrative trajectories. This feeling of *immersion*, of being inside and interacting with some story or stories, is an effect of this overflowing curatorial style. The objects all share the space with human bodies, and we too become additional objects together with all of them as we move into physical proximity, and then detach and move on to new associations while we traverse this embodied spacetime.

I hope to convey some sense for how folks might take up objects such as these, move through such spaces, and wonder and decide what to do among these images of science.

So, when you arrive at the *SAL* exhibit (as you could have, say, in 2003), you are hailed by four points of possible entry.

— **To your left is the hands-on science center**, if you are lucky, open and staffed; you can see through its large display windows that it is full mostly of children.

— **Directly in front and a bit ahead is the main entrance to the exhibit**, through which wide door, indicated by conspicuous architectural detail, you can glimpse a space packed with objects, full-scale *reconstructions*, and large, colorful graphics.

— **To your next right in the intermediate space** within which you find
yourself included, are wall backdrops of blown up photos, selectively
colored for effect, some collaged with other pictures, and a set of life-
size, freestanding photo figures of ten adult scientists and a couple
of children, in a conspicuous range of genders, races, ethnicities, and
nationalities. These scientists' *voices fill the air*, giving their own
opinions on "What is Science in American Life?" matched by pictures in a small video monitor at about knee level. A laminated
picture book will tell you about each individual scientist and child:
their proudest moments and what they find most exciting about
their work. A label tells you "Some of the scientists have more to say
inside the exhibit."[24]

— Meanwhile, **to your immediate right is a very plain door**, its unexcit-
ing notice says "exhibition exit only," although through it you can
glimpse a few exhibit stations with smaller interactive working areas
and you notice that almost half the folks coming through enter here
no matter what the sign says.

— A little farther down are **enormous large windows on the right**,
matching those of the science center on the left, open upon a full-
size, diorama-style reconstruction of an atmospheric study site in
the Antarctic. (In 2002 the Julia Child exhibit opened up across the
hall here.)

— **Graphics surround this whole entering area**: a stylized house,
human, leaf, microscope, and DNA strand. A title label explains:
"Science and technology are right in the thick of American history. . . . [They] stir up wide interest and heated debate." Other,
newer exhibits have brochures to pick up, but any such brochures for
this one were long ago taken and not replaced (along with the American Chemical Society's funding), although there are some for the
science center.

— **The wall backdrops in the intermediate space** introduce the large
thematic sections ahead in a narrative chronology:

> *Laboratory Science Comes to America, 1876–1920*
> *Science for Progress, 1920–1940*
> *Mobilizing Science for War, 1940–1960*
> *Better than Nature, 1950–1970*
> *Science in the Public Eye, 1970–*

Entrance to *Science in American Life*. Photo by Chandrasekher Mukk.

Large-scale photo figures in the anteroom: these are the so-called dummy scientists also seen throughout the exhibit. Photo by Katie King.

— **The last one is the one you see first:** it is a wall-sized photo of a demonstration, and the photo figure scientists and children appear to inhabit this contentious moment, the now. "Better than Nature" is illustrated with what seems to be a model homes fair. "Mobilizing Science for War" is backdropped by a group portrait of men working on the Manhattan Project, and "Science for Progress" is pictured as the New York World's Fair of 1939, with photo-figured girls collaged and the stand out, brightly colored figure of a conspicuously fashionable woman. "Laboratory Science Comes to America" is figured with a massive institutional building overlaid by the picture of a scientist working on the cover of an early copy of *Scientific American*.

THE NARRATIVE TRAJECTORY, AN INTERLACED DESCRIPTION, A PASTICHE

The sociologist Lynn Mulkey and the network management theorist William Dougan (who worked with Gieryn on the Cold Fusion Archive, which has a modest place in the "Science in the Public Eye" portion of the exhibit) create one possible narrative trajectory for this *SAL* exhibit. Their collaborative story differs slightly from another by Tom Gieryn, and I interlace these accounts that privilege somewhat different elements of this massively documented space, by starting with Mulkey and Dougan's numbered *outline* to which I add Gieryn's notes.[25] I connect both of these with my own indications of space and movement among interactive stations, video displays, life-sized recreations, and other notable features, spoken, as now, in the first and second persons:

As you pass through the main entrance, on your left is a (seemingly) full-sized *diorama* of Remsen's lab including two life-sized mannequins, while the air is filled with the supposed voices of Remsen and Fahlberg describing the discovery of saccharin.[26] To your right is a display contrasting and interconnecting two approaches to science: "The Pure Science Ideal" and "Life in the Laboratory."

I. "LABORATORY SCIENCE COMES TO AMERICA, 1876–1920"
   1 Chemist Ira Remsen pioneers a laboratory at The Johns Hopkins University in 1876; Remsen disputes with Constantin Fahlberg over the discovery of saccharin;
   2 Ellen Swallow Richards, one of a few women scientists, becomes a chemistry instructor at the Massachusetts Institute

Ellen Swallow Richards station. Photo by Chandrasekher Mukk.

of Technology; she and Charles Frederick Chandler devote
their energies to the chemistry of water sanitation;[27]

We encounter for the first time a duplicate photo figure we have met
already in the anteroom: the chemist Cynthia Friend, a professor at Harvard, whose life-sized figure speaks to us in her label, complete with her
personal signature, saying that "women like Ellen Swallow Richards made
my career possible." She is a white woman.

    3 Harvey Washington Wiley studies food additives;

    4 Intelligence testing (World War I) begins;

    5 A Call for Pure Science emerges;

    6 Science Enters Society: Some scientists concentrate on the
       practical value of scientific knowledge and make careers in
       government or private industry;

Hampton Institute
photo wall. Photo by
Lillian Doherty.

7 The Hampton Institute is a training center for dairy
hygiene.[28]

The Hampton recreation consists of a flat photo wall with two life-sized
photo figures, one working at a real table; the people pictured are black,
and one sees a woman among them.

GIERYN: Laboratory Science Comes to America, 1876–1920: Ira Remsen's lab from Johns Hopkins University, depicting his squabble with
Constantin Fahlberg over priority in the discovery of saccharin; the
practical fruits of the coal tar tree, from dyes to explosives; scientists
active in the social reform movement, featuring the Hampton Institute's instruction in dairy hygiene, James R. Murie's ethnography of the
Pawnee Indians, Charles Frederick Chandler and Ellen Swallow Richards's chemistry of water sanitation, and Harvey Washington Wiley's
research on food additives; and World War I intelligence testing;[29]

The next section is marked by dramatically altered space: a large circular wall in front covered with a striking photo from the New York World's Fair in 1939. Inside the small circular room that the wall creates is the Futurama video station, with chairs for an audience of about twelve. The distinctive voice of Linda Wertheimer from National Public Radio fills the air in the documentary presented there.

II. "SCIENCE FOR PROGRESS, 1920–1940"
1 In the Scopes trial of 1925, science challenges the traditional authority of religion over the issues of teaching evolution in public schools;
2 Science on Stage: The New York World's Fair of 1939–40, supported by industrial corporations, reaffirms the abiding American faith in science as progress (included, the Eastman Kodak firm is a supporter of basic science to create new products);
3 Dupont and nylon appears;[30]

We encounter the first of several "hot link" labels here: it directs us to another section of the exhibit, "Science and the Home," because products produced by wartime industries will turn up later in other guises as household consumer items.

4 A. C. Gilbert Company merchandises science toys to instill in the young beliefs of a scientific culture.[31]

GIERYN: Science for Progress, 1920–1940: the role of Science Service in popularizing and publicizing the accomplishments of science, culminating in Scopes (the WGN radio microphone is here); dusty old chemistry sets; DuPont's Wallace Carothers and the nylon story; bombast, better living, and "Futurama" from the 1939–40 New York World's Fair;[32]

As you leave this area, you encounter another of the photo-figure scientists from the front: the physicist S. B. Woo of the University of Delaware (DuPont country). He is an Asian man. His label describes his concerns for "selling science to the public": a telling metaphor for communication.

In an interstitial space, just around the corner from the "Laboratory Science" beginning section and just before entering the "Science for War" section, you come across a whole display area called "Coal Tar goes to War." It has a small interactive station to examine the chemical structure of the various derivatives of coal tar, among them saccharin, dyes, and explosives.

Things: Scopes window cabinet. Photo by Lillian Doherty.

As you enter the next section, on the left wall is a sign commanding "Proper Identification Required"; it heads a panel displaying ID badges worn for the Manhattan Project.

III. "MOBILIZING SCIENCE FOR WAR, 1940–1960"

1   National defense investments by the federal government give rise to "Big Science"; Physicist E. O. Lawrence invents the cyclotron (atom smasher); he had a Radiation Lab at the University of California, Berkeley, and helped plan the development of the atomic bomb at the Manhattan Project;[33]

Two videos appear here: one in a low monitor with a soundstick (you can only hear it with your ear to the sound piece) entitled: "Science Recruits Women and Minorities, 1940–1960"; the other is closer to eye level on a larger TV-style monitor, and its narration fills the air with an explanation of the chemistry and physics of "Two Paths to the Bomb."

2   Robert Oppenheimer, Enrico Fermi, E. O. Lawrence of the Manhattan Project; Enrico Fermi leads a team at the University of Chicago that creates the first nuclear reactor (Chicago Pile no. 1);[34]

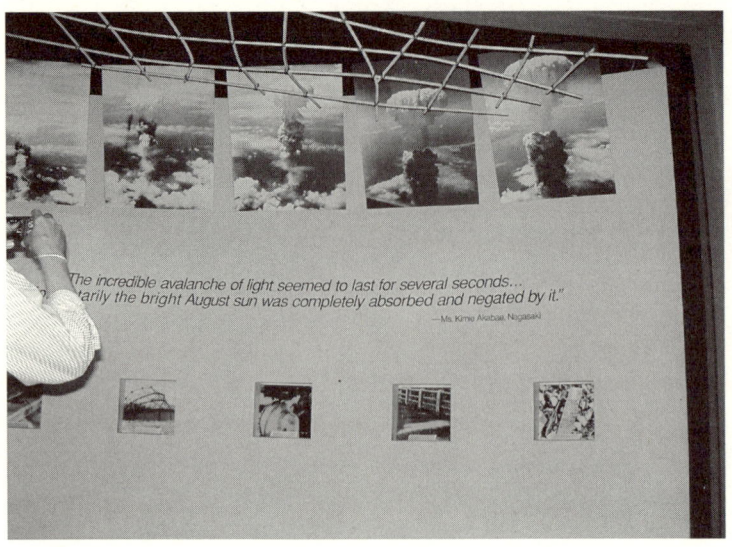

Hiroshima wall. Photo by Katie King.

Chicago Pile no. 1 is an almost full-scale, diorama-style recreation, fore-shortened for space and effect. It includes three close to life-size mannequins, with other figures painted in the backdrop; also included is a small-scale model. Across the visitor path is an interactive model of a cyclotron.

Into a further space is a display of the Hanford Nuclear installation, which includes the large object of an actual "Control Console" from the site. Another life-size photo-figure scientist, G. V. Martinez of the US Department of Energy, talks about safe disposal of nuclear waste in his label, entitled "Hanford, Then and Now." He is a Hispanic man.

3 Hiroshima;[35]

This is a slightly curved photo room: high up above us are photos of the blast; below them in artfully lighted recessed framings are photos of the effects of the blast: the shadows made by bodies illuminated by the overwhelming light, pictures of the destruction, a woman's body marked by burns, a picture of a plank written upon with information left behind for searching relatives.

4 The fallout shelter (Ft. Wayne, Indiana) comes on the scene.[36]

This artifact is set up in a recreation, with the kinds of stuff one would need if using it, a strange little "home." It is directly across from the plastics home recreation.

The large object of a Geodimeter from Cape Canaveral is set up in a little recreation with a photo figure using it in mapping. A "hot link" nearby connects this point to the "Information Age: People, Information, and Society" exhibition (once) on the same floor.

> GIERYN: Mobilizing Science for War, 1940–1960: diverse war-related scientific research programs such as the Massachusetts Institute of Technology's Rad Lab, the American Soldier studies, Skinner's Project Pigeon, and rockets; Lawrence's lab at the University of California, Berkeley, site of the first cyclotron; Chicago Pile No. 1 and a lot more from the Manhattan Project, Los Alamos, Hanford, Bikini, and Hiroshima; a Fort Wayne, Indiana, fallout shelter set amid debates over nuclear risk/reward;[37]

IV. "BETTER THAN NATURE, 1950–1970"
>   1 Rachel Carson writes, in *Silent Spring*, about the dangers of pesticides to the environment;[38]

This section actually comes *after* the home recreation, around the corner. Filling the air with Linda Wertheimer's narrating voice, this section includes a video documentary about Rachel Carson.

>   2 Plastic, as a new synthetic material, is a feature of suburban homes (the Princess Jeanne development in Albuquerque, New Mexico);[39]

This is a recreation of a kitchen and family room from this development. The TV set runs a loop of various video selections, among them a duck and cover drill. On the opposite wall, across the visitor path, is a wall-sized photo of the outside of a suburban home, with a recreation of its garden shed in full scale, brimming with pesticides and herbicides DDT and 2,4-D.

>   3 The birth control pill becomes popular.[40]

Part of this display includes as one object, a plaque emblazoned with the name of Margaret Sanger's newspaper, "The Woman Rebel." In another area of the display we meet another of the photo-figure scientists, the biologist Vijaya L. Melnick of the University of the District of Columbia,

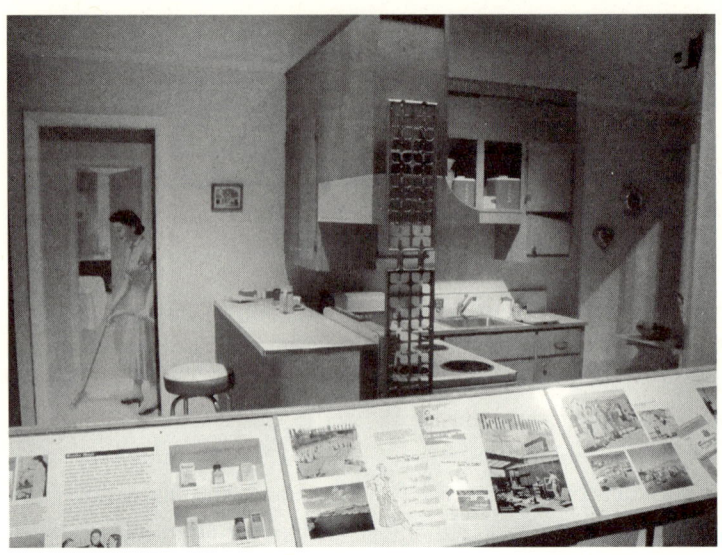

Suburban home, Princess Jeanne development. Photo by Chandrasekher Mukk.

whose label tells us she works for the "health and well-being of women and children," and that "we must be aware that seemingly 'simple solutions' often have implications that range from basic individual rights to global political and economic relationships." She is a South Asian woman.

> GIERYN: Better than Nature, 1950–1970: a suburban 1950s tract home made better by plastics and worse by careless use of lawn pesticides and herbicides; the birth control pill and its chemistry, politics, and demography; "Atoms for Peace" and Silent Spring; and[41]

V. "SCIENCE IN THE PUBLIC EYE, 1970"
1 The Challenger space shuttle explodes;
2 The partial meltdown of the nuclear reactor at Three Mile Island is an issue;
3 What is the relationship between sciences, technology, and progress?;[42]

These three notes connect only to references in the opening label of this section in 2003. No pictures or displays refer to them. There is a "hot link" to an exhibit at Air and Space "forthcoming 1996," the label still present in 2003. A small section of the wall resources the Cold Fusion Archive in which Gieryn and Dougan were collaborators.

Photo figure of the
biologist Vijaya L.
Melnick. Photo by
Chandrasekher Mukk.

4 Stanley Cohen, Annie Chang, and Herbert Boyer investigate
   recombinant DNA;[43]

A continuous loop video of citizen hearings of the Cambridge, Massachusetts, City Council in 1976 fills the air. A display on genetic engineering
and popular culture includes the large object of a human size Teenage
Mutant Ninja Turtle. We meet another photo-figure scientist, this one the
evolutionary biologist Matthew George of Harvard. He works on the DNA
of racial groups and on the heritage of the so-called African Eve. He is a
black man.

5 Susan Solomon, atmospheric chemist, leads the first National
   Ozone Expedition (NOZE I) to Antarctica, 1986, and finds
   chlorofluorocarbons as the cause of the ozone hole;[44]

The diorama-style recreation of this expedition site, visible through display windows from outside, includes two full-sized mannequins, one of

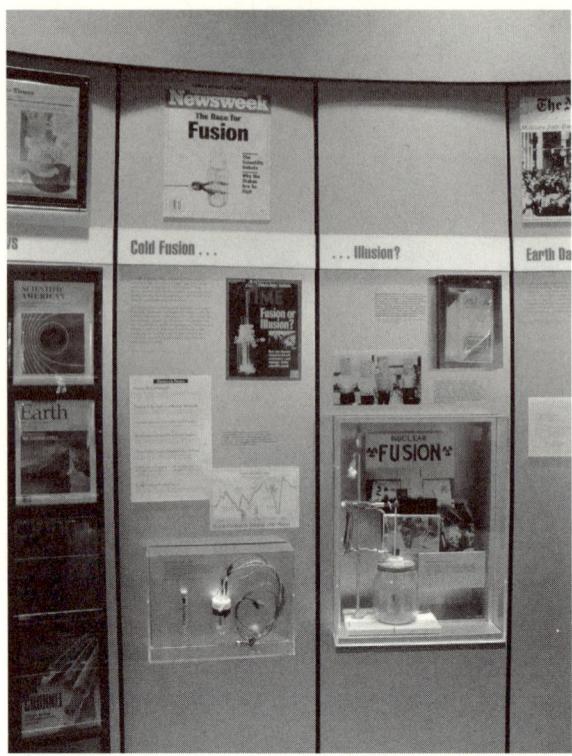

Cold fusion, wall
detail. Photo by
Chandrasekher Mukk.

Susan Solomon, a scientist we met at the entrance. She is a white woman.
On a low video monitor with a soundstick, Solomon narrates a discussion
of "Women in Science," which includes the work of four other women
scientists too.

> 6 The U.S. Congress shuts down the Superconducting Super
> Collider at Waxahachie, Texas.[45]

This area is dominated by the large object of a cross-section of an elec-
tromagnet, a prototype for the Superconducting Super Collider.

> GIERYN: Science in the Public Eye, 1970–: Moon landing, war on can-
> cer, Three Mile Island, Love Canal, cold fusion, and other incidents of
> science in high relief; DNA and its genetic engineering ("The Splice of
> Life"); chlorofluorocarbons (CFCs) and the ozone hole; the sad fate of
> the Superconducting Super-Collider.[46]

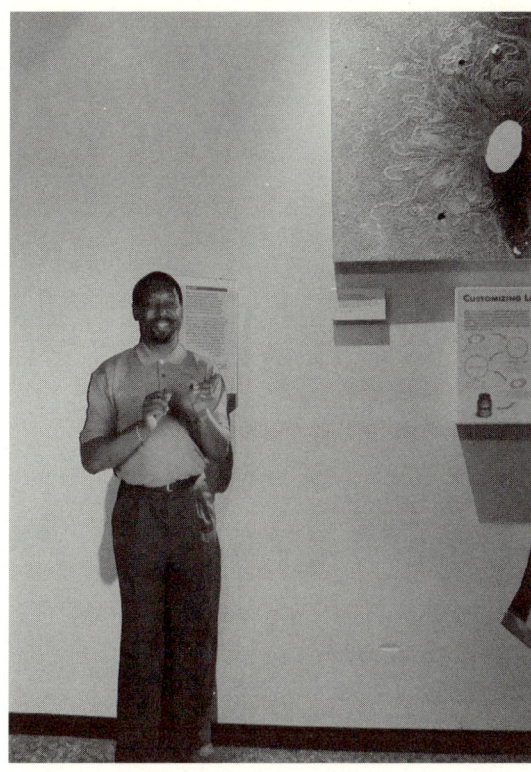

Photo figure of the evolutionary biologist Matthew George. Photo by Chandrasekher Mukk.

Only Tom Gieryn describes the last bit: "Looking Ahead is focused on biotechnology (engineer a tomato), whereas in the Hands-On Science Center visitors can sit with a docent at a laboratory bench and test for food additives (my thirteen-year-old son: 'cool') or locate themselves on some bell curve with old intelligence tests."[47]

In 2003 the "Looking Ahead" section had several broken-down stations, blacked out and empty. Their interactive screens and such seemed less censored than unrepaired. A bare listing gives you some idea of what the makeup of this area once was:

Starts with Engineer a Tomato
Basics: interactive choice of kinds of DNA spliced with tomato
Growing plastic and Blue Jeans for lunch
Stop and Think 1: What can you do? Among suggestions: decide whether
    or not to boycott Genetically Modified Foods

Diorama where Susan Solomon, atmospheric chemist, leads the National Ozone Expedition. Photo by Chandrasekher Mukk.

The garbage dilemma (this is now a blank, unrepaired station)

blank (something else unrepaired)

Stop and Think 2: What can you do? Perhaps join an environmental group

Getting New Genes, Gene Map

Tools of Biotechnology: includes large object, full size DNA Sequencer

Computational chemistry and Models (blank station, unrepaired)

Stop and think 3: Consider the work of the Recombinant DNA Advisory group

Play DNA: interactive station in which you play a DNA strand as if it were a xylophone

What's New? (blank station, unrepaired)

Video: "A Night at the Recombinant Opera," in which TV film critics Gene Siskel and Roger Ebert use the Marx Brothers movie to explain recombinant DNA

What do you think? (blank station, unrepaired)

In 2009, after the reopening of the museum, only this portion of the exhibit was renovated. Some elements in the main areas had been lost and

Added after renovations are wheeled robots. Photo by Chandrasekher Mukk.

not replaced, for example the Harvard chemist Cynthia Friend's photo figure was entirely missing. However, a new exhibit was installed here, including a station called "Wheeled Robots."

WHAT TROUBLED THE CRITICS? UN-BLACK-BOXED

Critics of *SAL* objected implicitly to *the tactics of problematization* employed throughout. "Tactics of problematization . . . contribute in a fundamental way to a network's longevity" point out the medical sociologist Vicky Singleton and the environmental ethicist Mike Michael in their analysis of the UK Cervical Screening Programme in a very technical *actor-network* study.[48] (Along with Michel Callon and John Law, Latour was among the principal architects of actor-network theory, styled ANT in science studies.[49]) They explain:

a network is rendered durable by the way that actors at once occupy the margins and the core, are the most outspoken critics and the most ardent stalwarts, are simultaneously insiders and outsiders . . . [such "durability" is an artifact of how] the whole system is unreliable. In [the actor-network theorist Michel] Callon's terms the *actor-world* can convert or revert into an *actor-network* . . . materials can suddenly become problematized (un-black-boxed). The roles and identities assigned by one entity to another may suddenly be challenged, undermined or shattered. Where once the "enrolling" actor had organized the obligatory points of passages for others, it finds itself forced to traverse the obligatory points of passages that are "dictated" by others. And it is not only social others who intervene; the heterogeneity of the networks means that any entity can begin to step out of semiotic character within the network—electrons, microbes, scallops, the Atlantic.[50]

Such "unreliability" is an index of the dynamic and unfinished processes that characterize how knowledges can be stabilizing or destabilizing in temporal trajectories; that is to say, how knowledges can be taken for granted or revised, in the way the apparently finished *actor-world* can swiftly shift into the process focusing *actor-network*. And the forefronting of such unreliability is the mark of that "postmodernist" analysis decried by conservative science critics, that inquiry into *how*, that is to say, *the means by which*, pivotal and enabling foundations can be offered by science as discovery and rationality and yet change over time. "Longevity" and "durability" are noted by analysts as, counterintuitively, the very *effect of problematizing*—for example, that having critics and stalwarts within memberships rather than characterizing their boundaries allows for long-lasting circumstances in which deep dynamic change occurs without necessarily calling knowledge and authority into question. The "things" that matter in order to authorize membership may well be among those entities that Singleton and Michael say can "step out of semiotic character" within a network; they could, for example, be considered foundational at some times and not at others, or for some purposes and not for others.

Paul R. Gross, another pro-science conservative, controversial coauthor of *Higher Superstition: The Academic Left and Its Quarrels with Science* (a text native to the "science wars"), and a life scientist at the University of Virginia, replied to Tom Gieryn's analysis of the SAL exhibit process and reiterated the claim that SAL was unbalanced. He supported his account with the following list of important *things* that were left out of the exhibit, things he considers foundational and essential. These are thus among what he understands to be markers of membership for authoritative science practitioners and things necessary for a proper exhibit:

> increase of the human life span (due, yes, to "public health improvements," but those are due to science); synergic explosions of pharmacology, organic synthesis, biochemistry, and microbiology to generate a rational chemotherapy; entry into medicine of physics and thus of diagnostic tools hitherto undreamed of; mergers of science with the clinical arts, thus, for example, rational anesthesia, open-heart surgery; radar (which, along with synthetic rubber, won World War II, whereas the atom bomb merely ended it); a comprehensive materials science; agricultural genetics—a key source of America's wealth—now deployed, indispensable, and feeding people around the world; planetary science and cosmology (not just Apollo) about which tens of thousands read with awe and pleasure in the Sunday newspaper supplements; every significant fact of a new science of ecology; an information revolution from mathematics and electronics and solid-state physics; the fusion of genetics, molecular biology, population biology, and evolutionary biology to help us understand our place in the biosphere.[51]

Gross's list here—it does indeed make one wish for these not included *things*—elides the only too brutal weight of "boundary work" that choosing from the universe of possibilities makes so effortful and unnerving. And of course we are talking about an already incredibly inclusive exhibition staged within finite financial, physical, and conceptual "space." Black-boxing (or not forefronting or making visible or not un-black-boxing) the work of negotiation and the fragilities of communities in practice collaborating to make the exhibition makes for a strong argument by Gross, and it allows for the assertion of his own alliances and commitments but cannot properly honor the integrity of others. And, of course, refusing to acknowledge such "good faith" practice is precisely Gross's intent, itself a signal of that intensity that is both affectively rhetorical and affiliatively enrolling.

The advisory board during the period of its work on the exhibit, together with the range of museum creators, including the chief curator, is made up of "actors [who] at once occupy the margins and the core, are the most outspoken critics and the most ardent stalwarts, are simultaneously insiders and outsiders" of the museum and its processes, of the exhibit and those constructing it. Gieryn explains: "Our job was to provide advice to museum curators about the general direction and technical details of the developing exhibition; in practice, we provided ammunition for Smithsonian staff and ACS representatives to use in higher level policy battles that we only heard hints about. Neither the chemists on the board, nor the STSers [science and technology studies folks], nor the Smithsonian curatorial team functioned as a unified bloc pushing for a party-line vision of SAL."[52]

Problematization, ambiguity, metacommunication—all these forms in which *telescoping* layers of locals and globals animate the *things* of the exhibit, those present and those absent—enlarge the several scales in which these things simultaneously reside. Some levels of problematization extend their temporality, of some moment to museum curators making permanent exhibits, as associations, assumptions, historical contexts, and other instabilities are explained and situated, as well as sometimes implicitly and explicitly critiqued. But other (or these same) levels of problematization, controversy, "noise" may endanger fragile stabilities.

VALIDATION FUNCTIONS

"In April 1995, the National Museum of American History (NMAH) asked the Smithsonian's Institutional Studies Office (ISO) to conduct a study of visitors to the *Science in American Life (SAL)* exhibition." Responding to any possibility that they would be asked to alter the exhibit, curators might properly hope the study would establish authoritatively that critics were incorrect in their claims that the public understood the exhibit as antiscience. Interpretation (published 1999) of the study (the data collection period was June and July of 1995) stated "conclusively that the visiting public entered the exhibition with a very positive view of science and technology and that their views were reinforced and confirmed by the experience of *Science in American Life*, rather than changed in either a positive or negative direction." Attitudes about science held by visitors entering (and leaving) the exhibit were similar to those held by the US population as a whole.

The effect of the exhibition on its visitors was subtler than a change of mind. It probably served to validate and confirm ideas that visitors brought with them. Nearly one in four (24%) visitors said that *they already knew everything* the exhibition had to say. We believe that this *validation function* is a key dimension of the museum experience. Part of the satisfaction people find in visiting exhibitions seems to reflect *the experience of having one's ideas validated in a serious public forum*, since *individuals tend to visit the exhibitions that agree with their viewpoint and to express indifference or hostility toward the ones that do not*.[53]

Visitors with children were especially drawn to SAL. Compared to typical NMAH visitors, visitors to SAL were more likely to be in a group with at least one adult and at least one child. The Hands-On Science Center (HOSC) may account for this difference. The Tracking Study confirmed that visitors saw HOSC as "child-oriented," since it found that 71 percent of all visitors to the center were in groups that included teenagers or children.[54]

In his description of the controversies surrounding the exhibit, the chief curator of SAL Arthur P. Molella remarked that,

> findings of this study were publicly accepted by the American Chemical Society as a "positive" development, leading it to reevaluate its assertions about the negative effect on visitors. This took some of the force out of an effort initiated by the ACS in spring 1995 to pressure the Smithsonian into revising the exhibit, an effort that was effectively abandoned a year later. Persisting in its claim that the presentation "conveys a significant amount of antiscience sentiment," the Society essentially washed its hands of the exhibit in March 1996 when its chairman, Joan Shields, declared that "further negotiations" with the Smithsonian to alter the exhibit "would be non-productive."[55]

Mulkey and Dougan's social constructionist analysis also places the exhibit within values of the US population as whole, although in alternate scales and terms, in layers of globals *at the level of epistemological abstraction* in which science itself is *normalized* culturally. Mulkey and Dougan interrogate not only the exhibition, but also exemplary "outside" critical voices as well as others engaging in the controversies surrounding the exhibit, *all as parts of the work that the exhibit does*. This capacious understanding of such work operates with similar intentions to my own extensive definition of reenactments.

"Facticity"—that is, the forms in which we make and share our social worlds and their things, and especially among them are so-called facts—

itself is held to be the subject of all these processes in Mulkey and Dougan's technical ethnomethodology:

> We conclude that issues of "nature" or "experiment" are distinct at one level of analysis, but that both comprise and are embedded in a single, radical, fundamental invariant social property that makes science what we know it to be. Evidence is never there apart from some kind of narrative. Reflexivity is a "social" practice and in that a narrative capability—*the structure of the story that makes the phenomenon recognizable as the "fact."* This level of insight about the sources and functions of social behavior chisels "absolute" norms from social practice. The practice makes facts findable reflexively through various forms of "secondary elaborations" that affirm in one way or another (in the laboratory, in a journal, or in museum exhibition) the "facticity" of the world. We need "facts" and "nonfacts" to make "facticity." There is no such thing as "just evidence." It must be shown to be evidence and the "must be shown" takes place in relations that occur as laboratory, journal, electronic bulletin board communication and museum exhibition practices. . . . The maintenance of science then is not determined by nature, but the natural is knowable solely through the social practices that name it so. In this way, when someone asks us as experts of just those human relations that result in things like "scientific discoveries," we can offer them another view of the matter, that *museum exhibitions and their critiques are not "about" experiments, they are "another version" of them.*[56]

Museum exhibitions and the controversies surrounding them, together with and as variants on experiments and laboratory practices, are elements in all that embodies scientific discovery, that great assemblage and material and conceptual infrastructure that is "science."

TELESCOPING LOCALS WITHIN A "GLOBAL" SCIENCE STUDIES

Mulkey and Dougan's ethnomethodological STS analysis, in *its priority of the "social"* and in its politics and intellectual apparatus, is a variant on other approaches that characterize divergent but interconnected communities of practice within a wide-ranging set of kinds of STS. Consider for example, "Haraway" and "Latour" as shorthand for ranging communities within and across feminist technoscience studies and ANT. Gieryn's notes hint self-interestedly at the *contentious* differences among those within such divergent communities of practice (with their different acronyms or shorthand exemplars) yet also within the larger field (understood captiously, however named). He hints at ranges drawn between authoritative and alternative knowledges, only too obviously relative, relational, and professionally particular: "I resist the temptation to disaggregate STS into a 'reasonable and prudent camp' and a 'lunatic fringe.' I have my own objections to some postmodernists, feminists, and constructivists. But the risk of being divided and conquered by those who wish to tame STS into a mere apologia for science requires that such disagreements entre nous remain latent here."[57]

DISPARATE EXPERIENCES AND VALIDATION FUNCTIONS

Each time I visited *SAL* accompanied by others, a different aspect of the exhibit seemed primary, a different scale of formal and informal analysis was necessitated, a different feature experienced of that validation function appealed to by the Smithsonian's Institutional Studies Office (ISO). Each person I visited it with prioritized specific concerns about the exhibit, and finally I could not help but notice how disparate my experience was with each one (I can only imagine how I changed the experience for them). The more they knew about the controversies surrounding the exhibit (and which over succeeding visits I came to study myself), the more the salience of alliances around these controversies seemed intensified and drew me in. My own cognitive and affective *sensations of validation and affiliation* were strikingly different with each person each time.

One person, a full "member" of the social worlds of science studies (although of course, not always pivotal, or even sometimes fully authoritative in *every* science studies community of practice), was in career terms "ahead" of me with considerably more academic and intellectual status; a person to whom at times I had been personally institutionally subordinate. She had been involved in professionally supporting the curators at a time when the exhibit was most threatened, possibly to be gutted or changed in other alarming ways as was the *Enola Gay* exhibit. In her company I first experienced some of those powerful allegiances mustered to protect the existence of the exhibit. Our own disagreements and differences examining or criticizing the exhibit felt somehow collapsed by this threatened outlook and became momentarily deeply uncomfortable, even though this period was conclusively past. In my ignorance of these issues and contexts I exacerbated our disagreements in haphazard unconscious and insubordinate resistances, trivializing critical elements of this exhibit in preference for other exhibits at NMAH that I had had more interest in and experience with instead. Without any such intentions I was inadvertently refusing to ally on the side of radical science studies and displaying my ignorance of what might be at stake for those who did.

I visited the exhibit later with yet another person in academic science studies, also "ahead" of me in career trajectory yet closer to being a peer, indeed someone with whom I had trained, someone also intimate with these controversies without having played a role in them herself. She was just then tentatively imagining herself as a possible curator of a very different collection of scientific artifacts. This time around I, now rather* more knowledgeable about all the controversies, experienced very different alliances in her company. These were alliances within which the exhibit was understood to exemplify previous and perhaps conservative communities of practice within the field of STS and among museum curators. I was responsive to such critiques myself and participated in them wholly in our discussions and observations together, enjoying these debunking pleasures and feeling validated by one kind of intellectual mastery.

But later, visiting it with others wholly outside STS, indeed with some of my own women's studies students in comparison to whom I was the most acquainted with these controversies and had the most institutional power and status, I experienced the exhibit as much more radical than I had in either case before. They appreciated it as often "in your face" and successfully debunking what we all understood to be commonly held popular (but not our own) opinions about specific scientific-cultural debates: on evolution and creationism, on the bombing of Hiroshima, on the social effects of the birth control pill, on the depletion of the ozone layer, on uses of biotechnology.

Thus, in the first visit I felt vaguely *attacked* and debunked myself, although I was mistaken in supposing I was a target; in the next I was *persuaded* by debunkings of the exhibit itself, and in the third, I was *confirmed* in my own political opinions by what I saw in the exhibit. Together with my increasing knowledge, the social worlds and communities of practice I virtually inhabited with others and within which I had different trajectories of membership and status at each visit required and offered different affective relations among those *validation functions* remarked upon by the Smithsonian's ISO.

WEIGHING ALL THE STUFF

Each time I visited the exhibit afterward, many more than just those accounted above, I was newly aware of elements I had not examined before, and each time, I discovered more and more and more *stuff* to examine. The *detail* of each section of the exhibit became increasingly obstructive to me as I found I could not read every label, interact with every station, or examine each item carefully, no matter how many times I came (it seemed). I found myself traveling through it more and more cursorily, picking out only one bit to point out, usually one I had already examined, becoming after a certain point more and more reluctant to see anything new and blasé about what was there.

I tried reversing the trajectory: entering at the door marked "exhibition exit only" and examining the exhibit backward. The varieties of scale making one could bring to, experience at, or take away from the exhibit seemed many layered: from the levels of epistemological abstraction of Mulkey and Dougan's large social process explanations to the micro-examinations of particular objects surrounded by other objects in order to create specific contexts.

In all these ways the exhibit requires and creates a *kind of consciousness* and a sort of *affective and cognitive environment*, in which one moves among such levels fairly freely if not always painlessly, and also permits—or requires—a great deal of selection among the overwhelming variety, to pick and choose those elements that interest one, confirm one, or debunk one. (And the ISO study suggests that such experience is hardly unique to this exhibit, if rather more studied here.) "Sharing agency" with such a "sea of actants" (Latour)[58] in "kinds of relatings, and scores of time" (Haraway)[59] is complicated but possible, if requiring various simplifications and, among agencies, alternate narrative schemes. Especially against the backdrop of the angry lamentation of say, Park or Gross, Latour's musings on scale, scope, perspective, debunking, and trust work to reframe ethically this affective and cognitive environment: "How can moderns be restored to ordinary humanity and inhumanity without being too hastily absolved of the crimes that they are right to seek to expiate? How can we claim—correctly—that our crimes are frightful, but that they remain ordinary; that our virtues are great, but that they too are quite ordinary?"[60] What roles might or do reenactments extensively understood possibly play here?

The life-size freestanding photo figures of *SAL* scientists work to *situate, create, and share scales of importance* all throughout the exhibit. They invite visitors to put themselves into the scene, and the kinds of scenes vary considerably. One can stand next to one of these figures, simultaneously inhabiting a space together with and also apart from them. They "speak" in exhibit labels written out or in video bits you have to initiate on monitors, commenting and making alliances across space and time with other figures described or reenacted in the exhibit. They inhabit re-created spaces set up as scenes in historical and epistemological mini-dramas.

For example, the Harvard chemist Cynthia Friend's label tells me more about Ellen Swallow Richards and allies with her as a woman scientist in the "Laboratory Science Comes to America" section. The University of the District of Columbia biologist Vijaya L. Melnick's label explicates the complexities of the political history of birth control for the well-being of women and children in the "Better than Nature" section. The life-sized mannequin of Susan Solomon in the diorama of the National Ozone Expedition site, speaks to us via video soundstick about the work of other women scientists in the "Science in the Public Eye" section.

Mulkey and Dougan call these figures "Dummy Scientists" and these processes "shadowing" and "witnessing." At the level of analysis they pursue, perhaps neutrally or perhaps in debunking description (both possibilities are in deferring tension here), they find these dummy scientists to be indications of, maybe impositions of, *universalism normalizing science*:

> Models and sketched caricatures and photographs of scientists are objectified images of abstract norms, such as, for example "universalism." From visual icons of persons of varied racial, ethnic, gender, and age origins emerges science. Science is important and witnessable against the backdrop of the unimportant attributes that change in relation to what is constant. This one is black and this one is white, this

one is female and this one is male, but they all do science. *To produce science, we ignore aspects or cues for how to associate—according to gender, race, age, and more.*[61]

But interlayered with different levels of feminist analysis, if we highlight agencies among *varying and telescoping* ranges of locals and globals, these Dummy Scientists *and* the people they represent simultaneously, might be understood also as *things* themselves in volatile fields of power. If things, as well as "witnesses" and commentators within and upon these very processes, they are *meta-communications and meta-communicators both, showing and telling such agencies* as well as making clearer for feminist analysis in particular the compelling subjugations that produce subjectivity ("gender, race, age, and more"). The work of "shadowing" as described by Mulkey and Dougan, could also open upon complex collective agencies not limited to the human, within an analysis of "situated" knowledges policitized in, for example, feminist technoscience studies. Donna Haraway's work is one touchstone for such intellectually political feminist intentions.[62]

On the one hand, Mulkey and Dougan explain:

Shadowing is a practice that styles, orders, shifts the observer's attention from "knowing" to "doing," by encouraging the process of *identification* with the speaker, what is said and what is known. The observer first sees the scientist—"looks over her shoulder"—and then is the scientist. In essence, shadowing encourages the observer to identify with the object it observes. The persons speaking are no longer heard but may become internalized as the observer speaking. *Shadowing distinguishes museum exhibition as a form of communication* by accomplishing the task of getting the dissociated, estranged observer to "act as if." Shadowing reaffirms facticity by making the observer a shadow of the object, science, scientists (the glosses employed by subjects communicating). . . . Particularly, the three-dimensional exhibits confront the observer with stark, life-sized scientist proxies. Viewers, in this case, *unlike in television communication* and in other forms of pictorial representation, are closely aligned with models of the subjects communicating.[63]

But "acting as if" could also open *other possibilities* in addition to these perhaps silenced others (as feminists might say) now internalized within an individual self. For example, *collective agencies* among actants produce a "polyphony" of receptions for varying viewers. Validations range *among* the particularistic. With apologies to Mulkey and Dougan, this kind of "acting as if" would be far more *like* than "unlike" those globalized TV agencies we have already been exploring, indeed would *link* TV communication to museum exhibition and shadowing at this range of reenactment in the nineties. This point should become even clearer in chapter 3.

MODEST WITNESSING

Shifted in valence to this ethnomethodological description is that of another sort of feminist technoscience analysis and an alternative kind of "witnessing," closer to the work of the ironic, impure "modest witness" Donna Haraway wrings out of any governing "normalization" of science—a different facticity of alternate modest liberations. Shadowing Haraway's modest witness might offer more ranges of agency—single, collective, partially interconnected, nonhuman—in lower or demoted registers or layers of abstraction and materiality (sometimes "local" or "concrete," but also sometimes not), not quite visible or un-black-boxed yet on the determinative and coercive high scale of "the social" in Mulkey and Dougan's analysis.

Haraway offers historical and transdisciplinary alternatives in her book *Modest_Witness*:

I have tried to persuade my readers that several apparently counterintuitive claims should have the status of matters of fact—that is, crucial points of contingent stability for possible sociotechnical orders, attested by collective, networked, situated practices of witnessing. Witnessing is seeing; attesting; standing publicly accountable for, and psychically vulnerable to, one's visions and representations. Witnessing is a collective, limited practice that depends on the constructed and never finished credibility of those who do it, all of whom are mortal, fallible, and fraught with the consequences of unconscious and disowned desires and fears. A child of Robert Boyle's Royal Society of the English Restoration and of the experimental way of life, I remain attached to the figure of the modest witness. I still inhabit stories of scientific revolution as earthshaking mutations in the apparatuses of production of what may count as knowledge. A child of antiracist, feminist, multicultural, and radical science movements, I want a mutated modest witness to live in worlds of technoscience, to yearn for knowledge, freedom, and justice in the world of consequential facts. I have tried to queer the self-evidence of witnessing, of experience, of the conventionally upheld and invested perceptions of clear distinctions between subject and object, especially the self-evidence of the distinction between living and dead, machine and organisms, human and nonhuman, self and other as well as of the distinction *between* feminist and mainstream, progressive and oppressive, local and global. . . .

What will count as modesty now is a good part of what is at issue. Whose agencies will revised forms of "modest witness" enhance, and whose will it displace?[64]

Putting Haraway's distinctively affective and cognitive apparatus and ethics to the work of describing SAL, we might note that collecting ten adult scientists and two children in the anteroom of SAL with laminated picture book at child or wheelchair level might facilitate identification or might make it a bit effortful physically, might work to honor children as potential scientists, or might suggest adults as authorities unquestioned or questioned. That these photo figures are conspicuously gendered, raced, and nationed might make the politics of multicultural national identity moot or validate it or call it to account. Choosing among these in a process of validation might be a simple choice or a more difficult one, highly conscious or utterly unconscious, wherever it ends up. What roles *call out* to be taken up is tentative here as well as attractively positioned. The modesty and ethics of small choices with visionary but unpredictable outcomes is made both as simple as a story in a picture book, and as difficult as growing up; whether to become a scientist or a science-savvy person, *seeing* and *standing up for* are mortal, fallible possibilities. Credibility, trustworthiness, is an ongoing project that science in the most capacious sense *normalizes*, yes, but that could be only from moment to moment, or in the anteroom, decade to decade.

PASTPRESENTS

Similarly we might alter the valence of other Mulkey and Dougan descriptions, not to substitute something else for these, but rather to work with them and against them, scaling and scoping between in a doubling gestalt, like that of a Necker cube. The practice they call "past present," as well as the sequencing of events amid cognitive sensations and affects they call "Hammock practice," might be worked with and against in order to un-black-box instead reenactment's *pastpresents*. They say:

> The "past present" is a mode of communication, a practice of museum representation that reflexively affirms facticity by depicting breaches of finding the phenomenon through images of past events. We are aware in the present of what to feel and act by modeling the past. The viewer might interpret the exhibits as documentations, the history of science and its applications, when, actually, the history consists of varied versions of one practice—to assert "science" by asserting it as separate from its applications. This practice of thinking about science as separate and self-evident is an act of producing science in the present by producing the past. . . . The Hammock practice sustains science by the sequencing of events, the presentation of events, again and again. For example, referents to exhibits appear according to date: 1876–1920, 1920–1940, 1940–1960, 1950–1970, 1970–present. The chronology constructs science by marking "it," identifying it "as this" repeatedly. This normalization is evident in the "back and forth" and "then and now" referencing of science in society. A panorama of exhibits can be visited and revisited sequentially or back and forth. Recurrency of the phenomenon is achieved by a here and there feature of Hammock practice. Science is here—"Laboratory Science Comes to America"—and there—E. O. Lawrence's Radiation Lab at UC Berkeley or Enrico Fermi leads a team of scientists at the University of Chicago. Science is sustained by talk that happens "back and forth," and "here and there."[65]

These are helpful insights about all the boundary work required and displayed that labor to separate science and nonscience. The trajectories of past present with science *here* and science and nonscience *there* are a bit less elegant, however, when, still taking Mulkey and Dougan to heart, one rescales such analysis to telescopically open up upon, say, the WGN radio microphone from the Scopes trial, and thus un-black-box even more chronologies of controversy. Mentioned by Gieryn and glossed by Mulkey and Dougan as "science challenges the traditional authority of religion" this microphone *thing* un-black-boxes out onto a more massive assemblage from which in 2005 the Scopes trial is newly retold, as religion challenges science in what might be varying reenactments of Scopes by school boards, for example, in Georgia, Pennsylvania, and Kansas in 2004, 2005, and 2006. In 2005 the trial offers a very different semifictive virtual event of 1925 and becomes instead the answer to a call from the ACLU for a test case, indeed one manufactured by civic leaders to bring publicity and economic incentives to the town of Dayton. Indeed Scopes himself likely never even taught evolution.[66] Recurrence and chronology here show and tell that any *pastpresent* is intermixed and continually changing, while the story told is only too unstable in small variations that may or may not normalize science for diverging audiences and interests out of the nineties.

Consider the large objects that connect *SAL* to the sites of their use and description. Rather than distinguishing museum goers, what happens if instead we interconnect them—as reenactors, shadows, witnesses—with television viewers? In chapter 3 we will take up television viewers as reenactors who play in games of being "there," on set, on site, in that past, in a past: mentally enacting, reenacting, experimenting, speculating, trying to find evidence for various pastpresents.

HOW TO PRACTICE SCALE MAKING AND SCALE SHIFTING: STRUCTURES OF SCALE

Scale making, time sequencing, and chronology are engaging partners, and together they make what the anthropologist Kath Weston calls "time claims": "There can be no *time claim* without a *time frame*: history, infinity, chronology, generation, era, future/past. Implicit in these claims are *modes of temporality* (regressing, moving ahead, modern traditions, coming back around) and *morality* (stolen futures, lost generation, better days). In relativizing fashion, time claims tether me, you, and our brother's keeper to our respective *timespots* (1990s butch, twenty-first century woman, follower of the old ways, old-fashioned). Time claims can even naturalize or denaturalize the very modes of reckoning embedded within them."[67] Situating our moment's globalization processes in which we are encouraged to make time claims by "traveling through a racialized, sexualized museum called the past," Weston is careful to point out that globalization is not a new phenomenon, although some of its current features are specific: "Since the days of the Silk Route, since the even earlier period of Buddhist maritime trade, the earth has witnessed many rounds of what could be called globalization. In the latest episode, capital flows and speculation cast a long shadow over trade."[68]

And Weston has a very different take on the telescoping salience of such categories as age, race, gender, and nation, rather than pitching them at the scale of their normalization by universalism as described by Mulkey and Dougan. Rather under globalization's layers of locals and globals, *salience* is dynamically scaled and rescaled, in terror and possibility:

> It can help to know that a genderless world is now and here. . . . In the nations that direct this global economy, *gender zeros out on a regular basis as bodies are called in and out of classification.* . . . During that flash of an instant when a person becomes unsexed, gender temporarily passes away, rather than bringing the curtain down on some world-historical stage. . . . Gender relations in the era of global capitalism constantly vanishing, never quite gone. . . . *The zero that is unsexed holds open a place for regrouping in the wake of those moments when things come undone.*[69]

When I pointed out earlier that "for exhibit makers, for teachers, for cultural critics, for analysts of all kinds, talking *about* something may appear to others to include *denying* that something, or include making talking *about* it more important than the thing itself"—it is scale making itself at issue, these levels of abstraction and *salience*, thus significance. Shifting scales makes possible that suggestion of Latour's: "The relevant question for the diplomats would no longer be, 'Is it or isn't it constructed?' but rather: 'How do you manufacture them?' And, above all, 'How do you verify that they are well constructed?' Here is where the negotiations could begin: with the question of the right ways to build."[70]

It is with related purposes in mind that Donna Haraway looks to a specific cognitive sensoria, that of optics, for an intellectual model, "diffraction," an alternative to that of "reflexivity," that self-conscious positioning of individual intention that attempts to ground ethical political practice. Haraway says: "Reflexivity is not enough to produce self-visibility. . . . Diffraction is the production of difference patterns in the world, not just of the same reflected—displaced—elsewhere."[71] A nested and relatively individuated notion of "reflexivity" is un-black-boxed by Haraway's substitute term "diffraction." Diffraction positions multiple actants, or agencies, including but not limited to people, among a ranging set of telescoping scales of abstraction or units of significance, while also always signaling strong commitments to finite materialities as "interference patterns," those constraining resources focusing our "effort to make a difference in the world." Although Haraway jokes that she has "pretty nearly an allergy to abstraction," nevertheless in the interactive and affective semiosis she practices, she is constantly shifting amid levels of abstractions and levels of concreteness in her layers of locals, globals, and tropes among theoretical jokes and her political evaluations.[72] Gieryn's defensiveness combined with explanatory curiosity is similarly a properly ordinary version of Leigh Star's multilayered injunction that we "do not abandon moral commitments even as we simultaneously forswear claims to absolute epistemological authority."[73]

In the anteroom of the SAL exhibit, where the dummy scientists assemble, and where their voices speak into the air without reference to any intention on our parts, Mulkey and Dougan's debunking of the multicultural universalism constructed by figuring scientists in mere accidental variants of age, gender, ethnicity, race, and nation makes one kind of sense. But that very sense is telescoped elsewhere, when the dummy scientists speak more directly and particularly (as Haraway figures it) "reaching into each other, through their 'prehensions' or graspings . . . constitut[ing] each other and themselves," and us, as we refocus their speech.[74] By implication they and we associate and dissociate these only sometimes "accidentals" with other interests, with situated knowledges in space and time. They offer commentary less amenable to such flattening out, and one feels more and less inclined to ally with particular folks thus articulating, on the basis of their differing implicit and explicit social and epistemological politics. Calling them and oneself in and out of alliance and its classifications, that momentary universalism shades into other ranges of affiliation and disaffiliation, such momentary universalisms occasionally holding "open a place for regrouping in the wake of those moments when things come undone." *Salience* becomes tangible, literal, experimental.

RICH CONTRADICTORY NESTINGS

These *flexible knowledges* create and depend upon what I called earlier "audience polyphony." Audiences and markets shift and converge in that complex address of multiple audiences, in that contradictory nest of niche political and epistemological "markets." While in the movies and TV shows for which I first described audience polyphony these very contradictions may be pleasurable—bundled with their spectacles of production and commercially exuberant remediations, having a great time making fun of it all in the very form of consciousness cultivated by such global products—in the national museum, displays of power in their necessary instabilities may be only too painfully contradictory.

Nevertheless, the results of the Smithsonian's ISO study of SAL also suggest that rich contradictory nestings *permit and require* visitors to select among possible salient stories by animating differently layers of locals and globals, activating intensively the "validation function" that the study claims "is a key dimension of the museum experience."[75] Tactics of problematization, un-black-boxing, a range of metacommunications in layers, mark instabilities in which a naturalizing "actor-world" at any moment can be tilted, telescoped, can "convert or revert" into a suddenly only too questionable and analytically explicit "actor-network," as controversy erupts and ethical membership becomes partisan.

In part 2 of this chapter we will examine moments of tension in which networks and worlds sway politically between precarious tensions and collapsed simplified narratives. It is possible for a spectacle of production to distribute along larger scale *stabilities*, to hold them in a deferred and precarious tension, or to collapse them into single simplified stories. At urgent moments accusations debunk or support political and epistemological alliances. SAL is only a piece of the Smithsonian controversies coming out of the nineties, controversies in which commerce, knowledge work, and national culture are inextricably intermixed.

PART 2.   TRUST, COMMERCE, AND THE EXHIBIT IN THE MUSEUM

RESPONDING TO ACADEMIC CAPITALISM

When, at the end of the nineties in community colloquia, I first introduced women's studies colleagues to the scholarship of such feminist technoscience theorists as Susan Leigh Star and Lucy Suchman, that their investigations had at times been conducted at Xerox's Palo Alto Research Center (Xerox PARC) deauthorized their work for some. These colleagues were skeptical and untrusting about the work of those involved in global industry. Collective research supported by such global commercial facilities was especially foreign to the epistemological alliances and political resistances in the communities of practice of those in the *humanities* in our public, state-funded university. For many academics, although unevenly, it has been only too easy to misrecognize in understandably partial resistance our own already existing, although sometimes invisibly blackboxed and certainly unevenly distributed and scaled, implication in enterprise culture under academic capitalism.[76] My own reactions are no exception to such cognitive and affective misrecognitions and resistances, and this book emerges from a desire to work through these at a historical moment when our implication in academic capitalism is intensifying.

Describing exactly such connections changing over time is the research detailed in *Academic Capitalism: Politics, Policies, and the Entrepreneurial University*, by the higher education and science policy studies analysts Sheila Slaughter and Larry Leslie. It is an examination of global restructuring of universities beginning in the eighties and intensifying over the course of the nineties, with an especial focus on the UK, Australia, the United States, and Canada. Slaughter and Leslie explain:

> We think the 1980s were a turning point, when faculty and universities were incorporated into the market to the point where professional work began to be patterned differently, in kind rather than in degree. Participation in the market began to undercut the tacit contract between professors and society because the market put as much emphasis on the bottom line as on client welfare . . . increasing the likelihood that universities, in the future, will be treated more like other organizations and professionals more like other workers. . . . The flow of public money to higher education was receding, in part because of increasing claims on government funds. In the 1970s the emergence of financial markets made possible the financing of ever larger debts in western industrialized countries. These moneys were used primarily for entitlement programs . . . for debt service, and in the United States, for military expansion. As borrowing increased, federal share of funding for postsecondary education programs . . . decreased. . . . After 1983, states periodically experienced fiscal crisis . . . that precipitated restructuring in higher education. In 1993–1994 the several states, for the first time, experienced an absolute decline in the amount of money expended on higher education rather than a decline in the share of

resources provided or in inflation-adjusted expenditures per student. Restructuring often put increased resources at the disposal of units and departments close to the market, that is, those relatively able to generate external grants and contracts or other sources of revenue. . . . When we talk about restructuring of higher education, we mean substantive organizational change and associated changes in internal resource allocations (reduction or closure of departments, expansion or creation of other departments, establishment of interdisciplinary units); substantive change in the division of academic labor with regard to research and teaching; the establishment of new organizational forms (such as arm's-length companies and research parks); and the organization of new administrative structures or the streamlining or redesign of old ones.[77]

When, at the end of the nineties in graduate courses, I first introduced women's studies students fascinated by feminist epistemological theories to the epistemological implications of global knowledge economies and divisions of labor among knowledge workers, they were openly bored. Despite their own experiences as teaching assistants increasingly directly affected by such divisions of labor in flux, I lost their interest until I learned to openly speculate conspiratorially on who benefited from their finding such concerns boring.

And, when I first started using the terminology from Bowker and Star of "communities of practice" in graduate courses, at least one student, a rather more knowing one, refused to take my course because of it. She positioned the origin of the terminology in the commercial interests of the managerial expert Etienne Wenger, a positioning that for her mandated a debunking critique and a renunciation of these terms in a refusal of my course—altogether an ethical feminist response. Katie Vann (a comparative human cognition analyst) and Geof Bowker (a science studies coauthor with Susan Leigh Star of Sorting Things Out) in 2001 clarify:

Today, the locution "communities of practice" is often invoked as a term for the kinds of social learning formations to which [Jean] Lave [in her 1988 book Cognition in Practice] called attention. A key moment in the trajectory we mark is a book by Etienne Wenger, a colleague and previous co-author of Lave. Wenger's Communities of Practice (1991) popularized a concept of practice in the managerial domain. . . . In the trajectory we mark, a particular knowledge about knowledge has become *robust enough to be instrumentalized differently.* In Lave's work it is instrumentalized as part of a critique of normative psychological testing in use in formal educational assessment. More recently, the locution "practice" has traveled into organizational management consulting communities. . . . In pointing to this trajectory, we mean to explore how a concept of practice is reinstrumentalized and reconfigured as a commercial object with specific uses. We trace one strand in a much larger configuration of interests and inquire how practice is instrumentalized in a particular academic formation, how it is there constructed as an object of knowledge, and how it is re-instrumentalized as a commercial object. Each mode of instrumentalization reflects imperatives of the two communities in their respective, particular historical moments. It appears that as we move between the two social formations, *"practice" is configured first as an instrument of a de-reifying critical theory, and then as an instrument of economic value creation.* We consider this configuration of interested relations and *how knowledge about knowledge is transformed as it moves between the two.*[78]

The term "communities of practice" is thus an example of a transdisciplinary *boundary object.* Bowker and Star describe boundary objects in *Sorting Things Out,* as "plastic enough to adapt to local needs and constraints . . . yet robust enough to maintain a common identity across sites . . . weakly structured in common use and . . . strongly structured in individual-site use. . . . [They] may be abstract or concrete. . . . The creation and management of boundary objects is a key process in developing and maintaining coherence across intersecting communities. . . . [They] arise over time from durable cooperation among communities of practice . . . [and] resolve anomalies of naturalization."[79]

In this book the transdisciplinary boundary object "communities of practice" is appropriated as a feminist *thing* with related and alternative uses. For metacommunication in a posthumanities it enables the mapping of things in their movements and transformations across communities of practice as it registers cognitive and affective *skills* required for *living among things* and sometimes *for living as things ourselves.* And, rather than normalizing our commercial implication under the term "interdisciplinary," instead it forefronts this implication in academic capitalism as these very trajectories of use of the terms "call out" and "un-black-box" only too mixed politicizing histories of the nineties. "Communities of practice" as a boundary object extends but also rescales the work that the term "interdisciplinary" has done and still often does in academic discourse. It allows description of a range and not only in the academy, of more particularistic local, identity-based, generational, subdisciplinary, or regionally specific units of analysis, *knowledge worlds*, built around defining "practices" rather than "disciplines," simultaneously telescopic and dynamic. Thus, it revalues as it un-black-boxes transdisciplinary intellectual work done outside or alongside the university in shifting globalizations of, say, knowledge workers and information management.

SELLING EPISTEMOLOGY

Sue Stafford is a "knowledge engineer," a consultant in artificial intelligence and knowledge management, as well as a philosopher of science at Simmons College, in Boston, and at the Simmons Graduate School of Management (which boasts that it is the "world's only graduate business school designed especially for women").[80] She reflects "on the process of commercializing epistemology as it occurred in the 1980s during the heyday of expert systems" (during which time, referring to Slaughter and Leslie, the sets for the production of academic capitalism are financially rearranged). Gaining insight from these experiences and their failures or misadventures, she extracts a set of heuristics:

> I apply these insights to current efforts to sell epistemology in the form of knowledge management. My analysis shows that knowledge is embodied and often dependent on the senses; a significant amount of it is tacit. Much valuable knowledge is revealed to be situated; it is the result of a complex interplay of contextual elements that are at once physical, psychological, social, political and corporate. The analysis also demonstrates that knowers are epistemically interdependent, making knowledge a social phenomenon. In addition, knowledge and values are shown to be intimately connected, and intellectual virtues such as perseverance and trustworthiness are found to be essential if knowledge is to be productive.
>
> Commercialization provides strong temptations to cut corners in our understanding and management of knowledge and succumbing to those temptations will surely result in failure of knowledge management enterprises. On the other hand, commercialization provides both

an incentive and a test bed for applied epistemology. . . . I view the process of commercializing epistemology through the academic discipline of what has been called analytic social epistemology. . . . I draw upon on my own experience as a knowledge engineer for major consulting firms in the 1980s. . . . I take seriously the analyses presented in the mainstream popular press—not because I consider them a source of "truth," but because they represent the operable understandings that drive the commercialization process.[81]

The epistemological alliances that worked in the nineties to produce and extend knowledge work and management, along with the forms of commercially inflected communication developed to create these alliances, mark a range of *flexible knowledges*, even including nationalisms. Indexing the trajectories of use of the term "communities of practice" un-black-boxes all of these.

SYSTEMS FOR COMMUNICATING SCIENCE AND TECHNOLOGY KNOWLEDGES

Flexible knowledges are negotiated, implicitly or explicitly and within spatial and temporal fields of power. Globalization processes and constraints reconfigure "public" and "private" funding for continuing nationalisms in the displays of power at national museum and park sites. Asking Latour's question—"What are the right ways to build them?"—telescopes among knowledge worlds and their *things* in layers of locals and globals. Indeed this question rescales units of agency for scholars and others interested in reenactments or involved in an emergent transdisciplinary posthumanities.

And commercialisms and nationalisms are also networked within an assemblage of communication infrastructures built upon itself over time. Bruce Lewenstein, an STS historian who examines public communication about science, tells a history that, zooming out farther in scale, helps to contextualize the *SAL* exhibit inside these infrastructures:

By mid-[twentieth] century a *broad, variegated system* for public communication of science and technology had emerged. As the various components had been doing since the nineteenth century, they complemented and intersected each other: the books and lectures directed at elites were both emulated and reshaped for broader audiences; writers moved back and forth between pulp magazines, educational institutions, museums, and public information campaigns; and audiences partook of different aspects for multiple reasons. Equally important, the *frequency with which people moved about among private, commercial, educational, and government positions* suggests the kind of interaction that replaces "policy" as a guiding principle for understanding the nature of public communication activities in the United States. It was not the existence or creation of national or even regional policies that determined the shape of public communication activities. Instead, it was the individual actions of particular people with particular goals and concerns that created an interlaced web of activities, supported by a range of institutions (both public and private).[82]

The term "policy" black-boxes the range and dynamism of this highly interactive and variegated system, over which national interests have quite limited control, and among which individual agencies, however essentially political—with apologies to Lewenstein—are also in quite limited control, of either this system or those national interests. We glimpse indeed a coevolution of knowledge work, nationalisms, and commercialisms working out among whole *ecologies* of communication.

Lewenstein also offers queries that help us zoom both in and out, telescoping to locate *SAL* in these ecologies across communities of practice:

> So what implications does this history have for attempts to integrate history of science more fully into efforts to improve public understanding of science? First, I think it points to the *variety of sites* to which one might look. We need not expect *science journalists* to suddenly include historical perspective in their stories (something that would be extremely difficult in today's media world); we can look instead to *exhibits*, plays, books, and other forums. Second, we should realize that our own instincts and goals as *historians of science* may be different than those of the *producers with whom we must work*; as I noted in my introduction, those differences do not prevent collaboration, but they provide *constraints on the kinds of products* that may emerge. Finally, I think we must *recognize the incredible amount of work* that goes into producing material for public consumption—the many activities I've chronicled here show a trend from "back-pocket" work by practicing scientists to full professional engagement by individuals committed to

public communication. We cannot expect that history of science will slyly work its way into public discourse without finding ways to reward and sustain people who chose to give such work their full professional attention.[83]

The rest of this chapter takes to heart Lewenstein's observations. It attempts to network among various sites and actants with their divergent agencies, "instincts and goals," in order to reflect on many mandated collaborations across essential differences, the constraints on products never easily handed off, and especially to "recognize the incredible amount of work" required but unevenly acknowledged, rewarded, or sustained. Thus it also takes to heart those exemplary "outside" critical voices as well as others engaging in the layered controversies at the Smithsonian, more of those actants that Mulkey and Dougan insist are *all parts of the work that the exhibits do and that science (as knowledge) does.* This capacious understanding of such work is essential to my explication of *reenactment*, as part of an always unevenly realized *fantasy* in which making, sharing, and teaching to use and using knowledge might be exuberantly managed, intellectually and commercially.

COMMERCE AND THE SMITHSONIAN: A NEW SECRETARY

A year before Sue Stafford and Katie Vann and Geof Bowker published their articles in a special issue of the journal *Social Epistemology* for which the theme was the commercialization of epistemology, that is to say, in 2000, the Smithsonian Institution's Board of Regents appointed a new secretary to run its operations. The earliest secretaries had been scientists, naturalists, and collectors, while recent secretaries had been academics and scholars, but this new secretary was the first to come from the corporate sector.[84]

> Prior to becoming Secretary of the Smithsonian Institution, [Lawrence] Small had served as President and Chief Operating Officer of Fannie Mae, the world's largest housing finance company. . . . Before joining Fannie Mae, Small worked at Citicorp/Citibank, the largest US banking institution, for 27 years, ending his tenure there as Vice Chairman and Chairman of the Executive Committee of the Board of Directors. . . . His service on nonprofit and corporate boards has been extensive, including the National Building Museum; Mt. Sinai-NYU Medical

Center and Health System; the Spanish Repertory Theatre; the US Holocaust Memorial Council; Brown University; Morehouse College; the Collegiate School; the Joffrey Ballet; the American Women's Economic Development Corp.; the International Executive Service Corps; the Instituto de Estudios Superiores de la Empresa in Barcelona; and the Greater New York Councils of the Boy Scouts of America. He serves on the Committee for the Preservation of the White House; on the boards of trustees of the John F. Kennedy Center for the Performing Arts, the National Gallery, the Woodrow Wilson International Center for Scholars, and is a member of the boards of directors of The Chubb Corp. and Marriott International Inc. He is chairman of the Financial Advisory Committee of Trans-Resources International, the parent company of Haifa Chemical, an Israeli firm. He also has been a board member of Paramount Communications Inc., an entertainment and communications company, and of Fannie Mae and Citicorp/Citibank, the financial service companies where he was previously employed.[85]

Twenty-first-century "crisis" at the Smithsonian has come to focus on this figure of Lawrence Small and this range of corporate financial and banking and cultural and entertainment interests. In his person Small comes to *both show and tell* the "commercialization" of the Smithsonian—"the largest museum and research complex in the world." In his policies Small is held to have actualized the Smithsonian as "a museum of American corporations."[86] Controversy and crisis flowing around Small's person and policies both within and without the Smithsonian resulted, for example, in the resignation of one museum director and the hiring of a new one.

In that example, the NMAH lost Spencer Crew, an African American historian responsible for the acclaimed exhibit *Field to Factory: Afro-American Migration 1915–1940* (1987). In *Field to Factory* Crew had worked with but somewhat shifted the epistemological melodrama of such life-sized dioramas as those common in past national museum installation practices, adding additional elements of what we have just been calling *shadowing* and *witnessing* to these (extensively understood) *reenactments*. Not being able to rely on missing African American historical artifacts to embody primarily individualized narratives, either because they were too few, no longer existed, or were yet uncollected, instead *Field to Factory* used its spectacular full-scale recreations to animate stories of large historical processes. In 2001 Crew left the NMAH after twenty years to become executive director of Cincinnati's National Underground Railroad

Freedom Center, acknowledging that Small's administrative policies were a factor in his decision to move to another institution.[87]

Replacing him was Brent Glass, an oral historian and museum administrator, formerly executive director of the Pennsylvania Historical and Museum Commission in Harrisburg.[88] Glass thus became director in 2002 of a recently renamed institution in the process of "transformation," now called the National Museum of American History, Behring Center, following the California land developer Kenneth E. Behring's gift to the Smithsonian of $100 million, $80 million of which went to the NMAH in 2000, $20 million to the NMNH in 1997.[89]

Thus Small got to officiate at the Smithsonian's "Biggest Single Donation in its 154-Year History," although presumably the courting of these funds predated his secretariat, and the renaming of the NMAH took place at the end of Spencer Crew's directorship.[90] Indeed Crew officially became director in 1994, the year of the opening of SAL, after two years as acting director, and he presided over a major reorganization of NMAH later that year.[91]

WITHDRAWN FUNDING

Even more hyped in the media was the fiasco in 2002 surrounding the Virginia businesswoman Catherine Reynolds' withdrawn $38 million dollars, funding that was "contracted" for a NMAH exhibit, *The Spirit of America*, focused on the achievements of individual Americans.[92] The Smithsonian Blue Ribbon Commission's recommendations in their report that year on the NMAH spoke to this debacle specifically, while at the same time rescaling the issues in general terms as "the reality of divergent interpretations of American history."[93]

The commission tried to clarify what the debacle was all about while lowering intensity among the various forms of partisanship across communities of practice:

> One of the many great virtues of American history is the liveliness of argument about it. Such argument exists—and is often heated—among professional scholars. Among the general public, the conflict between divergent interpretive frameworks is less scholarly, but no less intense. The stakes are not trivial. Interpretations can help shape history. And this reality presents a serious challenge for NMAH management. Advocates inclined to emphasize the role of heroic *individuals* vie with those

who would concentrate on less powerful figures and the larger historical forces that shape their lives. There is tension between those inclined to *celebrate* American achievement and those inclined to focus on America's failures to meet her declared aspirations. There is a related tension between those who see American history as a series of leaps from *triumph* to triumph and those who see the history as a more difficult and *troubled* journey. And there is a basic difference of perspective between those who see American values and experience as in some positive sense *"exceptional"* and those who do not. The opposition between these points of view is genuine. It is sometimes rooted in analysis and evidence, and sometimes rooted in contemporary politics. There is often *heartfelt distrust* among contesting advocates. They do not allow their differences to be washed over. Still, it is possible—often necessary—to use a combination of competing perspectives to produce a responsible historical presentation. So, the challenge for NMAH is to attend fairly to divergent frameworks—and to use legitimate arguments *about* interpretation to help make exhibits more interesting and engaging. That is more easily said than done.[94]

Without saying so directly, the commission named here the various charges brought by critics to plans for the proposed Reynolds-funded exhibition; in particular, that it would focus on individuals at the expense of social movements, that it would be celebratory and self-complacent, that its narrative would be a triumphalist one proclaiming American achievements as exemplary for the world.

Nevertheless, *the exhibit did not yet exist*; the complicated negotiations required over considerable time for making it work by many divergent communities of practice were yet just begun. Still, critics both inside and outside the institution were fearfully ready to predict its failures by virtue of the funding arrangements, its initial conception, and the public statements of those funding it, and all this within an atmosphere of "heartfelt distrust" already created around the figure of Secretary Small and both the existing and putative commercialization of the Smithsonian.

And indeed those public statements by the funders *were* provocative in exactly the ways the commission attempted to describe in the metaterms of "oppositional" points of view. For example, in an interview in 2002 with Mike Wallace of *60 Minutes*, explaining why they had withdrawn their money after all, Catherine Reynolds and her husband Wayne were astonished that such divergent viewpoints existed, that their own opinions were not obviously shared by others. And Wallace collaborated in making their astonishment seem only natural and respectable, and their partisan interpretations of others' opinions simple fact:

WALLACE: (voiceover) But Ms. Reynolds and her husband, Wayne, insist the curators were opposed to any exhibit honoring individuals, no matter who they were.

MRS. REYNOLDS: The curators would say to us, "Well, this is just a hall of big egos."

MR. REYNOLDS: We were told that the heritage of individual accomplishment in America is meaningless.

WALLACE: Wait, wait, wait, no.

MR. REYNOLDS: That individuals never mattered in American history, but only social movements mattered, that only institutions mattered. The American Revolution mattered, of course, but Jefferson, Adams, Washington, they didn't matter. See, even the civil rights movement. You won't find anything on Martin Luther King there, because they say Martin Luther King, "Yeah, he was great, but somebody else would have come along. He—it was the wave of the moment that swept history. But that individual didn't matter."

WALLACE: You really mean that you were told this by the curators with whom you worked?

MR. REYNOLDS: Oh, sure.

MRS. REYNOLDS: Oh.

MR. REYNOLDS: Oh, sure.

MRS. REYNOLDS: Many times. Curators refused to work on our project. Refused.

MR. REYNOLDS: I've never met people like this who said individuals never mattered in history. My whole career, my whole life, Cathy's whole life is based on one person can make a difference in America.[95]

Such public statements could only make critics of the now withdrawn gift feel justified in *their own* debunking partisanship. Trying to redraw such dual "oppositional" maps, Patricia Limerick—professor of history and environmental studies at the University of Colorado, Boulder—described her own conversations with the Reynoldses and her own hopes for the exhibit that never got into production. As she did so, she had to first authorize herself for a range of progressive communities, attempting to make her political alliances clear since she intended to counter the debunking that otherwise reassures partisan membership:

> Admittedly, I had only a brief opportunity for firsthand observation, participating last August in a two-and-a-half-day consultation with Catherine and Wayne Reynolds, the head of a foundation they have formed, Smithsonian curators, and outside consultants. In the months since, I have met further with the Reynoldses on two occasions. On the basis of what I have seen myself, I cannot categorize the coverage of *The Spirit of America* as our news media's finest moment. Indeed, my experience leaves me mystified by much of the reportage.
>
> My career as a historian of the American West has involved rearranging the field so that the experience of ethnic and minority groups is front and center. I am a museum-quality specimen of an unreconstructed, 1960s white liberal. And I had a wonderful time in 1991 defending the Smithsonian's *The West as America* exhibit against its overwrought right-wing critics, who saw its attempt to demythologize the West as an affront to our national identity. The fact that, with such a background, I found considerable common ground with Cathy and Wayne Reynolds is its own testimony that the latest situation must have been considerably more complicated than the public record has allowed it to appear.

Then she worked to redraw the map of oppositional dualities as complementary:

> The Reynoldses did want to focus on individuals. And yet, contrary to the stereotypes now deeply embedded in coverage of the exhibition they wanted to sponsor, this was not a fight between those who would have removed individuals from history to celebrate them uncritically and those who wanted individual life stories firmly embedded in the broader context of social history. Cathy and Wayne Reynolds agreed that portraits of individual achievement would make no sense unless the obstacles against which those individuals struggled received full

coverage. . . . Responsibility for the selection of the individuals to be featured was to lie with a panel on which scholars would be represented. Thus, rather than an unyielding demand from an uncooperative donor, Cathy Reynolds's much-mocked suggestion of including Martha Stewart represented only a moment of speculating on possibilities in a conversation with a reporter.

By current practices in the field of American cultural history, moreover, that was a suggestion worth considering. In the early 19th century, writers like Catharine Beecher played an important role in telling American women how to conduct themselves in their family relationships and social ties. Martha Stewart's success is the latest manifestation of a long history, considered significant by nearly every American historian, of women trying to find orientation and direction in changing times. Using the example of Stewart would, indeed, have offered an effective way of inviting museum visitors to think about a long-running practice and to get a sense of scholarly work in the history of popular culture.[96]

But the recommendations of the Blue Ribbon Commission are actually more complexly drawn (the following list is my restructured paraphrase with quoted bits).

Concerning "Balance in and among exhibits," the Commissioners:

— Advocate "intellectual order" "while avoiding gross simplification or inattention to . . . schools of historical thought"
— Advocate being "sensitive to traditional values" as well as to "diversity of American experience"
— Advocate using these very differences "to engage visitor's interest"
— Advocate depicting "diversity as inextricably entwined" with layers of "the American historical experience," rather than depicted by "separation or sub-categorization"
— Advocate not to "merely seek compromises," but rather "assure that . . . resolutions of issues of balance meet the highest standards of scholarship"

Concerning "Donor relations and public trust," they:

— Advocate "attracting donors on the museum's preferred terms" and that such "terms are clear in advance"
— Advocate "as fundamental," "the policy that reserves to the museum final control"

— Advocate remaining "mindful that their special national status" gives the museum "a comparative advantage in negotiating" with donors, while "resisting the general tendency toward commercialization"
— Advocate "timely public release" of the "concepts and contents of planned exhibits" and their "associated contractual terms"
— Advocate helping "donors prepare for" the "degree and character of public attention"
— Advocate that "tests of balance" (in previous recommendation) be "applied in the development of the new exhibits" given the kinds of public controversies likely
— Advocate that the choice of a new director who prioritizes "relations with both internal and external constituencies"[97]

CONTRACTS AND BOUNDARY OBJECTS

Consider as transdisciplinary *boundary objects* the terms "contract" and "contractual" ("weakly structured in common use" but "strongly struc-tured in individual-site use"; in other words, intensively or technically defined and meaningful *within* communities of practice but widely or extensively used in more general terms *across* many more).[98] These and associated terms were appealed to by the Reynoldses in other parts of the *60 Minutes* interview and named in the commission report. Secretary Small in his own representations to the public in *Smithsonian* magazine said: "Many of the criticisms leveled against recent donations are based on erroneous information. For example, critics charge that the terms of Ms. Reynolds' donation give her the power to appoint an advisory board for the exhibition. In fact, though, she has the power only to nominate candi-dates. No one may become a member of the advisory board without ap-proval from the Smithsonian's Board of Regents, and the contract docu-menting the gift explicitly says the Institution's staff will retain final control in the case of any dispute over the content of the exhibition."[99] The Organization of American Historians, for example, presumably rely-ing on reports by insiders, stated: "The donor's contract stipulated that of the fifteen American achievers represented in the exhibit, the Reynolds Foundation would select ten and Smithsonian Institution would select five. In various interviews Reynolds suggested names of individuals she would consider for the exhibition, including Oprah Winfrey, Martha Stew-art, Dorothy Hamill, and Sam Donaldson."[100]

Critics claimed that the terms of the contract had never been made public.[101] The commission called for transparency in such contract making, which would permit both insiders and outsiders to know authoritatively what the contract promised, and emphasized that the museum's unique status, and thus negotiating position, entitled it to set the terms of such contracts to its own advantage. Such control would warrant publicly the terms of "balance," negotiated in a contract and subsequently to be negotiated in any productions, both within its own internal communities of practice and also with external constituencies. Negotiations were advocated at *a very high level of synthesis*: compromise among disputing parties was held to be a lower standard, instead synthesis needed to be conceptually creative and integrated, and needed to include *meta-analysis* of the very differences to be synthesized or otherwise intertwined, and in *a way that itself would be an element of appeal across constituencies*. In other words, it would be presented as its own *epistemological melodrama*.

It is just this degree of optimal synthesis, the show and tell together, possibly attainable, possibly unrealistic, that characterizes fantasies to which (extensively understood) *reenactments* are held accountable. It is the work of boundary objects, Bowker and Star point out, to develop and maintain "coherence across intersecting communities" as they "arise over time from durable cooperation among communities of practice" and they work to "resolve anomalies of naturalization."[102]

Several layers of metacommunication were called for here, and much sophistication with negotiation skills, which would be required in any new NMAH director. Not only did direct communication need to occur across communities but they needed to *become educated about the practices of others*: for example, donors needed to become educated about the practices of public announcement and dispute, about media intensities and problematics, as well as about the effects of such public communication on the negotiations of which they were a part.

In other recommendations the commission advocated assuming fewer long-term contractual obligations, such as the "permanency" of the SAL exhibition, originally negotiated with the American Chemical Society as one provision of funding:

> In order to achieve its mission, NMAH is required to seek private funding. This would be true even if federal funding were substantially increased because federal funds are limited not only in amount, *but also*

in purpose. ["The Institution is approximately 70 percent federally funded," according to the Smithsonian website's "Facts about the Smithsonian Institution."] In general, federal funds have been oriented toward the support of basic operating expenses and infrastructure, *not the development of exhibits* per se. (While Congress and the President could change this limitation, many have welcomed it as a *protection against possible partisan or parochial politicization of Museum content.*) Private funding often requires long-term contractual commitments.... The accumulation of such commitments is now considerable. . . . Recent long-term commitments will allow the Museum's substantial renewal to move forward. [Behring money is intended for part of the current "transformation" of the museum after renovation and the creation of various "orientation" exhibits and structures.] And in general, long-term commitments can help relieve NMAH curators and exhibition staff from what might otherwise be *excessive time demands for future fund-raising.* But the accumulation of long-term commitments also has costs. . . . two of the unintended costs they may entail are especially noteworthy. First, insofar as they involve long-term contractual *commitments of large amounts of floor space*, they may limit the museum's ability to change in the future (even though they may serve as helpful change agents in the near term). Second, they not only *reduce the museum's ability to adapt in the future*; they also decrease the space available for *smaller and shorter-term exhibits.* They thus *reduce the number of exhibition topics* the museum may treat, and limit its ability to develop new exhibits in *emerging areas of interest or capability.* This, in turn, may have two further undesirable consequences. It may reduce the museum's ability to address a broad and representative *range of topics and themes.* And it may reduce the number of opportunities for *creative expression by the specialized curators* the museum must attract and retain in order to fulfill its long-term mission."[103]

THE WORK OF PARTS AND WHOLES

Lewenstein's work reminds us that we cannot expect one piece of a communication ecology or infrastructure to do the work of the entire system. Such work is distributed across the system in several dimensions and dynamics and among actants. Nevertheless sometimes special bits in the system are microcosmic segments that in miniature do structurally resemble the system as a whole.

In other words, within the historical ecology of public communication about science that Lewenstein analyzes, its US national museum subsystem today begins to take on more of the characteristics of the system as a whole. Within itself it is more differentiated, requiring greater sophistication of communication across its increasing numbers of communities of practice, some professionalized and some not. What counts as partisan or parochial politicization has (despite the hopes represented by the commission, perhaps ironically) moved beyond the sphere of party politics in Washington and now includes issues of diversity, of commercialization, of historical narrative, of scholarly standards, and of skills at metacommunication.

And its "national" character and its "historical" character are simultaneously long-term continuities but also relatively recently refocused priorities in politicized environments of the last half century. For example, it was not until the late fifties that these Smithsonian historical collections were gathered together as the Museum of History and Technology, and it was not until the early sixties that this entity was first designated as the *National* Museum of History and Technology, in its then new building. In the early eighties, the technology aspect was demoted in favor of national naming, when it became the National Museum of *American History*. And in the late nineties, of course, it added to that a new additional designation, the Behring Center. The fate of *SAL* is a little piece of this history of refocused, rescaled importance and a sometime microcosm of a ranging infrastructure in dynamic movement.

LITERALIZED RESCALING AND THE PROBLEM OF CHEAP CRITIQUE

Rescalings, such as the ones I have tried to both show and tell myself in this chapter, can be very literal and their metacommunications provocative. For example the NMNH first planned a photo exhibition, *Arctic National Wildlife Refuge: Seasons of Life & Land* by Subhankar Banerjee, for a downstairs hallway gallery space, then reconceived it up in the main rotunda area, but by the opening in May 2003 finally showed it in the original downstairs space.[104] That movement, up and down floors and from main area to hallway, became melodramatically significant for media and Congress as Smithsonian critics called it censorship and defenders claimed "the Smithsonian had a right to protect itself from political advocacy," including criticism of Alaskan oil drilling.[105]

Before a Senate panel Lawrence Small defended the Smithsonian not only for the location change but also for altering the photographer's captions. They too were rescaled: "[Randall] Kremer [spokesman for the Natural History Museum] said, 'There was a lot more detail than would have been used for any exhibition' in the original text. 'As with anything, the first text is not always the one that is used. There were quotations about protecting the wilderness.' Kremer said Robert Sullivan, associate director of public programs, thought the captions 'bordered on advocacy.' "[106]

Configurations of private and public funding as simple analogues of nonpartisan and partisan control are moot here. Other configurations are in the process of mattering as *grain of detail* comes to bear political significance. The grain of detail focused by a boundary object across extensive and intensive definitions signals alliances, memberships, and forms of authority and control and unevenly appeals to diverging audiences, niche, regional, and partisan, all of which may fantasize they are the global, general, or universal or that their memberships, however partial, must be central. Exempting my own extensive use of *reenactments* is impossible here.

MY NOT DEBUNKING DEBUNKING

Some progressive lobbyist and activist groups and individuals, such as Russell Mokhiber and Robert Weissman of Common Dreams, argue "there should be a stark dividing line between public and private institutions in America."[107] These editors respectively of the *Corporate Crime Reporter* and the *Multinational Monitor* and coauthors of *Corporate Predators: The Hunt for MegaProfits and the Attack on Democracy* are invaluable truthsayers within the politics of anticorporatism.[108] Similarly, the activist group Commercial Alert targets "ad creep," with a list of political successes that begins with the Smithsonian, and ends with the city of San Francisco:

> Commercial Alert was part of a campaign that led to new Smithsonian Institution guidelines on marketing sponsorships and business joint ventures. The effort was launched after Secretary Lawrence Small sold

the naming rights to several exhibits for the first time in the museum's history. . . . Last summer [2003] Candlestick Park in San Francisco became the first ballpark to reclaim its popular title from a corporate sponsor after citizen pressure, including [executive director of Commercial Alert Gary] Ruskin's. San Francisco is now the first US city to propose a complete ban on the sale of naming rights to public property.[109]

Un-black-boxing but not deauthorizing—that is to say, *my not debunking* —the very practices of debunking, among them, say, the work of Common Dreams or Commercial Alert, means practicing *rescaling* as a dynamic, politically progressive analytic. Such rescaling is required in order to mobilize the sort of feminist relationalism in which, as Susan Leigh Star says, we do not abandon our moral commitments even as we simultaneously and intentionally forswear claims to absolute epistemological authority. Exploring reenactments of the nineties mobilizes my own intentions to develop such relational feminist tools for progressive political work. Working with and exploring the limits of debunking as it and its limits become more and more intrusive in the nineties is part of what one might call a critique of critique. Others in the nineties took up this project as well, among them Bruno Latour. As with Latour, some victims of debunking wished to do more than repeat debunking in their turn; only too aware of how they themselves had come to depend upon debunking analysis, they worked to open up other styles of progressive analytic engagement too, neither simply debunking debunking nor abandoning political commitments.

It is as a question of scale and flexibility amid metaphors of expense and of industrial exploitation that, for example, Latour critiques critique:

It is not that critique is no longer needed, but rather that it has, of late, become too cheap. One could say, with more than a little dose of irony, that there has been a sort of miniaturisation of critical efforts: what in the past centuries required the formidable effort of a Marx, of a Nietzsche, of a Benjamin, has become accessible for nothing, much like the supercomputers of the 1950s, which used to fill large halls and spend vast amount of electricity and heat, are now accessible for a dime and not bigger than a fingernail. You can now have your Baudrillard's or your Bourdieu's disillusion for a song, your Derridian deconstruction for a nickel. . . . Conspiracy theory costs nothing to produce, disbelief is easy, debunking what is learned in 101 classes in critical theory. As the recent advertisement of a Hollywood film proclaimed "Every one is suspect . . . everyone is for sale . . . and nothing is true!"[110]

Such cheap and miniaturized critique is only too easily commercially democratized within systems of knowledge management, public history, education and entertainment; that is to say, among some of the flexible knowledges explored here. Yet would we want to make critique more expensive, as in, would we want to keep it elite? Signified in a list of the names of great male theorists? Hardly. But cheap formula critique, like the products of off-shored labor, has global effects. We do not just get the inexpensive shirt, we also get the systems of exploitation that go along with it. Formula critiques that cost the critic nothing cannot honor the complexities of living *with things* and *as things* among a sea of actants, nor can it honor the differences between ethical intentions and political control. Cheap critique and academic capitalism are comrades and finding additional kinds of analysis that labor together with them has to be a feature of a feminist transdisciplinary relationalism working out within any new posthumanities.

HOPE IN BEING IN ENOUGH DIFFERENT WORLDS SIMULTANEOUSLY

At the end of the nineties the anthropologist and feminist analyst of science and technology Lucy Suchman, in an interview about her work at Xerox PARC, analyzed the epistemological implications of paying attention to one's concurrent worlds in telescoping layers of locals and globals:

> I guess I'd locate my hope in being part of enough different worlds simultaneously. . . . I've tried to model a way of being in this kind of an organization that makes sense to me. It makes sense to me in the ways that it's been formed by all these other worlds that I'm part of. I don't see what else to do, and I think doing that is part of what makes for an interesting cross dialogue or traffic flow across some of these worlds. That might make things clear in some cases, open up new possibilities. I think real change happens through quite subtle and small events, but with large cumulative effects. In some ways I see my ties as a kind of an intervention in a place that would be different if I weren't here, just as I would be very different if I hadn't spent all this time here. That's going

on all over the place for different people in different ways. I'm obviously a strong believer in the importance of time, that things take a long time.

Her interviewer, C. Otto Scharmer on behalf of the Society for Organizational Learning, draws these connections:

> As I heard you, the picture that came to my mind is that our social world has two modes of operating. The first mode consists of highly fragmented autopoetic islands. Every system is totally decoupled and blind to its environment. And every individual lives in one and only one system. The other mode operates based on the primacy of relationships. The social worlds are interconnected and each individual participates in multiple worlds or systems. People are the nexus of exchange, where one world is relating to another one, or becoming another one. Your work and your identity are really about being this nexus, making these connections and allowing one world to slide into another and return.[111]

BRANDING

For her own analysis of corporate academies Suchman uses but rescales a critique of "branding," targeting the ubiquity of corporate logos in "ad creep," as she examines "Anthropology as 'Brand.'" Admiring the work of Naomi Klein, a Canadian activist of anticorporatism, she quotes her: "The astronomical growth in the wealth and cultural influence of multinational corporations over the last fifteen years can arguably be traced back to a single, seemingly innocuous idea developed by management theorists in the mid-1980's: that successful corporations must primarily produce brands, not products."[112]

Suchman herself continues:

> It is this basic premise as well, Klein argues, that underwrites the rapid rise of the "virtual" corporation, aimed at outsourcing production to various export processing zones around the globe, then attaching an image to the resulting assemblage of parts. Unlike their industrial ancestors, the in-house work of these companies is not manufacturing, but marketing. . . . Klein keys off the name "Spiders," adopted by student activists working to pressure multinationals not to engage in

business with Burma, to suggest that the web of what she calls the "logo-linked globe" might actually afford the threads through which a new wave of activism and re-spinning is emerging.[113]

But Suchman also notes: "Daniel Miller reminds us that, in his word, 'things matter.' . . . Unless our stories of consumption can come to grips with these specific materialities we'll have missed something substantial about the place of stuff and its power to enroll us, however unwittingly, in the increasingly asymmetrical and inequitable flows of labor, goods and capital around the globe."[114]

Suchman's analysis provokes me to rescale debunking as academic "stuff" without deauthorizing it, to rescale critiques to account for and position larger ecologies among knowledge worlds, communities of practice, epistemological alliances, and layers of locals and globals without abandoning feminist political commitments. Suchman's appeal to "branding," as an index for describing the work of academic disciplines among global products, should resonate throughout the next chapter as we examine knowledges created televisually for and across countries and knowledge worlds.

ENTRUSTING REENACTMENTS AND PUBLIC-MINDED HISTORIANS

In March 1997, following the controversies over the *Enola Gay* and SAL exhibitions, the American Historical Association's then president Joyce Appleby questioned "Should We All Become Public Historians?" This query ranged widely, addressing the many communities of practice that in themselves each constitute a career in public history; the history wars and the controversies at the NMAH; the "time-consuming, work-diverting, ego-deflating" opportunities to talk to nonhistorians; the crafting of state education standards; the uses of adjuncts in restructuring universities; and the talking with friends and family about the histories of the marginalized. Appleby advocated countering ahistoricist nostalgia with accounts of historians' actual practices and also reframing public debates on so-called revisionism: "To call something revisionist history is tantamount to saying that it is made-up history. Yet no one would characterize new findings in chemistry as revisionist chemistry."[115]

All of these are opportunities for becoming, Appleby urges in 1997, "public-minded historians." Later, in January 2001, in the midst of the Reynolds and Smithsonian debacle, the American Historical Association followed up on some of these concerns and established a new Task Force on Public History, jumping off from the Smithsonian's difficulties to its own reactions:

> The AHA has long demonstrated regard for the practice of public history . . . most recently, the AHA has affirmed the Standards for Museum Exhibits Dealing with Historical Subjects, originally developed by the Society for History in the Federal Government, in communicating to the Smithsonian Institution its concerns about the scholarly integrity of the proposed "Spirit of America" exhibit, to be funded by the Catherine D. Reynolds Foundation and mounted at the National Museum of American History.
>
> To build on these and other accomplishments, the Professional Division agreed that it is an auspicious time to examine more carefully the relationship between the AHA and public historians.[116]

And not too much later, in 2003, other, perhaps more partisan forces were in play as the Bush administration's efforts to privatize National Park Service jobs were raised critically and repeatedly in the press: "Under his 'competitive sourcing' initiative, 850,000 government jobs have been identified as commercial in nature [including many National Park Service jobs], and agencies must allow companies to bid on at least half of them over the next few years. The administration is finalizing revisions to regulations that are expected to shorten competitions to as little as 12 months and provide agencies greater leeway in privatizing jobs."[117]

Critics pointed out, for example: "The Park Service is not a business enterprise." So said Frank Buono, a former assistant superintendent of Joshua Tree National Park and a former manager of Mojave National Preserve. He continued: "There is a fundamental ideological binge that the free-enterprise system will heal all wounds and solve all problems. Ask Enron about the efficiency of the unregulated private marketplace."[118]

But even those in Bush's own party were coming to reject this particular extension of the logic of the market: "Late Thursday [17 July 2003], the House voted 362 to 57 to cut off funding of efforts to put the jobs of the 100 archaeologists at the centers up for bid [targeted by the Interior Department under the competitive sourcing plan]. The measure was attached to the Interior Department spending bill, which passed late Thursday, 268 to 152." "The margin was fairly remarkable," said Rep. Doug Bereuter (R-Neb.), whose district includes the Midwest center. "Here you have people doing an outstanding job, and all of a sudden you have bean counters trying to close them down. I've never used the word 'stupid' on the House floor before, but this was stupid."[119]

Partisan control, privatization, public trust, professionalism, outsourcing, particular forms of nationalism, and "co-branding" are mixed up and remixed "globalization processes" here amid a proper *call out* also for "public-minded" historians, for histories of flexible knowledges and science broadly understood and interconnected, and for diffracting practices in the display of "images of power" as *reenactments* in these complex ecologies identified by Appleby and by Lewenstein.

Political renunciations and attempts to keep private and public funding as analogues (in either direction) of nonpartisan and partisan control are insufficient responses—these ecologies are manifold and polyvalent—but they do make clear that strategies that reclaim public power from corporatism are very necessary. Examining and altering "Public History as 'Brand,'" might be done with subtle interventions sometimes intended to have larger and rooted (radical) effects, or maybe within collective agencies for which "intention" is quite meaningless. But such examinations require also new forms of public communication and metacommunication, also both intended and beyond the scale of intention.

What roles do the cognitions and transmission effects of *reenactments* play in these public communications and metacommunications? How are ecologies addressed? The next chapters will take up some examples of other reenactment venues to consider these and related questions.

Should the terms in which public history is valued be kept messy, obvious, and un-black-boxed rather than taken for granted and transparent? When implicit and when explicit? How are trust and epistemology understood as co-constitutive? How do we mine the terrors of globalizations for possibilities? Stafford speaks to trust and epistemology, commercial and not:

> The nature of trust and trustworthiness as they function in creating, using, and sharing knowledge is complex. . . . Mature trust is trust that is articulated and reflected upon. . . . [It is] not taken for granted, but is generated dynamically by the explicit and implicit understandings, demands, promises, expectations and dependencies that characterize

knowledge enterprises . . . knowers come to know which people and which institutions to trust about what. . . . The relationship that is mature trust is dynamic and ongoing, and continually requires re-negotiation and renewal that may be implicit rather than explicit.[120]

Trust and epistemology are co-constitutive, making each other work. Which institutions, which actants, which bits in assemblage to trust about what is only too dynamic, only too implicit. Trust is not a one time, all over, all or nothing "thing." Groups for which it is a condition of membership might themselves be only too untrustworthy, but working to generate fragile moments of trustworthiness across groups is a necessary risk.

Trust's naturalization is subject to proper denaturalizations, sometimes over and over, other times only at critical moments. Keeping messy many terms in which public history is valued and obvious needs ongoing habitation of many communities of practice simultaneously, by individuals, in seas of actants, among ecologies only partially mapped. Human instrumentalism is only too misleading. We cannot mine the terrors of globalization for possibilities unless we act as modest witnesses for what we are becoming.

What kinds of trustworthiness can modest witnesses cultivate? Witnessing, trust, and reenactment will be brought together again in chapter four. But first, the next chapter will look to another venue, science documentaries on television, for commercial exuberance among reenactments, for more dynamics of experience and experiment amid incommensurable knowledges, and for embedded technologies of the explicit.

THREE

TV AND THE WEB COME TOGETHER

PART 1.

TIME-TRAVELING TELEVISION AS SETTINGS FOR REENACTION

DIGGING FOR THE TRUTH, SEASON 3, 2007

I CLICK ON MY E-MAIL with the subject line "Discover the 'true' purpose of Machu Picchu!" Up comes a mini-website from the History Channel, "Machu Picchu: Lost City of the Inca / Monday, March 5 @ 9pm/8C"; time given in the style of an e-mail address. In very small letters, almost unreadable: "Test your knowledge in the *Digging for the Truth* Sweepstakes for your chance to WIN a 7-day/6-night adventure-filled trip to Atlantis, Paradise Island, Bahamas. Roundtrip airfare provided by JetBlue Airways departing from any JetBlue City to Nassau, Bahamas." On the left are links to podcasts for the show, screensaver downloads, and the online store to buy the two first seasons on DVD. Other links suggest one "Join the discussion" on a message board and download complete episodes on AOL. Of this episode we are told: "From the mountains of Peru, host Josh Bernstein will follow in the footsteps of Hiram Bingham. He builds a log bridge across a raging river, examines the stonework at the site, and reviews ancient manuscripts to discover the 'true' purpose of Machu Picchu."[1]

Thus in 2007 we are linked across time to Hiram Bingham, that charismatic collector, explorer, and archaeologist from the turn of the twentieth century who some claim is the model for the character Indiana Jones in *Raiders of the Lost Ark* (1981). The host, Josh Bernstein, reenacts Hiram

Bingham here in this *pastpresent*, but he also reenacts us fans of *Digging for the Truth* as educational virtual tourists in our own Hands-On Science Center at the museum exhibit Machu Picchu.

Watch out when you click the first link, "Off the Record: Machu Picchu," as sound and video erupt from it unexpectedly. At full blast and greater volume than I thought my laptop was capable of, my web browser springs to life. Suddenly I find myself in the video gallery of the History Channel, where, when my one-minute segment on the challenges of filming the *Digging for the Truth* episode on Machu Picchu in the mountains of Peru ends, Senator Edward Kennedy's speech withdrawing his nomination for the presidency in 1980 begins.

The lineup for NBC Universal's the History Channel has changed.[2] No one calls it "the all-Hitler channel" anymore. Although it still relies on a large dose of the military as do other reenactment venues, more and more new technologies have been added and remixed. My own favorites in 2007 were *Digging for the Truth*, alongside *Engineering an Empire*, *Ancient Discoveries*, *Lost Worlds* and *Cities of the Underworld*.[3] Each of these is a remix of (extensively understood) reenactments with science-styled history. They are often scaled and focused via experimental archaeology and draw upon computer graphics developed for games and scientific analysis, among them the imagery of 3-D virtual worlds. Other remixed reenactments can be found elsewhere on cable, broadcast, and public TV, on TV saturated venues on the web, on DVD, videotape and iTunes, and maybe *now* on other TV locations coming into being over the course of the production of this book.

In the mid to late nineties, all this TV reenactment styling was just cascading, just becoming available for remix, and colonizing the web. Videotape was still hot, DVDs were only just no longer "vaporware," and Netflix did not exist yet. The BBC and PBS, public forms of television making new commercial arrangements and partners in the nineties, pioneered some of the styles of reenactment TV thus "cascading" in more and more commercial forms in the twenty-first century in the United States and internationally, say, on Disney's Discovery Channel or on NBC Universal's History Channel.

All this puts into perspective why in the early nineties Bruno Latour could quip with some prescience, "Reason today has more in common with a cable television network than with Platonic ideas."[4] The joking literality of Latour's insight can be unpacked with the examination punctuating this chapter of two endlessly suggestive, humorous, maddening, and effortful *Nova*, WGBH Boston television series. The first series of five episodes, now called *Secrets of Lost Empires I*, coproduced in 1996 by the BBC with the collaboration of PBS, "tested hypotheses" in experimental archaeological reenactments of possible ways of making Stonehenge, a pyramid, an obelisk, awnings over the Roman Coliseum, and an Inca style rope suspension bridge.[5] A second set of five episodes, *Secrets of Lost Empires II*, produced by WGBH in 2000 in association with Channel 4 in Britain and La Cinquième in France, focused on additional do-it-yourself ancient technologies that included fashioning a Chinese Rainbow Bridge and a medieval trebuchet, revisiting the question of raising an obelisk, exploring how the moas of Easter Island were moved, and experimenting with and fighting over how a Roman bath was built.[6] With each series' companion book, *Secrets of Lost Empires* (1996) and *Mysteries of Lost Empires* (2000), respectively, and the home video versions then, and DVDs now, these shows offer a *template* for understanding and *remediating* a range of TV reenactment documentaries mid to late nineties and after.[7] Their traces will thread through all my examinations of the different shows I mention in this chapter and work to interconnect immersive environments as *reenactment*.

And note that each *Secrets* series has connecting and *styled* sites on the web, which in this time period become a venue for extending their range as various kinds of *immersion*. The *Secrets of Lost Empires II* site (2000) was and remained a substantive integrated system functioning with stylistic updates in 2007. In contrast, the *Secrets of Lost Empires I* site (1997) harkens back to an earlier moment as a set of concatenated web pages, now only embedded in other parts of the PBS web system, but also quite *stylishly*, or, in other words, in styles updated graphically with Cascading Style Sheets (CSS), a markup system for web browser appearance.[8] *Cascading* matters to these conspicuously fulsome educational websites, *materializing* their teaching plans and resources. The second series site even includes transcripts of each episode as well as video clips and other graphically sophisticated elements. (The first series transcripts are also available but embedded within a general *Nova* archive.)

And, as Latour's joke considered retroactively clarifies, these series jokingly and literally "reason," that is to say—speaking etymologically— call to account and hold in argument their very roles as nodes within TV networks in these cascading as well as telescoping layers of locals and globals. The television series themselves could be understood as nested within the historian Bruce Lewenstein's interlocked and layered infra- structural systems of science public communication;[9] in other words, they were created for the Peabody Award–winning *Nova* TV series, "now the longest-running documentary series in America."[10] *Nova* has become such a robust citation point that both WGBH, Boston's PBS station, and the American Association for the Advancement of Science (AAAS) explain themselves to the public by references to it: "WGBH . . . has built up a reputation as the flagship of the Public Broadcasting System, a reputation derived from the production of such high-quality programs as *Nova*"; and "AAAS had helped launch what has become the longest-running science program on television, *Nova*. AAAS used funds from a large NSF [National Science Foundation] grant for public understanding of science to provide seed money to producer Michael Ambrosino at WGBH in Boston."[11]

THE THREADS OF META-REALITIES AND IMMERSIVE TV ENVIRONMENTS FOR THE WEB

This chapter follows time-traveling television in and around *Nova* for a particular vista on that decade beginning in the mid-nineties, when TV and the web come to partner and encompass each other. Distributive economies of scale are partnered with proliferated economies of scope in branding and franchising. The cascading "skins" of browser interfaces and branded "strands" like *Nova* become some of the technologies centrally servicing the highly distributed processes of global television production. As interlocking media proliferate commercial products in many kinds of "repurposed" materials and objects, television and the web together take advantage of every possible sensory modality and every prospect for com- modification. Cognitive sensation, affective melodrama and remediated commercial products all together create immersive environments embed- ding spaces and worlds, each within the others.' These are the settings analyzed in part one for the work of reenaction, settings in which the heritage politics of a Celtic cultural package play roles in EU and Anglophone nationalisms, and in which *spacetimes* are linked in 2- and 3-D data visualizations and peopled by reenactors. The examinations of two TV shows build on and illustrate these points.

First, partial knowledges communicated imperfectly by properly limited forms of expertise, together with the disruptive agencies of materials and conditions, make up the epistemological melodrama of *Nova's* series *Secrets of Lost Empires.* The episode "Roman Bath" illustrates reenactment as an experimental knowledge practice that allows all these materialities to be lively actors, no longer "gypped their due." Indeed, they are honored with and as makers, in labor intensive responsibilities for and emotional highs and lows of managing and moving among authoritative and alternative knowledges, in a practice of *speaking with things.*

Then, social and object technologies of authenticity and chronology are demonstrated, scoped, and scaled, in the four-part series *Surviving the Iron Age*, a BBC reenactment of one of its own prior TV shows. Its gaming time challenges animate political choices for claiming *spacetimes.* Breached authenticities structure its epistemologies of inclusion, rivalry, safety, and refusal. Its display of various sorts of reenactors are a setup for the discussions of part two of this chapter about how the work of reenaction also always includes those who create the environments for reenaction and its conditions of reception.

So, in part two of the chapter the manifold and various forms that the work of reenactors takes alters who and what we understand reenactors to be. First, we explore how they embody a complex ethical and political path of re-representation in which they are both bearers of meaning they work hard to create and bearers of many additional meanings they may never even know. Thus they both illustrate and help us question how it is that objects can inhabit multiple contexts and have both local and shared meaning, as well as how people can communicate across knowledge worlds. An ethnography of Colonial Williamsburg teaches us ways to care about the agencies of reenactors and the range of their individual efficacies, as well as to explore difficulties and misrecognitions of critique.

Then, the work of feminists Susan Leigh Star and Kate Hayles allows us to consider reenactors as exemplary of distributed forms of human agency and of human being, as well as within large systems of distributed cognition. All of these agencies are scoped and scaled both within and beyond individuals. Star, Hayles, and others working with these concerns are indebted to pioneering analysis by the father and daughter anthropologists Gregory Bateson and Mary Catherine Bateson. All of these scholars have collectively built one sort of groundwork for articulating contemporary sciences of *emergence* while recognizing altering human subjectivities. Terms like "posthuman" and "posthumanities" have become nodes for an examination of who we are becoming and what kinds of knowledges can help us understand these changes.

The chapter ends with examples of how a feminist posthumanities might work with networked reenactments. First, it traces a path of re-representation of women warriors across knowledge worlds of television, commercial heritage industries, militaries, fandoms, and academies. Then it finishes up by looking at reaggregations of gender and race in the time-traveling DNA technologies of three different kinds of television reenactment documentaries: Spencer Wells's *Journey of Man*, Henry Louis Gates Jr.'s *African American Lives*, and Jeannine Davis-Kimball's *Secrets of the Dead*, "Amazon Warrior Women." Skills for sorting among authoritative and alternative knowledges require us to scale and scope in ranges of detail accessibly elegant and specifically important as we examine with others DNA boundary objects traveling among incommensurable knowledge worlds.

NOVA CASCADING GLOBALIZATIONS

So we begin with that flagship PBS station central to *Nova* histories, WGBH, which itself opens onto a longer history of science public communication. Its parent organization, the Lowell Institute Cooperative Broadcasting Council (LICBC), was founded in 1941 by Ralph Lowell, connected with the famous Lowell Institute through which John Lowell Jr.'s bequest in 1836 made possible free "public lectures for the benefit of the citizens of Boston." (His death was two years after the Lowell mill girls went on strike against the factory system pioneered by this textile manufacturing family.[12]) By 1946 the Lowell Institute had cooperatively arranged with six Boston colleges to broadcast educational programs on commercial stations, then in 1952 the first TV channels began to be assigned for noncommercial use. The LICBC created WGBH radio in 1951 and WGBH-TV in 1955. In 1967 the Public Broadcasting Act was passed by Congress, which established the Corporation for Public Broadcasting (CPB), leading to National Public Radio (NPR) and the Public Broadcasting Service (PBS). October 1970 saw PBS's first season, shown over a national network of 198 public TV stations. *Nova* was launched in 1974; its "science adventures for curious grownups, some from WGBH, some from the BBC, and some joint efforts, give *Nova* a breadth previously unknown on American TV."[13]

WGBH's Science Program Group got its first season support not only from the AAAS's NSF seed money but also from the CPB, the Carnegie Corporation of New York, and Polaroid. Michael Ambrosino, who developed *Nova*, is described as "one of a growing number of persons whose professional lives have been spent almost entirely within public television, people whose careers began soon after the first channels were assigned for noncommercial use in 1952."[14] It was during a CPB fellowship in London observing BBC "production procedures," especially those of the BBC's *Horizon* documentary series, that he came up with the ideas that evolved into *Nova*. "*Nova* became the first of many WGBH *strands*." As what we might call one sort of productive *distributed agency*, Ambrosino described a "strand" as "a continuous run of broadcasts that a [BBC] unit presents and administers. Some are freshly produced, some are coproduced, some purchased, and some repeated. This method allows flexibility, lowers costs, increases quality, enhances communications with foreign broadcasters, and spreads the responsibility of administration."[15]

As narrated by David Steward in 1998 for PBS's own trade newspaper *Current*, available online (with more said the next year in his traditionally published book on PBS's history):

> Of *Nova*'s first 50 programs, 19 were made by WGBH, nine coproduced and 27 acquired through purchase. . . . The operation had been partly based, of course, upon the advantages of cooperation with the BBC and other production sources. The number of WGBH productions represented 36 percent of the total. . . . In the first three years *Nova*'s staff looked at 150 foreign-produced documentaries to purchase 22. They were drawn from four BBC documentary series, from the British companies Yorkshire TV and Granada, and producers in Sweden, Yugoslavia, Switzerland, Germany and Canada. [The] Australian Broadcasting Corp . . . eventually became a major source of program material. . . . Ambrosino's objective [was to develop] long-term relations with producers outside the US.[16]

Robert Reid, former head of the Science and Features Department of BBC, became *Nova*'s chief consultant. Not surprisingly the three production team leaders were British, two of whom had worked for the BBC.

Nova's premier program was from the BBC, "The Making of a Natural History Film." It demonstrated filmmaking techniques used for BBC nature sequences in "an extraordinary film-within-a-film tour de force"— a conspicuous *spectacle of production* embracing that pleasure in meta-realities upon which the infrastructure of commercial TV depends. *Nova*'s second program was its first WGBH in-house production, "Where Did the Colorado Go?" In examining Colorado water management it set a station agenda to address national science policy issues together with interests in basic science.[17]

REPURPOSING TELEVISION: CASCADING AND BRANDING IN TV ECOLOGIES

The immersive environment networking e-mail, the web, and TV for *Digging for the Truth* with which this chapter began is an example of what the cyberculture theorists Jay Bolter and Richard Grusin call "repurposing," a vibrant form of the commercial exuberance we examined in chapter 1. (Repurposing is only one sort of "remediation" or cycling through media that they explore.) The vertical integration of corporations requires and inspires an appeal to all the senses at once: content is controlled and displayed in as many media forms as possible, producing a network of commodities that taken together are strangely akin, Bolter and Grusin point out, to Wagner's ideal Gesamtkunstwerk, or total work of art.[18]

Repurposing is also an everyday term used by web designers who somewhat similarly take content from one format and restructure it for another. Some mechanisms for content repurposing involve software developed in the nineties using CSS. CSS allowed designs and displays using the same text to be perceived by a web browser in different "skins" or graphically styled environments, "cascaded" in priority for particular purposes. CSS required and permitted the distribution of web design as well: for example, when content and styles are stored on different servers, each separately produced by different workers and artists, CSS could provide unifying graphical interfaces that service these multiplying and differentiated contents, styles, and forms of work. Distributed production thus depends upon these servicing interfaces.

So, such interfaces are fundamental to doing the kind of repurposing that means taking content from one kind of website or web page and using it in another kind of website or web page, or more broadly, taking content from non–web forms and putting it up on the web. For example, a museum might be repurposing old brochures that became obsolete when exhibitions were taken down. But if such exhibitions or some of their objects are included in online sites, then these brochures have a new salience extending their lifetime, and their content is worth the labor of putting them up on the web. (The National Museum of American History [NMAH] may well have done something like this over the period of its renovation.) Such repurposing may mean altering both style and content for this new use to such an extent that something new has been created in the process. In the UK an e-government initiative attempted to require that by 2005 public services be delivered electronically and interactively, effectively mandating such repurposing. In the same spirit public history sites in the United States (and probably elsewhere) are pressed to repurpose their "legacy" materials and encouraged to see this as creating new value for their institutions.[19]

In the United States television cable and broadcasting industries *repurposing* has an intensively narrower but related meaning. For this community of practice it specifically refers to taking a broadcast television series episode and, within a specified window of time, say, ten days, showing it again on a cable network. (The short time frame is one way of differentiating it from reruns or selling past seasons in syndication.) The idea is to enter into broadcast-cable partnerships so that production costs can be spread out and further distributed. Reverse repurposing means similarly showing an episode from a cable network produced series on a broadcast channel. Either kind of repurposing may involve the inclusion of additional content and be specifically packaged with "value added" for the new venue. In 2002 Rick Holzman, then Universal Television Group's senior vice president of strategic research (which owned the USA Network on cable), pointed out that "for certain shows the more you play them, the stronger they get. There's not a ton of [audience] duplication back and forth on an ongoing basis. It builds the show as a brand."[20]

"Branding" might be considered shorthand terminology for such servicing of the entire environment of commercial Gesamtkunstwerk in its extended infrastructures. "Franchise" is a related term used for the properties branded, say, *Star Trek*, or *Highlander* and *Xena*, including all the many commercial products that can be spun out from and for their repurposed multiple TV series, movies, and fandoms.

In 2007 in another repurposing one can "subscribe" to the current season of a small group of TV series on iTunes and automatically download their episodes very shortly after they air on broadcast or cable TV. Although certainly not limited to it and playable on any computer with the right software, nevertheless these are intended as content serviced for collection by Apple TV, a product alternative to TiVo, which is a subscription TV temporary library automatically personalizing one's TV viewing by time-shifting favorite programs. TiVo, another of NBC Universal's properties, in its turn is an alternative to the more traditional and largely outdated videotape time shifting of the nineties. For those no longer living in a world of videotape all these have become taken for granted and now naturalized Latourian *things*. Such experiential universes are generation and location as well as resource specific in layers of distributed accessibilities.

What *Nova* did, following the BBC in creating a *strand* of new original productions, coproductions, and repeated episodes, might be understood as a different but related kind of repurposing, an activity we might call *cascading*, in which the distributed production elements are administered centrally and archived in these various *Nova* skins or styles. As we will see toward the end of this chapter with reference to the "Amazon Warrior Women" episode of PBS-styled *Secrets of the Dead*, cascading is one mechanism that produces or contributes to the kinds of effects that create that contradictory nesting of niche markets described in the first chapter in connection with the film *Disclosure*.

TV HISTORY POLYPHONIES

In television the democratization of knowledge and its pedagogical commercial exuberance have become one. Consider from the end of the nineties such BBC history shows as *Surviving the Iron Age* or *The Ship: Retracing Cook's Endeavor Voyage*—each shown 2001, in the United States on public television member stations or in Canada on History Television—and compare them in the same time period to signature producer Wall to Wall's cascading *History House* format shows such as *Regency House Party*, *1900 House*, *Frontier House*, and *Colonial House*, some created in production partnerships with PBS in the United States, others in partnership with the

BBC or Channel 4 in the UK. All these shows recruit volunteers who are put into environments conspicuously uncomfortable for late twentieth-century or Millennium folks as elements highlighted from past lifestyles dramatize historical continuities but especially discontinuities. An emphasis on participants' surprise at the difficulties of daily life and a previously unexamined and thus taken for granted assumption of physical comfort is the formula for melodrama in these kinds of shows. *Surviving the Iron Age* is an example of this type of *time-traveling* TV and one we will examine more closely later.

Compare them all to the *Nova* do-it-yourself ancient technologies shows, *Secrets of Lost Empires*, and, half a decade later, to the commercial programming of *Ancient Discoveries* on the History Channel.[21] The you-are-there history shows and the do-it-yourself, science-styled ancient technologies shows are related forms of so-called reality programming on TV. All of them are one part soap opera, one part period recreation—and with folks from our time who invite audience identification as "us," viewers mentally enacting too, playing at, reenacting, shadowing, experimenting, speculating, trying to provide evidence for, various understandings of varying pasts. Their chronological anachronisms interweave pastpresents. Indeed media and viewers often call the participants in these TV shows "time travelers." "Science" and all it stands for—knowledges broadly understood or our everyday knowledge-managed technologies—are especially lively players in the action in the second set of these, although defined, displayed, communicated with, and emphasized differently in intensive meanings among specific communities of practice. It is to this type of history "reality" programming we turn to first as we follow up on the globalizing histories of *Nova*.

INCOMMENSURABLE KNOWLEDGES AND SPEAKING WITH THINGS, "ROMAN BATH"

An episode from the second series of *Nova*'s *Secrets of Lost Empires*, "Roman Bath," literalizes what Latour celebrates as "the Parliament of things."[22] In this episode a group of experts work to recover "lost" and "advanced" ancient technological knowledge. How might a heating system for a Roman bath operate? For example, how should the roof help to vent gases, and how hot should we understand a Roman bath to have been? These are working points not deduced from past knowledge, from archaeology or documents in archives, although substantive speculations are possible. Theorized variously on the basis of very distinct forms of experience and practice, such concerns are now put to an experimental test in reconstruction as the TV show experts represent debates on these and related points. Desires to know such particular details become shared and valued in the labor of reconstruction.

Experts' arguments on-screen dramatize that different knowledge worlds properly have different reasons for their speculations, use different forms of knowledge itself to work with and from, and have different interests in any answers, or even what counts as an answer. "Reconstruction" and "experimental archaeology" are two terms associated with this sort of knowledge generation process. Affect and sensation play parts in the melodrama also expertly edited and displayed in distributed television production. The melodramas of heated argument and bruised egos work to manage and manipulate expertise among divergent memberships in communities of practice. A particular sensory repertoire for inspection, problem solving, and enjoyment of the bath is built conspicuously for this set of events from human bodies and devices, by time-lapse photography, sensing technology, and physical effort. Knowledge worlds are honored in parallel but without being rigorously collapsed into one integrative form, and the Roman bath built among them comes into being, yet, perhaps, not entirely in equal satisfaction to all.

And it is the melodrama itself that makes it possible to move back and forth between a televisually expert "black-boxed" and elegant "story" and the conspicuous formula stagings and editings depending upon and teasingly un-black-boxing a range of crucial and contingent actants and processes. As with the other episodes of the *Secrets* series, the "Roman Bath" episode's distributed production is peopled by folks from a variety of communities of practice: academics and professionals, craftspeople and archaeologists, some folks indeed from communities living and working adjacent to the filming sites, not to mention the camera crew and production people making the documentary. Across the series people are gathered transnationally, in this episode from three places: the United States, the UK, and Turkey.[23]

First there are the three *academics* from different disciplines, ranks, and kinds of institutions:

— One is Fikret Yegül, a Turkish art historian and researcher of Roman architecture, now teaching in the United States. He is among those scholars responsible for a Harvard University–backed architectural study and partial excavation of the Imperial Bath-Gymnasium Complex at Sardis, Turkey, and has long-term commitments to reconstruction as an experimental practice (he also brings along his engineer colleague, Teoman Yalçinkaya, from Sardis; see below).[24]

— Second is Garrett Fagan, a historian and classicist, natally Irish with a Canadian PhD, and also now working in the United States. He has a specialty in Roman baths and is a lively presence as a lecturer for the Teaching Company, a business that provides commuters and others with intellectually entertaining summaries of university level scholarship (intentions not dissimilar to those of *Nova*, out of different but overlapping media).[25]

— And third is Peter Aicher, a professor of classical languages and literatures with a strong focus on undergraduate teaching, who had just written a field guide to Roman aqueducts. Since the broadcast he has led tours and seminars for teachers, book groups, and community audiences and has out another intellectual guidebook, supplemented for scholars with original evidence and texts.[26]

Then there are the three *engineers* from different kinds of businesses or practical experience and with greater and lesser connections to the academy and investments in archaeology specifically:

— The first, Max Fordham, is a world-renowned British engineer with awards in sustainable building projects and an expertise in complex climate control systems (he brings along a colleague helper, Tristan Couch).[27]

— The second is Tony Rook, a British practical archaeologist and author, founder and leader of a rescue archaeological society with an expertise as a building technologist and structural engineer (he also brings along another working friend, Bryan Scott).

— And the third is Teoman Yalçinkaya, a Turkish engineer and excavation archaeologist and possibly the most crucial figure in the practicalities of the reconstruction. As a colleague of Turkish art historian Fikret Yegül, he has worked for more than thirty years as architect for site work at the Sardis excavation nearby. In the role of construction foreman for this reconstruction and a local, he supervises the actual building of the Roman bath itself.

More black-boxed are the folks who perform the *physically skilled labor* involved in the actual building and firing of the Roman bath:

— A dozen local farmers from the village of Sard (the only one named is Ibrahim Akyar) come with previous experience laboring at the Sardis excavation. Working nonstop with only a couple of hours off weekly for prayers during the seven weeks of the shoot, they finish the bath (and watch over it afterward) under the direction of Teoman Yalçinkaya.
— In addition, there are the unnamed tile makers who fire the tiles that end up cracking because they were not given enough time in a tight shooting schedule to dry them properly.
— And, by no means least but also unnamed is the local village baker, who steps in at a crucial moment in the drama of the episode with the know-how to light the fires for heating up the bath.

Even more black-boxed in the narration but essential to the existence of the show at all, and all named in *production* credits, are:

— Nancy Linde, the writer, director, and producer of this particular episode; and other producers, such as the associate producer Deborah Fryer and the executive producer Paula Aspell; not to mention a range of productive others, all of whom work together to put the episode in the context of Michael Barnes's two connected series.
— Also crucial and on the ground are the three-person TV production crew, filming near Sardis, Bath (England), and Rome: Mike Coles, camera; Keith Rodgerson, sound; and Richard Comrie, assistant camera.
— Combined together with all these are the rest of the production and the postproduction teams, among them the editor James Rutenbeck, and other workers and administrators, all of whom are responsible for creating the episode as a television show. They are named in production credits at the end of the episode, some fifty-four individuals, three companies, and a range of sponsoring or helpful agencies.[28] The voice of narrator Stacy Keach stands in for all these in the

dramatic interpretation of the televisual action. His (or rather Nancy Linde's) narrative first-names the academic and engineering protagonists of the drama in a conspicuous leveling action.

And finally, crucial to the drama and essential actants in production processes, are those agencies that, while conspicuously not at all black-boxed in the show itself, are the sorts of agencies almost always otherwise black-boxed in cinematic or televisual analysis:

- — A range of *materials* such as those that make up the cement and tiles, and those that provide heat and water. Indeed a discussion of cement is part of the narrative of the program.
- — As well as the *interactivities* connecting such materials with such other *worldly processes* as weather, chemistry, firing, and more; all these critically important to the drama of building of the bath and— black-boxed—to the making of the television program itself. Indeed as pivotal elements *they are played up explicitly in epistemological melodrama* within and indeed as that spectacle of production, the immersion in meta-realities, interwoven into the show.

"EXPERIMENT" AS FORMULA

The BBC producer Robin Brightwell describes the formula of all the episodes of *Secrets of Lost Empires* as "a series of experiments on screen" in which the disagreements among experts provide the drama: "Our archeological experts did not always agree with the historical accuracy of the stonemasons' or engineers' schemes. The engineers, it turned out, were often less practically minded than they liked to admit. We . . . always brought along as close as a modern equivalent as we could find to an ancient foreman. The result was not welcomed by our building teams, but was a bonus for us film-makers: disagreement is always a good ingredient in a documentary."[29] In other words, the drama of each episode of *Secrets*—its soap-opera hook—is strategically created by displaying and animating the *incommensurability* of knowledges, worlds, languages, forms of evidence, affective valances, cognitive sensations and cultural meanings across communities of practice. And it is in the context of these purposes that expertise is valued in various forms, although its hierarchies of attention in the TV show are often more dependent on "good TV" (that is, melodrama) than on, say, conventional academic standards.

By 2007 whole social worlds of exacting labors were spun off by TV to invest in the pleasures of experiencing similar incommensurabilities. For example there were immersive details of work as viewed by, say, crabbers in the Bering Sea in Discovery's *Deadliest Catch*, or haulers near the Arctic in History's *Ice Road Truckers*, both created by the US company Original Productions. Or, other displays of technical detail set to test presuppositions that amount to superstitions, such as the debunking experiments of Discovery's *Mythbusters*, filmed in the United States for Australian Beyond Television Productions. Or, exacting forensic devices and procedures real or imaginable played up in the skins of broadcast TV, in shows like CBS and Universal Studios' *CSI: Crime Scene Investigation* and its spin-offs, comics, computer and board games, magazines, novelizations, toys, and even museum exhibition in its branded franchise.[30]

All these are examples of and nested within those distributed agencies that characterize not only the common processes of television production for each *Secrets* documentary itself but also, at the next level, each spectacle of production—that is to say, their meta-reality melodramas contrived from setting communities of practice together in both staged and uncontrollable ways, with the lines of authoritative and alternate knowledges played out or un-black-boxed, then recombined. Which knowledges are authoritative? Which are alternative? What counts as each is clearly contingent, recentered in movement from one community of practice to the next. In addition, many sorts of labors are represented as skilled and respected as such, no work comes across as simply unskilled. Expertise is reframed and knowledges are commercially democratized.

Thus a variety of different kinds of (extensively defined) "professional" knowledge are elevated as expertise while their boundaries of membership are threatened. Together they are valorized and even (unevenly) democratized because attending to practical, intellectual, and constructive knowledges is given relative and relational importance, and this happens within cognitive and affective melodramas of reenactment and experimentation in which they each have competing ranges of efficacy. Thus, these incommensurable worlds of knowledge and work are opened up for inspection and sometimes respect, although this opening up permits this inspection by particular others who do not necessarily share authorizing professional objects and values, languages, and rules for membership. Such "professionals," "experts," and "specialists," among them academics, long for, fear, and are now commercially required to produce, practice, and be held accountable for such "accessibility" amid the concomitant (mis)under-standings of their "others." Both accessibility and entertainment are man-datory in these TV shows.

In "Roman Bath" the reenactment is characterized by partial knowl-edges imperfectly communicated among the participants and by the very visible limitations of expertise, the contingencies of productive processes, and the disruptive agencies of the very materials and conditions. These together comprise that *sea of actants* that Haraway, Latour, and other science studies folks analyze.

The story of "Roman Bath" goes something like this: a team of so-called experts made up of historians, engineers, and archaeologists come together to plan and oversee the building of a Roman bath in Turkey, near the excavation at Sardis. Yet everyone knows that they have only seven weeks to do this, a timeframe that makes it clearly impossible to do it the way the Romans would have. There are important reasons why they have only seven weeks: television production is too expensive to do it in a longer timeframe, and these experts involved must combine this project with all their other professional duties in other countries. Nor is it com-mon knowledge how the Romans did build such baths: each expert has different kinds of knowledge to offer—some as "direct" as one can have centuries later, from documents and objects still around—others as edu-cated speculations based on worldly processes and materials that conform to rules they still know despite the passage of centuries. In some ways it looks like a *collaborative* problem-solving issue: combine partial knowl-edges to create a common understanding and then test that out. Or, alternatively, set up *competing* lines of speculation and see which works out best. Both of these end up happening.

And of course, none of this is at all simple. That there would be prob-lems was foreseeable and, for TV, desirable, even if some of the details were hazy beforehand. First, can the experts agree on the plans for the bath? The art historian and Sardis excavator Fikret Yegül puts his exper-tise on the line, outlining his plan for the construction here on his home turf. Immediately the indefatigable engineer Tony Rook challenges it. Tony, with his excavation experience at Bath, England, claims that Sardis cannot stand for all Roman practice. But the truth is, Fikret's plans have already been set into motion. Indeed they were part of preproduction planning and were going to be the model all along. Fikret, with both priority and the most status in this particular dispute, is personally forceful enough to maintain these on camera. Yet Tony is also another practical archaeologist as well as an engineer. He delightedly predicts that this plan will not work, and indeed in seven weeks, it cannot, at least not wholly. He clearly relishes the gadfly role in the drama on camera even when over-ruled. Fikret displays his frustration at meeting time schedules; his attempts to signal "authority" verge on "authoritarian."

At this point the formula for the episode is explicitly described by Fikret: this will be an experimental laboratory to test out new concepts, with an eye to the details of roof vault construction, water and heating, as well as also to display the Romans' development of concrete. The idea of a *reconstruction as an experimental laboratory* is a line of analysis and justification Fikret has been using ever since his early publications in the seventies on the excavation at Sardis.

However, the (black-boxed) television crew cannot afford to just sit around at the building site for the whole seven weeks—there are long periods in which the most important contribution to the bath is the physical labor of the Sard village workers under Teoman Yalçinkaya's direction. To chronicle their labor a time-lapse camera is left to run automatically so as later to rapidly review this work (in twenty seconds in the final TV version), while the production team sets off for Italy and England to shoot images, commentary, and historical context and backgrounds on aqueducts and on social aspects of bathing and sanitation with Peter Aicher and Garrett Fagan.

When they all return material processes have become complicated. The tiles to be used in the bath, made and fired locally, were dried much more rapidly than usual in order to meet the shooting schedule. They are also larger than similar tiles produced nowadays. They have cracked. But luck-ily Teoman in the role of construction foreman has come up with a practical workaround and has set the cracked tiles into steel frames to support them. Then they will look and act the way they "should." The British gadfly Tony agrees, although he cannot resist making comments about what the Romans knew that we do not. The grain of detail for what counts as authentic practice properly yields to the resources and materials at hand. In a laboratory some processes matter more than others.

Then a clump of experts have to leave temporarily for other professional commitments, and Teoman is left (with the television crew of course) to oversee the next steps by local workers. Unanticipated wet weather conditions make curing the concrete almost impossible; parts of the walls, roof, and other elements of the heating system are threatened by too much moisture. Teoman has to depart on his own responsibility from the plan to ceremonially light the fire for the bath water when everyone (that is to say, the "expert" protagonists) returns. He decides instead to start the fire earlier and for a longer period, hoping it will also then counteract all this moisture. But he does not know exactly how a fire should be lit. He successfully seeks out the alternative expertise of the local village baker to get the fire started. But will drying occur? Was the original design workable in fact? Will the gases flow properly? Will more building elements crack? Events demonstrate his decision is the right one: the drying does make a good difference and the smoke shows that the gases are drawing properly; the design of the bath has been vindicated. When the rest of the "expert" protagonists return, the climate specialist Max Fordham brings an infrared camera to check on the flow of gases. All is working well.

Now they all examine the boiler, created specifically for this project, and again the two excavation experts Fikret and Tony differ over details: the English gadfly is also a materials engineer and suggests that this boiler should be modified for greater efficiency. He and the famous climate specialist Max want the bath to be heated to fifty degrees, and the boiler needs to be altered to make that possible. This is the temperature such a boiler is capable of according to professional standards set by Max's references. Fikret feels the alteration to the boiler is unnecessary and that this temperature is not historically attested. He points out that Turkish baths are not as hot as this nowadays either. But Tony and Max support each other as the historian Fikret vainly attempts to claim his own publications as authority. The boiler is changed and a compromise about the heating level settles on forty degrees.

A final crisis is made much less of and quickly averted: just as everyone (meaning Fikret, Tony, Max, Peter, and Garrett) prepares for the ceremonial first bathing together, it is discovered that the water has all leaked out from more cracks. Teoman's silicon sealant works around this problem too, and "the experts" collectively and modestly enjoy the bath for the camera. Fikret sums up the experience again as an experiment he hopes will come to be known in scientific and humanist knowledge worlds. As such it models one type of transdisciplinary practice.

The trailer and introduction to the episode as it appears later on TV includes a brief costumed actor reenactment of a Roman bath sort of "party." This signals "reenactment" in its most popular sense and offers a simple beginning to the experimental archaeology that makes up the bulk of the episode and that creates the formula for these two *Secrets* series in particular.

The very requirement for melodrama as a commercial medium in this particular case allows for the making visible or un-black-boxing of the epistemologies Latour jokingly recasts thus:

> Any constructivists worth their salt should be ashamed to see that everywhere things have been gypped their due . . . if the word constructivist has any sort of meaning, it is because it leads us to agencies. . . . Yes, [things] act, yes they order, yes they resist, yes, they are plastic, but what has proved interesting are all the intermediary positions they are able to simultaneously occupy. . . . I have never met scientists at the bench who were content to choose between "realism" and "constructivism," except of course when giving science war pep talks. . . . Show me one single programmer who would think herself in full command of the software she is writing. . . . Everywhere, building, creating, constructing, laboring means to learn how to become sensitive to the contrary requirements, to the exigencies, to the pressures of conflicting agencies where none of them is really in command. Especially not the "maker" who spends nights and days trying to live up to his or her responsibility.[31]

Such knowledge "making" in metaphoric and literalized forms provides the epistemological melodrama for reenactment in the *Nova* episodes of *Secrets of Lost Empires.*

WELCOME TO THE IRON AGE

In September and October 2000 the BBC aired *Surviving the Iron Age*, a show with a novel generational hook, and one representing another sort of time-traveling "reality" documentary. Three of its "reality" participants in 2000 were children of people who in 1977 were involved in a similar but yearlong BBC Iron Age TV project *Living in the Past*.[32] In 2000 they and the rest of its seventeen volunteers took up a seven week residence at Castell Henllys in West Wales, an Iron Age Hill Fort sited in the Penbrokeshire Coast National Park, where they lived in archaeologically reconstructed roundhouses, the largest of which was finished only a few months before filming began. On their website UK National Park people recounted that they "supplied the volunteers with materials, clothing and food similar to those of the Iron Age based on archaeological evidence."[33] This show is an example of that style of reenactment TV that works with a formula of discomfort and discontinuity.

Around the time of broadcast the homepage of the BBC's companion website to the TV series (long gone) bundled together in their spectacle of production, that characteristic reenactment immersive remix of education, entertainment and soap opera:

> Welcome to the Iron Age / *Surviving the Iron Age* was an experiment in living history. Seventeen volunteers, including three children spent seven weeks experiencing life as it might have been in an Iron Age Hill Fort in West Wales. The series has now finished. / The British Museum created a tour on Iron Age Britain to accompany the series, featuring some amazing objects from its collections. / The BBC is not responsible for the content of external websites. / The *Surviving the Iron Age* book is published by BBC Worldwide and is available from the BBC Bookshop. / When it was all over, could the volunteers survive the modern age? / Anne, Bethan and Chris talk about the reality of life in the hillfort and a typical day. / Video—final thoughts. / Could you have survived the Iron Age? Get talking in the message board and send a postcard of the series. / Check out the transcript from the live chat with five of the villagers. / Read the biographies. / Peter Firstbrook, BBC series producer on making the programme. / Find out who won a prize in the competition.[34]

The BBC website was the most thoroughly saturated immersive version of the series, reaching out in as many media, sensory and temporal modalities, and educational and commercial mixtures as possible, repurposing all the other forms in which the series also existed. The TV show itself (as of this writing not available in DVD) probably most carefully elaborated the soap-opera *melodrama* of its events. And the large, brightly colored, and visually resplendent companion book, published and sold by the BBC, offered itself up as thoroughly historical, albeit admittedly introductory.

It interweaves narratives of TV series production with historical con-
textualizations such as maps, timelines, pictures of ancient objects, short
historical commentaries on various subjects, and bibliographies.

BREACHED AUTHENTICITY AND REENACTOR HOBBYISTS

The TV show was arranged as a mini-series in four episodes, three with a
common structure: in each of these the melodrama of the episode is
constructed out of some unexpected catastrophe that requires the closed-
world "authenticity" of the time-travel TV convention to be breached. So,
in episode one some volunteers become surprisingly sick as they try to
settle into Iron Age living, and a doctor has to be sent for. In episode two,
first women in two families with children come into conflict, and then two
group members leave the project, one for a week because of illness, the
other permanently. So a motivation expert is sent in to facilitate group
organization and morale. By episode three some illnesses are revealed to
be food poisoning. At that point official public health regulations mandate
the arrival of a food safety officer who insists that certain twenty-first-
century sanitation measures are taken. One of the mothers and her two
children finally decide to leave (eventually her husband leaves as well).

At the end, the structure of the final episode also pivots around outside
people coming in, but in this last celebratory show these folks from the
outside are Iron Age hobbyist reenactors from Kent. They come to show
and tell their own particular version of reenactment and share the skills
they have learned in order for the two groups to stage a fictional encounter as if between Iron Age tribal groups. Then the whole series is capped
with an observance of Samhain, an ancient festival loosely related to our
own Halloween and an important event in contemporary neopaganisms.

Thus this show incorporates a range of reenactment forms, including a
couple of the commonly taken for granted ones, those intensively defined
versions by hobbyist reenactors and in national park recreation simulations, as well as my extensively connected TV remixes, all together in a
wide array of layered infrastructures that includes neopagan reenactment
spiritualities and alternative histories and religions. Authenticity is re-
staged among these varieties of reenactment and interactively collabo-
rates among *things*.

Surviving the Iron Age's BBC in-house production team organized the activities of their volunteers through a series of game-styled events in what they called "time challenges"—messages written out from the production team with instructions for action. A first communication introduced the volunteers to the camp and gave instructions for setting up their settlement:

> *By the afternoon* you must learn how to look after your livestock, including how to milk your cows and goats. . . . *Before the sun sets* in the west you must also select your chieftain. He or she can be of any age. This person will have an essential function: through them you will be informed of the tasks you are required to perform to survive in the Iron Age. You already have many skills between you. Share your talents well, work together and plan for the future. . . . *Between now and Samhain*, you must all master the skills of the Iron Age people. Support and advice on how to survive will be passed to you through your Chieftain in messages such as this one.[35]

Such time challenges included making honey beer, making charcoal, preparing to feast the Cantiaci (the Iron Age reenactors' own group name), preparing for the observance of Samhain, making tallow, firing pottery, and creating a wicker man—a symbolic effigy set ablaze during Samhain. *A range of social and object technologies* were interwoven in the time challenges that required the volunteers to assess their groups' knowledges, share them and teach each other, and encounter and engage various objects—some familiar, some unknown; thus to create new objects and processes (*things*) as well as new identities and cooperative interactions (which also become Latourian *things*). Skills they learned and taught each other and themselves included: grinding wheat, cooking over a fire, milking goats, organizing themselves as a group and practicing leadership, making jewelry, making pots, weaving and dyeing, practicing "druidical" rituals, games and oralities, ploughing, forging a sword, beating a chalice, casting a bronze figure, firing a shaft furnace, and finally the characteristic and paradigmatic skill of smelting iron. Skills and tasks were distributed and reassembled, not everyone did everything, nor were all the tasks completed as instructed, nor were all the attempts successful. Smelting iron comes to represent and embody as a Latourian *thing* this entire new knowledge infrastructure in its layered assemblage of locals and globals, that is, all these folks taken together with skills, devices, and processes.

Referring to these as *social and object technologies* animates further the multiform meanings and histories of that marvelous word "thing"— setting out its current, latent, and obsolete definitions as described in the *Oxford English Dictionary*. As a noun the word "thing" draws together some currently counterintuitive meanings that emphasize interaction, deliberation, and process in fields of power, as well as the more common sense contemporary meanings indexing various entities. The *interactive* processual meanings follow because an ancient assembly or parliament was called a *thing*, therefore the word also comes to mean a legal case or process; and more loosely connects to that with which one is concerned, or that which is done, said, or thought. The second sense forefronts various *entities*: individuals, signifieds rather than signifiers, beings without consciousness or inanimate objects, but also living beings, creatures, persons. Indeed as applied to a person it may be in affective registers ranging from contempt and pity to affection or honor. As a verb, "thing" may mean to plead a cause or to bring to reconciliation; or to represent by *things*. It is also an obsolete form of the verb "to think."[36]

So when the science studies scholar Bruno Latour puts out his call for a "Parliament of things" honoring hybrid entities such as these, he and his translator are indulging in a bit of etymological punning. But we might consider these historical "reality" documentaries with and as *parliaments of things*: assemblages of entities and beings, living and not, conscious and not, individual and not, and their intra-actions among themselves and with worldly processes in what the feminist technoscience and animal studies scholar Donna Haraway calls "naturecultures," and what I have been calling so far pastpresents.

LOCALIZING AUTHENTICITY

Reenactment so-called authenticity is continually reconstructed in articulations by and with such *things*. *Things*, as interactive contexts and resources, all mutually and simultaneously constrain (one could say "bilaterally," or, instead multiply among a "sea of actants") all those reenactments and the "world" or worlds (as in knowledge worlds) to which the reenactments are (supposedly) referring. In other words, authenticity is always local, always built out of the resources locally available at a given moment. The limits of authenticity are sometimes obvious to those generating reenactments, and other times quite invisible because local membership often includes some consensus on what is and is not important, what can be "black-boxed" in creating *authenticity*.

A caveat on authenticity is introduced at the beginning of the *Surviving the Iron Age* series: "The BBC takes on a moral and legal responsibility when people become involved in a filming project, so living in *totally* authentic Iron Age conditions was never an option."[37] And that the producers invite the children of the earlier series *Living the Past* to volunteer for this project makes conflating the pastpresents of such dynamic articulation generationally literal:

> The BBC therefore decided that this *new experiment in "experiential history"* should start by repeating the Iron Age period. Not only is this a fascinating period of British history, but there would be the additional interest of comparing the experiences of the volunteers in the late 1970s with those of the people selected for the new project. . . .
>
> Mark and Jody Elphick, together with Tom Little, were invited to join the series because their parents had been involved with the original Iron Age project twenty-three years previously. Most of the "Iron Age" families had stayed in touch over the years and the children who were born after the original television series was made were brought up almost like cousins, seeing each other once or twice a year. The "Iron Age children," as they came to be known, had often talked of *repeating the experiment* which had become such a big part of their parents' lives. . . .
>
> "We've always wanted to do it. All the kids have always nagged at mums and dads and said couldn't we do a children's Iron Age thing, ever since we were little."[38]

The collection of people designated as reenactors and the collection of people gathered with them and as them to create the TV show was more fluid than was always initially planned. The knowledge worlds they necessarily crafted together in this experimental filmmaking televisual history actually depended on this fluidity. Although, for example, the role of the community chieftain was intended to *mediate* separations of volunteers from TV crew, separations intended to ensure one kind of authenticity, this division was not maintained in practice but rather breached over and over. Indeed, one of the volunteers actually worked for the BBC and on the series itself: "Emma has since [after studying radio and television production and social anthropology] worked on many popular BBC series. . . . In many ways, Emma had the most difficult job of all: she was not only expected to live in the Iron Age conditions, but she also had to film for the series when the main television crew was not on location."[39]

Similarly, when Chieftain Anne was collecting urine as mordant for dyeing, "any passing male (film crew included) were invited to contribute." And when Ron and Brenda were smelting iron "the bellows had to be worked constantly. Everyone got involved—the volunteers, the BBC team and the staff at Castell Henllys all took turns to pump air into the furnace." Ultimately, the "BBC project was always intended to be about how twenty-first century people coped with living under prehistoric conditions and *there was never any expectation that we would learn much about how the Iron Age people actually lived*" concludes the companion book to the series.[40]

One classicist friend joked to me when I mentioned this TV series to her, "We're *still* in the Iron Age!"—laughing at *the indeterminacy of what counts as Iron Age* cultures, peoples, and timeframes, as such scale making continually needs to be refreshed. Indeed one of the volunteers referred to the event as "this Iron Age twenty-first century."[41] That the production team officially communicated their time challenges in our own alphabetic writing in English marked these communications as both in our time and out of time simultaneously. A range of series writing technologies of various sorts allow for the *playful intervolving across times* that create the effect of "this Iron Age twenty-first century." Such hybrid entities are what all along I have been pointing to as pastpresents.

IDENTITY PACKAGING AND THE WORK OF ARTIFACTS

Critics of heritage culture publics and corporations lament that popular media represent artifacts as "timeless" or even as "timelessness" itself.[42] But knowledge worlds or communities of practice understand their own and others' artifacts in definitions arrayed simultaneously intensively and extensively. When in popular media or nationalist struggles such artifacts stand for the *ontological continuity* of peoples and cultures—as essential evidence of their existence across time—then easily, even necessarily, such artifacts are positioned to represent timelessness itself. This, even though for, say, professional archaeologists the constitution of artifacts and the very marks upon them, marks in and of time and use, are scaled as material evidence for *time-inflected* and *time-nuanced interpretations*. And of course, even this seemingly most abstract and generalizable ontological continuity is highly contingent and material: that some artifacts continue and others do not also matters, and what the artifacts that did *not survive* might have "said" to and for heritage culture *media nationalisms* is unavailable now.

Strong correlations between a material or archaeological culture and the identities, boundaries, self-namings, and tribalisms of peoples are made easily and mistakenly.[43] How and why artifacts are preserved or unearthed and interpreted is perhaps always already mired in the interests of states and factions as well. Michael Dietler, a University of Chicago archaeologist sensitive to these issues, points out how the interests of the state, together with various nationalisms amid ideological factions, condition materially the means of archaeological discovery:

> The state is concerned to finance excavations, designate and preserve "national sites," and sponsor museums and exhibits that display the "national heritage." Moreover, given that the state is the major owner of the means of production for archaeological research, it is hardly surprising that the pattern of support for archeological excavation and museum displays has been conditioned by national mythologies of identity . . . it is subtly operative in the demands placed on archeologists today as they seek to justify the significance of their sites in the competitive process of requesting grants for excavation or in attempting to protect the archeological record. . . . The subtle demands that condition a nationalist archaeology are likely to be shaped by complex, historically evolving, factional contests as much as by overarching state interests.[44]

CELTIC NATIONALISMS IN A REENACTED EUROPE

With all this in mind generally, *Surviving the Iron Age* draws upon what the UK Celtic studies specialist and geographer Angela Piccini impressively specifies in the mid-nineties as "a Celtic cultural package," one particularly created and displayed in that moment *televisually*:

My present work [in 1996] involves exploring how people consume heritage representations in Wales. Go to any heritage site or "living history" museum, such as the Museum of Welsh Life at St. Fagans outside Cardiff, Castell Henllys Iron Age Hill Fort in north Pembrokshire, or Celticas in Machynlleth [Montgomeryshire], and you will find people filming. What they are filming is all about who they are in relation to their ideas about the past and who they may once have been. . . . Their video productions, then, are about placing themselves in some relation to the past which bears on general notions of their own identities.[45]

Only a couple of years earlier the US archaeological theorist Dietler examined what roles a Celtic cultural package plays for the new EU collectively in a large material infrastructure of funding and distributed agency, at what he called "several contradictory levels":

It is my contention that such appeals to an ancient Celtic past have played and continue to play a number of important and often paradoxical roles in the ideological naturalization of modern political communities at several contradictory levels, including: (1) pan-European unity in the context of the evolving European Community [now become the EU as an entity], (2) nationalism within member states of that community, and (3) regional resistance to nationalist hegemony. An understanding of this complex process requires exploration of the ways in which language, objects, places, and persons have been differentially emphasized to evoke antiquity and authenticity *at each of these levels* in the process of constructing and manipulating emotionally and symbolically charged traditions of Celtic identity. As an archaeologist specializing in the study of those societies of ancient Iron Age Europe that serve as a touchstone of authenticity in the invocation of Celtic identity, I have an interest in examining the ways that archaeology has been appropriated, or has collaborated, in these "invented traditions" and its potential role in sorting out the competing claims of what Benedict Anderson has called "imagined communities."[46]

Piccini properly critiques a range of television documentaries, including BBC documentaries of the eighties and early nineties, which construct "the Celt as an appealing, market-friendly, and resoundingly apolitical object for public consumption, a pan-European entity ripe for marketing the European Union as it did during the 1991 *The Celts: The Origins of Europe* exhibition at the Palazzo Grassi in Venice." Mostly, "these Celts . . . belong to no specific time or place, as their associated reconstructed material culture is a pastiche of continental and British." And indeed this is a pastiche only too appropriate to signify contradictions and dangers of pan-European identity throughout the nineties.[47]

Such manipulations of Celtic identity were, for example, essential to the French and Canadian TV show *Highlander*, participating in its redirected antiracisms. Similarly, they were even played upon, despite its "ancient Greek" mindscape, in the remixed invented traditions of US produced but shot on location in New Zealand *Xena*, the theme music of which was described by fans as a kind of "Celtic fusion": "The blending of Celtic, Arabic, Bulgarian, and African melodic structures give the music a timeless, stateless feel appropriate to a show about a Warrior Princess who 'travels the timelines.' "[48]

REFUSING TELEVISION

In the early nineties Piccini's critiques motivated her to search heritage documentaries for evidence of "the ways in which competing histories are constructed, are made tangible, accessible to viewers, thus empowering them." But she realized soon that a cultural studies formula just *filling in* what we have already seen bundled in commercial exuberance as the spectacle of production, is inadequate to realize *significantly* empowered individual viewers across a simple range from active and passive: "It is not a matter of whether viewers are active readers of televisual text; what is at stake is whether that activity is significant." Her analysis concludes: "The real problem is how we as academics approach the public presentation of archaeology. We have to *question seriously why we want to televise* our activities and their productions in the first place."[49]

In political and ethical frustration Piccini redraws for academics involved in heritage television in the UK in the mid-nineties that same line corporate monitors Russell Mokhiber and Robert Weissman do for Smithsonian and other public agencies seeking corporate funding in the United States in the late nineties; that is, a line between commercialization and public history aims. At these two points in time, in these places, amid the history, science, culture, and image wars, opting out of commercial interconnections under varieties of globalized privatization might still seem, perhaps, possible. Or at least being clear about one's own alliances and making visible the dangers involved feels urgent in specific knowledge worlds. (As it feels to myself, if differently, now.) But Dietler in contrast, describes how academic work itself is and has been, unevenly and multiply appropriated, with a call for another kind of reflexive self-consciousness instead, for archaeologists in particular "to develop a critical awareness of their own situation in this process in order to understand how it informs their practice by conditioning research goals, interpretation, and evaluation of knowledge claims and in order to recognize their responsibilities in presenting the past in the midst of rival appeals to its use in authenticating modern collective identities."[50]

Piccini in the mid-nineties alternatively struggles to articulate an ethic and politics of renunciation and refusal: let us give up these televised stagings valorized as public pedagogy. But this cultural studies political strategy overvalues these televisualizations at the expense of accounting for a cascading infrastructure of remediation. Refusing television projects (and perhaps a kind of entrepreneurial self-aggrandizement) may be voluntary at the scale of individual scholars in any particular "right now," but refusing academic capitalism, of which such projects are a piece, both metaphorically and in reality, is no longer feasible. Dietler works at a different *scale*: he assumes that configurations of power, knowledge, and yes, love, including a range of identity projects, are produced within an apparatus that cannot be purified of its state and factional interests and the complexities of funding requirements, private, commercial, national, and so on, however much he also cautions all to inspect their accountabilities in these very circumstances.

Surviving the Iron Age teaches us to inspect the remediations that Piccini understandably overlooks at one moment in time: it does not exist only as documentary on film, or even only as the set of events, things, or people that create that product. It does not end with that product or even with its viewing on television by more and less active and sophisticated viewers. Its visuality is not its essential property, however powerful and important, since its sensorium is (however optically) diffracted amid materialities not centered in the documentary film itself although certainly including it. It is for the practice of just such inspection that I offer my extensive use of the term "reenactment."

Assemblages such as *Surviving the Iron Age* are dynamically scoped and scaled, and their analyses must be too. For example in this instance, its "Celtic package" of contemporary politics and their commodification is also articulated among layers and levels of multiple identity projects among an array of knowledge worlds as Dietler accounts. And such politics are not evacuated by identities either, for the material resources for making are dramatized too. Just to note a very few points within this assemblage, some of those cascading recombinations of media, objects, senses, and affects involving *Surviving the Iron Age*, its range of venues and *skins*: the TV documentary version, the TV "reality" show version, the educational gift book version, the you-are-there experiment book version, the teacher's resource website version, the play Iron Age the game website version, the historical reenactors version, the living history at public park version, the publicly funded history version, the work of academics being publicly recognized version, the "look at us—we deserve funding" version, and one could go on piling on these distributed agencies and audiences presented in one skin or another.

Collaborating, indexing, being accountable for, engaging, familiarizing oneself (perhaps not even consciously) with one's own movements among layers of locals and globals is one kind of consciousness (or perhaps several) cultivated by such variously remediated products and processes as *Surviving the Iron Age*. Although implicated in European identity politics, it also strangely offers communities of *practice* in addition to, or alternating with, communities of *identity*: what we are, what we name ourselves, shifts multiply as what we *do* variously with different each others connects us to multiple pastpresents. This kind of political possibility offers bits of utopianisms in a very different way than that of telling us who we should be and what we should do; instead it attempts to recognize *who we are becoming*.

These do-it-yourself pastpresents invite identification and dis-identification, on edge: communities brought together and also pushed apart as the "us" moves around. This is in distinction to some pastpresents where who you are and what you do are more or less conflated. Reenactment viewers play at being "there" as I have said, on set, on site, in that past, in a past: mentally enacting, reenacting, experimenting, speculating, trying to find evidence for various pastpresents. Nothing *guarantees* political possibility here, but neither are new possibilities by debunking category simply absent.

Honoring and perhaps identifying with Piccini's frustration when political possibility is only too easily transformed into the spectacle of production, we might look beyond some formula for an empowered viewer or for a critical politics of renunciation. Dietler's paradoxical roles, and contradictory, telescoping, and cascading levels among locals and globals of Celtic identity in a reconfiguring Europe, cannot assume resolution, even as a political good to be struggled for. A willingness to inhabit these and other uncertainties, volatilities, opens up frames without resolution and with shifting generalizability, but not without agencies.

MAKING SPACETIMES

Pastpresents amid scoping and scaling Google remappings are dynamic and immersive versions of what the anthropologist Kath Weston calls "spacetimes." In chapter 2 we looked to Kath Weston for ways to reframe at another level of scale Mulkey and Dougan's ethnomethodological situation of science work normalized as universal. In this chapter we look in closer detail at the workings of what she calls "time claims" by examining how spacetime is constructed in remediated forms in *Surviving the Iron Age* among: the TV show, its companion book, and with its reenactors. The grain of detail here may appear a bit obsessive, but I ask you to humor me. We examine this *timespot* at this level of detail in order to un-black-box a set of spacetime immersive technologies that will come to be taken for granted and stand in for each other after the nineties in other or later TV shows. And it is at this level of detail that we can feel out as a kind of *cognitive sensation* what Weston theorizes. This is also a lead-in to the second half of this chapter, where the figure of the reenactor and the work of reenaction are also scoped and scaled among infrastructures, some of longer duration and some emergent.

SPACETIME LITERALIZED: COMPARING ADDITIVES, SPACE + TIME

Surviving the Iron Age offers three remediated literalizations of spacetime —a table, a set of images, and, more complexly, reenactors and reenactments practicing reenaction—the first two found in its book variation, and the third, a subject in the second half of this chapter, distributed among all its variations.

The table version of spacetime is found in the BBC companion book to the show, also entitled *Surviving the Iron Age*, under the title "Chronology."[51] I will describe it so readers will not need to "see" the book, but I also put it into words so that the words work to defamiliarize and make explicit what one ordinarily grasps in a tacit visual gestalt. The table's very visuality allows it to play its important role as a boundary object communicating and resolving anomalies of time claims among many communities of practice. The seeming immediacy of such visual grasp belies the long training we need to have to actually take it in and the specifics that particular communities need to make the information work.

Across the top of the table extends "time" in the sequence 800BC to AD300 in one hundred year increments, and along the side we have "space" from top to bottom: Ireland, Britain, France (Gaul), Southern Germany, and Central Italy. Britain is colored differently, as the focus of "space" for the TV show.

The textual discussion of "Chronology" begins with the *lack of written language* of "the Iron Age people" and that thus "not one single Briton was known by name before [the Romans first arrived]" in comparison to "the Greeks, Romans, Egyptians, Assyrians and other early civilizations, all of which pre-date Iron Age Britain." *Other writing technologies* have come to manage past temporal division today however, even if they do not recover the "names" or actions of individuals in historical narratives. Instead they offer to name peoples. The ones discussed in the companion book are "radiocarbon analysis," "tree ring analysis, or dendrochronology," and especially "stratigraphic sequence" and "distinct periods" based upon "typesites."[52] Typesites are a technical technology of historical importance and, to some extent, come to essentialize peoples and places in a specialized spacetime.

The table draws time periods across spaces: for Ireland—Late Bronze Age, Iron Age, Roman Iron Age. For Britain—Late Bronze Age, Early Iron Age, Middle Iron Age, Late Iron Age, and Roman Iron Age. *Lines* temporalize specific excavated sites and associated names: Hengistbury harbour, Arras culture and East Yorkshire cemeteries, Lindow Man, Snettisham Hoards, Maiden Castle hillfort, Danebury hillfort, Deal Warrior, Castell Henllys hillfort to farmstead. *Dots or bullets* punctuate historical reference moments: Cantiaci tribe (the name the hobbyist reenactors of *Surviving* use in their living history enjoyments) migrate to Kent, Caesar's raid on Britain, Roman attack on Anglesey, Boudica's revolt, Hadrian's wall built. For France and Southern Germany we get periods based on typesite levels at Hallstatt in Austria and La Tène at Lake Neuchâtel in Switzerland. For France—Final Bronze Age, Hallstatt I, Hallstatt II, La Tène I, La

Tène II, La Tène III, Romans; while a dot or bullet marks Caesar's Gallic War. For Southern Germany—Hallstatt B, Hallstatt D (1, 2, 3), La Tène A, La Tène B (1, 2), La Tène C (1, 2), La Tène D (1, 2), Romans. For Central Italy—Etruscans, Romans; while dots mark Gauls sack Rome and Hannibal crosses the Alps. All the "Iron Age" space/times (in separated axes) are *colored* pink and beige alternately, while the Roman space/times are colored purple, the British Late Bronze Age is green, and the French Final Bronze Age, the German Hallstatt B, and the Italian Etruscans are colored lavender.

This lengthy verbal remediation emphasizes the table's scale-making technologies: of colors, of site level in a range of gradations, of time over lines and time punctuated by dots, of proportion within intersecting variables of space and time along two axes. That some might properly skim over these details without attending to them while others might recognize and know them well precisely demonstrates how such a table works as a boundary object among communities of practice. A visual gestalt allows one to "read" such shifts across detail (once learned) relatively easily and without having to bring this second-level knowledge to consciousness. Scoping and scaling among details is a taken for granted aspect of learning to read tables.

And the table's considerable detail is more than adequate, indeed quite excessive for its text discussion or for references from the companion book as a whole, even more for the TV show. Such granularity adds "texture"—Steven Johnson's term for irrelevant details added tacitly in games and television or, say, in fanfiction, for the pleasures of varying realisms cast among *in-the-know* kinds of jokes.[53] As texture the table displays details at a finer grain than used in the book, television series, or website. The texture works to authorize the contents of the companion book even though its grain of detail in such technical specifics is unusable by the casual readers for whom it is intended. Among those for whom such grain of detail is the proper environment for their specialized labors, such a book is not likely to be read. Here this over capacious texture, like the overstuffed display in *Science in American Life* described in chapter 2, is an example of a different sort of mechanism that makes that contradictory nesting of niche markets I spoke of in connection with the film *Disclosure* possible and mandatory, although in this case casual and specialized audiences are unlikely both to have investments in detail in this object. In this case it works with academic and other professional communities of practice that *authorize* the historical knowledge that all these remediations draw upon, while keeping the intersection of space and time relatively uncomplicated and clean. (This part is really only a setup for contrast with the next set of cognitive sensations that take space/time to another dimension.)

The anthropologist Kath Weston describes one aspect of this additive sort of space and time: "An *additive understanding (space-plus-time)* pictures time and space as two geometric planes that intersect, two streams or dimensions that flow together, with the eye trained on their confluence. The analyst brings the two together after the fact by first imagining them as separate but interdependent, then investigating the effect that one has on the other . . . [treating] time and space as two discrete entities . . . [which] creates the problem of bringing them back together again."[54] But my verbal remediation suggests that even just such a reenacted space and time is built from other meta-dimensions as well: the typesite names and references refer to specialist technologies that in their knowledge worlds make interactive and animate the archaeological layers at the excavation sites, named, ordered, and otherwise rationalized in a common system for dating artifacts by the use of other exemplary artifacts and layers. In other words, spacetime has been laboriously taken apart in excavation practices themselves to become space/time, then that new technology's separate but interdependent planes are intersected in order to *compare* spaces and times. This table compares spaces and times, after they have been carefully intersected in the first sort of spacetime. Several paradigmatic sets of spacetimes are cascaded among layers, each another knowledge world with its own distinctive epistemology.

SPACETIME LITERALIZED:
TELESCOPED RE-REPRESENTATIONS

The book version of *Surviving the Iron Age* displays another, additional sort of reenactment spacetime too. To produce this one photos of the reconstructed park site are set back to back and side to side with computer-generated 3-D virtual worlds images "of how Castell Henllys would have looked around 300BC." The *reconstructed* site today has been denuded of trees (justified as "for defensive reasons"), a wooden palisade has been imaged along with an elaborate entrance and double-entry stone gateway, and many more and larger roundhouses are imaged together within the computer-generated virtual world of this compound.[55]

The text itself offers additional, if intended as complementary, *meta-versions*. It describes the stages of construction and reconstruction of the hill fort over the long period of its continuous occupation from 600 BC to 1 AD. This narrative is interlaced with the narrative of the site's excavation, also in stages, from 1981 on. These interlaced descriptions draw in as another set of threads reenacted, recent professional reinterpretations of the site, which replace earlier understandings of the hill fort as primarily a defensive structure, with new narratives of its importance as a storage site for grain, and thus its conspicuous displays of power and status. Such reinterpretations of scholarly material are conveyed visually as reenactment and represented as authoritative for audiences for whom such interactive virtual worlds 3-D display will become more and more a taken for granted televisual feature after the nineties.

Spacetime in epistemic layers is remediated as reenactments here, not as some originary unity but rather as *forms of practice and attention* in telescoping and cascading ranges of expertise and interaction. Scholarly debates are naturalized but their *technologies* are dramatized. Such computer-generated reconstruction is the hallmark of History Channel TV shows in 2007 such as *Engineering an Empire* and *Lost Worlds*, where such reconstructions have now become *things* taken for granted by viewers, no explanation needed. Learning how to read such displays is now accomplished less consciously. When taken for granted such professional excavation knowledges are only tacitly represented in these nonetheless intensively produced simulations cascading 3-D computer generation styles.

SPACETIME LITERALIZED: REENACTORS

It is with these styles in mind that I turn to the third literalized reenacted remediation of spacetime, distributed among each variation of *Surviving the Iron Age*; that is to say, I turn to the reenactors of various kinds, that is, reenactors intensively defined within communities of practice nonetheless very differing. Reenactors in the nineties are another spacetime technology and agency, another set of dynamically cascading *things*.

The park site is a stage for the reenactors of the BBC production, who simultaneously reenact the whole period of continuous occupation of the hill fort, the punctuated moment of their own occupation for the cameras, and the earlier BBC production—elsewhere in an Iron Age when and, for three of them, among recovered memories of family importance. The BBC reenactors are visited by another sort of reenactor, the Cantiaci, "one of several *voluntary Iron Age 'living history' groups* in Britain." A frisson of desiring anxiety is generated between the two groups as the BBC reenactors are both "keen to see any new faces" while "unsure how they would match up against enthusiasts who had immersed themselves in the period for years."[56] And, in a third sort of intensively defined reenactment, workers are involved in the site of the park and its reconstruction of roundhouses, its professionals' gathering together of materials for the BBC reenactors. All three intensively but differently defined forms of reenactor are elements of reenactment upon which park personnel in particular bring their professional expertise to bear.

These hobbyist, semiprofessional, and professional historical interpreters are important players in reenaction, but not at all, as I hope the book so far attests, the locus of the essential meaning of reenactment. I have taken pains not to center them, to enlarge the circle of who can count as reenactors, to continually locate all of these in layer after layer of infrastructure, both long term and emergent, and to point out how the television settings of reenaction do much of the work these particular reenactors are held to represent. What their agencies are, how the limitations of such agency are ethically and politically represented, and at what scale their work is effective, are subjects that begin the next, second part of this chapter.

PART 2. EXPERIMENTAL HISTORY, REENACTORS,
AND THE WORK OF REENACTION

PEOPLING SPACETIME, VARIETIES OF REENACTORS

The "living" part of living history sites and epistemologies depends upon historical reenactments of various sorts, only some of them focused on or involving peopling by costumed history interpreters. In the next part of this chapter, discussing the training of interpreters in Colonial Williamsburg, we will see how within this ecology the ethos of "peopling" such sites is complexly contradictory and involves layers of good and bad faith as well as creativity and (often thwarted) aspirations to professional knowledges of various kinds.[57]

But first I want to stress that these peopling reenactors are amazingly various—some in their relationships to such professional aspirations and trainings, and others in relation to periods, alternative forms of reenactment, and peopling. Nor do I want to forget to mention all the personal identifications involved, from hobbyist creative expressions to other affective and cognitive pleasures. Nevertheless, costumed history interpreters collectively, whether hobbyist or professional, are not the *essential, ideal type* versions for the meanings of reenactment, despite the stakes in such intensively defined meanings of reenactment for particular communities of practice. At the very least and most literally, focusing primarily on them leaves out the visitors, viewers, tourists, and other peripheral participants upon which living history sites also depend, not to mention the enormous staff of those creating these especially elaborate "sets" for reenactments. Restricting "reenactor" to those hobbyists who seemingly do it all replaces interlocking virtual industries and their massive distributions with that romanticized (and essentialized) commodity with its unquestioned seeming "accessibilities." Thus, such ideal type reifications of reenactors as these persons leave out the many processes among a much larger range of people and things in telescoping or cascading infrastructures I have been discussing already and hope now to entangle further.

Relatively and relationally authoritative communities of practice for peopling reenactments include at the very least: professional actors likely to people TV documentary embedded mini-reenactments; national park employees who take up peopling historic sites, sometimes with the help of volunteers; former academic historians who take up historical reenactment as a new and rather marginalized profession to be hired by museums, parks, and schools; current academics who serve as talking heads in documentaries and occasionally people as resident meta-authorities TV or other simulations; as well as, the weekend reenactors who travel to battle sites and fairs to entertain themselves and others and to make, sell, and trade technological artifacts and materials, including websites with which to inhabit their pastpresents.[58] The degree to which any of these sorts of reenactors include with themselves as reenactors, visitors, tourists, viewers, or other peripheral participants, or, in alternative authorities, the very professions comprised among those working to stage reenactments, from curator to camera person to computer simulation expert, varies considerably.

Spacetimes are richly layered in such pastpresents peopled by reenactors, from examples where Iron Age European pastiche re-cultured meanings are played in various locations, historically sited or exemplary, to examples where, say, reenactors might shift which sides of strategic World War II battles between the United States and Germany they will fight on and where the specters of neo-Nazi survivalism and historical revisionism haunt their playacting.[59] "Time travel" is a term often used by all these various reenactors to describe what I would call the kind of *cultural work* reenaction is. Toward the end of this chapter we will examine an even wider range of time-traveling technologies as they are represented televisually.

DISTRIBUTED COGNITION AND DISTRIBUTED HUMAN BEING

Throughout this book I have discussed forms of distributed productive processes of many kinds, some coming into new intensive uses in the economic restructurings of the nineties. Two additional forms of distributive process are contexts for movement among knowledge worlds today. In an only too tricky mapping problem for my describing them, these are terms and forms of agency that some knowledge worlds will properly (intensively) refuse. I use the cognitive sensations of scoping and scaling to work out how to honor such refusals while repositioning them. But, how to present alternatives, without a debunking replacement? I hope my intentions are relatively clear even if this practice is not simple, is unevenly effective, and always politically and ethically complex.

So the two additional forms of distribution that I claim need to be taken into account here among recognitions of reenactors could be called "distributed cognition" and "distributed human being." The first is slightly less controversial than the second. Both are the subject of a range of books, journalistic and scholarly, for a wide, unevenly authoritative, and highly distributed audience.[60] These are the very sort of audience sets I claim become intrusive in the nineties among some communities of practice and the ground against which reenactment properly has its extensive meanings. These are the audience sets I use the term "transdisciplinary" to describe.

In the mid-nineties the feminist social interactionist and classification theorist Susan Leigh Star works to name *distributed human being* in this way:

> Analytically, it is extremely useful to think of human beings as locations in space-time. We are relatively localized for many bodily functions and for some kinds of tasks we are highly distributed—remembering for example. So much of our memory is in other people, libraries, and our homes. But we are used to rather carelessly localizing what we mean by a person as bounded by one's skin. . . . The skin may be a boundary, but it can also be seen as a borderland, a living entity, and as part of the system of person-environment. . . . Parts of our selves extend beyond the skin in every imaginable way, convenient as it is to bound ourselves that way in conversational shorthand. Our memories are in families and libraries as well as inside our skins; our perceptions are extended and fragmented by technologies of every sort.[61]

In her introduction to a scholarly collection she calls *Ecologies of Knowledge: Work and Politics in Science and Technology*, Star examines the infrastructures of knowledge work that come out of her ethnographic engagements among forms of commercial research and industrial science in the eighties and nineties at Xerox's Palo Alto Research Center (Xerox PARC), and then she analyzes the infrastructures of knowledge work that come out of scholarship in the nineties among the information sciences of library and classifications systems as they become more and more embedded among the knowledge workings of new technologies. These give her an exquisite sensitivity to emergent shifts in these institutional and cognitive infrastructures; and she struggles to evaluate, share, and network these among knowledge worlds that sometimes have little contact and that often have diverging values. She turns to the complex systems theory of the cyberneticist Gregory Bateson, among others, to work out, in medias res, what is going on. (Her title is an homage to Bateson's book from the seventies *Steps to an Ecology of Mind*.)[62]

What Star in the mid-nineties describes as distributed human being and what the feminist cyberculture historian Kate Hayles in the late nineties calls "distributed cognition" attempt to explain as clearly as one can in medias res some of the ways we network among these vital but highly distributed associations. I pointed out in the introduction that being inside and moved around literally by the very material and conceptual structures you are analyzing and writing about is a kind of self-consciousness, only partially available for explicit or direct, discussion. We need the term "transdisciplinary" today in order to both befriend and to pay attention to what we experience in networking engagements across knowledge worlds, as we necessarily *feel out* in cognitive sensation the complex contradictions of diverging values, entailment, and analysis among a range of academic and other genres of writing and professional product.

So, during and after the nineties, a range of others also come to be working out these transdisciplinary practices now attached to or near the term "posthumanities." They do so among networks in complex knots and alternate communities of practice, some in connection and some in virtual isolation. My own exploration of reenactments over this period and *now* brings one sort of viewpoint to bear upon this posthumanities, as it comes into being or "emerges" (using that term in a technical sense) out of the semichaotic conditions of global restructuring. Such a posthumanities is not, *surprise*, unrelated to another also uncomfortable term, "posthuman," and for some the term "posthumanities" is an attempt to reference the term "posthuman" without wholly identifying with it. The crucial point here is that agencies of the emergence of a posthumanities are most certainly not restricted to human instrumentalism, individual or even collective. Worldly processes, some set into motion by people, some not, as well as people and beings, skills and devices that together constitute *communities of practice*, are all elements of these emerging processes; that is to say, elements in *new units of agency* characterized by features of self-organization not captured adequately under the term "human" (thus posthuman).

The cyberculture historian Kate Hayles, for example, reframes a philosophical notion of "human will" or individual human agency, associating her thinking with that of others this way (note the use of the term "metaphor," which I will return to shortly):

No longer is human will seen as the source from which emanates the mastery necessary to dominate and control the environment. Rather the distributed cognition of the emergent human subject correlates with—in [Mary Catherine] Bateson's phrase, becomes a metaphor for—the distributed cognitive system as a whole, in which "thinking" is done by both human and nonhuman actors. "Thinking consists of bringing these structures into coordination so they can shape and be shaped by one another," [Edwin] Hutchins wrote. To conceptualize the human in these terms is not to imperil human survival but is precisely to enhance it, for the more we understand the flexible, adaptive structures that coordinate our environments and the metaphors that we ourselves are, the better we can fashion images of ourselves that accurately reflect the complex interplays that ultimately make the entire world. . . . As [Gregory] Bateson, [Francisco] Varela, and others would later argue, the noise crashes within as well as without. The chaotic, unpredictable nature of complex dynamics implies that subjectivity is emergent rather than given, distributed rather than located solely in consciousness, emerging from and integrated into a chaotic world rather than occupying a position of mastery and control removed from it. Bruno Latour has argued that we have never been modern; the seriated history of cybernetics—emerging from networks at once materially real, socially regulated, and discursively constructed—suggests, for similar reasons, that we have always been posthuman.[63]

That means, as Gregory Bateson (my own teacher in the seventies) used to say, we do not end with our skin. "Skin" at this moment in time has so many different meanings and associations among diverging knowledge worlds that the dramatically different implications for considering what it means to say to any particular group of people that, "we don't end with our skin," becomes an example itself of transdisciplinary movement across knowledge worlds. Engaging and networking such a "riot of association," comes to be *the work to take up in a posthumanities*.[64] Hayles's distributed cognition and Star's distributed human being name attempts to explain as clearly as one can in medias res some of the ways we network among these associations. "In medias res," in the middle of things, as these things themselves resolve or not, as we look to see things as they exist for others, in different degrees of resolution, of grain of detail. And attention to any particular grain of detail provokes response and affect. And that matters.

Mine are claims that require paying attention to *layers of locals and globals*, all of which are materially significant as well as literal and concrete. Among these, as we have seen, are layers of *infrastructure*, some of it conceptual, some of it institutional, some of it economic. This sort of attention works toward a kind of *complex systems analysis*, a goal for analysis I learned to value myself from Gregory Bateson in the seventies. Such a goal for analysis has been somewhat marginalized over the last two decades in some circles in favor of bounded, seemingly more focused or practical, applied, and local forms of examination. These kinds of examination are often quite necessary and very valuable, and I do not wish to replace them but rather, as I have said, to scope and scale among all these levels. Such scoping and scaling are among the practices I wish the term "transdisciplinary" to hold onto and share.

Reenactors as I analyze them, are themselves "meta-phors," bearers across, for themselves and for others: bearing the burden of the *transfer* of certain meanings (signaled here by a punning etymology). And this is a peculiar kind of agency: a sort of agential work in which individual humans are either not in control or in very uneven forms of partial control. Indeed this is a form of agency that a transdisciplinary posthumanities becomes positioned over and after the nineties to examine and analyze, one in which control and agency exist at different levels of analysis within complex systems. The rest of this chapter is intended to show at a finer grain of detail and with several sets of rich examples just how this might be so.

Alternatively, in another sense the term "metaphor" is precisely not the right one for considering the work of reenaction. In common use the term "metaphor" connects two things that are most emphatically not the same. Yet, reenactment is all about connecting things that are "sort of" the same. And for some knowledge worlds this is precisely their problem and the reason why these knowledge worlds refuse reenactment. "Sort of" the same is not one of the proper forms of management among their *things* of membership, their trajectories of authority, sometimes of authenticity. A transdisciplinary posthumanities has stakes though in forms of knowledge that work along networks of "sort of" the same.

BATESONS ACROSS TIME, AS PIONEERS IN A TRANSDISCIPLINARY POSTHUMANITIES

Throughout the fifties, and after, Gregory Bateson (and, of course, others) attempted to work out the complexities of emergent behaviors and the role of human conscious attention and intervention. He understood these in the fifties to be urgent issues in which a new field of cybernetics could contribute to an out of control Cold War arms race and later in the sixties and seventies also to a range of alarming changes in local and global ecologies. He understood cybernetics to have the potential to impact fields that otherwise appeared to have little relationship among themselves: communities of practice without objects or memberships in common, yet caught up in complex systemic processes together. During these decades he himself moved among knowledge worlds ranging from mathematical cybernetics and game theory to behavioral psychology and cetacean communication to evolutionary theory and anthropology, traveling among communities academic, new age, religious, artistic, and entrepreneurial. Authoritative and alternative knowledges mixed around him in an array often deauthorizing, sometimes demoralizing, and always pungent and arousing.[65]

In the fifties he had attempted to write about and share the complexities of thinking about processes in medias res in an intermittent series of unusual essays he called "metalogues," not published together until the collection of his work entitled *Steps to an Ecology of Mind* came out in the seventies:

> A *metalogue* is a conversation about some problematic subject. This conversation should be such that not only do the participants discuss the problem but the structure of the conversation as a whole is also relevant to the same subject. Only some of the conversations here presented achieve this double format.
>
> Notably, the history of evolutionary theory is inevitably a metalogue between man and nature, in which the creation and interaction of ideas must necessarily exemplify evolutionary process.[66]

The theories of emergence we reference today appear retroactively implicit in what Bateson meant by evolutionary theory, as he understood it in transformation within a cybernetic epistemology. In such metalogues as "Why do things get in a muddle?" and "About games and being serious" he attempted to share some of the insights of, for example, game theory and critiques of behaviorism, with audiences uninterested in or unable to work at the grain of detail that specialists in these fields properly communicated within. But describing his intentions so is not quite right: it was not because these fields were full of jargon that could be translated into some popular vernacular. Not at all. Rather the very insights of greatest importance here were ones Bateson understood to be subtly and tacitly misrepresented when too directly or consciously managed. In other metalogues, like "Why do things have outlines?" and "Why a Swan?" Bateson worked at the edge of his own understanding to share thoughts and connections in emergent formulations. His metalogues were conversations between a father (F) and daughter (D). This daughter becomes Mary Catherine Bateson, linguistic anthropologist, feminist, and popular writer and biographer. One of these father authored conversations takes up the issue of what a relationship of "sort of" might mean:

F: Well—I think it is sort of a secret.

D: You mean you won't tell me?

F: No—it's not that sort of a secret. It's not something that one must not tell. It's something that one *cannot* tell.

D: What do you mean? Why not?

F: Let us suppose I asked the dancer, "Miss X, tell me, that dance which you perform—is it for you a sacrament or a mere metaphor?" And let us imagine that I can make this question intelligible. She will perhaps put me off by saying, "You saw it—it is for you to decide, if you want to, whether or not it is sacramental for you." Or she might say, "Sometimes it is and sometimes it isn't." Or "How was I, last night?" But in any case she can have no direct control over the matter.

. . .

D: Do you mean that anybody who knew this secret would have it in their power to be a great dancer or a great poet?

F: No, no, no. It isn't like that at all. I mean first that great art and religion and all the rest of it is about this secret; but knowing the secret in an ordinary conscious way would not give the knower control.

. . .

D: Daddy, what has happened? We were trying to find out what "sort of" means when we say that the swan [in the ballet *Swan Lake*] is "sort of" human. I said that there must be two senses of "sort of." One in the phrase "the swan is a 'sort of' swan," and another in the phrase "the swan figure is 'sort of' human." And now you are talking about mysterious secrets and control.

F: All right. I'll start again. The swan figure is not a real swan but a pretend swan. It is also a pretend-not human being. It is also "really" a young lady wearing a white dress. And a real swan would resemble a young lady in certain ways.

D: But which of these is sacramental?

F: Oh Lord, here we go again. I can only say this: that it is not one of these statements but their combination which constitutes a sacrament. The "pretend" and the "pretend-not" and the "really" somehow get fused together into a single meaning.

D: But we ought to keep them separate.

F: Yes. That is what the logicians and the scientists try to do. But they do not create ballets that way—nor sacraments.[67]

For both Batesons, Gregory and Mary Catherine, the terms "metaphor" and "sacrament," as used here in 1954, continue to be useful and to overflow meaningfully in their subsequent writing and research. In 1967 Gregory participates in London in the Congress on the Dialectics of Liberation, a "curious pastiche of eminent scholars and political activists" among them the feminist performance artist Carolee Schneemann, the psychiatrists R. D. Laing and David Cooper, the structuralist Lucien Goldman, the gay artists and writers Paul Goodman and Allen Ginsberg, and politicos of such different activisms as Stokely Carmichael and Herbert Marcuse.[68] The following year Mary Catherine participated with her father in a Wenner-Gren Foundation for Anthropological Research Conference that Gregory organized on the theme of "The Effects of Conscious Purpose on Human Adaptation," about which Mary Catherine writes as the subject of her book *Our Own Metaphor*, which is the book Kate Hayles comes to reference concerning distributed cognition in the late nineties.[69] The theme of the conference echoes the title of the address Gregory made in London for a very different set of audiences and disciplines, "Conscious Purpose versus Nature."[70]

Metaphor as a "sort of" relationship mixes together, in an engagement with a Bateson use of "sacrament," ideas that literary scholars and others often keep taxonomically apart in the terminologies of metaphor, simile, model, and simulation. Reenactments extensively understood traffic among these meanings as well. I find it especially valuable to consider the ways in which grain of detail comes to bear on these: to what extent the "sort of" relationship of reenactments are ones in which what is reenacted is not wholly different from its referents but rather more and less elegant in grain of detail (or authenticity), more and less "black-boxing" a complexity of *things* amid their processes. I see a relationship between TV and the web coming to work out and among such distributed, branded, and cascaded boxings or, perhaps, modelings in the nineties in very concrete and material ways. I see reenaction and reenactors as networked nodes in agencies properly attended to in an emergent transdisciplinary posthumanities.

LITERALIZING METAPHORS IN A
PATH OF RE-REPRESENTATION

So let us examine reenactors as Bateson-style "metaphors," bearing the burden of the transfer of certain meanings in a sort of agential work, that "sort of" relationality, in which individual humans are either not in control or in very uneven forms of partial control. The layers of agency of reenactors range along one axis from bearing official meanings they have no place in creating, to bearing idiosyncratic meanings they have created themselves, yet carry also as large social and cultural narratives beyond themselves. Thus along other axes, their sense of instrumental individual agency may be misleading: from the coincidence of unconscious meanings, to the purveying of social mis- and disinformation, to misrecognitions of collective agencies, and to misunderstandings of the limits of such conscious purpose. Consider the complex ecology of "the path of re-representation" they embody. Here I draw upon such a formalization by Geof Bowker and Susan Leigh Star, using their terms and structure of analysis but filling it in with particular agencies of such reenaction:

1 How objects [in this case the reenactors themselves, but we might also consider the complex assemblages of *things* as well, of which reenactors and others are one kind] can inhabit multiple contexts at once, and have both local and shared meaning [individually and collectively generated, historically locally valued and historically nationally valued, meanings for fun and entertainment and meanings for commerce and barter, and so on].

2 How people, who live in one community and draw their meanings from people and objects situated there, may communicate with those inhabiting another [consider as an example those strategies used in pamphlets by academic historians and park historians to encourage the inclusion of women's narratives at national history sites by park officials and volunteers, some of each reenactors].

3 How relationships form between (1) and (2) above—how can we model the information ecology of people and things across multiple communities?

4 What range of solutions to these three questions is possible and what moral and political consequences attend each of them?[71]

Putting all this into one kind of perspective in concrete terms is the pointed chronicle of Colonial Williamsburg by anthropologists Richard Handler and Eric Gable, *The New History in an Old Museum*, which uses ethnographic participation and observation as well as interview and archival materials to examine and produce an academic spectacle of production. Its many critical academic satisfactions emerge from its lively debunking narrative of corporate assumptions unintentionally derailing the social justice concerns explicit in the "new social history" espoused by enthusiastic historians turned corporate managers over the course of the nineties, exposing one version of Colonial Williamsburg as a sort of Republican Disneyland. And Handler and Gable give us a strong sense of how personalized Williamsburg recreations become for those reenacting, for example, in their pride and creativity in their particular versions of character or in their display of artifacts in action.

UNCOMFORTABLE PLEASURE, AFFECTS, AND INTENSITIES AMONG COMMUNITIES OF PRACTICE

But Handler and Gable believe that for (semiprofessional) historical interpreters at Colonial Williamsburg during the period of their ethnographic study over the nineties "the training emphasized good vibes while eliding a critical social history." "The trainees learned, for the most part, not by reading but by imitating." They note that examination and questioning, relating past and present, were the ostensible goals of social history, academic and institutional at Colonial Williamsburg, but since real questioning from an academic perspective (critique) involves discomfort and conflict, in fact the sorts of questioning that produced such discomforts was in practice reduced to mere style. What mattered instead was peopling the site: inviting visitors to identify with its people, while also getting visitors to interact with artifacts and characters on the site. (Note the foundational presuppositions that neither imitation nor identification are as philosophically respectable as a dispassionate practice of critique. Feelings and cognitions are properly managed separately in communities of practice sharing these values. Shadowing and witnessing as discussed in chapter 2, for example, are not associations in play here.)

In their analysis of Colonial Williamsburg, Handler and Gable come to the conclusion that trivial questions with fixed responses were more valuable then than the kinds of questions that would display or create critical reflection: thus "questions should be used primarily for stylistic effect [Johnson's 'texture' servicing realisms and authorities] and to encourage an all-important sense of mutual and egalitarian involvement [the Smithsonian's 'validation function']."[72] Handler and Gable note the continuities between these practices and other pedagogies today, but with intentions to distinguish them from better teaching practices: "to point out the similarities between training at Colonial Williamsburg and generic educational practices is not to invalidate the lessons we can draw from it. In this vignette there is an almost obsessive emphasis on 'comfort.' This is the pedagogic version of 'the customer is always right.'" They report, for example, that parent complaints of interpreters' critical commentary were borne on the back of individual interpreters, one of whom remarked: "you can't ask the questions that are really painful. You don't have the institutional, the structural support for that."[73]

So Handler and Gable conclude: "To us, this meant that a critical history—the kind the social historians claimed they were teaching on Colonial Williamsburg's congenial streets—was a virtual impossibility. But when we presented such a view (in seminars, in conversations, in published papers), frontline employees, their managers, and the museum's professional historians were almost unanimous—in their public statements, at least—in disagreeing with us." In the end though, they resolve their own discomforts with these questionings of and by others when they decide that these disagreements with them are made in bad faith by straitjacketed employees and corporate managers: "corporately managed and disciplined frontline employees are a poor conduit for complex historiographical narratives."[74] Indeed, when some employees go on strike, they pointedly question: "In becoming managers, in learning to speak the language of management, have the new social historians lost their ability to hear the lessons their own historiography is intended to teach? . . . Though Colonial Williamsburg officially embraced a new social history aiming, among other things, to recover the conflicts of the pasts, it never intended those past conflicts to seem continuous with present-day conflicts like labor disputes. To confuse the boundaries of past and present was 'anachronistic,' it was a sin against mimetic realism."[75]

One reviewer, a museum curator, after commending their clear analysis of the tensions "inherent in the very structure of museums," which "create contentious dynamics among museum personnel," recommends the book for "the museum community at large" and especially for "students pursuing careers in history outside the academy." However she continues:

> My appreciation for the comprehensive work done by Handler, an anthropologist, and Gable, a sociologist and anthropologist, does not mitigate one of the glaring limitations of this study. The authors never seem to articulate an understanding of how difficult it is to do public history. Some empathy would not have marred the quality of their observations or usefulness of their critique. This limitation is indeed unfortunate for an industry that is struggling to find its voice in the midst of attacks on multiculturalism and social history. The struggles faced by museum personnel—curators, researchers, educators, docents, administrators, and trustees—do not have easy solutions. Bringing these diverse points of view into harmony remains part of the daily challenge of working in historical institutions. This is to say nothing of the responsibility of caring for the collections—artifacts, historic properties, and archival materials—that are the centerpiece of history museums. That so much of it comes out as well as it does is probably the greater surprise. And, the task is getting increasingly difficult as dollars become harder to raise, competition for audience increases, and a variety of museums beckon a public that insists on play with its learning experiences.[76]

In other words, Handler and Gable have it right but also wrong; that is to say, right and wrong at different scales of analysis, at different ranges of a "sort of" relationality. Those uncomfortable, questioning disagreements may not only have been made by straitjacketed employees or disingenuous corporate managers (although that too), but also by those whose agency is variously limited and ecological in range, who act not as instrumental individualists as the analysis of Handler and Gable seems to require of them, but who experiment with and push the edges of limitations, failing and succeeding within ranges of efficacy.

What does such negative critique demand of museums, and frankly, of an increasingly managed corporate academy? It is easier to make such

critiques than it is to inhabit responsibly and accountably the communities of practice analyzed; indeed the critique operates to sharpen the
edges between communities analyzed and communities analyzing, delim-
iting responsibility and escalating distinctions of membership among the
necessarily distributed processes of production.

The very distinction that works to ground the critique, one between
the hybrid corporation and a serious educational institution, breaks down
under academic capitalism. To what extent is such critique or critical
renunciation now virtually a nostalgic appeal, and such serious education
actually a phantasm of a never existing institution, if admittedly also a
critique in which elements quite justly criticized are intensifying within
the academy itself? Handler and Gable themselves misrecognize the very
sphere of their critique: its applicability beyond its site of analysis to the
very site from which they produce such analysis. They are themselves
caught in the very processes they critique and for which they appear to
those in museum communities to have so little sympathy. Like other
academics they are in struggle, and that struggle over and over mislocates
its range, its agencies, and its critical understandings.

Such academic debunking critique in the political climate today fosters
such misrecognitions. Academic negative critique isolates itself from both
the distributed elements producing, here, the whole apparatus of Colonial
Williamsburg, as well as isolates itself from equally misrecognized distributed elements of intellectual production among styles of analysis for
transdisciplinarity in a globally restructuring academy.

WHOSE COMFORTS ARE BEING CENTERED?

Reenactors indeed may be quite limited in their abilities as instrumental
agents to pose critical social questions across communities of practice and
engage profitably (especially) with all the attendant discomforts. As bearers of meaning across communities of practice the cultural work they do,
to very different political purposes, is often quite uncomfortable. Not
always to themselves or their interlocking audience markets, but more
broadly, to larger and often unanticipated "audiences"—those in "hearing" distance, or those connected through other remediated versions:
producing together, layered in myriad distributions, joined and disjointed
across forms of consumption citizenship. Such questioning discomfort,
for example, is the very subject of a magazine piece from a *Washington Post*

article in 2002 entitled "Attack of the Clones; They dress like Nazis and drive amphibious vehicles. And they wage their own Battle of the Bulge on a US military base. Does the Pentagon know about this?"[77] In other words, to begin to understand the cultural work that reenactors do one has to look much more ecologically, telescoping and scaling layers of locals and globals, to begin to engage paths of re-representations.

Reenactors are themselves communication technologies or metaphors: as objects "inhabiting multiple contexts at once," with both "local and shared" meanings, and as people communicating across communities of practice; thus in relationship, how do the relationships form between themselves as objects, objects and selves with multiple meanings, and themselves as people talking across communities; and finally in paths of re-representation, how do we model such relationships? What kinds of models are possible, what ranges of technology do we use, and what moral and political consequences do we all—all these entities and beings here acting together, like it or not—what consequences do "we" set into motion? How can we be accountable for them?

SETTING CHANGES INTO MOTION

Thinking back to the BBC TV show *Surviving the Iron Age*, note that just by unexpectedly choosing a woman, Anne, as their local leader, the reenactors of *Surviving* shifted the path of re-representation such that the companion book then must be positioned to argue also for women's leadership in Iron Age societies (yes, where, when, and with what interconnections to these Iron Age twenty-first-century pastpresents?). The choice of Anne also sets into motion requirements that the companion book work to center technologies that, because they have been associated with women in various gender divisions of labor, have dropped out of public discussion and history as technology. Calling the learning of and interactions between various technologies "time challenges" in a game-style reality show allowed all kinds of technologies to be displayed, shared, experimented with, altered, moved around, and otherwise acted with, upon, through, and deconstructed. How little the reenactors know and how much they know about practices in pastpresents are dramatically consequent as such knowledges and the lack of them, for example, make them ill and disrupt their relationships. Such knowledges and their lack are remediated in the companion book with such boxed-off discussions as "Medicine in the Iron Age," "Iron Age Crops," or "Storage Pits."

Here we might now shift back to recall and compare several levels of reenactment and re-representation mobilized in the TV Show *Highlander*, introduced in chapter 1. To enumerate, there were first the historical reenactments on film that were a central part of each episode as the principal characters' lives over hundreds of years were narrated. Then there were the fanzine writers' reenactments as they recast the official stories, filling in their own versions, complexly and creatively interwoven into the television story lines. Then there were the costume contests at cons, where prizes were given for costumes. Only some of these connected directly with the *Highlander* spacetimes. Most of these costumes were additionally woven into communities of reenactors of various sorts, principally folks of the Society for Creative Anachronism, although there were also costumed *Star Trek* reenactors speaking Klingon for example.

All these folks belonged to overlapping communities of practice and their skills and enthusiasms upon which all these remediated forms of reenactment depended were shared, displayed, studied, bought, taught, and pictured in various ways. Let us work out in some detail a kind of agency displayed among these "sorts of" reenactors, one not scaled at the level of individual intention or instrumental control, but rather ecologically produced in a networked form of reenaction.

WORKING OUT A RE-REPRESENTING
ECOLOGY OF WOMEN WARRIORS

During the course of my *Highlander* and *Xena* research both gender and sexuality were recast unevenly in *Highlander* communities, altering the path of re-representation. In chapter 1 I described how homosexuality went from "forbidden topic" to "marked topic" as Same Sex Sex on the *Highlander* listserv. When I first engaged the *Highlander* listserv, although many representations within the television program were actively disputed and reworked there, most folks were dismissive of those of us who occasionally wondered in this particular local public sphere (which included internationally distributed fans) about the women warriors of the Immortals. Some of the earliest television episodes, the ones least satisfying in production values and backstory, had inadequately depicted women warriors, focusing mostly on displaying female rock stars with perhaps waning international reputations and varying acting abilities, such as Joan Jett or Vanity.[78] Women Immortals were depicted during the first season in 1992–1993 as surviving by wiles and deception rather than by sword fighting. Even those who fought did so with less skill.[79] Nor did fan writing reflect much more in the way of other possibilities, despite the thoroughly imaginary worlds created.

The great exception was the story arc that began on television with the Immortal Amanda, who became a continuing character over and after the first two seasons. Although the first episodes depicted her as cunning rather than a skilled warrior, by the end of the second season in 1994 her backstory was filled in and we learned of her relationship with her slain mentor, Rebecca.[80] Even though both actors' sword skills were patently small, their abilities were greater within the story itself, although mostly comic in depiction. However in fan writing their stories became deep and rich.

When we first talked about women warriors on the *Highlander* listserv, fans were skeptical of the roles women could have played as warriors, claiming that the inadequate depictions in *Highlander* were reflections of *how it was in the past for women*, properly delimited within desires for authenticity. Some of us had already been influenced by such fantasy novels as those of (later revealed as transgendered author) Jessica Amanda Salmonson, depicting the female samurai Tomoe Gozen, and by her *Encyclopedia of Amazons*.[31] But the late eighties and nineties had also exploded in new materials about women warriors. Those of us arguing differently pointed to new press and books about women who had successfully disguised themselves as men in the US Civil War and elsewhen, or who had become leaders of pirates, as guarantors for the authenticity of representations of women warriors.[82] Much of this material had probably been motivated, at least in part, by greater and more regular participation by women in US and European militaries, indeed the recovery of women's past military history was becoming increasingly important to justify such service in national ideology.[83] But some of this material was also in process to be published a bit later in academic discussions of female masculinities and commodified in both academic and popular transgender histories.[84]

Not until the end of the third season of *Highlander* in 1995 did we get a depiction of a woman warrior with equivalent sword skills and a backstory of power, the Immortal Ceirdwyn, in an episode interestingly (for feminists) entitled "Take Back the Night."[85] What counted as a woman warrior in *Highlander* thus suddenly shifted up several notches, and fans and fan writing were altered by Ceirdwyn's appearance on the scene. I think fan writing elaborating the story of Amanda beyond what appeared on television made it possible for Ceirdwyn to exist on *Highlander* television, and certainly after she appears, fan writing became much more daring in its use of women warriors.

Yet probably most important in remediated television representations was the eruption of *Xena* onto television also in 1995.[86] *Xena*'s deliberate anachronisms and patent fantasy orientation—which, although present in *Highlander* as well, are flexed by simultaneous pleasures in low budget mimetic realisms—gave it much greater scope for elaborating historical and imaginary possibilities for women warriors, a different range of authenticity. Remarkably enough, with *Xena* on television, with popular and academic books circulating histories of women warriors, and with women's increasing participation in the US military, only just momentarily earlier but nonetheless quite deep skepticisms that women's roles could have been different in other spacetimes were countered in movements among layers of locals and globals, and such re-representations quickly normalized among *Highlander* fandoms.

DEFLECTING NOISE, CONSENSUS HISTORY, AND ITS FANS

Such normalized or consensus histories are highly valued by reenactors. As a historical conservatism, investments in consensus histories by reenactors are not intended to promote mimetic realism at the expense of anachronistic blendings of pastpresents, as Handler and Gable locate the political conservatism of Colonial Williamsburg historians. Low budget mimetic realism is not incompatible with blended pastpresents in most reenactments because although authenticity is a keyword for many, perhaps most reenactors, what counts as authenticity is extremely various. Bilateral articulation, or that set of local resources and material and conceptual infrastructures that create the horizon for authenticity in any community of practice, allows for many kinds of local success in producing authenticity.

Rather what many reenactors desire as consensus history is something generally agreed upon, precisely to offset the controversies that on listserv lead to flame wars and in other public spheres lead to history wars. Reenactors want to get on with their intensively defined reenactments, not fiddle with controversies, unless the controversies actually make working the enactments more fun or better according to their community of practice's values. Alternatively, however, in many academic or politically progressive communities of practice, controversy is a very mark of cutting edge research or vibrant political critique and alliance building. Yet, of course ironically, there are academics and progressives, as well as other professions and conservatives, among many sorts of reenactors.

Controversies for reenactors as reenactors are more generally the "noise" that has to be filtered out to create the *momentary stabilities* for reenactment. Among some communities the enjoyments emphasized through knowledge *transmission* may trump the sharper edges of scholarly knowledge *production*. Historical novelists also often work with consensus histories, although sometimes controversies might give them alternate narrative possibilities. Many historical television documentaries, although not all, also value consensus history for the same reasons, without worrying too much about whether the consensus is a popular rather than a scholarly one. (This is something that drives academics mad!) *Typicality* and *generalizability* are highly valued too as marks of such consensus history, and they indeed are often highly valued as standards in academic communities as well. Normalized histories, consensus histories, authorized histories, normative histories, and official histories overlap or collapse in layers of locals and globals. The strategies of some social change activists, and alternative storytellers of many kinds, may instead emphasize speculative history, counterhistory, and even counterfactual history. (And what appears to be counterfactual at one historical moment turns out to be "factual"—in a range of meanings—in another, as the American Historical Society president Judith Appleby pointed out in 1997 in her joke about so-called revisionist chemistry, mentioned in chapter 2.)[87]

COMMERCIAL EXCAVATION: ADD TO WOMEN WARRIORS NOW WOMEN GLADIATORS

All these forms of history can be ecologically interconnected within highly commercialized remediations in the nineties and after across culture industries, including academic ones. For example in 2000, Disney's Discovery Channel takes up a controversial excavation of an unknown woman by the Museum of London, making a documentary entitled *Gladiatrix*, which aired in 2002, pointedly narrated by *Xena*'s Lucy Lawless. The documentary was anticipated by a *Discover* magazine article on the same topic.[88] Penguin Putman recruited Amy Zoll, an anthropology graduate student and University of Pennsylvania IT staff person, to write a companion book, which, like the documentary, is subtitled: "The True Story of History's Unknown Woman Warrior."[89] Commercial education sites at the same time post materials on female gladiators.[90] Meanwhile the Museum of London quietly removes the materials on the excavation from its website as ranges of alternative and authoritative knowledge shift among their remediated forms, and they find an association with all these popular and commercial forms deauthorizing.

Yet both enterprise and heritage cultures are complexly interwoven in the Museum of London's archaeological work itself. Redevelopment and construction in London has to take its turn through the heritage industries first:

> Applications for new building are scrutinised by the Greater London Archaeology and Advisory Service (a department of English Heritage) or by archaeological officers in borough planning departments. If the site is of archaeological interest, the developer will be required to pay for an archaeological evaluation. If archaeological remains are found during the evaluation, it may be necessary to re-plan the development so that they can be preserved in situ—or, failing that, to commission a full-scale excavation. Evaluations, excavations and other forms of field-work are not normally carried out by government agencies but by commercial or semi-commercial archaeological contractors—of which the Museum of London's Archaeology Service is the largest in Europe.[91]

It is interesting to note that in 2007 the History Channel's *Cities of the Underworld* remediates these commercial and heritage interests as it dramatizes great international cities built upon layer after layer of previous habitation, sometimes rendered in virtual worlds 3-D imagery.

The day after the documentary *Gladiatrix* airs in the United States, the *Washington Post* reports "Rome Puts Modern-Day Gladiators (and Caesars) Under Its Thumb." Gladiator reenactors in Rome, both male and female, from this point on will be required to be licensed and to conform to city rules for authenticity. Reenactor groups, the Roman Centurions Association, and the Roman History Group with its Gladiator School, thus gain semiprofessional status in a move "to protect Rome's tourist image."[92]

Entertainment reenactments may very well be ephemeral in ways that maximize the desire for consensus stabilities but at the same time sharply limit their temporal period of authority and salience (commercial, educational, national). The reenactments of, say, museum exhibitions, in contrast or in combination, create a greater range of *temporalities in play simultaneously*, and thus their temporal delimitations are more broadly flexed in scale-making practices intended to widen and expand such salience and authority. In other words, their stabilities are intended to be longer, to cover more content, indeed may hope to "democratize" knowledge.

Controversy as publicity might in limited cases be helpful, but controversy as "noise" that needs to be filtered out to achieve such stabilities may be damaging or even devastating. How are stabilities and consensus, on the one hand, telescoped, opening and collapsing in black-boxed elegance or over capacious detail, or, on the other hand, cascaded and branded in multiple ranges of accessibility, servicing well or ill all the necessarily distributed processes and things of flexible knowledges under globalization? In the final section of this chapter we will consider DNA time-traveling technologies as used in a series of TV shows to explore emergent popular formulations of race and gender. These attempt to network among transdisciplinary knowledges that labor with different grains of detail, among very divergent knowledge worlds, and without a contemporary consensus that authorizes ethical practice or maintains representational stabilities. These networkings are literally displayed and mobilized in movements between the web and television, all of which become materially "networked" among commercial, scholarly, and entertainment infrastructures.

TIME-TRAVELING TECHNOLOGIES:
SECRETS OF THE DEAD'S SKINS

At the time of the broadcast of *Secrets of the Dead*: "Amazon Warrior Women" (August 2004), the website for PBS's series *Secrets of the Dead* was a graphically and conceptually sophisticated CSS-skinned conjunction of an ongoing temporally diverse range of TV shows. Offered as "Crime Scene Investigations Meet History" it listed shows as "case files," "current" and "active," with drop-down menus for cases and links for educators with

"Media-Enhanced Lesson Plans." This style or "skin" changed April 23, 2008, but sections—including those for "Amazon Warrior Women"—as of 2010, are still active online, while main pages are archived as updates with this skin via the Internet Archive's Wayback Machine, a digital time capsule of web pages.[93]

From this site itself in 2007 it was impossible to figure out easily any broadcast order for these "cases": this skin had consolidated them all in its forensic crime scene investigations (*CSI*) style, servicing them as cases with pedagogical entertainment at the middle school and high school levels. (CBS's *CSI: Crime Scene Investigation* depends upon pleasures in forensic reenactments; it set the style for a range of its own CBS spin-offs as well as for similar shows created elsewhere.) However, that the *Secrets of the Dead* shows were produced starting in 2000 and that this *CSI* skin came to link them over time became clear, with a bit of web archaeology: if you persistently clicked on "background" and "about" links for each show in its "case" format, the site's archaeological web layers (typesites?) were still available and became apparent.

The first version of this website still around then was Flash driven (that is, Adobe Flash or Macromedia Flash, an animation software). You could see its game-based and still visually arresting if somewhat dated simulation environment if you clicked on the "about" links for what turned out to be one of the first four shows. There these animated titles moved around in an early *Secrets of the Dead* site environment. (You can see the entry page still on the Wayback Machine's links for 2000.) Now constituting "Season 1," these shows were: "Catastrophe," broadcast in two parts May 2000, and "What Happened to the Hindenberg?" from a year later, with "The Lost Viking" and "Cannibals in the Canyon" sometime in 2001. Another show included in the *CSI*-style site has its own alternative website with some minor Flash elements (in its "timeline" pages) as well: *Secrets of the Pharaohs*, a three episode series of its own, now incorporated into this skin as another title in *Secrets of the Dead*.[94]

The skin in 2007 appears to owe this *CSI* configuration to the lively lesson plans and other school curriculum- and resource-driven elements now "value added" to the airing of the shows themselves. Classroom "use"—reenactment experience value rather than Flash game "animation"—reenactment experience value is added here. Credit pages still active include not only the TV production credits and the web credits but also the pedagogical credits: "Victoria Babcock lives near St. Louis, Missouri, where she has taught science for 10 years, including high school biology, botany, zoology, and physical science, and middle school general science. She has started and coached Academic Teams at the high school level. Before becoming a public school teacher, Victoria was involved in informal science education as part of the St. Louis Science Center's Outreach team."

Thus this *CSI*-style site was an analogue to the Hands-On Science Center at the Smithsonian's *Science in American Life* exhibit, with its own web ontology and televisual connections and complications. Its strategies for "democratizing" knowledge are pedagogical. As Latour teaches us to ask: How do they manufacture this knowledge and how well? How does the *CSI*-style repurposing accomplish this?

FORENSIC ANTIRACISMS AND DNA TIME-TRAVEL TECHNOLOGIES

Not all but many of the shows in the ongoing PBS series *Secrets of the Dead* involve DNA analysis as their time-travel technology. In this they participate in a range of PBS-styled documentaries, on either public television or on Discovery or the History channels, or maybe, say, National Geographic Channel or Animal Planet. The *Journey of Man* from the UK Tigress Productions, in which Spencer Wells, head of the (US) National Geographic's Genographic Project, "uncovers vital pieces of the genetic jigsaw puzzle that at last solve the mystery of how Homo sapiens peopled the world," is paradigmatic.[95] Others might include *African American Lives*, coproduced by PBS/Thirteen and Kunhardt productions, which, in addition to PBS, History, Discovery, and the Learning Channel, produces documentaries for Bravo, HBO, and AMC, not to mention CBS and ABC.[96] (Peter W. Kunhardt previously worked at ABC News. He is a cofounder of the International Freedom Center, the proposed museum intended to memorialize 9/11 on the site of the former World Trade Center.[97])

Such DNA time-travel technologies are gender and evidence specific and are incorporated into a range of racializations and antiracisms as well as into heritage histories and culture. For example, UK Tigress's *Journey of Man* does not mean "man" generically. While it stands for "human" here it does so in a pointedly gendered form, that of the heritage investments in the trail of the male Y chromosome and the genetic markers that operate its time-travel, tree-branching machinery.

Spencer Wells's *Journey of Man* narrative includes melodramas of sharing and comparing presuppositions in alternative or conflicting social worlds. Although the framing narrative does not destablize a normative universal science operating its DNA machinery, in his interactions with those whose DNA samples he has been given and to whom he returns to discuss his results, Wells represents his science not as universal, but as a kind of story that matters to his own people, comparing it to stories that matter to various people from whom he has asked for genetic samples. Some groups he talks to are only men, some include both men and women. With some he comes to a kind of agreement about the meaning of the DNA histories he has extracted, others flatly disagree, and some interactions reveal misunderstandings about the purpose of the samples taken, represented in fairly respectful but still comic relief.

Intended, with the strongest forms of evidence, to epistemologically reposition biological race in a range of worldly processes, some of *Journey of Man*'s televisualities may nevertheless inadvertently participate in essentializing race and gender, as when it honors its participants by valorizing the images of particular men whose DNA provides evidence and in its taste for a utopian photographing of people of mixed race who conform to pan-European conventions of beauty, drawing heavily on that Celtic fusion heritage package of the European Union. Not coincidentally Spencer Wells's US National Geographic Society's Genographic Project is working hard, with some but limited success, to address criticism that it exploits the biological and cultural property of indigenous peoples, a charge of biocolonialism. This project is a laboratory not only for mapping the peopling of the globe, but also for the politics of biopower and for one sort of strategy for reordering "race" among remixed, indeed recombinant biological categories.[98]

In a US Kunhardt variant, *African American Lives* adds to such PBS styles additional elements of HBO and AMC celebrity entertainment, commercial advertising heritage campaigns, academic intellectual entrepreneurship, all along with the travelogue tourisms essential to most documentary TV. The host, Henry Louis Gates Jr., serves as a model for one sort of intellectual entrepreneurship under academic capitalism in his role here and elsewhere of startling innovator of a particularly packaged form of "accessibility" in cross-race academic and mainstream broadcast forms. (Indeed Gates had used the phrase "intellectual entrepreneur" to name himself in 1999.[99]) This TV show, according to its companion website, "takes Alex Haley's *Roots* saga to a whole new level through moving stories of personal discovery. Using genealogy, oral history, family stories, and DNA analysis to trace lineage through American history and back to Africa, the series provides a life-changing journey for a diverse group of highly accomplished African Americans: Dr. Ben Carson, Whoopi Goldberg, Bishop T. D. Jakes, Dr. Mae Jemison, Quincy Jones, Dr. Sara Lawrence-Lightfoot, Chris Tucker and Oprah Winfrey."[100] With similar intentions—that is, redisplaying what counts as evidence—to those inspiring Spencer Crew's variant dioramas of the eighties at the NMAH in the *Field to Factory* immersive exhibit, Gates and his producers (melo)dramatize in this documentary a range of genetic and other historical methods and scholarly innovations, filling in gaps in the personal histories of specific and variously famous African Americans. Many such gaps are the result of the effects of slavery on what counts as historical record. Such scholarly methods are depicted among varying forms of reenactment, as are the travelogue elements pulling them all together.

Strikingly similar to the (commercial) curatorial practices fantasized by the Reynolds Foundation for the NMAH, in her own enterprising way Winfrey has spun off her own materials from this documentary in *Oprah's Roots, An African American Lives Special*.[101] It has its own companion book, authored by Henry Louis Gates Jr., while the DVD version, with only thirty minutes of excerpts from the broadcast, concentrates on the scholarly imaginations of "genealogists, historians and geneticists featured in the program and in the original *African American Lives* series." That it also "uncovers Winfrey's maternal great-grandmother Amanda Winters's remarkable achievements in the field of education" justifies Winfrey's interests in the Oprah Winfrey Leadership Academy, intended to produce as leaders an elite cadre of young women in Winfrey-similar styles of intellectual entrepreneurship in South Africa.[102]

DNA technologies used in *African American Lives* are carefully contextualized on the *African American Lives* website in (un-black-boxed) detail not possible within the series itself, given levels of (black-boxing) simplicity and dramatization required for its aesthetics of narration and its effects of accessibility. The television explanation as reenactment is scaled as much as possible at a "black-boxing" elegance of "show, don't tell." But offering additional verbal levels of telescoping detail, the website is remarkable not just for clarity, but also for the ranges of proportion and perspective possible when both "showing" and "telling." Scope and scale are opened, closed and shifted with promoting and demoting hyperlinks either associative or increasing in depth; for example, in explanations of Y chromosome and mitochondrial DNA lineage testing and population proportion "admixture" testing of nonsex specific chromosomes. The whole *African American Lives* series works to reenact implicitly what the website says explicitly: "The results of DNA testing, admixture and lineage testing alike, are in themselves relatively difficult to make sense of. Without an understanding of their cultural, genealogical and historical contexts, it is hard to make sense of what the percentages and genetic markers might mean."[103]

Gates's own genetic heritage test results especially require technologies of scale and scope, provided not only by the additional databases needed for more specific comparisons of markers associated with populations, but also that of experts on the slave trade and on the history of African Americans in Colonial America. And the results are used on the website counterintuitively to belie (and sometimes confirm) assumptions about race, history, and slavery:

> His mtDNA [mitochondrial DNA] tests revealed the most matches in northern Europe and only a single match on the African continent, in northern Africa, near Egypt—very unusual for an African American; who would expect to find European matches in his Y-chromosome lineage, among his male ancestors. [Referring back to website descriptions of white owners' sexual abuse of slave women.] But Dr. Thornton and Dr. Heywood, working with documentation of Dr. Gates' family, parts of which had lived as free people since the time of the American Revolution, developed a well-supported hypothesis: that Dr. Gates is probably descended, on his mother's side, from two indentured servants, living during the colonial period, a black man and a white woman. . . . [Admixture] test results were then compared against a database of individuals from several West African ethnic groups. The results of the analysis show where the subject's markers are clustered relative to a known African ethnic group. In this way, he found a close match for Dr. Gates among the Mende people—introducing him to his distant relatives and revealing, at last, his roots in Africa.[104]

Such observations about various framings of DNA time-travel technologies, and the labors required to scale and scope them, variously ranging along lines of some possible and simultaneous "realities" and "fictions" of race and gender, are tools we take up as we turn to an episode of *Secrets of the Dead:* "Amazon Warrior Women." Two emergent fields referenced by these DNA time travels shift scales and scope among "race" and "gender" there: the field of phylogeography, that is, the genetic study of the origins and dispersal patterns of humans, and the field of archaeogenetics, or the analysis of ancient DNA.[105]

ARE THEY MYTHICAL OR REAL?

In 2004 Washington, DC's Story House Productions produced *Secrets of the Dead:* "Amazon Warrior Women" in association with Thirteen/WNET New York, National Geographic Channels International, and ZDF, one of Germany's, indeed Europe's, largest broadcasting companies.[106] In that complex ecology re-representing warrior women in reenactment it literalizes questions about how all these entities and beings here act together, are set into motion and animated in and among social worlds with radiating out consequences for intellectual, moral, and political meanings.

"Amazon Warrior Women" reenacts a research expedition of the "second-career" archaeologist Jeannine Davis-Kimball, perhaps one female inheritor of the mantle of such entrepreneurial explorers as Hiram Bingham (mentioned at the beginning of this chapter as perhaps the model for movie adventurer Indiana Jones). With a PhD in art history and archaeology from Berkeley but not afterward on the faculty of a university, Davis-Kimball is executive director of her own nonprofit institute and organizations, among them Zinat Press and the Center for the Study of Eurasian Nomads.[107] Exemplifying a career path alternative to some academic disciplines in one sort of typicality, she exploits the much more capacious history of alternative institutionalizations realized within archaeology, as a field only sometimes academy specific and many times most unevenly supportive of women. As a researcher, talking head, or participant she has appeared in the Learning Channel's *Russian Amazons, Nova*/Channel 4's *Mysterious Mummies of China,* the History Channel's *Amazons,* Channel 4/Discovery's *Gladiatrix,* and Discovery Canada's *Ancient Clues.*

Necessarily an intellectual entrepreneur, Davis-Kimball's work shifts among layers of alternative and authoritative knowledges relative and relational among various communities of practice. She herself creates institutions and collaborations that continually refresh and reposition her work along these axes. She maintains her own website, a venue from which vectors an array of social worlds: scholarly and museum vectors out of the United States, the UK, Eastern Europe, and a recombinant Russia after the fall of the Soviet Union; popular press and television interconnected out of her Time-Warner book *Women Warriors: An Archaeologist's Search for History's Hidden Heroines*, which might be thought of as a companion book to "Amazon Warrior Women" and these other TV shows, although not marketed as such; and articles on the web and in collector enthusiast venues like *Archaeology* magazine, but also some in what could only be called "cult" worlds of feminist goddess interest.[108] Her website attempts to facilitate access to funding opportunities for students and excavators, and itself solicits funding "from history buffs and archaeological and ethnographic aficionados to help students financially participate in an archaeological excavation, necessary to complete their school requirements."

Davis-Kimball is only too well aware of the entrepreneurial skills required for any kind of archaeological funding today, academy centered or nationalisms addressed or property inflected, as an interview with her from the *Secrets of the Dead* website explains: "There are several factors involved in excavating—you have to have a site you want to excavate that has the potential for new discoveries, and you have to consider the cost. It has become extremely expensive to put together an excavation, and a lot of the focus on research in the Middle East has gone to contemporary issues—Islam, terrorism—which don't affect me in archaeology, but decrease the availability of funding."[109]

The documentary opens with a *Xena* reminiscent mini-reenactment of women warriors "beautiful, graceful and blond." The excavation of a burial site is reenacted for 2004 as a "live" happening by Davis-Kimball, her collaborator from the Russian Academy of Sciences, Leonid Yablonsky, and their students digging as we watch. A mid-point tour of the Munich Antiquities Collection is cast by Davis-Kimball as a search for "blond and tall killer beauties" amid the vase paintings; "they had their television too," she jokes. And it is a young "blond" girl whose discovery completes the documentary, looking very much like Davis-Kimball herself, clothed in matching red and with similar personal coloring, connecting them together as pastpresents across the image of a woman warrior.

Davis-Kimball's understandings and the production's mobilizations of DNA time-travel technologies forensically and phylogeographically are dramatized at two pivotal narrative moments in "Amazon Warrior Women." First, having realized—that is, now taking up opportunities to *make real*—the possibility that a person uncovered in the reenacted grave site excavation with the weapons that usually signify a warrior might be a woman, she and the German (captioned) "forensic anthropologist" Joachim Burger, of the University of Mainz, collect DNA samples of this and similar burial remains from a bone archive and genetics lab in Samara, southern Russia, as part of their effort to test whether such persons are female. After six months of analysis at Berger's own ancient DNA lab in Germany, they find out that they are. Second, having hypothesized that the buried woman was a warrior priestess, and having manufactured an associative "lineage" of Amazon representations—from the Munich Antiquities Collection, among artifacts from the Ölgii, Mongolia museum's nomad family collection, and with reenactments by an archers group of Ölgii office workers displaying weaponry and costumes similar to those found in pit graves and depicted on Greek vases—Davis-Kimball predicts that a group of present-day Mongolian nomads might be genetically related to this buried woman, and she goes in search of a "blond" and "Caucasian" individual in that group whose DNA might be related to that of the woman buried. She finds such an individual, a young girl, who indeed via DNA analysis turns out to be genetically related to the "woman warrior."

The documentary narrative produces all these associations grouped together as authorizing evidence for the historical existence of Amazon women warriors, as do most popular web interpretations of the material, and indeed at least one interview with Davis-Kimball on a feminist goddess website hyperlinked from her own. Davis-Kimball does appear to warrant this interpretation in her talking-head support in the documentary. However, her own scholarly and popular work is actually somewhat more circumspect about what counts as evidence and argument, addressing specific and more demanding forms of scholarly persuasion. And genetic, linguistic, and goddess speculations are remixed in this networked reenactment of a range of scholarly and other controversies collapsed and telescoped in an uncomfortable word, only and flexibly used by Davis-Kimball in the show, but displayed and implicitly reframed in the production, the word "Caucasian."

The scholarly figure never mentioned but always present in this documentary is the charismatic, both valorized and trivialized, Lithuanian American feminist archaeologist, Marija Gimbutas.[110] Women, gender, and archaeology are haunted by her methods, speculations, and influences, and Davis-Kimball's own person and figuration cannot escape from these lingering comparisons, present, even for those viewers who do not know of Gimbutas, in the kurgan, or pit grave sites, of these possible women warriors.

With a PhD in archaeology from Tübingen, Gimbutas was professor at UCLA from the sixties almost to the nineties. She combined archaeology, linguistics, and mythology to support her "kurgan hypothesis" of the origins and migrations of peoples speaking Proto-Indo-European language, influences still fundamental if differentially controversial within and about Indo-European studies today. "Kurgan" is a (now) Russian term for burial mounds and is associated with pit graves like the one Davis-Kimball excavates in "Amazon Warrior Women." Toward the end of her life Gimbutas contributed to a particular and popular feminist version of prehistory in which patriarchal nomadic warriors invade peaceful goddess-worshipping matriarchal agriculturalists.

Stronger and weaker versions of this explanation, or other points of focus among Gimbutas's work, also vary along axes of authoritative and alternative knowledges, as associated with particular subfields common to several disciplines and using specific types of scholarly evidence, linguistic, archaeological, and DNA based. For some scholars, perhaps a majority in classics for example, the matriarchal focus of the kurgan hypothesis or related speculations are now unquestionably superseded. For others—ranging from studies in prehistoric religion, to current phylogeographic studies, such as those anchoring Wells's genographic project—several recombinant elements, especially linguistic ones, are prioritized and are still quite viable, even understood as one necessary context to the examination of these communities' "things" at fine-grained levels of detail. Davis-Kimball's own cascaded Amazon warrior women refuse any easily debunkable simple split between warrior men and agriculturist women, remixing warrior, woman, priestess, nomad, raider, and trader in a variant feminist intervention into Gimbutas's history of patriarchy, a variant simultaneously accepting as foundational at a different level of detail some naturalized uses of Gimbutas's work in archaeogenetics.[111]

Thus, at one pitch of detail and controversy Gimbutas's work might be thought of as one especially powerful thread through *varying* strategies by feminists for combining women, gender, feminism, and archaeology in flexible reconstructions of its ranging fields, subfields, and communities of practice, attended by some careful and some not so careful debunkings.

And, at an alternate pitch and range of detail and controversy and across another recombinant spectrum of weakly and strongly structured versions, for various others Gimbutas's work is still lively, although quite embedded, in controversies in linguistics, genetic population histories, and excavation archaeologies.

And then, on top of all this, we add Davis-Kimball's use of the word "Caucasian" in the documentary, a term in this context only too infused with all these meanings, local and global, around the geographic and ethnic venues and significance of the pit graves, but also infused in layers of locals and globals with *additional* lively and deadly possibilities. Still used popularly and governmentally as a synonym for "white" in the United States, it and the word "Caucasoid" are also strongly associated with now discredited forms of racial classification and for systems of biological racism, among them Nazism and neo-Nazism. While far more sophisticated and more internally "split" among many subcategories linguistic, regional, genetic, and ethnic, the kurgan hypothesis uncomfortably still can be used to "lump" "Caucasian" in forms with only too many possible white supremacist associations. In racial classification registers these associations are interconnected among Germanic Celtic fusions of race and ethnicity.

Around this word "Caucasian," then, are played in "Amazon Warrior Women" a range of nested contradictory receptions. These are those polyphonies described in chapter 1, in polyphonic use not available for un-black-boxing for audiences, those alternative and sometimes mutually exclusive scenarios. They are produced in "Amazon Warrior Women" by an impossibility of stabilizing consensus at this time among various practices and their relatively bounded communities indexed by the term "Caucasian." Davis-Kimball uses both Caucasian and Caucasoid in the documentary, and in this German-heavy production the terms are *only* used when *she* says them. Both terms can be understood in telescoping layers of locals and globals along the lines of technical languages collapsing deeper and deeper academic subspecialities, sometimes also together with more and more broadly transnational professional practice knowledges. None of these are entirely innocent, and all still bear the burden of and possibly transfer the racisms of past classifications.

All this inflects the DNA time-travel technologies of reenactment in this documentary's epistemological melodrama, only partially available to viewers yet wholly present amid ecologies of re-representation. (This is also true, if differently black-boxed and un-black-boxed, of the Wells's and Gates's documentaries described earlier.) *Showing* and *not telling* has important naturalizing implications among the various practice communities brought together. Not just elegance of narration or effects of "clarity" are at stake. Rather, in addition to these, often desirable, effects, each practice community effectively and accessibly appealed to assign its own naturalized meanings to the objects displayed—objects it recognizes because they are needed for its very own practices, among them debunking —objects such as this term "Caucasoid." At the same time the affective and cognitive sensations of *belonging* or *affiliation* produced by "accessibility effects" makes these "things" (disputable objects) feel more generalizable and stable than a larger ecology of reference, one of many differentially bounded communities, warrants.

One primary use of "Caucasoid" in "Amazon Warrior Women" is as part of a forensic typology used in the United States, where the evolutionary explanatory instabilities and sociological issues and concerns surrounding the term are demoted in favor of its heuristic applications in US courts of law. The differences among juridical so-called racial groups in the United States in craniometry or skull measurements are, arguably within some practice communities, relatively specific and possible to delimit because of (and naturalized by) histories of segregated populations in the United States. Popular and expert meanings are not simply differentiated across authoritative and alternative knowledges amid the multiple practice communities' ranges of use of various boundary objects.

For example, how applicable such practical skull measurement–based racial attributions are beyond such US court-specific identifications is disputed in horizontally mixed community venues such as the "talk" section of the Wikipedia entry on "Craniofacial anthropometry." There distributed authority is displayed amid rancorous debunking discussion of "how the classification that American forensic anthropologists pretend describes race would likely fail, in say, Germany."[112] The transnationalities of such practice classifications are black-boxed by the term "forensic" in "Amazon Warrior Women." But black-boxes are opened, not resolved, not even able to be mapped among forms of authority and popular uses in mixed venue knowledges exemplified by Wikipedia. Boundaries between "science," "nature," and "culture" are challenged in naturecultures of distributed authority. Is this meaning of Caucasoid unquestionably applicable for the purpose of even similar forensic description in a post–World

War II Europe, for example? For political and historic as well as practical reasons? Which naturecultures are in reference here? What sorts of "science" are generalizable or "natural" here?

Thus perhaps not surprisingly, but hardly noticeable, Davis-Kimball is the only one who uses either "Caucasian" or "Caucasoid" in this documentary variously set in southern Russia, western Mongolia, and Germany. The German, captioned "forensic," anthropologist, and (not named) ancient DNA specialist Burger restates Davis-Kimball's use with the phrase "European appearance," while her disappointment with the look of the facial reconstruction of her woman warrior (not blond) is offered for another niche reception as misled, presented by the narrator recapitulating the results of the computer-generated work of the German Federal Police's laboratory in Wiesbaden. "Caucasian" in some venues of "Europe" is carefully, increasingly, specifically tied to actual inhabitants of the Caucasus region, and even there current terminology for an associated biogeographic region is likely to be named the Steppic Region, which is the appropriate reference made by the narrator, Liev Schrieber, when mentioning "ancient Steppe nomads." The histories of Nazism and of African slavery are of course pertinent to if not determinative of all these careful namings that are also responsible to a range of technical professional languages.

However, it is also clear that Davis-Kimball's use indexes other possible and somewhat overlapping, sometimes technical and definitely still debated, treatments for the term "Caucasoid" or for associated DNA "lineage" time-travel technologies. In the climax moments of the narrative, Davis-Kimball exclaims in excitement watching the nomadic young blond girl riding horseback, that she is a "true admixture," a "throw back to Caucasoids who lived in this area," and thus "a reenactment of the ancient warrior women of the past." This documentary sequence is only too available for appropriation by white supremacists, as at least one pan-Aryan website's use of it attests.[113] It is not just Amazon warrior women who may or may not be "real" but also the ghostly matter of "race" inhabiting authoritative and alternative knowledges among DNA time-travel technologies.

Human phylogeography, or studies in human migrations over time and space, of which Wells's genographic project is one sort, deal in complex lattices of haplogroups of either mitochondrial or Y-chromosome DNA; mirrored among taxonomies, these may reenact histories of movement of various genetic lineages. Put most simply, haplogroups are based on differences among nonrecombining portions of DNA. Single-nucleotide polymorphisms (SNPs) that can be traced back in time to the last mutation in that combined set of points on the DNA molecule, and thus back to a common ancestor among all those with this set of variations, are called haplotypes. The term "haplotype" can simply refer to a set of points on the DNA molecule inherited together (as in medical studies), to a gene together with its regulatory sequence (as in genetic studies of animal breeding), or to these portions of the DNA molecules as they have been classified for tracking genetic heritage information. This kind of haplotype information is collected in three ways: by studying genealogical lineages, analyzing molecular data, and making inferences from large genetic databases. Both mitochondrial DNA from one's mother and Y-chromosome DNA from one's father can be analyzed for haplogroup information. Genetic admixtures map multiple haplotypes existing together onto kinds of peoples, usually in complications of race, ethnicity, nationality, and biogeographic regions. At least seven systems for naming and defining haplogroups have existed and there is still no single standard.[114]

The time frames of the National Geographic's Genographic Project are much longer than those for which these latticed haplogroups, along with associated "admixtures," are referenced in the genetic heritage genealogies of *African American Lives*. Even when haplogroups are "roughly" mapped onto US social racial groups in heritage genealogies, their complexities defy any simple one-to-one correspondences, and the resulting confusions are sometimes instructive for participants, as such epistemological confusions present opportunities in *African American Lives* for pedagogical engagement.

With somewhat similar shorter timeframes and practical intentions, that is, specifically scaled and scoped, are the pharmacological and other implications of remixed versions of "race" in medical genetic population studies. Here debunking versions of race as fictive, and heuristic, juridical, heritage, and civil rights investments in realities anchoring whatever "race" is, come together in epistemological melodramas in which denaturalizing and deauthorizing dance about in many couplings. Attempts by professional groups, say, sociologists or anthropologists, in ethical concern to authoritatively anchor biological race as fictive—or to say, with Latour perhaps, improperly constructed—meet with others who may misrecognize, or quite properly recognize, these denaturalizations.[115] They may feel these as erasing their own experiences of racialized discrimination or, alternatively, as producing taboos for research, say medically intended genetic research, or explanations involving racializations social and biological in recombinant dynamics. Scale and scope matter enormously here. Such epistemological reaggregations telescope, cascade, black-box, and use various technologies of accessibility to enormously important purposes. They range over communities of practice so disparate as to make consensus-style stabilities impossible, at least now.

"Amazon Warrior Women" very modestly and perhaps inadequately attempts to destablize the most dangerous of these meanings and to only lightly touch upon some possibly more useful in its production reframings of Davis-Kimball's maybe careful, probably not very careful, use of the terms "Caucasian" and "Caucasoid" in her DNA time travels. The cascading CSI-branded, commercially exuberant pedagogical website instantiating the series as a whole is not a help here, although it might have been, as such websites are becoming one possible location for learning some skills of scaling and scoping. Such skills sorting authoritative and alternative knowledges amid black-boxed or overfull epistemological melodramas are possible and required for responsible movement among communities of practice with their telescoping and cascading meanings and boundary objects, layers of locals and globals under globalization. How to scale and scope in ranges of detail accessibly elegant and specifically important is as much my own problem here in this section as it is that of *Secrets of the Dead:* "Amazon Warrior Women."

ON NOT REFUSING TELEVISION

In the nineties television had to learn not only to "show" but also to "tell," in forms newly interactive and participatory. It accomplished this in not altogether voluntary partnership with the web and, beyond that, in activated partnerships with assertive fans, un-black-boxing educators, and intellectual entrepreneurs who took jobs of "reception" seriously and practiced them in detail. It became necessary to *both* show *and* tell, in new divisions of hyperlinking labor. Multiple products that expanded sensory ranges for commercial reasons were also tasked with hyperlinking responsibilities in embedded and immersive layers among cascading infrastructures. Reenactments became a particular way to both show and tell, reenactors a kind of communication technology themselves, scaled both as persons and also as moveable elements in immersive seas of actants now eddying among knowledge worlds. Reenactment melodramas demonstrated transdisciplinary knowledge practices such as *speaking with things* as well as the affects and ethics of sifting through and managing authoritative and alternative knowledges in a posthumanities.

The boundary work of pitting cultural criticism, or a set of "best" educator practices, in any simple way against the liveliness of commercial exuberance, or the enjoyment of popular comforts and pleasures—as in refusing television or enlisting in negative critique—became moot. Academic capitalism made only too explicit what was already historically a complexly interwoven and multisystemic layering of public infrastructures for education and entertainment.

Now we come to the final chapter, in which we will see how scholarly historiographies end up using TV drama idiom in ways that work to sensitize us to these very alterations in knowledge production under global academic restructuring in the nineties and after. And a core group of academics, after potentially disillusioning experiences with reenactment television, as reenactors themselves, labor to communicate with publics why work with pasts matters and to create a new field, reenactment studies. What kind of transdisciplinary narrative is this? How do new interdisciplines practice close negotiations among memberships? And what kinds of other transdisciplinary practices are also important?

FOUR

SCHOLARS AND INTELLECTUAL ENTREPRENEURS

PART 1. TV DRAMA IDIOM, ACADEMIC HISTORIOGRAPHIES, AND THE MEANING OF RESTRUCTURING

How to evoke the flavour of an obsessional sect of fervently committed Jews from Qumran, the site of the Dead Sea Scrolls, discovered in 1947? . . . The Dead Sea Scrolls are repetitive and difficult to understand. So here I try to capture both the intensity of their religious passion and the difficulty of reporting it now, by using a quintessentially modern idiom, a TV drama, in which all that we see/read is mediated by a simplifying process, of (mis)interpretation. This TV play is set partly in ancient Rome, partly in the modern world. . . . The hero of this play is the TV camera itself, which, like a historical source, arbitrarily selects what it chooses to show, never lies, and never understands.—Hopkins, *A World Full of Gods*

AT THE END OF THE NINETIES a Cambridge economic historian and sociologist, getting ready to retire from his professorship in classics to become vice provost at King's College, produced a dual history and historiography entitled *A World Full of Gods: Pagans, Jews, and Christians in the Roman Empire*. TV drama was one idiom Keith Hopkins chose for working out cognitive sensations such as "immediacy," "intensity" and "empathetic identification" in historical practice and to communicate second-order cognitions in, for example, local and global evaluations of evidence. His chapter 2 on the Dead Sea Scrolls was a reenactment script of the making of an imaginary BBC documentary, called, tongue in cheek, "Dialogues with the Dead."[1]

Also in that same year, 1999, a professor of English and the director of the Center for the Study of Gender and Sexuality at New York University, Carolyn Dinshaw, who discussed "touching on the past" in *Getting Medieval: Sexualities and Communities, Pre- and Postmodern*, described the impact, after the historian John Boswell's death, of coming across in his papers aborted plans from the early eighties for a PBS-style TV documentary based on his book *Christianity, Social Tolerance, and Homosexuality*.[2] In her analysis of this project and the many letters she read among his papers, Dinshaw tenderly and firmly displaces a critique of a "transhistorical" and essentialized gay identity leveled at Boswell's work then and now with a compelling alternative argument for an already-in-place practice of non-essentializing "partial connection."[3] Reflecting upon assumptions underlying scholarly interventions that, at Boswell's expense, valorize "alterity," or the otherness of the past, she remarks how "the distant past is assumed to be too far away to have any relation to the present, while inversely the homosexual is not assumed to be different enough."[4]

A year earlier, in 1998, another transdisciplinary medievalist and pioneering new media scholar, Kathleen Biddick, reprinted as a chapter in her book *The Shock of Medievalism* her 1992 article "Bede's Blush: Postcards from Bali, Bombay, Palo Alto."[5] Originally published in an interdisciplinary collection, this essay spanning the nineties worked out of but reshaped experimental metanarratives associated with postmodern theory, adding to them a particularly literal performative staging, one that layered institutional exigency and multicultural pedagogies and theory.

And Biddick's staging too was "in tension" with "the contradictions of pastism and presentism." She had already noticed how these scholarly urgencies were mixed with other affects and questions in a "double bind" that "divided medieval studies into camps . . . who debate over the epoch in which to locate radical 'past' alterity instead of questioning desires for such a boundary."[6] The third vignette of her article animated genres and figures of feminist postcolonial and postmodern scholarship amid academic restructuring, performing its fictional conversation among four scholars in an institutional moment of the nineties: a dean at Stanford University, where a requirement in Old English had recently been dropped; the Venerable Bede, the eighth-century historian first writing a history of England in the vernacular English language; an Old English professor; and a Chicana feminist theorist chairing a humanities curriculum committee.

The Chicana theorist and Bede, at first gingerly and gradually more companionably, talk about what it means to be "a go-between" among knowledge worlds and among multiple theoretical, linguistic, political, sexual, and racial identities and values in interconnecting webs of power. The Chicana theorist mentions the dual names for Malinche, the emblematic Nahua woman translator for conqueror Cortez and the Aztecs, one decrying her as sellout, the other recognizing her as victim raped. When she asks Bede about his nicknames among his own people, Bede blushes.[7]

With his blush, Bede "admits to his fear and anxiety at the thought of imagining himself as a go-between. He finds the comparisons with Malinche particularly unsettling. . . . As she speaks to Bede, the Chicana theorist ironically realizes that she too has reenacted the art of go-between."[8] Biddick concludes her essay, "The time has come to mark my own performance as a go-between negotiating feminist and postcolonial theory." Her final paragraph quotes, unnamed in the main text, Chicana theorist Gloria Anzaldúa, describing how mestiza consciousness, emblemized by the dual and maybe undecidable characterizations of the go-between Malinche, energizes creativities that examine, restructure, and work with new paradigms as they emerge.[9] Cognitive sensation and affect here skillfully outline webs of power as well as make explicit the risks of translation, cultural brokering, and movement across knowledge worlds.[10]

Naming Gloria Anzaldúa in a delicate performance of the notes allows Anzaldúa, and by extension other literary artists and scholars such as Cherríe Moraga and Chela Sandoval, to model the Chicana theorist for this period over the nineties.[11] If so, read *now* this citation also layers another self-conscious *blush* about the function of a go-between, in or through a restructuring academy. Despite Anzaldúa's remarkable emblematic status in academic feminist theory, when she tragically died in 2004 from complications from diabetes, it was without yet completing her PhD or ever having had the tenure track job in the academy that Biddick's Chicana theorist has. Whether Anzaldúa would have wanted that particular kind of job is yet another question about the practices, tasks, status, and institutionalizations of academic or feminist go-betweens as understood in the midst of changes just on the edge of apprehension. Anzaldúa had had various visiting teaching jobs and was focused full time on her writing while offering writing workshops and traveling on a lecture circuit. She had cobbled together a flexible career among roles and institutions. Whether a regular job with health care benefits might have kept her alive is another question.[12]

Biddick's article is tantalizingly sensitive to emergent issues, open to subtly inflected and differential readings over the decade as academic and feminist interests converge and diverge. It reenacts effects and disappointments that various versions of multiculturalism created and experienced in academies in the United States during the nineties. Debates in women's studies over accessibility and style in academic language and theory; opportunities among careers and careerisms; new positionings of standpoint theory, postcolonial subjectivity, and transnational feminisms; and queer racialized uses and rejections of postmodern method were all elements in changes in academic environments for US feminisms.[13] These shifts are directly reenacted, in the third person, in the interplay between Bede and the Chicana theorist and, in the first person, in Biddick's self-location and disclosure interconnected with the quotation from Anzaldúa. At another scale these shifts are indirectly animated among the venues of its three vignettes: Bali, as node for the anthropologist Clifford Geertz's own transnational reenactment genre of thick description, valorized in medieval studies in the early nineties; Bombay, as site of British colonial administration and education reenacting medieval England's colonization with and by Latin Rome; and finally also, Palo Alto, where, as in this imaginative scene, multiculturalism and its new student and faculty constituencies have their impact on even elite private higher education, in California and throughout the United States. Sensitivities to these changes, barely conscious at the beginning of the decade, are explicitly and literally read from the article by its end.

The density of implication and allusion in Biddick's reenactment, part of its perpendicular performative genre and method, arise not from coy intentions—although there is a lot of sly humor and considerable reflective sadness here—but out of the difficulty of making, and of making *explicit*, these and many more tacit or half-conscious "partial" connections across distributed audiences and genres of analysis important to feminism. Over the course of the nineties this increasingly transdisciplinary range, even just among US feminisms, is actively proliferating and diverging among disciplinary, artistic and commercial literatures, and activist and scholarly political communities. Responsibility to an entire range as it expands, but without control over, or perhaps even knowledge about, its varied contexts of reception and use, motivates both subtle and showy experiments such as those in Biddick's corpus of scholarship, which travels among feminisms, new media practitioners, interdisciplinary medi-evalisms, and histories of technology.

There are also generational knowledges in play, accessed and skilled within a history of televisual experiments in educational entertainment. For US academics schooled in the fifties, sixties, and seventies some old TV shows haunt this vignette as well. Two are Walter Cronkite's *You Are There* (CBS, 1953–57) and Steve Allen's *Meeting of Minds* (PBS, 1977–81). During the mid-century decades either or both could be found on the TV screen and in US secondary school classrooms.[14] Even *now* the thought-fully presentist *You Are There* reenactments can be viewed on DVDs from Netflix; you can be personally addressed and included as Cronkite inter-views Socrates about his choice to poison himself with hemlock rather than submit to exile after ostracism in ancient Athens. Cronkite's inter-views, scripted by blacklisted Hollywood writers, were specifically charged with messages against McCarthy-style witch hunts that were "felt" rather than spoken out.[15]

In contrast, a specifically seventies tone marks *Meeting of Minds* reen-actments, a joking political edge nevertheless quite serious too. *Meeting of Minds* costumed actors spoke, when historically available, quite literal quotations from the figures they re-created—say, as in one episode, from Theodore Roosevelt, Cleopatra, Thomas Aquinas, and Thomas Paine. Hosted in a dinner party style by comedian Steve Allen, these oddly col-lected historical figures created funny new meanings out of anachronistic congruities not exactly accidentally drawn in conversations about contem-porary issues of the seventies.[16] Audiobook versions of the companion book series are now available for download on the web, in a literal and commercial "hypertext" relationship across sensory channels. Cognitive sensation, tacit and contingent knowledge, entrepreneurial intellectual-isms, and deliberatively presentist histories are displayed in such TV drama idiom.

BOTH SIMULATIONS AND REALITIES

This chapter is about how TV becomes a model for, and a simulation and reality of, scholarly activity under global academic restructuring in the nineties and after, as a "posthumanities" comes into being. Some of the scholars described in the chapter, humanists and more, may, blushingly or not, find themselves taking up roles as intellectual entrepreneurs in order to speak to publics in the languages of heritage and enterprise.

The first part examines TV drama idiom as a conceptual sensorium—a way of *feeling out* tacit and half-conscious "partial connections" among histories bundled with their own historiographies, their own ways of being made. Cognitive sensations associated with such reflexive transdisciplinary practices—the anxieties and reluctances of unlearning, the cares and difficulties of collaboration, the weight of responsibility among only too fragile negotiations adjudicating forms of evidence and authority—are all handled with recursive humors in a range of epistemological melodramas. The classicist Keith Hopkins's work is richly suggestive of some of the rigors and idealizations of transdisciplinary scholarship, and the evocative usefulness of TV drama idiom for scholars working out how practices making, sharing, demonstrating, and using knowledges are changing for them. His funny metaphors for intellectual discovery and interpretation in the idiom of time-traveling reality TV draw upon his experiences with BBC TV history and academic capitalism in the nineties and after. Thoughtful presentisms poke fun at naive assumptions about methodological warranties in professional historical practice.

But why are these appeals to TV drama idiom conveyed at the edge of apprehension? Why are they so allusive and performative rather than beacons of clarity and plain style? Surely television is precisely all about appeals to popular audiences, commercially mandated? This chapter also argues, all the way through, that television is a model for distributed cognition across levels of infrastructure among varying systems materially interconnected as that *thing*, so-called globalization. Responsibilities among ranging networks—through distinctive knowledge worlds, among politically volatile alliances, between niche audiences, among processes and communities just coming into being—position creative actors and agencies not as in control over or perhaps even able to know about all the varied contexts of reception and use of the knowledges they labor to co-create and communicate, but as themselves elements in these processes. Distributed cognition belies assumptions that knowledge is fully available to consciousness or open for elegant management. And cognitive sensations of agency do not have to be limited to feelings of control.

Part 2 of the chapter takes up these issues of distributed being and knowing, of transdisciplinary practice under globalization. And it does so by examining the making of a new field, intensively interdisciplined among close memberships as "reenactment studies," and extensively mobilized among its many infrastructures of cocreation, especially those threaded together by activities surrounding the term "knowledge transfer" in the United States, the UK, and Australia. Academic reenactors are maneuvered by double binds both in a BBC reality TV production and within competing and contradictory local and national mandates to explain what they do, the work of the academy and of humanist scholarship, to publics of entertainment and worlds of work, to federal legislators and restructuring administrators, to governmental and private funding agencies, and to other professionals inside and outside national academies for transdisciplinary social projects.

Transcontextual confusions and gifts are required for a double conscious "play" of learning in mandated forms of transdisciplinary action, education, research, and development. Humor, fun, gaming, and their ironic fears as well as pleasures all materialize in TV drama idiom and reenaction, all themselves elements too in whatever those *somethings* once called the humanities are becoming.

Toward the end of part one the serious play of Cold War gaming over time proliferates among an entire commerce in cognitive technologies, and the term "immersion" reveals another layer of meaning, as that very horizon of realisms terms like "authenticity" and "rigor" in their respective knowledge worlds attempt to manage. Reenactment relies directly on and moves about into this strange history. So in part 2, a discussion of Gregory Bateson's work on play, levels of learning, and double binds provides a backdrop for understanding how games and play are being leveraged for many networked reenactments amid all these flexible knowledges under globalization.

ONE-OFF ARTISTRY OR INTELLECTUAL DEVICES OF USE?

Keith Hopkins's experimental historiography, *A World Full of Gods*, was, he offers, the outcome of a failed research collaboration on early Christianity at King's College, Cambridge. The five scholars attempting it discovered that differences among specializations, religious approaches, and even nationality kept them reluctant to synthesize collaboratively or to relearn, that is, to engage in good faith other local meanings. Noting his own "deep resistance to be open-minded, to unlearn the half-unconscious absorptions of childhood and adolescence" even while enjoying the pleasures of historical engagement, Hopkins muses: "So why then don't we incorporate this empathetic wonder, knowledge, pseudo-objective analysis, ignorance, competing assumptions, and disagreements into the text of the book?" These and other "irreconcilable tensions" are *felt* rather than resolved in this transdisciplinary book's various reenactments across chapters— "different methods of historical reportage, description, and analysis, and some of my colleagues' objections."[17]

Hopkins varies reenactment forms as genres of communication across chapters and they include:

— a *report* by hired time-traveling witnesses of Pompeii just before Vesuvius's eruption, paired with a King's College classicist colleague's *letter* evaluating this chapter's scholarship;

— a *screenplay* about the production of a TV documentary on the Dead Sea Scrolls together with a fictional internal *memo* summarizing fictional scholarly reviews of the first cuts of this documentary;

— a framed "objective" *interdisciplinary analysis* intercut with a social scientist's nonreligious *reflection* on what religions package and market;

— a series of retold apocryphal "secret" *stories* of early Christianity, split around a *reaction* from a German theological historian objecting to storytelling as a substitute for disciplinary analysis;

— another *report* from the time travelers who escape judicial torture in Ephesus by using their fictional technology providentially to return to *now*;

— a *letter* from the author announcing the fictional discovery of a letter from an early Christian convert, which includes the text of the discovered letter itself as a series of stories within stories, together with *letters of reaction* to the staging of this essay by a couple of theological friends—one the German historian and the other a US Jew, sophisticated in story style among commentaries such as the Mishnah;

— some self-consciously reflective *retellings* of the not quite Christian Gnostic and Manichaean origin stories, topped off by a fictional *deathbed secret statement* by St. Augustine of Hippo, wondering about the effects of his writings against them;

— and finally, a *formal analysis* of Jesus as a mythological rather than historical figure, together with a *reaction* by a believing British vicar and scholar considering how to use and test scripture for its spiritual values.

Conveying my sense of a scaling or resolution across layers of facticity performed by Hopkins here in genres is tricky, and I mean by "fictional" so very obviously fictional as to be immediately humorous. Hopkins claimed to be delighted when readers mistook less obviously fictional but still imaginary academics' reports, for example, to be actual ones.[18] The ironies here are playful, creative, and cautionary.

And, to add another layer of complexity, the very argument in part one of this chapter is that examining Hopkins's joking about scholarly products also as simulations with varying degrees of resolution across actuality and imagination is precisely *not* about humorously disabling historical skill and forms of authoritative value. Simulation-styled thinking, both Hopkins's and my own, conveys cautions but also makes it possible to value work for varying uses across shifting grains of detail and resolutions of actuality, paying attention to the differential interests in these, as genres among communities of practice in varying knowledge worlds.

Indeed, knowledge worlds come to be so densely packed in Hopkins's book that any attempt at listing them here in some orderly fashion would improperly restrict or fix them. The very experience of being daunted in the face of their fecundity is affectively important. The point of such overwhelming variation is not specification but the cacophony of knowledges in contrast to attempts at close, careful, and controlled analysis by communities of practice.

Hopkins's sensuous depictions with and among knowledge worlds also enroll collections of *things* that their inhabiting communities of practice care about. Things are the very subjects and outcomes of disputation instantiated in objects and methods, assumptions and values. Working as many processes of cognition and institutionalization, the things of Hopkins's book depend upon nonconscious adaptations—simultaneously intellectual, cultural, religious, political, embodied. His many reenactment styles serve as "flashing arrows" for why a particular attempt at collaboration across even some of these knowledge worlds might properly fail. Transdisciplinary scholarship is burdened as well as creatively propelled by double binds, including those in which commercial and academic value are disciplined within a restricted set of niche audiences where authority, reputation, style, grain of detail, and enabling assumptions can be closely negotiated and semiconsciously naturalized and forgotten.

When pivotal *things* should be left implicit or made explicit, in disciplinary or transdisciplinary collaboration, may well be contested on a basis of a proper scaling across grain of detail or on a basis of sufficiently scoping out and relearning when, where, and for whom making assumptions explicit is taken to disable them. Each scholarly reviewer in Hopkins's book simulates, in telescoping and collapsing resolutions of detail, realism, and actuality, how authority recenters itself as it manages its alternative knowledges. Over and over this is the metanarrative across chapters that variously adjudicate among alternate knowledge worlds and the specific things of their communities of practice, some displayed as currently naturalized and conventional but to be newly attended to, others displayed as atypical and assumed to be questionable but here reopened for consideration from various points of view. Although sometimes intellectual "rigor" may be as phantasmatic as "authenticity," it is similarly useful when exquisitely sensitive to its own horizon of possible resources and infrastructures, local exigencies, and differential memberships.

The first extended example of how Hopkins presents himself together with his scholarly reviewers as working at different grains of detail amid varying scales of perspective comes at the end of chapter one of *A World Full of Gods*. Keith and his colleague Mary exchange letters assessing the value of his explicit inclusion of details such as these from chapter one's time traveler's reenactment, from the section, "Room at the Inn (James)":

> Luckily I remembered there was a large public toilet just behind the Forum. Wizened hag at the door took my money . . . made for the nearest seat, incredibly low, but made of stone and clean. Instant relief and looked round. God! I thought, and saw a Goddess looking down, painted on rough plaster, presiding over her twenty-seater. . . . No privacy, just functional, and flushed, intermittently. Men and women mixed; just as well it had been an emergency, might have hesitated otherwise and looked for a quiet corner. Some people went in the street, you could tell from the stink, and the occasional notices painted on walls: "Piss or shit here, and you'll have all the gods after you." . . . I went to a small loo in a bar in Pompeii, with a large painted Goddess Fortuna in a red dress towering over a naked male shitter, squatting on a pair of entwined snakes, the normal emblem of prosperity (plate 1). Symbolically, he was shitting exactly where the household altar normally would have been. So you squat, just as he does, with the Goddess Fortuna looking down at you. Above him, the words are scratched/painted: 'Shitter, shun evil' (*cacator, cave malum*). Is it meant to be

scary, or funny? To complete the ensemble, underneath the painting there was a cheap terracotta altar. So these guys have Gods in (what we would think of as the strangest places) toilets, baths, bars, make fun of them and worship them at the same time.[19]

Positioned as Hopkins's time traveler in his debriefing travelogue, we imagine some of the smells, physical positions, feelings of discomfort and comfort, temperature and texture, on first encountering this reenacted past, detailed empathetically on the basis of a fresco with graffito from Pompeii (reproduced as plate 1) as compared with other excavations connected within this chapter's notes. Intuiting jokes piled upon in-jokes, we also participate in poking fun at the once unspoken but nowadays conspicuously answered typical tourist questions, those that make explicit reactions to alternative systems of privacy and shame as tourists literally see that urban waste disposal systems are not just modern. (Indeed, a similar but less graphic scenario is also narrated by the classicist Peter Aicher when, broadcast the next year, he and Garrett Fagan display for the camera the water systems of ancient Rome in the episode of *Secrets of Lost Empires*: "Roman Bath," described in my chapter 3.)

In other in-jokes we mime typical student humor and Latin scatological display, cultivated in reaction to bowdlerized vocabularies in classics, say, the delicate translations into Latin rather than English within Liddell and Scott's massive Greek dictionary's entries on sex and shit. Both what usually goes unsaid implicitly, as well as what differentially goes for saying in which linguistic register, are sent up in this reenactment. Jokes here move us around and between insider memberships and peripheral participations. They are able to redraw nonessentializing partial connections when this kind of empathetic identification refuses to essentialize alterity, and when it demonstrates practices able to make fun of, worship, and fear all at the same time.

In this chapter's concluding scholarly simulation, Keith's letter to Mary focuses attention on and revalues these *things* conventional historiography leaves out, all these sorts of cognitively embodied sensations at the edges of consciousness, while Mary's letter returns attention to and insists on what authoritative history puts in instead, consensus frameworks of analysis and depth. And, while "immediacy" is something they both value, each speaks of it with varied intonation. Is it mostly a *style* of lively and entertaining transmission for what is already corporately acknowledged, or a continually to be reexperienced and denaturalized *condition and effect* of the making of new knowledge? Mary's postscript suggests books Keith might mine for details that preempt facile receptions by untutored readers, and Hopkins slyly but respectfully adds a note to her sentence that refers to volumes of a recent commanding publication on Roman religion by his Cambridge colleague M(ary) Beard. Although this jovial intellectual sparring occurs in two agonistic views, only one of which "Keith" takes up, nevertheless Hopkins's is actually an animation of a relational range of scholarships, not just a valorization of "Keith's" views, as well as a wistful idealization of professional communication.

Is Hopkins's book too introductory for scholarly colleagues but too scholarly for general readers? Too full of in-jokes and postmodern meta-attentions for many of either? Is it akin to a work of conceptual art, in which its reified end product is but the tiniest bit of the actual labored assemblage in its entirety and where process and intentions are paramount? Or more like a Disney cartoon movie, simultaneously entertaining parents with in-jokes while providing for children apparently innocent narrative? If so, does that make it a one-off work of art or perhaps an educational package strategically marketed, rather than an object or model for scholarly use? Do we really need simulations of scholarly process and activity or reenactment R and D—research and development—*now*? And what role does Keith Hopkins play in all this? Intellectual entrepreneur? Go-between among knowledge worlds? Who is blushing now?

"MORE TOLERANCE THAN I DESERVE"[20]

Before his death in 2004 Keith Hopkins's associations with reenactment and TV drama idiom were personal as well as professional. His son, Ben Hopkins, is a British screenwriter, director, and filmmaker, known for an experimental full-length historical feature, as well as for television and film series and documentaries made around and for a multiple cultural Europe; that is to say, one that includes the UK's EU rivals, such as Germany, as well as Europe's edges and aspirants, Eastern Europe, the former Soviet republics, and Turkey.[21] During the so-called British television history era during and after the nineties, Keith Hopkins also was variously involved with film and television production. As "talking head" he worked with the documentary filmmaker Phil Grabsky in two very different formats for television history, one for the "straight" documentary series *I, Caesar* (1997) and the other for the reenactment-heavy, serious-but-played-for-laughs show *The Hidden History of Rome with Terry Jones* (2001). He was also associated with a BBC/Discovery Channel documentary partially based on his own research, Tilman Remme's *Colosseum: A Gladiator's Story* (2003).[22]

Throughout *The Hidden History* series the former Monty Python comedian Terry Jones acts as historical interpreter, meta-analyst, and trickster; in this particular episode, wearing a simple costume, he humorously demonstrates Roman ways of doing things in various present-day settings of ancient activity and engages in interactive commentary with scholarly authorities, one of them Keith Hopkins. *A Gladiator's Story*, in contrast, delivers a re-created drama with voice-over third- and first-person narrations, in which the first-person narration, taken literally from archival materials, together with costuming, set design, and location sequences, computer animation, stunts, and fights, are intended to create as "true-to-life" a historical experience as current scholarship and the technologies of "realism within attainable budgets" allow, all unpacked in bonus feature interviews with the filmmaking crew. For this documentary, Keith Hopkins worked as historic consultant.

Earlier, in 1985, the year Hopkins was elected to the Cambridge chair in ancient history, he did a videotaped interview with Moses Finley, the expatriate self-described "anti-anti-Marxist" scholar fired from Rutgers in 1952 during the second US Red Scare, who had taken up that same chair fifteen years earlier. Produced for the University of London's Institute of Historical Research and their *Interviews with Historians* educational films series, Hopkins's interview noted Finley's eccentric career as the very resource for his celebrated and once iconoclastic insights and methods, most widely known in such works as *The Ancient Economy*.[23]

Finley argued from his own experience for the special value of a broad theory-driven and largely self-taught graduate immersion in many fields, reflecting on his small group of fellow students at Columbia in the thirties informally grappling with "social theory of all kinds." He credited the nomadic democratic socialist and Hungarian expatriate Karl Polanyi for showing him how to take up anthropological literature as a "seed bed for ideas." When Hopkins asked for some central message emerging from his reflections on methodology, evidence, and models in ancient history up through the eighties, Finley replied he had two. One was that surviving documents in Greek and Latin should not be exempt from "rules of rubbish," in other words, not assumed to be exemplary or normative just because they are still around and happen to be all that we have to work with. The other was that "complete skepticism" was called for concerning (any) current corporate knowledge of the ancient world, because what scholars think they know is "not epistemologically possible with the evidence we have."[24] In other words, speculation, always subject to change and always partially ("sort of") fictional, is an integral element in scholarship precisely in connection with whatever currently is available as, or counts as, evidence, and this condition is not something to be denied or elided to produce *effects* of authority and rigor. (This is that liveliness of "revisionism" that Appleby jokes about, as I recount in my chapter 2.)

Like Finley, Hopkins also had an eccentric academic career. He passed more years as a sociologist attentive to economies—at the University of Hong Kong, the London School of Economics, and Brunel University in West London—than in the institutional role of ancient historian. Still, his original undergraduate and graduate degrees were in classics and from King's College, and his most recognized sociological work from the seventies and early eighties analyzed demographic data on Roman society. Two volumes charted the political economy of empire, including slavery, and studied structural interrelationships within the Roman cult of death, including gladiatorial combat and religious sanction. Like Finley, Hopkins challenged the very structure of argument in studies on the ancient world, calling into question the assumptions of inductive logics and epistemologies and forefronting the limitations of evidence and method while yet enthusiastically still committing scholarship.[25] The reenactment R and D of *A World Full of Gods* makes all this virtually palpable and imaginatively economic.

A TRIPLE HELIX

Making knowledge costs money. During the nineties across the Anglophone academies this was no longer taken for granted as neoliberal policies made politically explicit some of the roles states intended their educational systems to play in global economic positioning. *A World Full of Gods* is interlaced all through with jokes about an entrepreneurial post-Thatcher Cambridge where sharing research with new publics is both a requirement and an opportunity. Fictional BBC documentary parodies in Hopkins's chapter 2 show how television takes up the work of scholars and offers it to publics. But they also use that parody to simulate serious materialities of knowledge production in the nineties amid neoliberal imaginings of globalization. And, globalization, it turns out, does not just happen *now*. Multitemporal histories create lively interactions with other globalizing times and places, in varying degrees of proximity and connection.

Hopkins's imagery works among multitemporal histories that do not stabilize easily and do entangle promiscuously:

> The structure of the book is like *a triple helix* of multi-coloured and interwoven strands. The three major strands, Judaism, paganism and Christianity, were each in themselves diverse, complex and changing. They continually interacted, both inside themselves and with their own variants, and externally with each other. . . . To re-experience the thoughts, feelings, practices and images of religious life in the Roman empire, in which orthodox Christianity emerged in all its vibrant variety, we have to *combine ancient perceptions, however partial, with modern understandings, however misleading.* That is the tension and *excitement of recreating and reading a history of a vanished world,* which was once full of harsh realities, dreams, demons and gods.[26]

Metaphor, analogy, simulation—for the nineties, the triple helix offers an incomparable conceptual range for processes of coconstruction. For sociologists of an economic bent it cannot help but be entangled with the influential Triple Helix series of workshops, biennial conferences, and publications associated with Henry Etzkowitz and Loet Leydesdorff. (Their first paper in 1995 on the subject led to their first transdisciplinary conference in 1996 and an edited collection in 1997: *Universities and the Global Knowledge Economy: A Triple Helix of University-Industry-Government Relations.*[27]) More generally the figure of the triple helix is often confusingly entangled with imagery of the DNA molecule. A triple helix structure for DNA had been first hypothesized by the chemist and X-ray crystallographer Linus Pauling in 1953, but within several months the structure for DNA was correctly retheorized in double helix form by subsequent Nobel Prize winners James Watson and Frances Crick.[28] Beginning in 1990 the Human Genome Project came to embody post-physics "big science" in the United States, becoming a "race" between public institutional collaborations (academy with government) on the one hand, and flexible capital private adventures pressuring technological innovation on the other. The excitement of this "race" often dominated what counted as public culture science during the nineties, not only in the United States but elsewhere, with the result that helical DNA imagery became widely available to stand for a range of intricate processes in global knowledge production.[29] For example, the evolutionary biologist Richard C. Lewontin uses the image in the title of his popularizing book *The Triple Helix: Gene, Organism, and Environment* (2000), while DNA helical imagery and knowledge economy analyses were brought together by Etzkowitz and others in transnational forms in the theme paper and opening plenary for the Fifth Triple Helix conference in Turin, "Third Academic Revolution: Polyvalent Knowledge; the 'DNA' of the Triple Helix."[30]

So helical DNA works for Hopkins and transnational others in the nineties as one conceptual sensorium, a venue of and for embodied "reasoning." The classical historian Hopkins works it directly, engaging its resources to grasp at complex mutualities among Judaism, paganism, and Christianity, his history's three main strands, "in themselves diverse, complex and changing. They continually interacted, both inside themselves and with their own variants, and externally with each other." And the economic sociologist Hopkins works it more allusively, virtually at the edges of consciousness, to intuit some forms in which we develop such processes *now*, working and feeling these out within our own flexible cultural economies of knowledge, technologies, and states, because an understanding of this mutuality had become in the nineties also entangled with the triple helix.

ACADEMIC CAPITALISM AND R AND D

The failed collaboration that begins Hopkins's book animates both the opportunities and new industrialized requirements among even humanities scholars, some now enlisted through technology projects and other infrastructure funding efforts for work in groups across institutions or in public-private partnerships in styles of corporate industrial science. Failed or troubled academic collaborations tell us as much as successful ones about politics, training, specialization, and reasons for synthesis among healthy and vigorous intellectual diversities. A *posthumanities* is coming into being.

Hopkins's history is virtually teaming with fruitful and failed collaborations. Their epistemological discomforts are among the book's subject matter. Refusing to resolve discomforts but instead continually reframing them is a new sort of contribution to the kind of methodological work done once by Finley. In this case, it means addressing what can be said to be known about the Roman Empire and its peripheries, given the evidence and material infrastructures corporately available *now*, and attending to, without debunking, what is imaginatively "filled in."

In the collaboration in chapter 1 the time travelers Martha and James are recruited from an ad from 1997 in London's *Time Out*, an actual lifestyle magazine and website, for imaginary "Academic coordinator" Hopkins's expensive, public-private technology history team project. They give his academic startup, "KH Inc.," "sole publishing, film and TV rights" to the written report based on this secret journey by "holographic time-machine," although after January 1, 2000, they are allowed to use it in their own scholarly activity and writings. Which bits of the project count as results, what form they take, how valuable they are for what kinds of reward, and how secrecy figures for products and property or processes and scientific release are all elements of academic capitalism dressing the set for this reenactment.[31]

Later, in chapter 2 of *A World Full of Gods*, we find out that the academic coordinator Hopkins had intended to send the time travelers Martha and James to Qumran, the site of the settlement now associated with the Dead Sea Scrolls, and had applied for funding from the private Leverhulme Trust. But this time-traveling method of ethnography was rejected by the trust as neither practical nor ethical: the board advisors asserted that thoughts and feelings of faith are not inspectable through participant observation and, anyway, covert research was not something they would countenance. So, seeking alternative commercial funding, the academic coordinator instead sends out for review the screenplay of the BBC TV documentary production set out in Hopkins's chapter 2; it is read by a "commercial TV producer interested in religious affairs. In Britain, TV stations have a statutory obligation to produce religious programmes, though I imagine only the pious watch them, so they're always on the look-out for something to fill the screens. . . . The words 'Dead Sea Scrolls' . . . were enough in themselves to catch his populist eye for that micro-second before he junked it."[32] Although in a fictional funding frame it is junked by the BBC, this reviewed TV treatment simulation of a BBC production of a documentary called *Dialogues with the Dead* is the material that takes up the larger part of chapter 2.

These failed funding efforts parody various forms for capitalizing knowledge over the course of the nineties, some already available and others newly emerging. The upper levels of management of multinational Unilever, created in the thirties when palm oil interests in British soap and Dutch margarine merged, make up the trustees for charity Leverhulme as specified by its Victorian founder, William Hesketh Lever. It was on his death in 1925 that the trust was created. Shares in the $60 billion company Unilever provide the trust's income, and the trust actually has funded several projects in ancient history at Cambridge. Other projects have been funded by the public British Arts and Humanities Research Council, restructured in 2005 to take up for a posthumanities what is increasingly called "knowledge transfer" in a broader variation on the more widely recognized and more specific term "technology transfer." Technology transfer names a movement from university *processes* to market *products* that is the basis for what comes to be called in the nineties "academic capitalism."[33]

The fanciful idea that ancient history research might be funded through partnering with culture industries like television is just unlikely enough in the nineties to make this a somewhat painful joke. For one thing, television development projects are usually just as starved for funding as are academic ones, as Hopkins's son Ben knows well. Who would fund whom? And each might or might not actually generate income, together or separately, at best perhaps just breaking even in a university-industry partnership. Yet the entrepreneurship of the idea is also just parallel enough to the startups, spin-offs, and public-private partnerships innovated in the nineties for academic science and technology interests to be able ironically to represent the many double binds of funding "curiosity-driven" humanities scholarship under academic capitalism.

The higher-education analysts Sheila Slaughter and Larry Leslie coined the term "academic capitalism" and described its progression from the UK to Australia to the United States and then to Canada, with hopes that "the concept of academic capitalism will enable faculty, other academic personnel, and administrators to make sense of their daily lives." Over the course of the nineties they researched "the increasing 'marketization' of the academy" and detailed "the rise of research and development (R & D) with commercial purpose." Consolidating this research in 2007, Slaughter and Amy Metcalfe note that the "entrepreneurial units" participating in technology transfer are elements in "new circuits of knowledge that connect the academy to the knowledge economy and make universities an integral part of the innovation process."[34]

Collaborative product-driven technology transfer not only attracts funding, it hopes to generate income. Academic capitalism projects a neo-liberal vision of the university becoming an active market player rather than a passive beneficiary of state support. Yet net benefits of academic capitalism are still in dispute: "The calculus for determining who bene-fits and who pays as a result of these transactions is not yet clearly es-tablished, although the university, as institution, probably puts more into innovation than it receives in return."[35] How can humanities-styled, curiosity-driven research fit into this marketized academy? Is knowledge transfer analogous to technology transfer? Will the values of the knowl-edge worlds closest to the market trump the values of those less able to marketize? And how does TV drama idiom figure in a sort of reenactment R and D for a transdisciplinary posthumanities?

A DECONSTRUCTED MARKET

The feminist technoscience theorist Lucy Suchman analyzed her own ex-periences of corporate collaboration in the nineties at that emblematic site for industrial knowledge work, Xerox's Palo Alto Research Center (Xerox PARC). The labor of newly resident sociologists of knowledge did not seamlessly fit within either a literal or metaphorical production line of products and services. Defensively in good faith they worked to account for this: "We came to see that the problem lay neither in ourselves nor in our colleagues, but in the division of professional labor and the assump-tions about knowledge production that lay behind it. The discontinuities across our intellectual and professional traditions and associated discur-sive practices meant that we could not simply produce 'results' that could be handed off to our colleagues."[36] A proper inability to hand off results simply as "products" may mark many failed scholarly collaborations, in-cluding perhaps the one claimed to initiate Hopkins's book. Literal and metaphorical production lines cannot properly figure a much more com-plex, chaotic, multisystemic range of distributed agencies, skills, practices, and tools now networked among globally restructuring academies, as aca-demic capitalism vies with or includes *other* resident and emergent forms for making, sharing, and using knowledge. In this essay from 2000 Such-man projects out of her former difficulties not yet understood optimal possibilities that could come into being, possibilities she calls "new working relations."

Which metaphors for knowledge making will literally come into being under global academic restructuring is at stake in what at first appears to be just the dressing of sets for Hopkins's entertaining historical reenactments. Emergent forms vying with or included among academic capitalisms recombine assumptions and prescriptions underlying industrial knowledge work as well as underlying variant histories and visions for national academies. Deconstructing such assumptions and prescriptions is precisely what is taken seriously in Hopkins's funny forms of scholarly engagement. What is not exactly a critique, and what is certainly not a simple refusal to participate in new circuits of knowledge, is instead a not really voluntary willingness and resistance to unlearn and relearn conducted at the edges of actuality, consciousness, and adaptation. This is what is now required both of those who think to take control and advantage of changes in process across sectors of knowledge work, as well as of those just now finding their most cherished reasons for doing such work left out. For their part, in and for one range of knowledge worlds and with some urgency, Slaughter and Metcalfe advise scholarly women to alter academic capitalism and "to deconstruct the market," "a difficult task in an era when the 'market' is reified, normalized, and increasingly unquestioned."[37]

But for his part, ten years earlier in a different range of knowledge worlds, after a scholarly career engaging historiographies of markets and at the point of another career shift in administering in the academy, Hopkins does not advise or predict but, instead, jokes around. Multiple possibilities in various degrees of resolution are explicitly and tacitly displayed in admittedly rather pessimistic humors. In Hopkins's epistemological melodrama(s) silly as well as serious futures are narratively set into motion while chance and individual acts of malice are given power too. Leaving up in the air how unique or typical any of these possibilities are "marketwise" keeps markets as useful explanations without universalizing them; the play of deliberative presentisms makes it clear that they are somehow both unique and typical. Hopkins's junked reality-TV treatment depicting this fictionally in-production BBC documentary on the Dead Sea Scrolls is offered simulation style for the work of thinking about making history—its puns all possibilities across reflexive scales. TV drama idiom has become a base upon which Hopkins and other scholars have and are building a conceptual sensorium to experience both emergent roles among academic capitalisms as well as cognitive sensations of agency not limited to control.

ONLY SOME

Globalization changes who we are. Not only does it alter which groups of folks count as any "we" in continually rescaling constituencies and connections, but it also changes the very edges of personhood. Bodies, selves, persons, individuals, humans are neither simply equivalent or singular; they only very roughly map on top of each other in alternate epistemologies, Google style. Even when we do attempt to inhabit these as simply as possible, we find ourselves among add-ons and others too. More and more obviously we are only some of these very objects, devices, things, processes, and trial and error reassemblages that participate in various patterns of self-organizing "learning" happening at differential scales; in other words, we too are elements in emergence. Effects of this realization and our "feeling out" within them are deeply personal and deeply impersonal. They register as cognitions, sensations, and affects. One way we are expressing and developing them is as epistemological melodramas created by reenactment.

Global academic restructuring is a species of globalization process. Universities are venues packing in simultaneous realities in multitemporal histories that interlace, variate, and shift range. Distributive processes of making, sharing, using, and modeling knowledge reach out among networking knowledge economies such that creating a product, addressing readers and audiences, and finding communication styles are all more difficult. In some venues it is assumed that all this entails more carefully or narrowly reified "audiences," even though systems of publication and teaching alter or dissolve amid new technologies of delivery and even while marketing what it is academies can do is only one of many processes for democratizing knowledge.[38]

As just another node in networking knowledge economies, how universities are accountable and how they are funded is also redistributed and repackaged. Closer and tighter adjudication processes may involve mandated collaborations, and authority or productivity measures participate in state imposed audit regimes. On the one hand, in academic *disciplinary* reconsolidations, what were interdisciplinary eclecticisms are shaped into interdisciplines with scrutinized edges, and interdisciplinarity inside disciplines is valued only once it is emptied of antidisciplinary critique.[39] Simultaneously, on the other hand, *transdisciplinary* values in communication, allusive in multiple shorthand bits across knowledge worlds and only roughly mapping together with academies, provoke experiments in oblique performances or writings or of alternative services or products.

This chapter is intended to provide many examples of these. Hopkins's and others' reenactments or uses of TV drama idiom are some. Strange histories come together among these experiments too, histories in which funding and infrastructure mark out a commerce in cognitive technologies.

SERIOUS PLAY

A strange serious "play" of simulations and their associated cognitive sensations of *intensity and immediacy* was investigated and structured in a particular form in the fifties and sixties in the wake of the formation of the US postwar research university, as studied in the early nineties by the science and military cultural historian Sharon Ghamari-Tabrizi in *The Worlds of Herman Kahn: The Intuitive Science of Thermonuclear War.*[40] Subsequently, with funding from the National Science Foundation (NSF), Ghamari-Tabrizi studied simulations produced by Disney and the Pentagon for training troops for Iraq and elsewhere. Previously, for her Herman Kahn book and also with NSF funding, she investigated the initiating US military interest during the forties, fifties and sixties in war games at the RAND Corporation, a nonprofit military policy think tank that can stand as a reminder of funding collaborations producing the research university in the United States. At RAND they needed to know what were these war games, created by a military and university "Cold War avant-garde," and what were they good for?[41] Were they predictive of events? Could their outcomes be used in policy analysis? How "valid" were any of these uses? In the fifties these were all questions without clear answers and without methods for analysis.

> The quality from which the war game derived its realism was its dynamism, that is, its "process and playability." This was the first meaning of serious play. . . . Typically, players finessed the problem of gaming's validity by emphasizing *the intensity of the experience*, itself an untidy anti-concept. . . .

[Lincoln] Bloomfield [former State Department official, MIT Professor of International Studies, and a principal developer of the basic game design at RAND] called the war game "a laboratory in which [crisis] events can be lived through experimentally." [The formidable game designer Clark] Abt suggested that gaming provided "anticipatory experience." . . .

[The Cold War nuclear strategist Herman] Kahn stressed the gestalt of scenario. "[Scenarios] help to illuminate the interaction of psychological, social, political, and military factors, including the influence of individual political personalities . . . and they do so in a form which permits the comprehension of many interacting elements at once."[42]

"Finesse" is an interesting term here, given its associations with card games and strategic play. All the actors involved with these war games had to "finesse," not just those designing the games and those figuring out how to use them, but also, as especially noted by Ghamari-Tabrizi, those attempting to justify the many resources needed to play and evaluate them. Even before war games became the vogue, it was clear that they were very expensive, both time and resource intensive. Nor could they be justified by "outcomes"; outcomes did not yield information not already known.

In other words, war games could not hand off results. The results of games could not be understood as simple outputs for others who had not played the game. Games were more like art forms or craftwork, and there was no "independent way to validate the findings from any game." And the reason they were so labor intensive was because it was never clear how much included detail was enough, how much "rigor" or "authenticity" was needed: "Since a major war would batter every department of life, [game designers] were tempted to expand their model into infinitely complex details in the simulation of reality." Yet, they did have impact. It was their intensity especially, emotional and filled with detail, that altered reactions, fostered both self-awareness and a "feel" for crisis, and just maybe produced "insight"—that "indefinable good, the fruit of the players' tacit knowledge."[43]

Still, the more gaming had to be evaluated by those inhabiting the knowledge worlds of policy outputs, the less it seemed worth the cost. Finer grain of detail and greater resolution could take up weeks of labor by scores of researchers designing the game and its library of "carefully prepared background, strategy, and game-classified papers." Sides justified moves in a series of policy notes, each adjudicated by referees. At the end participants assessed an entire dossier of what had happened. The game itself could take three or four weeks. Having to justify these expenses—the computer time, the months of research work prior to the game itself, the labor of assessment afterward—officials were embarrassed to tell Congress or the media that the State Department was "playing games." Terms like "exercises," "simulations," and "serious play" were used instead, and it was for these sorts of reasons that US war gaming ended up "a somewhat clandestine affair." By the sixties all this was packed together as "the problem of realism," and not being able to claim realist validity was what finally discredited the RAND war games, Ghamari-Tabrizi concludes.[44]

A COMMERCE IN COGNITIVE TECHNOLOGIES

Realism is a horizon that infinitely recedes as its technologies of creation emergently improve. It is so much easier and so much less expensive to debunk realism than to work it, yet investments in realism, over time, can be highly profitable. And what counts as validity, or value, for which users of what "games" among communities of practice? By the nineties the clandestine babies of a Cold War avant-garde had become ubiquitous and were still evolving. The problem of realism or "authenticity" anxiously attending different sorts of gaming (and reenactment) did not hold these emergent processes back. Realism is also, it turns out, imaginatively easy to "fill in." Interactivity allows games to continue to be more and better than their instantiation as "products." Outputs continue to be less important than "process and playability." And gaming is all about contingency as well as about sensations of agency that do not map in some simple way onto conceptions of individual control, although game practice, in various forms or scripts, deliberately works with desires for control and the fulfillment and frustration of expectation. In fact, feeling in control, individually and vicariously, can be an elusive, even hypnotic *reward*, a deliberately deferred reward that hooks right into an embodied neurology and endocrinology of pleasure and action.

"Gaming" has come to refer to objects, practices, and skills in a number of knowledge worlds, from mathematical, economic and systems analysis and modeling, to cultural studies with and of computer and Internet communities, to casino and lottery industries, to university-industry partnerships for gaming software research and development. And television has played some roles in many of these, usually in computer and Internet combinations, although, of course, game shows have long been among the stuff television puts out anyway.

REPOSITIONING INTENSIVE FORMS OF
REENACTMENT AMONG EXTENSIVE ONES

Various intensive meanings of reenactment as understood in particular communities of practice are intertwined here too. Understandably differing communities of practice work to center their own fabrication, conventions, and explanations of reenactment, and there are more and more such communities and practices. Each in itself properly understands its version of reenactment as the most significant, real, or central. And, each of these communities of practice (both scholarly ones studying reenactment, and reenactors producing reenactments) has a history or taxonomy through which this *intensive* version of reenactment is vitally produced. Each may feel that reenactments are objects that they, perhaps alone, are uniquely qualified to address. "Reenactment" may or may not even be the term they prefer for all the things I enumerate as reenactments; in fact, it may even be a term *against* which some define their own special and significant activities. Nonetheless there are some continuities that network among all these, and overlapping concerns can be understood to animate them; indeed the strange histories of militarized gaming offer nodes for attachment. Let us unknot some of these entangled and *extensive* associations.

For most, as intensively used within their own communities to describe their own activities or those of others, the term "reenactment" centers on those *hobbyists meeting together on the battlefields* of, say, Manassas, recreating in their persons and material objects and actions an American Civil War confrontation. These reenactments are usually military in focus, although they also include important concerns about the material culture and place-shaped character of everyday life during the time periods depicted, even more especially as they come to or do include women playing a variety of parts. And somewhat similar reenactments, partly or wholly shorn of military associations, instead focus especially on artful and pleasurable elements of everyday life in historical periods—food, music, crafts, stories, and games—and are re-created for *festivals, fairs, and other celebrations.* Usually separately or even competitively, but sometimes together, these two strains of reenactment produce their own hobby cultures in which research into historical events and objects, community building in person and on the Internet, and volunteer or semiprofessional work for living history sites may be generated. Heritage interests or nationalisms can be represented in these, although some explicitly intend to refuse such associations. "Authenticity" may be used to distinguish between these, or to rank some practices among these over others. This form for reenactment stands for many as its "pure type," what one ought to mean by the term. My own use is often disappointingly diffuse for those who long to address this form of reenactment most carefully and in enough satisfying detail.[45] I hope however that this book will successfully even work with that sort of fulfillment and frustration of expectation, the very stuff all kinds of gaming depend upon, and at this moment offer one deferred reward, a vista very much worth working through levels of analysis to come out upon.

So, to continue with such goals in mind, for some the term "reenactment" might range among such hobby recreations not only in person, but extending out also to *war game simulations* of varying degrees of impersonation: from board games with dice and cards reenacting a specific military battle, to graphically sophisticated computer simulations also with military-style objectives and movements, to the newly under construction war games simulations produced by Hollywood for the US military for training purposes. And to this mix might also be added other similarly constructed simulations with less or without obvious "military" significance. These are often *multimedia fantasy games* modeled upon versions of *Dungeons & Dragons*, which over time have come to include sometimes more or sometimes less media, telescoping, or collapsing among multisensory, kinesthetic, and proprioceptive creativities, from drawing, playacting, game board making, costuming, event celebration, and so on, as well as including, or limited to, sophisticated computer graphic versions.[46] And explicit fantasy elements may be more appreciated in this mix, as groups such as the Society for Creative Anachronism may play deliberatively with issues of realism and authenticity in savvy, joking forms. In some ranges, any "military" elements may shift intensively and alternatively into various styles of contestation or fighting, from individual combat to street-style gang encounters to apprehending criminals and beyond these, merging with other *tournament games*, like baseball or golf.

Despite my way of explaining these here, exactly how these are all materially and historically intertwined with war gaming is reasonably open to question, although emphasizing the intertwined cocreation of military-based and culture-based reenactments might be important. Gender, race, nationality, and nationalism are all evaluative elements in differentially emphasizing some kinds of reenactments over others across a wide range of communities of practice.

More extensively—and this is the level at which my explorations of the work of reenaction are positioned in this book—there are new television versions of reenactments, some of them included within the scope of so-called *reality TV*, others are variations on *documentary TV* techniques. They range from historical documentaries with intensively defined mini-reenactments positioned to illustrate historical points to documentary TV in which the whole show is somehow a reenactment. Sometimes they actually include hobbyist reenactors, sometimes they also mix in an alternatively intensive range of *professionals, semiprofessionals and volunteers, doing first- or second-person impersonations or role-playing* as for living history sites. Other times, inside the reality TV rubric, people chosen in a contest of admission are engaged to "time travel" to another period and try to take up life within material and physically difficult constraints that interactively count as "authenticity" for that program.

Of course film and television might also be understood as always having been kinds of (extensively defined) reenactments anyway, as, for example, when situating TV's historic roots in vaudeville or film's in Lumière-style fantasy.[47] And indeed some gaming analysts detail other fictions of many varieties as simulated worlds in literary products.[48] This most extensive, fully telescoped meaning of reenactment, *modeling "reality" in simultaneous media*, is culturally powerful: the play between realities and things clearly not whatever that thing "reality" is, and things only too closely like "reality," are pivotally entertaining with varying degrees of cultural value and neurological and hormonal pleasure.[49] Which differences between these make a difference—sharply drawn differences or only too shaded transitional meanings, all embracing and even ritualizing constraints or rule-governed systems—these matter enormously in knowledge work. Validity, objectivity, rigor, standardization, explanation, modeling—all these and other essentials of knowledge in production, transmission, and pleasure are at stake when we extensively interconnect reenactment, entertainment, and scholarly production.

For example, historicizing *dioramas in museum practice* centers on epistemological melodramas of collection and colonial appropriation, as the lives of such collectors as adventurers in *travelogues* of places visited and revisited are framed as reenactment with critical meanings and scholarly weight.[50] This sort of critique as it moves among and together with (as objects of study or, better, *things*) the interpretations and interpreters peopling space in *living history sites* and for heritage industries or publics are probably the most academically recognizable form for scholarly interrogation of reenactment (although perhaps without using that term). And the combinations of entertainment subordinated to pedagogical purposes and the transmission of consensus histories, nationalisms, research new and old, are controversial in ways that produce cognitively intensive *feelings* on a "cutting edge." Where entertainment pleasures figure in pedagogical transmission (and for whom) is increasingly impressive in these venues: museums, collections, libraries, websites, historical places and monuments, commemorations of many kinds, even excavation sites. And, of course, universities.

My analysis of reenactment depends quite literally on such insights as Bruno Latour's witty suggestion that "Reason today has more in common with a cable television network than with Platonic ideas."[51] But I would add "a *nineties* cable television network," so that the tense of *now* builds in a clear multimedia and economic historicity for reasoning through a TV drama sensorium. That simultaneity of cable TV's monopoly alongside alternatives for its displacement matters too. And, traveling out of the range of Platonic ideas is also a justification for my assertively *partial connection* to "pure types" of reenactment. Instead, and only too obviously, the stories in this book offer nodes for attachment among those cable networked, season-ending *reenactment aesthetics of production* that *now* inhabit many forms of knowledge management, authoritative and alternative. They characterize sometimes estranged flexible knowledges on the edge of validity, authority, membership, as they border communities in transdisciplinary practice. At stake for my analysis are the only too strangely variant invocations of authenticities or rigorous assessments, these among the infinitely receding realisms that reenactments aspire to and, thankfully, only too obviously can never encompass. Gaming, modeling, serious play, and simulation each name a different Google-style "map" that, densely stacked, creates, across worlds and epistemologies, a specific and material commerce among cognitive technologies.

LEVERAGING GAMES AND PLAY

The anthropologist and cyberneticist Gregory Bateson's transdisciplinary work has been taken up among practitioners and theorists of gaming too. Indeed the term "serious play" is often especially associated with Bateson's research from the forties to the early seventies on formal structures of relationality in social planning, play and fantasy, family systems, learning, and selfhood.[52] This range of Bateson's work has been used in counterintuitive reframings of realism, immersion, consciousness, learning, and system hierarchies, as in the game theory of Katie Salen and Eric Zimmerman.

Salen and Zimmerman's book *Rules of Play* (2004) is a massive textbook, reference, and "conceptual guide" written for "game scholars, game developers, and interactive designers" and is "the first comprehensive attempt to establish a solid theoretical framework for the emerging discipline of game design" (says the blurb on the back cover).[53] Its authors are professionally positioned at a very nexus of transdisciplinary restructuring: simultaneously teachers in universities and schools of design, as well as game industry developers and entrepreneurial educators. Salen is also a film animator and curator as well as the executive director of the Institute of Play, while Zimmerman is the CEO of development company Gamelab and the host of an annual innovation competition for a professional conference of game developers. All these venues for action are among those "new circuits of knowledge that connect the academy to the knowledge economy and make universities an integral part of the innovation process."[54]

Salen's institute, for example, describes its mission thus: "Working across a diverse community of players, the Institute of Play leverages games and play as critical contexts for learning, innovation, and change in the twenty-first century. We bring non-traditional audiences into innovative spaces of production and learning through partnerships with the game industry, academia, government, science, technology, and the arts." In fall 2009 the institute opened Quest to Learn, a new secondary school funded by the MacArthur Foundation and located near the NYC New School campus where Salen is associate professor:

Quest to Learn uses the structure of games to create powerful educational tools. . . . Games work as rule-based learning systems, creating worlds in which players actively participate, use strategic thinking to make choices, solve complex problems, seek content knowledge, receive constant feedback, and consider the point of view of others. . . . Quest is designed to enable students to take on the identities and behaviors of explorers, mathematicians, historians, writers, and evolutionary biologists. . . . Quest is not a school where children spend their day playing commercial videogames. . . . [Instead it] combines what researchers and educators know about how children learn best with the principles of game design to create highly immersive, content-rich game-like learning experiences.[55]

In a form of academic capitalism in which "knowledge transfer" really does work as a broader variation on that movement to products called "technology transfer," Salen and Zimmerman very creatively work the edges of education, art, craft, industry, and university disciplines in the making, although still without making any actual university a player in commercial markets.[56]

THE IMMERSIVE FALLACY

Salen and Zimmerman use Bateson's work on play, and the work of Jay Bolter and Richard Grusin on remediation and repurposing, to counter what they call the immersive fallacy, the "idea that the pleasure of a media experience lies in its ability to sensually transport the participant into an illusory, simulated reality." This idea assumes that increasingly realistic simulations are more pleasurable as they require less and less suspension of disbelief. They quote the literary theorist of electronic textuality Marie-Laure Ryan: "The history of Western art has seen the rise and fall of immersive ideals." And they note "within the digital game industry, belief in the immersive fallacy remains alive and well."[57] To counter these lively assumptions Salen and Zimmerman use Gregory Bateson's work on play to question the whole notion that deep engagement in immersion depends upon its realism, instead asserting a more complex structure of "double consciousness":

On one level, the immersive fallacy actually does make intuitive sense. When we play a game, we feel engaged and engrossed, and play seems to take on its own "reality." This is all certainly true. But the way that a game achieves these effects does not happen in the manner the immersive fallacy implies. A game player does become engrossed in the game, yes. But it is an engagement that occurs through *play itself*. As we know [from their analysis of Bateson], play is a process of metacommunication, a double consciousness in which the player is well aware of the artificiality of the play situation.[58]

As animals and children learn to play they come to know that there are some ways a play self *can* and must be separated from an everyday self, and they learn to perform this separation in interactive cognitive and social communication forms of "not": they amuse themselves by performing the communication "this is not it." The puppy nips, but not hard enough to injure. (Violence? Not.) The teen kisses in spin the bottle, but not necessarily the person they like the most. (Sex? Not.) Yet at the same time there are also other ways in which these selves simply *are not* separated, in certain physiological processes and psychological equivalences. The nip actually hurts a bit, the kissing blush and stammer. A double consciousness of being in both these states at the same time is possible, as Bateson puts it in formal terms, because *play* creates its own commentary in itself about itself as an *intense* and pleasurable interactive dynamism—communicatively social, as well as neurological and hormonal. Such *metacommunications*—or communications about communication—are performed by embodied selves at multiple "levels" of organic and social system, some sequentially, some simultaneously.[59]

Salen and Zimmerman point out that when Bateson explained his theory of metacommunication in logically formal terms he deliberately chose to use in his examples intense and "emotional statements about love and hate [or we could say, nonpejoratively, sex and violence], statements seemingly addressed to someone else outside the frame." These "remind us that the questions of play and paradox . . . are not just abstract philosophical chatter." Such affectively charged examples address "the emotional and social realities games reflect and construct. The metacommunicative state of mind [including body across Bateson's work] is deeply intertwined with the unique pleasures and experiences of play."[60] Intertwined, yes certainly, and together with pleasures are intertwined an entire *range* of affects and experiences: frustration and anger, for example, can tip over into violence in play. An entire range of products and effects in gaming even depends upon this double consciousness of "Violence? Not," "Sex? Not," and "Reality? Not." Play is all about this edge of discrimination and about the shifting of context that makes it meaningful.

Salen and Zimmerman also connect to double consciousness and a sense of something "outside the frame," the socially technological play of remediation described by Jay Bolter and Richard Grusin. Bolter and Grusin describe how *immediacy*, in its successfully experienced illusionism, psychologically and historically continually oscillates with *hypermediacy*, that virtuoso performance that calls attention to the very technologies creating illusionism. "Although," say Bolter and Grusin, "each medium promises to reform its predecessors by offering a more immediate or authentic experience," as these technological claims are realized what also simultaneously develops is a connoisseurship of such creation, which "leads us to become aware of the medium as a medium. Thus immediacy leads to hypermediacy." Salen and Zimmerman point out: "We can also analyze games within this model. The double consciousness of play finds a strong parallel in the process of remediation, which mixes transparent immediacy with a hypermediated awareness of the constructed nature of play."[61] (Real? Not.) Cognitive sensations associated with immersion thus depend upon this double consciousness amid "meta" levels—such as the levels Bateson analyzed as "learning" that I discuss below, levels in hierarchical frameworks logically formal and, as we see here, materially embodied. Some analysts of games note parallels between such formally described levels of learning and the hierarchical structures in which one plays and one creates computer and video games themselves.[62]

You might note here that throughout this book I have used a work-around that addresses some problems with the immersive fallacy as analyzed by Salen and Zimmerman—using "immersion" and "immersive" for a play of metarealities *conspicuously* artificial for reasons explicitly described as historically remediated and repurposed. In terms both economic and technological I connect reenactments within "levels" of infrastructure and system. Thus for my analysis, immersion works as a *commerce in* as well as a *commercial horizon of realisms*, and I situate immersive practices as repurposing cognitive sensation for multiple commercial media.

Bateson's theories of metacommunication—from analysis of play, from abuses of communication in family systems that contribute to schizophrenia, from schematics of learning and paradox—formally work out and among "levels" of abstraction and recursion to show how every object of analysis includes as a possibility enacted within itself (recursion), and simultaneously also at the next level of abstraction (reflection), a necessary frame or context in which it becomes meaningful. This is why scoping and scaling matter so much. This insight was shared in varying kinds of professional detail and formalization among a range of philosophers, anthropologists, game theorists, systems analysts, and mathematicians gathered together in the fields of cybernetics in the fifties, sixties, and seventies. In a kind of shorthand Bateson referred to the whole set of these quite detailed knowledges with a statement by Alfred Korzybski, the founder of general semantics theory: "The map is not the territory."[63]

Bateson's jokes about this tended to animate one side of this dynamism, correcting tendencies toward paradox as one kind of "formal error."[64] Indeed, his was a "playful" emphasis on the "not," like the puppy's bite that signals "I am not attacking you." He also joked, "Language commonly stresses only one side of any interaction."[65] The whole point of making the statement, of course, is because these *things*, various sorts of maps and territories, in practice can be quite difficult to distinguish actually. (The assessment of the learning becomes as important as the learning, say.) And the joke of using the statement in the way Bateson does is that "the map is not the territory" includes as play, in the double consciousness of simulation, *both* the communication "don't mistake the representation for the thing" and *also* the communication "don't take the thing for everything it is about." Bateson was aware and also always communicated that what counts as a map and what counts as a territory is always dynamically shifting up and down levels as one scopes and scales in infrastructural layers of complex systems and among systems in both chaotic and regulated interaction. This latter contrast of systems is the very basis of the term "cybernetics," etymologically commenting on systems both "steered" by a pilot and those "not."

Bateson continually demonstrated concern about the effects of both philosophies of science and theories of political agency that *overvalue* conscious intervention or individual instrumentalism at the expense of a necessarily *non*conscious action of or *partially* conscious attention to what today we call emergence. Emergence is that "learning" that takes place throughout a system and includes as agencies not only people but "worldly processes." It may also include our hopes and intentions for "human flourishing," as Donna Haraway puts it in her transdisciplinary feminist work for a liberatory "posthumanities."[66]

For his part, when Bateson "was laying down very elementary ideas about *how we can know anything,*" he went on to say, "in the pronoun we, I of course included the starfish and the redwood forest, the segmenting egg, and the Senate of the United States."[67] Indeed Bateson insisted that epistemology was "a branch of natural history" and so actually *"bits" in* our material world, not something apart from and only representing it as we usually assume. (As in, for example, common sense distinctions drawn between a binary "abstract" and "concrete.") In fact Bateson claimed that as you become aware—"without being fully conscious or thinking about it all the time"—of epistemology and its abstractions, "you become in a curious way much closer to the world around you" in "a region where you are partly blown by the winds of reality and partly an artist creating a composite out of the inner and outer events." He admitted and joked that, however, "only at very brief moments, in flashes of awareness, am I that realistic."[68]

Please notice here that pointing out that something is overvalued is not equivalent to saying it is not valuable. These are ranges and perspectives, scoping and scaling, not "on" and "off" switches or debunking critiques in which one tosses out the thing critiqued or demonstrates one's pivotal alliances by taking up sides. Nor are those actions always wrong or improper, although they may be in particular "contexts" as Bateson used the term. Scoping and scaling require a transdisciplinary movement or a particular sort of double consciousness in which one promotes simultaneously the proper, say, politics of individual action, while also being open to "feeling out" how such action rarely is determinative. (Preventing the confusions of infinite regress is one reason to keep one's attention on the "not" in "the map is not the territory." Making the important point of acknowledging the dynamic nature of what counts as each, tends to take us to the brink of potentially paradoxical recursion. But double consciousness trains us to be aware of both, simultaneously; that allows us to acknowledge and labor with recursion rather than work to deny it.)

In other words, such movement trains us to investigate as well as understand *how it is that* human instrumentalisms matter without "steering" events wholly, and how many *things* (including nonhumans and processes —some unforeseen, some simply too numerous, or too unfixed and not yet materialized) have yet-to-be-realized elements of agency without being determining in their turn. The grain of detail at which one addresses these issues—disciplinary, locally political, or theoretical—matters too. Some of these processes of agency, including ones yet to be realized, are among what we mean by terms like "self-organizing"—because out of chaotic systems and noise emerge new and, for a time, undecidable patterns, on the edge of terror and possibility. Bateson was well aware that "all that is not information, not redundancy, not form and not restraints—is noise, the only possible source of *new* patterns."[69]

Of that denaturalization or metacommunication that is mistaken for deauthorization or debunking Bateson also joked around (rather than mocked), saying, "Americans . . . have a strange response to any articulate statement of presupposition. Such statement is commonly assumed to be hostile or mocking or—and this is the most serious—is heard to be *authoritarian. . . .* Consequently, to make any statement of premise or presupposition in a formal and articulate way is to challenge the rather subtle resistance, not of contradiction, because the hearers do not know the contradictory premises nor how to state them, but of the cultivated deafness that children use to keep out the pronouncements of parents, teachers, and religious authorities."[70]

LEVELS OF LEARNING AS FORMALIZED BY BATESON

This brings us to Bateson's levels of learning, and, first of all then, this caveat. Logical types, or orders of abstraction from individuals to classes of individuals, provide the basis for Bateson's understanding of levels of learning.[71] Typing both can provide valuable protocols for clarity that reduce logical tautologies and paradoxes but, if taken too easily for representations, may distort specific *dynamics* of relationship in that range of complex processes they could be taken to represent. Bateson was only too well aware of this problem with the kind of formal description he also still found usefully clarifying. And, as we have already discussed, he was well aware of the distortions of conscious description and explicitness itself, as if they were *as exhaustive* as their descriptions attempted to be explanatory. He addressed these issues in various ways over time, making jokes like, "To get from the *name* to the *name of the name*, we must go through the *process* of naming the name."[72] He was perfectly capable of saying this with a straight face and meaning it seriously, although the edges of his eyes would crinkle as the silly repetitions and recursive humor were evident in the words he chose to make his point. He did also say straightforwardly: "In the absence of the distortions of logical typing, humor would be unnecessary and perhaps could not exist."[73]

> It is not intended that the explanations of the phenomenal world which the model [of levels of learning] affords shall be unidirectional . . . within the model it is assumed that higher levels are explanatory of lower levels and vice versa. It is also assumed that a similar reflexive relation . . . obtains among ideas and items of learning as these exist in the lives of the creatures which we study. . . .
>
> It follows that a next task will be to look for examples of learning which cannot be classified in terms of my hierarchy of learning but fall to the side of this hierarchy as *learning about the relation between* the steps of the hierarchy.[74]

In 1979 Bateson said that no conventions for description or explanation of biological organization and human interaction yet existed, "no existing science whose special interest is the combining of pieces of information."[75] He had faith that his work and cybernetics itself offered some steps in that direction (as in the title of the book *Steps to an Ecology of Mind* in 1972). Perhaps what we are beginning to call emergence is becoming that science or, better perhaps, those worlds of knowledges.

So, now the levels of learning as described by Bateson. "Zero learning" is the first piece of what we ordinarily understand as learning, that is to say, it names that receiving of information that can be replicated. It is, however, not yet subject to correction by trial and error and by intention, which is the second piece of a common sense understanding of learning. This "change in the process" of zero learning Bateson names "Learning I," which he says "contains those items which are most commonly called 'learning' in the psychological laboratory."[76] "Context" is what enables attention to this difference between zero learning and Learning I (and to each next level of learning); and context is a metacommunication, up one level or *about* something or itself (reflexive and recursive): "We may regard 'context' as a collective term for all those events which tell the organism among what set of alternatives he must make his next choice. . . . An organism responds to the 'same' stimulus differently in differing contexts, and we must therefore ask about the source of the organisms's information."[77]

Chance and probability, that is to say, stochastic process, always play a role in "choice" here, and context markers and intention may also. So "choice" here is not exhausted by intention, which is only one possibility among several, because all learning "is in some degree stochastic . . . [and thus] contains components of trial and error."[78] Clearly Bateson uses "learning" as an extensive term, one that includes but is not restricted to either humans or individuals. This extensively animated "learning" is broader in meaning than common sense assumptions are likely to allow for, being instead *the very change coming into being* among a particular set of relations and patterns of transaction. You can also see that play and learning are versions of each other, in some ranges of resolution properly treated as the same, at other grains of detail distinguished with appropriate context markers.

Change in the process of Learning I then similarly characterizes "Learning II" as well. At this level correction happens "in the *system of sets of alternatives* from which choice is made." Context markers signal information about these sets. This continues up each level, for "Learning III" and "Learning IV." Learning II may alter "how the sequence of experience is punctuated," Bateson claims, while of Learning III he says, "to demand this level of performance of some men and some mammals is sometimes pathogenic." Both levels include possibilities for exceptional creativity as well as for delusional understanding. Of Learning IV he says it "probably does not occur in any adult living organisms on this earth. Evolutionary process has, however, created organisms whose ontogeny [or developmental abilities, in the meaning here] bring them to Level III. The combination of phylogenesis [evolutionary development of whole species across the span of their occurrence in the world] with ontogenesis [the development of individual organisms over their life span], in fact, achieves Level IV."[79] In other words, Learning IV is a kind of learning that whole species do, not individual organisms. This is one example of the learning of whole systems as one element of emergence, a truly embodied learning in which both embodiment and learning are distributed across an entire species. (Like "distributed cognition" and "distributed human being," embodiment is also a distributed process. Bateson was especially interested in distributed embodiments.[80])

Bateson understood how these levels worked out in formal patterns as here but also that "our immediate task is to give substance" to these definitions.[81] For example, we can say that Learning II is what educators call "learning to learn," that is, when you know how to learn one thing well, it increases your abilities to easily learn more of that thing and also to learn something else. This second sort of learning to learn requires the *transfer* of kinds of learning from one context to another, and that requires using context markers to distinguish among sorts of learning, noticing which apply in particular circumstances. Nor is all learning optimal either: you can learn mistakes that will make functioning difficult as you repeat them over and over, or you can be taught abusively, so that you are punished for understanding what is happening. This second possibility is the basis for Bateson's famous double bind theory (discussed in more detail below).

> Phenomena which belong to the category of Learning II are a major preoccupation of anthropologists, educators, psychiatrists, animal trainers, human parents, and children. All who think about the processes which determine the character of the individual or the processes of change in human (or animal) relationship must use in their thinking a variety of assumptions about Learning II . . . what is learned in Learning II is a *way of punctuating* events . . . [which] is not true or false . . . [and which] have the general characteristic of being self-validating. . . . Such learning is almost ineradicable.[82]

We are getting at the results of Learning II, Bateson thought, when, say, we talk about someone's so-called character. What we are drawing attention to with that term are the *relations* between prolonged or repeated experience and *transaction in particular environments*. In Bateson's words: "His characteristic, whatever it may be, is not his but is rather a characteristic of what goes on between him and something (or somebody) else."[83] Similarly, if we call someone "dominating" for example, we describe how one sort of relation with another person may be transferred to a whole class of relationships with others. Or we can see in the phenomena of transference another example, in which one might produce particular cues to entice another to act in familiar ways one tends to repeat because of the results of earlier Learning II experiences. We can be "aware" of these patterns without knowing their origins or being able to describe the transactions that animate them. Indeed because Learning II is so difficult to alter and its precipitating elements so interactively complex, the change in the process of Learning II that would constitute Learning III is equivalent to, says Bateson, a "profound reorganization of character."[84]

> Learning III . . . must lead to a greater flexibility in the premises acquired by the process of Learning II. . . . If I stop at the level of Learning II, "I" am the aggregate of those characteristics which I call my "character." "I" am my habits of acting in context and shaping and perceiving the contexts in which I act. Selfhood is a product or aggregate of Learning II. To the degree that a man achieves Learning III, and learns to perceive and act in terms of the contexts of contexts, his "self" will take on a sort of irrelevance. The concept of "self" will no longer function as a nodal argument in the punctuation of experience. . . . Even the attempt at level III can be dangerous, and some fall by the wayside. These are often labeled by psychiatry as psychotic, and many of them find themselves inhibited from using the first person pronoun. . . . For others, more creative, the resolution of contraries reveals a world in which personal identity merges into all the processes of relationship in some vast ecology or aesthetics of cosmic interaction. That any of these can survive seems almost miraculous. . . .[85]

We are talking then about some sort of tangle in the rules for making the transforms and about the acquisition or cultivation of such tangles. . . . There is nothing to determine whether a given individual shall become a clown, a poet, a schizophrenic, or some combination of these. We deal not with a single syndrome but with a genus of syndromes, most of which are not conventionally regarded as pathological. Let me coin the word "transcontextual" as a general term for this genus of syndromes. It seems that both those whose life is enriched by transcontextual gifts and those who are impoverished by transcontextual confusions are alike in one respect: for them there is always or often a "double take." A falling leaf [or] the greeting of a friend . . . is not "just that and nothing more."[86]

We are back here at the brink of paradox, surveying the worlds of sublime confusion in sacrament, art, and madness. As Bateson came to appreciate the deep significance of levels of learning among all the entities and agencies of chaotic and controlled systems, in his life he found ways to "give substance to these definitions" by moving within and among communities of animal researchers, artists, contemplatives, and schizophrenics. The very different worlds of scholars and others engaging psychedelics, animal communication, and new age imaginary and actual worlds became resources for thinking with and through transcontextual experience. And it was not so only for Bateson: out of the sixties and seventies such lineages are tacit for generational "character," part of conceptual and material infrastructure for a wide range of cybercultures, media experiments, and intellectual entrepreneurships amid *a commercial commerce in sensation*, as well as among *wide scale forms of social learning* today. These latter among their extensive ranges include even the "learning" accomplished across multiple species as well as the self-organizing feedback found in worldly processes. Maps charting these genealogies may also be bits on scaled out maps for engaging an emergent transdisciplinary posthumanities.[87]

DOUBLE BINDS

This all brings us back then to the notion of a double bind. A double bind is a precisely technical term for Bateson. His work on double binds came out of a stint beginning in 1949 as resident ethnologist at the same VA hospital in Palo Alto that was one inspiration for Ken Kesey's novel *One Flew Over the Cuckoo's Nest*.[88] (Bateson even claimed to have known Nurse Ratched.) In the fifties Bateson was working simultaneously on theories of play, levels of learning, and the communication dynamics of schizophrenia, with funding coming variously from the Rockefeller Foundation, the Josiah Macy Jr. Foundation, and the Family Psychotherapy Foundation's Fund for Research in Psychiatry. (This was during and just after the collaborations he participated in at the so-called Macy Conferences, 1946–53, that established the field of cybernetics.)[89] Doing this work together created intertwined preoccupations with learning and play and how these can go wrong. At the time he was teaching not only the graduate medical students resident at the VA hospital but also folks at Stanford and the California School of Fine Arts.

While at the VA, Bateson developed double bind theory, for which he won in 1961 the Frieda Fromm-Reichmann Award, given for research in schizophrenia by the Endowment for the Advancement of Psycho-therapy of the American Association of Directors of Psychiatric Residency Training.[90] For this work and what developed from it, Bateson is still con-sidered one of the central theorists inspiring family systems therapy. (Frieda Fromm-Reichmann was famous in the sixties for the therapeu-tic technique that occupied the dramatic center of her patient Joanna Greenberg's autobiographical novel *I Never Promised You a Rose Garden*.[91] Fromm-Reichmann had fled the Nazis in World War II after having estab-lished with her then husband, Eric Fromm, a psychoanalytical training institute and hospital in Germany. Bateson was as proud of having known her as of getting the award named in her honor; he offered a eulogy at a memorial service for her in 1957.[92] I remember his great pleasure too when Greenberg shared reminiscences of Fromm-Reichmann in a letter of appreciation for *Steps to an Ecology of Mind*.)

By 1955, in the course of his work for the Rockefeller and Macy grants, Bateson had come to the conclusion that the so-called ego weakness that then was held to characterize schizophrenia, was "induced by experience" and could be understood as

> trouble in identifying and interpreting those signals which should tell the individual what sort of a message a message is, *i.e.*, trouble with the signals of the same logical type as the signal "This is play." For example, a patient comes into the hospital canteen and the girl behind the counter says, "What can I do for you?" The patient is in doubt as to what sort of a message this is—is it a message about doing him in? Is it an indication that she wants him to go to bed with her? Or is it an offer of a cup of coffee? He hears the message and does not know what sort of order of a message it is.[93]

In the talk for a VA conference from which this analysis comes, Bateson illustrated this point with a story of meeting the mother of a particular pa-tient from the hospital, one he had taken for his first home visit in five years. Noticing as he dropped the patient off that the home was furnished like a model home set, complete with artificial vegetation, when Bateson returned to pick him up he presented the patient's mother with some flowers and the comment that he wanted her to have something "both beautiful and untidy." She replied, "Those are not untidy flowers. As each one withers you can snip it off." Bateson recounted at the conference that what he thought was even more interesting than the possible castration metaphor was that she had reclassified the kind of message he was offering, changing

> the label which indicated what sort of message it was, and that is, I believe, what she does all the time. . . . If he [her son, the patient] says, "The cat is on the table," she replies with some reply which makes out that his message is not the sort of message he thought it was when he gave it. His own message identifier is obscured or distorted by her when the message comes back. And her own message identifier she continually contradicts. She laughs when she is saying that which is least funny to her, and so on.[94]

Bateson schematized the ingredients for double bind transaction:

— "Two or more persons"
— "Repeated experience"
— "A *primary* negative injunction"
— "A *secondary* injunction conflicting with the first at a more abstract level, and like the first enforced by punishments or signals which threaten survival"
— "A *tertiary* negative injunction prohibiting the victim from escaping from the field"
— "Finally, the complete set of ingredients is no longer necessary when the victim has *learned to perceive* his universe in double bind patterns"[95]

In other words, whatever the content of the communication itself, all of the metacommunications accompanying it are punitive, nonconsciously conveying the sense that life itself is at risk and that escape from the situation is impossible. This last condition for such abusive interaction is most likely to occur in situations of power, such as when children are wholly dependent on parents for survival, or when adults must work or live under authoritarian conditions. But once this pattern of transaction has been absorbed, even more modestly risky environments will appear to be, or will be revealed to be, similarly structured in double binds. An exquisite sensitivity to the possibility of double binds has been learned.

Although Bateson's work was first and primarily conceptualized at the level of individual patients' own life histories, the theory is adaptable to whole other scales of complex contradiction in multileveled metacommunications. Indeed Bateson's own sensitivity to larger scale social pathologies was part of this analysis as well. Family systems, organizational systems, and social organization are all scales at which double bind theory can be applied and the "schizophrenia" of variously scaled and distributed entities identified. Although the neurology and endocrinology of what today is diagnosed as that class of disorders called schizophrenia is new and powerfully explanatory, Bateson might well argue still that such explanations work to include microlevels of neurological and hormonal metacommunication at other scales of embodied systems. Even the title of Bateson's original talk to the VA in 1955, "Epidemiology of a Schizophrenia," signals that in this extensive meaning schizophrenia is a condition of systems, not a label for a kind of person. At one range it is epidemiological and a matter properly analyzed in terms of public health and ethics among large-scale social systems. (The raucous and ultimately tragic absurdities in that emblematic book of the sixties, *One Flew Over the Cuckoo's Nest*, depict a range of schizophrenic transactions at multiple levels of system.[96])

And, of course, Bateson was developing these theories during that national period in the United States now known as McCarthyism. Such double binds characterized whole structures of political life at this time, and the conditions of risk, survival, and escape were unevenly distributed and appreciated. Some McCarthyites were vocal critics too of public health measures, notably mental health services. (Although according to Gallop polls in 1954 some 50 percent of the US population supported McCarthy, 1954 was also the year in which McCarthy himself came under attack in the course of the Army-McCarthy hearings. ABC television's unprecedented public broadcasts of the hearings were a turning point in public support for McCarthy.[97])

Bateson was also aware that double bind effects might not be simply debilitating or pathological. Normal versions of double binds occur all the time and may impede anyone's ability to distinguish between logical types. Bateson characterized these as being *intense*, that is, needing fine discriminations between kinds of messages for urgent appropriate response; *contradictory*, and this at two different orders of message, each of which denies the other; and finally, *unvoiced*, that is to say, not permitting the metacommunicative statements that check one's choice of what kind of message is appropriate for response, or otherwise making such checks of context impossible, inappropriate, or meaningless. And both sorts of double binds—these relatively common ones and those of much greater abusive effect—also create, in ranges of circumstance to the almost intolerable, conditions that *may* produce new creativities, if survived. Terror and possibility are on edge in double bind experiences, as "transcontextual confusions" require "transcontextual gifts" one may or may not have. Schizophrenia, in Bateson's scaled out meaning, is a likely outcome; enlightenment—perhaps—a possible one.

Religious practices, entertainment, game design, learning, and professional environments may also deal at this edge of double bind, where abusive practices and challenging ones only too easily can be mistaken for each other and in which the crucial context markers distinguishing one from another may be unrecognizable, contradictory, or fraudulent. The next section elaborates this point within another range of applications, where we reexamine some time-traveling television reenactments and their mobilizations of gaming and realism amid the complexities of public communication.

LITTLE SHIP OF HORRORS, HISTORIANS AS HUMANISTS ON THE SHIP

I can see now that we historians were recruited less to provide interpretation or insight than a fig leaf of authority for a fundamentally antihistorical enterprise. All along it was assumed too that history, unlike botany or navigation, could be assimilated by some sort of effortless osmosis. It was not real work: stealing away from deck-scrubbing duty to consult with our books and charts was viewed as malingering. And when we were asked to perform for the camera, it was to answer questions that forced us into banal orthodoxies. Yet even under these dismal conditions, I don't think any of us rejected the reenactment enterprise as intrinsically valueless. Had the program been more open to critical and heterodox interpretations, it might have generated more passion among the viewers. Had it chosen openly to explore the intellectual and emotional challenges of trying to represent the past through contemporary reenactment, it might have been better TV and better history. If we'd been allowed to be openly reflexive about the imperatives of the present or skeptical about our ability to recapture the past, the series might have been enhanced, not derailed, by the intervention of the events of 9/11. If the voyage had explored the passions of the mind as well as of the body, if it had been what Jonathan

Lamb calls "sentimental" rather than "extreme" history—interrogating our psychic interiors as well as our aching muscles—it might have been less one-dimensional and repetitious. Instead, it seems to me to have succumbed to an identity crisis, unsure whether it was historical documentary or reality TV.[98]

In August 2001 a set of academic participants were maneuvered into what can only be called a double bind situation. For a BBC reenactment of Captain James Cook's voyage in the South Seas, they were recruited, reality TV style, to be specialist volunteers and to live on his ship, The Endeavour (reconstructed for the Australian bicentennial in 1988), in circumstances the director, Chris Terrill, was to call "extreme history."[99] As one of them put it, it was only when they arrived for filming that they found out they were to be put through the physical demands of being crew rather than a more protected status of professional. Their inability to escape the situation was heightened on September 11, 2001, when any fun of reenactment was pitted against desperate desires for information about the attacks in the United States and, for some, the desire to be home with loved ones at a moment when individual and national survival seemed to be at stake.[100]

The executive producer for this six-part BBC2 reenactment series titled The Ship was Laurence Rees; formerly head of BBC History, Rees is now creative director of television history. An award-winning filmmaker Rees is best known for books and documentary television on the Holocaust. In fact, his own professional website strictly focuses on this expertise and makes no mention of The Ship at all. (Interestingly enough, back in 1995 he had worked with Terry Jones on The Crusades, and in 2003, the next year following the first broadcast of The Ship, was coexecutive producer of Tilman Remme's Colosseum: A Gladiator's Story, for which Keith Hopkins's scholarship was a source and for which Hopkins worked as historic consultant.) The director, producer, and cameraman of The Ship was Chris Terrill, a former anthropologist and BBC World Service specialist on Africa, who has produced seventy television documentaries since joining BBC television in 1989. Associate producer was Simon Baker, who had joined BBC History in 1999 and had worked with Rees on the award-winning BBC2 series Timewatch. He also wrote the companion volume for The Ship in 2002, and, more recently, the companion volume to a BBC1 series on Ancient Rome in 2006.[101]

Of course the director, producers, and other film folks were not in control of all the distributed agencies set into motion in the course of making *The Ship*. Certainly all were blindsided by 9/11, which threatened the possibility of continuing production at all. Nevertheless in other ways the format of this type of show was already in the process of becoming conventional: a band of volunteers with only partial knowledge of what was entailed were to be didactically required to undergo surprising physical hardships in front of cameras in the service of a kind of historical authenticity. Added to this were conditions in which their everyday social statuses were to be inverted by blatantly uneven distributions of autonomy, of kinds of work, of the possibilities for meeting simple necessities of cleanliness, sociality, and getting things done. Although usually accompanied by claims that *strict* authenticity was never the goal, all these discomforts were positioned nevertheless as prized cognitive sensations, elements in epistemological melodramas still valued for "time-traveling" reenactment.

And to top it off, all of this was to be "fun" and "playful"—adventurous. The participants were to be good sports who showed their mettle, and got face time in the final version, by backing the production one hundred percent—sifting through the experience for parts that were redeemed by "learning" and reframing the show as a kind of game. Such TV double bind gaming has taken this particular reality reenactment form between 1999 and *now*.

Surviving the Iron Age (2000), discussed in chapter 3, was a relatively friendly example of this type of reenactment documentary, and there a follow-up from something similar produced by the BBC in the seventies, *Living in the Past*. However the most dramatic shows in this format were the amazing Wall to Wall "House" documentaries, created from 1999 to 2006, usually in cooperation with Channel 4 in the UK, and inspiring similar public television ventures in Canada, Australia, the United States, and Germany.[102] Each varied these elements slightly, for example, the didactically justified and just on the edge of humiliating shifts of status and autonomy figuring especially in, say, *The Edwardian Country House* (2002, Channel 4) and *Frontier House* (2004, Channel 4/WNET); while a dating game show style humorously commented on the political economy undergirding Jane Austen's novels in *The Regency House Party* (2004, Channel 4/WNET). Being a good sport about, at the very least, having to unlearn things you thought you knew is a feature of all these shows.

Anger, frustration, confusion, manipulation, and even effects on physical and mental health are all filmed deliberatively as play, entertainment, learning, and spectacle, offered and removed in immersive variations on "Authentic? Not."

But in the case of *The Ship* a core group of academic participants eventually were able to turn the tables on at least some of those responsible for their discomforts, by, in their turn, capitalizing on whatever good faith production folks did have in these enterprises. Eventually they reciprocally involved a few of them directly or indirectly in a series of academic conferences and events that took place in the UK, the United States, and Australia from 2004–2008, and which in Australia culminated in a research platform theme at the Australian National University's (ANU) Humanities Research Centre and in the UK fostered a venue for "knowledge transfer" at York University's Institute for the Public Understanding of the Past (IPUP).[103]

I participated in one of the early conference events and contributed to a special issue of the academic journal *Criticism* devoted to the topic of that US conference in 2004 at Vanderbilt University, entitled "Extreme and Sentimental History."[104] At that point three years had passed since the reenactment was filmed but the emotions stirred remained, demonstrated in Iain McCalman's quotation above from his contribution to that special issue, entitled "Little Ship of Horrors: Reenacting Extreme History." Evaluations had shifted back and forth in the knowledge worlds brought together in a transdisciplinary project. These had been and were then being shaped by global academic restructuring in the UK, the United States, Australia, and Canada and by interconnected political economies in television and new media, as well as among national heritage sites, including museums with curatorial imperatives to compete for audiences with entertainment technologies.

A TRANSNATIONAL GROUP OF FOUR

A core group of academics, all present for this Vanderbilt conference in 2004, all represented in the journal special issue, and all participants in the television reenactment of *The Ship*, were: Vanessa Agnew from the German department at the University of Michigan, with interests in music, travel, and racial discourses; Jonathan Lamb from the English department at Vanderbilt University, with interests in maritime travel in the eighteenth century; Iain McCalman, then in the history department at the ANU and an academic policymaker, with interests in multimedia histories and curatorial methods; and Alexander Cook, a PhD student at King's College, Cambridge, but working in Australia as a research assistant to McCalman, with interests in French and British history.[105] All were transnational academics who had in various ways moved among national academies: Agnew with education and fellowships in Wales, the UK, and Germany; Lamb with education in the UK and teaching in New Zealand and the United States; McCalman educated in Zimbabwe and Australia; and Cook educated in the UK and researching (and finally teaching) in Australia. McCalman had at the time just finished a stint as director of the Humanities Research Centre at the ANU, was still then president of the Australian Academy of the Humanities, and very much a nationally recognized public figure, undoubtedly the person with the most academic and social status among this group; although only just followed by Jonathan Lamb, a prominent senior faculty member in an endowed chair at Vanderbilt with an international scholarly reputation. Agnew was then a junior faculty member, although one with unusual and striking credentials, and Cook was still working on his PhD at Cambridge.

The term "historian" was used in its most extensive meaning by the television professionals creating the show and later publicizing it. As individuals among the forty-one volunteers and fourteen working crew described in *The Ship*'s press pack, this group of four were included under the collective classification "British and Australian historians together with scientific specialists including a botanist, botanical artist and astronomer," and first-named in the listing of fifteen "specialist voluntary crew members" as: "Alex, PhD History student (British) . . . Iain, Historian (Australian) . . . Jonathan, Historian (British) . . . Vanessa, Historian (Australian)," while other specialists were tagged as naval historian, doctor, navigator, Royal Navy, botanical artist, anthropologist, and botanist. In a section of the press pack called "The 21st Century Adventure—Crew Members Talk" McCalman and Lamb are quoted as saying, good sport style, and now with full names and some credentials:

> *Iain McCalman—Professor of History, National University of Australia, Canberra:* "We mostly live in our imagination, we mostly live through texts. . . . We don't know what it's like to have to get up aloft and furl a sail or ungasket a sail. It's an impossible fantasy for most people to go

back, physically back in time into the vehicle of the very period that they're studying and that's what we're going to be doing on this voyage. It's a fantasy come true."

Jonathan Lamb—Professor of Humanities, Vanderbilt University: "The project was invaluable: in my work I had sentimentalised life on board an eighteenth-century sailing ship—billowing sails, exotic shores, deep blue seas. I had even sentimentalized the food, the work on watches, washing on deck. . . . However, in reality, I soon found out that you cannot sentimentalise salt pork with bristles still in it, or cracking your head against a beam every time I got up for night watch, and nothing to wash in but the water that came up in a canvas bucket hauled over the side. But the harsher sides of life at sea made the landfalls exquisite. This taught me why so many "paradises" have been discovered by navigators in the eighteenth century. This was a rare insight into my very own area of research and I could only have learnt it by going on the voyage."[106]

Such rhapsodies of learning and fantasy come alive were matched at later moments by other memories, according to McCalman:

In retrospect, I see that I failed to heed some early omens . . . when our muscular, bare-torsoed director decided to tamper with history by making us walk to the *Endeavour*'s mooring through a leech-infested swamp. During the process, he dropped a heavy camera on his bare foot and smashed several toes. Though they were blue-black and contorted, he showed no signs of pain. Up until that moment I had thought that the prospective hardships would be faked for the camera. . . . The historians' complacencies lasted only until we first clambered onto the deck of the *Endeavour*, where we discovered that, unlike the other experts, who were to be treated as supernumeraries with cabins and offices, we would be serving as full-time able seamen. The status of humanists had pursued us onto the high seas. Quite apart from the ignominy, there had been no test to see if we really were able.[107]

And, with due respect to Jonathan Lamb's reflections, the term "sentimental" comes to have many extensive and intensive meanings over the course of events associated with *The Ship*, from the rather common trivializing associations as the term is popularly used, to its professional genre and period associations that sometimes are equally if differently critical, to its rhapsodic uses at particular historical periods, to its increasing associations with a scholarly turn to an analysis of emotion, sensation, and various "affects." "Interrogating our psychic interiors" is how McCalman ascribes its meaning as according to Jonathan Lamb in their collective reflections on the series, in a contrast between the extreme and the sentimental. But that first Vanderbilt conference description seemed rather to conflate these in the last of its six aspects of reenactment as: "extreme or sentimental history, in which the importance of the past is seized on as a personal and affecting experience, more akin to sympathy than to cognition."[108] It seemed to me at the time of that conference that the term "sentimental" was invested with a great deal of debunking intensity—but I was then only partially aware of what had actually happened on *The Ship* and certainly not able to foresee all that this core group of academics would come over time complexly to articulate with the help of this term.

CLASHING KNOWLEDGE WORLDS? DEVILING DETAILS

This was an unusually emotional conference, in fact. Small, indeed a sort of workshop, in the process—I can see retrospectively—of building upon or even creating a new "community of practice," it took up emotional topics, analyzed them with great intensity, and performed its scholarly practices in an atmosphere that sizzled. I was aware of little subgroups plotting together, with spokespeople attempting to mediate. One person who did a great deal of such mediation work was among the three folks from the BBC: Helen Weinstein, later to become director of the University of York's IPUP, was there with both Laurence Rees and Simon Baker. For example, at the time I knew nothing about the particular production people associated with *The Ship*, but Weinstein attempted to clue me in, especially pointing out Rees's stature in the industry. Weinstein had expertise in both radio and television and was particularly known for her work at BBC Radio 4, especially the series *Document*, begun in 1997. With the exception of Otto Sibum, from the German Max Planck Institute, who was scheduled to participate but unable to attend, myself from the United States in women's studies, and Mark Harding, a US independent scholar, all the academics on the program were from English, history, or German departments. With the exception of McCalman, Cook, and Sibum, all the invited academics were in positions in the United States at that time, whatever their native nationality. An additional knowledge world was instantiated by Toby Haggith and Robert Blythe, British curators at, respectively, the Imperial War Museum and the National Maritime Museum.

A recurring point of friction among academics, BBC folks, and the museum curators involved the large interconnected questions of transmission and accessibility: to whom were the fruits of historical research to be communicated and in what forms? Although no one spoke of it in these terms, one element at stake was grain of detail. Concerns about the importance of and the effects of working at a particular grain of detail were pejoratively polarized—either as a criticism of jargon and elitism or as a critique of illegitimate forms of popularization—although all attending were, in principle, in favor of democratic and progressive knowledges created and communicated accessibly. That knowledge has to be made as well as transmitted was only acknowledged occasionally, and then almost immediately bracketed. Even so, the fantasy of reenactment that haunted the discussions was that through reenactment we all might be able, *somehow*, to create, share, and demonstrate the use of knowledges together, in a single democraticized and commercially entertaining package. *How* this might be done however was at stake, and the devil was definitely in the details.

The BBC and museum folks became one constituency for whom particular materialities of production were properly most engaged with the transmission of knowledge. The commercial realities of television, whether public or not, as well as a focus on audiences, sometimes markets, was communicated as populist as well as popular. Attempts at sharing older and newer traditions of television documentary and their complexities were sometimes pitted against a range of fidelities: to historical scholarship and especially details of accuracy and rigor, to representation and an ethics of possibility, to memory and its necessary shifts across affect and changing meaning, and to time-traveling immediacy—or just how close does one get to the past?

Even as one aligned constituency the BBC and museum folks were outnumbered by the academics, although the academics were continually refracturing their allegiances, sometimes siding with a populist emphasis on transmission, teaching and learning, sometimes splintering along lines of discipline and scholarly method. Working archives? Or working simulation for new insights? These approaches were emotionally polarized but in fantasies of reenactment brought together. At what grain of detail? And with what import for scholarly consensus? The only just grasped alternatives for the making of knowledge did not by any means affiliate academics easily. Rigor and clarity were often pitted against each other, even though everyone appeared to believe that there ought to be a way to companion them easily, and even if no one really claimed they could be "assimilated by some sort of effortless osmosis."

I wanted to foreground the materialities of academic capitalism as they affected how we even asked these questions, but my talk was scheduled at the end of the conference and my attempts to bring up these issues all through the talks and discussion were—it seemed to me—marginalized. But I was hardly the only one who felt—accurately or not—that the concerns they wished to make central had become marginalized. While indeed the core academic group from *The Ship* supplied a great deal of the energy for the conference and probably much of the intensity of affiliation, clearly they too were frustrated at getting across some of the collective critique they had mustered following their experiences. And it was also clear that the BBC and museum folks felt deeply misunderstood and misrepresented, positioned on the edge of debunking partisanships. Even more, other subjects and issues not directly related to television or museum forms of reenactment were positioned to the side of these only too arresting and intense engagements.

What counted as "history" scaled across detail from the most extensive uses to several competing intensive uses in professionally technical forms. What history had meant to the makers of *The Ship*, as they named their participants for imagined audiences and positioned them in its epistemological melodrama, was retrospectively quite different from what the core academic participants meant in self- or institutional description and sensibly quite different among scholarly practices. Who owned "history"? Knowledge worlds in transdisciplinary collaboration and competition were outlined in the very emotional investments dramatized in angry or frustrated interchanges, often participated in or overheard sotto voce in semipublic spots. Such affect transmitted various subtexts when some important *thing* affiliating members of particular communities of practice was preempted for boundary work outlining what was "historical" or "antihistorical." Everyone seemed to believe *there was a right way* to do "reenactment." And, although how one affiliated shifted around considerably, most felt that their own community of practice had, if not the answer, at least the best approaches and the most important constraints to be taken into account. Together in this with everyone else, I too felt then, and even now, that, working out from my own communities of practice, I also had some special insights into these issues, insights unmatched by the work drawn from other lines of examination.

INTELLECTUAL ENTREPRENEURS AS AGENCIES

This "Extreme and Sentimental History" conference on reenactment was held in Nashville in April 2004. Two months later, in Canberra in June, at a meeting of the National Press Club, Iain McCalman gave the Telstra Address, televised live on the Australian Broadcasting Corporation's public network to a large national audience. John Byron, executive director of the Australian Academy of the Humanities and inaugural secretary of the Council for the Humanities, Arts and Social Sciences (CHASS), commented later that the "Telstra Address is recognised as one of the key policy vehicles for taking an important message into the public arena, and it provided a perfect context for the establishment of CHASS as a vibrant new participant [as a stakeholder policy entity] in the education, research and practice arena." Under the title "Making Culture Bloom," McCalman told stories that valorized Joyce's *Ulysses* and the commercial and festive celebrations of Bloomsday in Dublin, in a bid to claim for a CHASS economic and educational "sector" a unique offering to Australia's federal agendas in research for innovation. Positioning the CHASS as practitioners of cultural expertise valuable to culture industries, McCalman also pointed to culture industries fueling the Celtic Tiger of Ireland's economic boom and, similarly, an "arts-led economic strategy" in film and television raising GDP in New Zealand. He enthusiastically celebrated these as indicators of the economic value of the cultural expertise that the sector of arts, humanities, and social science as policy player had to offer Australia as well.[109]

Retrospectively, after the global financial crisis of 2008 and with the very visible waning then of the Celtic Tiger, for example, such transsectoral enthusiasms looked, if not actually naive, then maybe premature or perhaps bounded in time or scope.[110] Nevertheless, something that McCalman did here, analyzed instead at a different grain of detail, was to perform or demonstrate a particular kind of agency, one rather similar to that of technology evangelist, that is, a person who publicly promotes a new technology or technological standard, in an effort to build a constituency of early adopters whose practice will in turn work as a kind of demonstration marketing of the devices, brands, skills, and infrastructures involved.[111] Nationalism is expressed in the role McCalman takes up here in both enthusiasm for commercial enterprise and in sincere appeals to national character, resource constraints, and a cultural heritage both unique and transnational. All this is also articulated for the benefit of one's communities of practice, honored, explored, and explained in a bid for attention and meaning on the national stage and for federal decision making.

McCalman did here what humanists all over the world in this last decade are being told they must do: "communicate to the public" why their work matters. And the mandated language for this appeal continues to be that of "enterprise culture" and "heritage culture," the twin motors for translating knowledge work into commercial innovation and for pitching innovation, commercial, and "knowledgeable" (that is, coming from sectors of knowledge production), as the proper instrument for assessment of national value.[112] One might speak of this new cultural role as "intellectual entrepreneur." The African American studies scholar at Harvard Henry Louis Gates Jr. used this term to describe himself in 1999, and with some reference then to simultaneous activities in the academy and with television. (Since then "enterprise culture" and "heritage culture" continue to be the languages he has mobilized for such knowledge evangelization in television sites as described in chapter 3, acknowledging his role in PBS's *African American Lives* in 2006 and its DNA time-traveling technologies.[113])

In 2004 the promise of such intellectual entrepreneurship was palpable. April saw the reenactments conference in Nashville, June saw McCalman's Telstra address, and in between, in the Shrine Dome on the Canberra campus of the ANU, May saw the Fenner Conference on the Environment. It was called "Understanding the Population-Environment Debate: Bridging Disciplinary Divides." These Fenner environmental conferences were begun in 1988, and this one added a somewhat unusual meta-analysis of disciplinary knowledges and collaborative practice to the normal thematic focus on a particular environmental theme. The Fenner conferences instantiate one version of academic capitalism in which tackling large issues at the national level happens in the language of science-knowledgeable economic analysis, while at the same time partnerships are encouraged and partially mandated through funding mechanisms among a very wide range of industry, government, nongovernmental organizations, and academic people, skills, institutions, and infrastructures.

From that conference the products of two other intellectual entrepreneurs illustrate some of the meanings accumulating around the term "transdisciplinary" as it scopes and scales at different resolutions of detail in material contexts of global academic restructuring. One such intellectual entrepreneur is Julie Thompson Klein, a truly amazing institutional actor and scholar from the United States. From the 2004 Fenner conference website:

> Julie Thompson Klein is an award winning Professor of Humanities in Interdisciplinary Studies at Wayne State University in Detroit, Michigan (USA). She holds a Ph.D. in English (Uni. of Oregon) and is past president of the Association for Integrative Studies (AIS) and former editor of the AIS journal, *Issues in Integrative Studies*. Her numerous books include *Interdisciplinarity: History, Theory, and Practice* (1990), *Crossing Boundaries: Knowledge, Disciplinarities, and Interdisciplinarities* (1996), *Transdisciplinarity: Joint Problem Solving among Science, Technology, and Society* (co-edited, 2001), and *Humanities, Culture, and Interdisciplinarity* (forthcoming). In addition to considerable consultancies across North America, including the development of tertiary interdisciplinary programmes, Klein has been very active internationally. She represented the United States at an OECD [the Organization for Economic Cooperation and Development, an offshoot of the administration of the 1947 Marshall Plan in Europe, headquartered in Paris]-sponsored international symposium on interdisciplinarity in Sweden and at UNESCO [the United Nations Educational, Scientific and Cultural Organization, founded 1945 and also headquartered in Paris]-sponsored symposia on transdisciplinarity in Portugal and in France. She has been a visiting or invited lecturer to Japan, Nepal, New Zealand, Brazil, Mexico, Canada and Russia. She was a member of the planning board for the Swiss National Science Foundation's international conference in 2000 on transdisciplinary approaches to sustainability, and in 2003 delivered an inaugural address for a UNESCO Summer School in Uruguay on local development and environmental sustainability in Latin America and the Caribbean.[114]

Klein spoke in one of the two opening plenary presentations; the other was given by Paul Monk, a former academic and Defense Intelligence officer, a cofounder of and managing director of consulting at Austhink, "a critical thinking skills research, training and consulting firm." In their plenary addresses Klein and Monk each offered a set of "tools" for use in the conference: Klein promoted the "big integrative toolkit" and "large family of proven methods" of interdisciplinary *integration*[115] while Monk promoted his firm's proprietary software for creating *argument maps* or "box-and-line diagrams that lay out visually reasoning and evidence for and against a statement or claim. A good map clarifies and organizes thinking by showing the logical relationships between thoughts that are expressed simply and precisely."[116]

For practice, these could be understood as similar entrepreneurial "products" at the conference, offered with analogous instrumental intent for use by participants in workshop fashion. Although the bundles of "practices" they each offered differed, along with their venues of production, each product bundle manages cognitive sensation among connecting infrastructures. Klein's presentation especially worked to realign *resistance* and *openness* across boundaries between disciplinary knowledges ("permeable" and "patrolled" are two boundary conditions she mentions). She presented a history of disciplinarity and a sheaf of handouts to reframe some of the cognitive sensation experienced by participants, that is, to reorder affect, including discomfort, confusion, frustration, even anger, for the purposes of collective problem solving.[117] Monk's software is intended to rationalize the process of translation across various technical languages that characterize the disciplinary knowledges prioritized at the conference. Confusion, irritation, impatience, and similar affects that accompany the cognitive sensations of such translation are to be minimized with claims to simple and precise statements of evidence and authority, displayed in trees of black-boxes to be opened and closed in embedded hierarchies.[118]

What might "knowledge transfer" from humanists (including social scientists among the alliances of, say CHASS) on the order of "technology transfer" from scientists look like? Of these two instantiations, Monk's company would come the closest to a direct analogy with spin-offs and start-ups in a technological mode. (And, although on a different scale, reminiscent of Keith Hopkins's jokes on the subject in 1999.) At this conference his company's product was offered to professionals to rationalize their own work of interdisciplinary integration promoted by Klein. (Since then the product has been promoted as a more common software tool for primary, secondary, and tertiary educators to offer to students, and so rather less ambitious in its claims and uses.[119])

Klein's consultancies are another example of knowledge transfer in the mode of intellectual entrepreneur here. What counts as "transdisciplinarity" in all this is still up for grabs. As are inter-, multi-, cross-, pluri-, anti-, postdisciplinary, and, for that matter, disciplinary formations, practices, institutional structures, cognitive territories, products, or services. Klein has been an indefatigable adjudicator among all these, with relational variations of each across time and for varying venues and uses. Her books from 1990 to 2005 constitute one map for how these terms shifted in their uses and meanings over this time on various global stages.[120] Focusing closely on practices of *integration* for the Fenner conference, Klein pinpointed three variations on all these for the purpose of clarifying strategic interdisciplinary collaborations at this conference (retaining the website's typographical emphasis):

Multidisciplinary approaches juxtapose disciplinary/professional perspectives, adding breadth and available knowledge, information, and methods. They speak as separate voices, in encyclopedic alignment. The status quo is not interrogated, and disciplinary elements retain their original identity.

Interdisciplinary approaches integrate separate disciplinary data, methods, tools, concepts, and theories in order to create a holistic view or common understanding of a complex issue, question, or problem. "*Instrumental*," "*strategic*," "*pragmatic*" or "*opportunistic*" forms focused on economic, technological, and scientific problem-solving differ from "*critical*" and "*reflexive*" forms that interrogate the existing structure of knowledge and education. Theories of interdisciplinarity premised on *unity of knowledge* differ from *a complex, dynamic web or system* of relations. Scope also differs. "*Narrow interdisciplinarity*" involves disciplines with more or less the same paradigms and methods. In "*broad interdisciplinarity*," they differ.

Transdisciplinary approaches are comprehensive frameworks that transcend the narrow scope of disciplinary world views through an overarching synthesis, such as general systems, policy sciences, feminism, ecology, and sociobiology. More recently, the term also connotes a new structure of unity informed by the world view of complexity in science, a new mode of knowledge production that draws on expertise from a wider range of organisations, and collaborative partnerships for sustainability that integrate research from different disciplines with the knowledge of stakeholders in society.

Two overriding considerations arise from this terminology: what is the degree of integration, and what is the purpose of integration?[121]

Klein offers her taxonomy so that the conference members can scope and scale among contexts as she positions the tasks the conference plans to take up. She situates this particular conference within these contexts primarily as needing to practice interdisciplinarity as a kind of instrumental and pragmatic problem solving, while still leaving open reflexive tools required for deciding what is possible among types of integration. Should it be a kind of disciplining unity requiring consensus or a more captious contextualization of semiautonomous systems brought into networking alliances? These are nonpejoratively positioned on each hand with "narrow" and "broad" interdisciplinarity respectively.

Klein's toolkit of proven methods made explicit at the table along with the work of integration itself includes twenty-eight tasks in five areas she outlines under: "Negotiating, brokering, and leveraging knowledge." For example, in the "initial phase" task three is: "Envision a spectrum that is neither too narrow nor too broad for the task at hand"; while in the area of "social learning and communication" tasks twelve and thirteen are: "Craft a hybrid interlanguage" and "Use conflicts creatively to refine and advance the work." And in the final area of "evaluation and dissemination" task twenty-seven is "Articulate findings and recommendations in the public sphere, using all appropriate media from electronic means to informal community-based networks."[122]

May 2004 also saw the publication of Klein's article for the journal *Futures*, "Prospects for Transdisciplinarity," which ends with its own kind of evangelization:

> Forms of multi-, pluri-, and interdisciplinarity do not call into question disciplinary thinking. Transdisciplinarity does, through the principle of articulation between different forms of knowledge. . . . It requires that disciplinary thinking evolves to match the complexity of the issues facing science today. The realization that reality is multidimensional has implications for unity of knowledge as well. The older notion of synthesis, which perpetuated the principle that an object has only one reality whose unity must be reconstituted, is no longer possible. Transdisciplinarity requires deconstruction, which accepts that an object can pertain to different levels of reality, with attendant contradictions, paradoxes, and conflicts. [It has the capacity] to take into account the

flow of information circulating between various branches of knowledge, permitting the emergence of unity amidst diversity and diversity through the unity. A systematic and holistic approach is still possible . . . but in a mode of coherence rather than unity. . . .

Transdisciplinarity was once one of many terms. It has become a major imperative across all sectors or society and knowledge domains, making it more than a fad or fashion. It has become an essential mode of thought and action.[123]

While acknowledging that "transdisciplinarity requires deconstruction," that it works with "different levels of reality," and indeed that these are attended by "contradictions, paradoxes, and conflicts," Klein's entrepreneurial or evangelizing efforts themselves tend to be prescriptively visionary, pushing toward integration and product. (Such a push to product is also how she manages uncomfortable recursions. The difference is clearer if you match this product-driven style of intellectual entrepreneurship to the funny reenactment-style deconstruction Keith Hopkins practices. Hopkins's requires explicit transdisciplinary contradiction, paradox, and conflict to shape and humor its recursive epistemological melodramas. You may remember that these, rightly but uncomfortably, keep taking us to the brink of paradox, one of the nice literal-metaphoric points also made in consequence of his "time-traveling" tropes.)

In 2006, the Australian Government's (then) Department of Education, Science, and Training put out a report titled "Knowledge Transfer and Australian Universities and Publicly Funded Research Agencies." The report examined the state of knowledge transfer funding practices in the UK and the United States as well as evaluating those in Australia. It distinguished between knowledge transfer needed "to enhance material, human, social and environmental wellbeing" and that needed "to enhance the success of commercial enterprises." In each case it called knowledge transfer "the process of [universities and publicly funded research agencies] engaging, for mutual benefit, with business, government or the community" but noted that the term "transfer" tended to imply that this engagement went only one-way.[124] (This is a point that could be connected to the one made by Slaughter when she suggests that universities put much more into technology transfer than they ever get out of it, at least in revenue.[125])

The report noted that although the United States had pioneered technology transfer with the Bayh-Dole Act of 1980, it had not moved beyond that, and indicated that knowledge transfer terminology or funding practice was not a dedicated policy in the United States. In contrast it reported that, for example, in England "in recognition of the importance of university knowledge transfer to the UK's innovation performance, the Government has now committed to a permanent 'third stream' funding programme £238 million . . . for the two-year period 2006–08 . . . 'third stream' funding should be allocated in a way that provides universities with greater certainty about future funding levels and reduces the administrative burden associated with repeated bidding rounds."[126] (This would make the "transfer" less "one-way," at least in one sense.)

It also suggested "that effective knowledge transfer usually requires the intervention of knowledge intermediaries who are able to translate and contextualise academic knowledge to make it 'useable' by non-academic communities" and that a "recent study on knowledge exchange networks . . . emphasises the importance of the human interface in networks, noting that paradoxically the greater opportunity for the transfer of knowledge through the Internet, the greater is the need for skilled facilitators, trusted advisers and 'honest brokers' who can bridge the cultures and interests of the parties to an exchange."[127]

McCalman, Klein, and Monk are all positioned as various versions of such culture brokers, and how they make claim to good faith and fair dealing cannot just be taken for granted. Transdisciplinarity positions standards of all kinds as relative and relational and fair dealing as specific to communities of practice *in formation*. As the epistemologist Sue Stafford points out: "Mature trust is trust that is articulated and reflected upon . . . not taken for granted, [it] . . . is generated dynamically by the explicit and implicit understandings, demands, promises, expectations, and dependencies that characterize knowledge enterprises."[128]

Indeed McCalman's retrospective narrative of his little ship of horrors is an account of trust violated, of communities of practice taking each other for granted, of tacit understandings not shared, of literally divergent levels of reality experienced in unevenly distributed working relations, all together making up that particular television project. And this really was (mostly) the epistemological melodrama *intended*, coming into convention and offered on screen as a reality TV challenge. Yet this melodrama was also coming into companionship, in odd, emergent forms of complexity and transdisciplinary articulation, with other, unintended or differently intended, melodramas among extensively produced and materially distributed epistemologies at other levels of scale and detail. Among these were national projects for knowledge transfer, strangely twined with this intended "reality" drama, where trust, divergent realities, and being taken for granted figure too.

Consider again Kate Hayles's comments on distributed cognition as the framework among which such layers of locals and globals can be scaled:

> the distributed cognition of the emergent human subject correlates with—in [Mary Catherine] Bateson's phrase, becomes a metaphor for— the distributed cognitive system as a whole, in which "thinking" is done by both human and nonhuman actors. "Thinking consists of bringing these structures into coordination so they can shape and be shaped by one another," [Edwin] Hutchins wrote. To conceptualize the human in these terms is not to imperil human survival but is precisely to enhance it, for the more we understand the flexible, adaptive structures that coordinate our environments and the metaphors that we ourselves are the better we can fashion images of ourselves that accurately reflect the complex interplays that ultimately make the entire world.[129]

Networked reenactments as recounted in this book precisely offer demonstrations for understanding *how* some of these flexible, adaptive structures might "coordinate our environments and the metaphors we ourselves are." The academics of *The Ship* quite literally, as well as metaphorically in Mary Catherine Bateson's meaning, worked up an entire set of transcontextual complexities, confusions, and "gifts," coordinating all these in environments promoting knowledge transfer. The skills that the *intended* melodrama of *The Ship* depended upon—among them, the good faith of its participants, even their (properly only sometime) willingness to sift through their experiences for "learning" on the style of trial and error gaming—were also put to use in ranging contexts of national, professional, and personal importance. All of these then could even be made strangely "fun"—as in intellectually satisfying and as in valuing new cognitive sensation. (Although, of course, "fun" has its unpleasant ironies here too.) All of these added-on experiments in knowledge making, sharing, and demonstrating actually became the also rocky but ongoing projects of reenactment in conference after conference and the new institutionalizations animated within such collective intellectual entrepreneurship.

REENACTMENT STUDIES BECOMES REAL

In 2006 Helen Weinstein, another of the participants at the Vanderbilt reenactments conference, became director of the IPUP at the University of York in the UK. The institute's mission is ambitious: not just to transmit academic knowledges coming into consensus but also "to establish and embed new findings and methodologies relating to the matrix of knowledge, education and culture." Notice then, that means to establish and embed new ways of *making* knowledge together with the new knowledges *themselves*. "Establish and embed" also implies structural integration into already existing infrastructures. And the sorts of knowledges pinpointed here are those emerging from the now explicitly inter-defined culture industries into which education has become incorporated by means of the mandates of enterprise and heritage. As it says in its website, the institute works

> to promote academic partnership projects across museums, galleries, heritage and the media . . . [and] draws together researchers, practitioners and audiences. . . .
>
> IPUP bridges academia, the heritage sector and the public to generate new understandings of how identities are constructed and how narratives of the past function in our society. The focus of research goes beyond contemporary and national boundaries, analyzing the uses of the past in earlier and comparative societies.[130]

Notice then also how the term "history" is bypassed in the institute's name and description. As we have seen and discussed so far, nations are ranking education as one element for global economic positioning, scoping and scaling within what we can call the enterprise linkages of neoliberalism. At the same time publics, perhaps unsurprisingly, turn out to be less interested in history, that disciplinary *thing*, than in heritage linkages, especially prizing their own family generations and the contexts that make these meaningful. These then are the very intersections of enterprise and heritage so brilliantly animated for popular use (and learning and play) in, say, Henry Louis Gates Jr.'s *African American Lives*.[131] Such animations, both those of Kunhardt and Gates, and those of Weinstein and IPUP, are direct responses to realities made explicit by one line of scholarship taken up in the midst of the so-called history wars.

For example, they are all indebted to a series of surveys in the early nineties conducted by Roy Rosenzweig and David Thelen that charted several ranges of popular uses of this *thing*, history. Emphasize here the term "use." Rosenzweig and Thelen found that most of those surveyed would not use the term "history" for those practices they most valued revolving around pasts. Even to gather a proper range of data, the surveys themselves needed to use extensive language, needed to refer to activities concerning "the past," because in popular understandings the word "history" belonged to intensive, mostly professional memberships, and for those outside these memberships it meant something "formal, analytical, official, or distant."[132] Two-thirds of respondents valued most *their own* history making, revolving around their own circles of family and friends, and *trusted* most, for truths about pasts, the oral accounts of relatives or the objects viewed at historical sites and museums. Respondents felt *least connected* to pasts depicted in books, movies, television, and in classrooms. They felt *far more connected* to what they saw and interacted with at historical sites and museums and *most connected* to pasts constructed out of their own *uses*. One-fifth of respondents belonged to communities of practice specifically devoted to making, sharing, and demonstrating knowledge of pasts, while two-fifths intensively engaged individually in hobbies or collected materials engaging pasts.[133]

Clearly interactivity, making, and participation are all key to this sort of public feeling for connection with pasts. Rosenzweig concluded that popular historymakers enjoyed most their own versions of history, and while he felt cautious about the extent to which these intensive versions of popular historymakers could be "privatized" narrowly, he actually compared such privatizations to similarly intensive and narrow versions by professional historymakers. He foresaw a participatory history already coming into being, an "active and collaborative" venture between popular and professional historymakers, one that involves "redistributing and redefining the meaning" of historical authority.[134]

In my own contribution to that special issue of *Criticism* titled "Extreme and Sentimental History," I pointed out the ironies by which the critiques by professional historians of so-called presentism are themselves presentist. That is to say, are bought with the coin of a professionally prescriptive "alterity" or imposed "otherness" on that only too wide range of ways of relating to, describing, and using pasts in these very "other" times and places. Such times and places do not just *not* prescribe or even value such critique but positively create and respect many presentist pasts in abundant variety. I used the term "pastpresents" for these, among them many reenactment pasts, to suggest the difficulties of maintaining boundaries between pasts and presents and to question the circumstances of doing so.[135] IPUP's transdisciplinarity similarly rescales, reaching out to redistribute historical authority when it includes "analyzing the uses of the past in earlier and comparative societies." Standing at the brink of these sorts of recursion and paradox however allows for a panorama of transdisciplinary view, momentarily rescaling a professional critique still intensively proper at particular moments for urgent purposes.

You can see that all the television experiments described in this book pick up from such findings and ironies—or intuiting them, work with their implications—and attempt to capitalize (quite literally) on the kinds of shadowing, witnessing, and reenacting we examined in museum installations, bringing all these together into alignment with the distributed working relations of television. And you can also see how reenactment, reenactors, and reenactment studies are themselves also transdisciplinary articulations realigning layers of locals and globals—all these together working out *how it is that* historical authority comes to be produced *among a sea of actants* in old and new distributions and cocreations.

Allying with two ethnomethodologists of science Lynn Mulkey and William Dougan when they point out "museum exhibitions and their critiques are not 'about' experiments, they are 'another version' of them," we too can witness and shadow, point to and understand reenactment, reenactors, and reenactment studies as rescaling versions of each other.[136] Thus the reenactment scholars represented in eddies waving out from or networked around that Vanderbilt reenactment conference in 2004 are actants together with their own *repurposing forms of knowledge in transfer.* Among these are: six transdisciplinary conferences (plus associated graduate workshops) in three countries, gathering together academics, artists, and various other culture industrial professionals, together with a research platform theme at the ANU's Humanities Research Centre;[137] a publication series in reenactment history at Palgrave Macmillan, with two edited book collections, as well as that special issue of an academic journal;[138] and some newly developing projects, not only IPUP at York, but also Donna Landry and Gerald MacLean's "The Evliya Çelebi Ride, a project of historical re-enactment, leading to the establishment of an UNESCO European cultural route, The Evliya Çelebi Way," which is "primarily an equestrian route designed to generate interest in Turkey's vanishing horse culture. . . . Combining the romance of horseback travel in remote but stunning landscapes with rediscovery of Turkey's historical past, it must appeal to all who are concerned to preserve Turkey's heritage through sustainable tourism."[139]

This is transdisciplinary *immersion*—that play of often transnational metarealities historically remediated and repurposed, that commerce in as well as a commercial horizon of realisms, authenticities, and authorities. Indeed, the reenactment conferences all take elements of immersive practice as their topics as well as enact repurposing of these each year: in 2004, "Extreme and Sentimental History: A Conference on the Re-Enactment of Historical Events" (USA); in 2005, "Re-enactment and the Question of Realism" (USA, with graduate workshops at CalTech, Humanities Research Centre Canberra, and ANU House Melbourne); in 2005, "Settlers, Creoles, and the Re-Enactment of History" (USA); in 2007, "Re-enactment History and Affective Knowing" (UK); in 2007, "Art and Re-enactment Conference" (part of research theme at ANU's Humanities Research Centre, "Historical Re-enactment and Public Memory"); and in 2008: "Once More With Feeling: Re-enactment and the Capture of the Past" (UK). The two Palgrave reenactment history collections are entitled *Settler and Creole Re-Enactment* and *Historical Reenactment: From Realism to the Affective Turn*. Such transdisciplinary immersive practices engage in repurposing all this described and enacted cognitive sensation for multiple commercial, academic, governmental, and other public media.

One way to follow trajectories of process as this new interdiscipline of reenactment studies comes into being (using "web action" as described in my introduction) might be to begin now to map it with Google's Flash-generated Wonder Wheel, a data visualization tool debuted in May 2009 and another literally metaphoric form in commercial experimentation with which to practice scoping and scaling. As a baseline, consider that in August 2009 Wonder Wheel maps out three deeper associations for the only seventy-five hits on the term "re-enactment studies" (using quotation marks and hyphen). Among these seventy-five hits are IPUP itself and also one of its interviews, with, in fact, Jonathan Lamb, and about these conferences and this new field. Two associated groupings led out then among other extensive and intensive versions of reenactment as understood in this book. Click on the grouping "re-enactment events"—I got close to eight million hits distributed among: viking, victorian, gettysburg, battle of hastings, revolutionary war, enacting festival, reenactment groups, and historical reenactment. Click on the grouping "re-enactment forum"—mostly linking reenactor discussions and groups on the web—I got almost two million. These were pretty well recursively looped among: allied, nederlands, third reich, ww2 reenactors, ww2 reenactment, axis reenactment, and enactment groups. (The other third, "studies," offered 171 million links to various other fields of study or to empirical case studies of various kinds.) Google mapping data visualizations matched against this baseline and undoubtedly changing over time, could dynamically trace some trajectories of process in layers of locals and globals as various emergences across and including this particular field shift and alter.

In this dynamic version of transdisciplinarity, to be found in other knowledge areas as well, extensive meanings of, here, history and reenactment, cocreate with intensive ones. A new intensive community of practice works out among its close and specialized membership a newly named interdiscipline, in this case so-called reenactment studies (sometimes with a hyphen, sometimes without it). Those members turn up again and again in each repurposing version. At the same time, other extensive inclusions ripple out, engaging a range of knowledge worlds, these not possible to "discipline" or even "interdiscipline" at these other levels of reality and other scales of infrastructure and context. This form of transdisciplinarity permits the play between extensive and intensive repurposings at these different levels of detail, system and innovation, all relative and relational, all scoping and scaling among honored commitments and distributed authority. This is the double consciousness of immersive play, of levels of learning, and of the recursive paradoxes that create and take advantage of transcontextual meaning sensitized by double binds.

CONCLUDING QUESTIONS, CONCERNS, AND INTERESTS

In 1999 the transdisciplinary medievalist Carolyn Dinshaw tacitly contrasted that moment in the early eighties, when two producers seriously considered making a PBS television mini-series based on John Boswell's book *Christianity, Social Tolerance, and Homosexuality*, with the last half decade of the nineties out of which she was writing, when the "absurd projects" of congressional culture warriors worked to eliminate queer art and history and defund the National Endowments for the Arts and for the Humanities.[140] Ten years later, I pick up the *Washington Post* to read how President Obama is forced to work within a complex political double bind set into motion for himself and for his LGBT supporters, as his administration's Justice Department defends the thirteen-year-old Defense of Marriage Act despite the president's declaration that the law is discriminatory. The *Post*'s article uses casually a term unthinkable in the early eighties, "same-sex marriage law."[141] In the mid-nineties, as he died of AIDS, another book by Boswell, *Same-sex Unions in Premodern Europe*, was just being published.[142]

Dinshaw helps us to work transcontextually, at different grains of detail across complex incommensurabilities in time, sometimes in alignment, sometimes not. Her notion of "getting medieval" both allies honorably with alterities—those intensive othernesses Foucault-inspired historiographies work to sharpen and among which "the homosexual" is often understood as a local phenomenon or *thing* of the last few centuries only— and also allies honorably with the "filling in" work an extensive connective tissue of associations and identifications does, in that kind of experimental reconstruction among pasts for which Boswell had to reframe what counts as evidence, in order to display and demonstrate new pastpresents.[143]

"Appropriation, misrecognition, disidentification: these terms that queer theory has highlighted all point to the alterity within mimesis itself, the never-perfect aspect of identification. And they suggest the desires that propel such engagements, the affects that drive relationality even across time," muses Dinshaw.[144] She even mentions the fan letter for *Christianity, Social Tolerance, and Homosexuality* that Foucault himself wrote in rough English to Boswell's publisher in late 1979 (smoothed out eventually as a blurb for the book): "I receive John Boswell's work with thankfulness. . . . It makes appear unexplored phenomenons and this because of an erudition which seems infaillible."[145]

Boswell's book also reached out to popular historymakers and readers who found their identifications to be one element of their interactive engagement with his work. Dinshaw combed through these letters, wondering and reflecting, allowing them to alter her own understanding of historiographic method. A philosophy professor wrote: "Whereas I have often felt intellectual 'friendships' across the centuries—historical thinkers with whom I have felt such strong affinities that I feel I know them and that we speak for one another, I had never felt—until I read your book—that I had *gay* friends across the centuries." Other letters were from people who, isolated, wrote out their own narratives of self- and other exploration in a "brief, private, supportive contact with another gay man."[146]

And Dinshaw's analysis of the exchange of letters about a possible project between one of the TV producers and Boswell speculates about what it means to pivot, first, around alternative, and then, around authoritative knowledges, working among those consensus histories television projects claim:

> Both Boswell and the producer use history as a foundation for gays' assertion of a place in culture now; but while Boswell delineates how it might change the notion of what that culture is, the producer presumes only that history will reinforce the present. There was no doubt a variety of reasons that this television project didn't go forward, but I suspect that this difference may have been one of them; it pointed to limitations of the standard PBS-style documentary and the way it sought to guarantee legitimacy in an already established cultural field. Boswell's history sought "tolerance," and expansion of the mainstream, not a revolution—but it was going to require pushing beyond the reinforcement of present cultural categories, which is all the documentary producer could envision. As it turned out, even this reformation would not be televised.[147]

"Getting medieval" for Dinshaw is about the re-coordinating articulations among intensive and extensive memberships, authorities and alliances in the processes of making, sharing, demonstrating, and using knowledges. For example, the transfer of knowledge from her own field of medieval studies to other fields only now learning to take it into account for their own projects. Or how the thinking and feeling of a queer medievalist "can point out crucial links between ideologies that are usually kept quite separate," and this in ways that only sometimes include its special *things*, such as "the homosexual." In fact all the levels of system involved in the making of queer medieval histories—funding, national ideology, schooled curricula among them—"none will be the same once an articulation of one with another has taken place. The process of touching, of making partial connections between incommensurate entities . . . that process [she calls] . . . getting medieval."[148]

Actor-network theory (ANT), used among the interdisciplining science studies of Michel Callon, John Law, and Bruno Latour, works out *how* a sea of actants inhabits these sometimes black-boxing and authoritative actor-worlds and those other times un-black-boxing and problematic, alternative and processual actor-networks. All of these actants enliven their multiple realities as they variously flip back and forth among nonlinear trajectories or spacetimes: "The *actor-world* can convert or revert into an *actor-network* . . . materials can suddenly become problematized (un-black-boxed). The roles and identities assigned by one entity to another may suddenly be challenged, undermined or shattered." Yet paradoxically and recursively, what is problematic also offers an invitation to durability, because "a network is rendered durable by the way that actors [devices, skills, ideas, beings, worldly processes] at once occupy the margins and the core, are the most outspoken critics and the most ardent stalwarts, are simultaneously insiders and outsiders."[149] Such are these networked re-enactments that I have labored among in this book.

Hopkins shares with us the cognitive sensations of immediacy and the conditions of repurposing immersion that are actually *both* lively and entertaining *styles* of transmission for what is already corporately acknowledged, and also a continually to be re-experienced and denaturalized *condition and effect* of the making of new knowledge. These are cognitive sensations of agency not limited to control.

In a continually shifting environment of flexible knowledges, where so much chatter, so many unrecognizing objects and beings, so many layers of context and spacetime are bewilderingly chaotic about us, I blushingly offer my own one thread through terror and possibility. With others, I too push my way forward in what is not exactly a critique and what is certainly not a simple refusal to participate in new circuits of knowledge. Mine is also a not really voluntary willingness and resistance to unlearn and relearn conducted at the edges of actuality, consciousness, and adaptation. When do I think to take advantage of changes in process across sectors of knowledge work, and when do I not? I have my own worries that my most cherished reasons for doing such work may be left out. No matter what, I must labor with others anyway, to see where all this is taking us and consider, with all the good faith I have, just what my role may be among cocreators of a feminist transdisciplinary posthumanities.

TOWARD A FEMINIST TRANSDISCIPLINARY POSTHUMANITIES

REENACTMENTS ARE SOMETIMES MAPS AND SOMETIMES TERRITORIES

IT MAKES FOR AN ODD sort of book, this reenactment R and D. At one level it is a demonstration of how one sort of case study within a feminist transdisciplinary posthumanities might work. Reenactments are sometimes then an object for illustration, but never only that. To take reenactments up seriously as dynamic relationalities, including the very coming into being of a field named reenactment studies, requires all the recursive paraphernalia of an emergent feminist transdisciplinary posthumanities. Of course this book is not *the* way to do such a study: it is only one way. But it is one way within an approach that values such work and traces out this doubled coming into being.

Like many good (and bad) things, it could be some other way. And this matters too. The extensive examination I do here does not suggest a particular program of research or offer a template for proper method, even if my concluding subtitle here might seem to promise this. But there are intensively focused communities of practice who may properly bring themselves into being around exactly such prescriptive projects producing networks of association, standards, literatures, genealogies, or metrics. Of these, I would myself consider most useful and "rigorous" the ones exquisitely sensitive to their own horizon of possible resources and infrastructures, local exigencies, and differential memberships. Ones that understand Bateson's joking around with "the map is not the territory"— understand that it includes as *play*, in the double consciousness of simulation, *both* the communication "don't mistake the representation for the thing" and *also* the communication "don't take the thing for everything it is about." Whoops! How prescriptive is that? Well, as I understand it, purging paradox and contradiction is not what extensive examination is about either.

So my conclusions may be a funny mix of the hopeful and the pessimistic, the making fun of prescription while allowing it to leak in, a sort of passionate soapboxing taken together with real anxiety and a terrible delight in switching context and having to unlearn which "side" I am on, or seem to be on, or are supposed to be on. A funny kind of feminism then too, oddly relative, oddly decentered, oddly grounded. Relational or differential, I and others might call it.

EMERGENCE KITS: LEARNING TO BE "AFFECTED"

Emergence kits? What are they? Well, they are a fantasy and reality inspired by another essay by Bruno Latour, only there they are "odor kits," training devices that allow a person to progressively acquire body parts: "through the training session, she learned to have a nose which allowed her to inhabit a (richly differentiated odoriferous) world. Thus body parts are progressively acquired at the same time that 'world counter-parts' are being registered in a new way. Acquiring a body is thus a progressive enterprise that produces at once a sensory medium and a sensitive world."[1]

It is a piece of my argument in this book that science-styled television reenactment works with cognitive sensation to examine and create sensitized worlds, as it too offers "training sessions," these very programs themselves, in which "world counter-parts" are newly registered or indexed. Among such worldly counter-parts are the emotional engagements that manage knowledge worlds by foregrounding particular epistemological melodramas. These television reenactments are bits in "kits" that allow us progressively to become more embodied and more sensitive to such melodrama. Enacting each sort, we vicariously and directly experience alternately embodied epistemologies, for example, those hooked in neurologically and affectively as gaming structures, while coproducing "a sensory medium and a sensitive world." "Cognitive sensation" works out through such sensory media in an augmented "cognitive sensorium," another set of parts in a body we progressively work with these programs to acquire. And a good thing. We find ourselves among actively distributing embodiments now. And we need sensitizing worlds.

So, add to these "TV reenactment kits" my fantasy- and reality-inspired reenactment "emergence kits," which together with the TV ones come to be made up out of layered assemblages of reenactment infrastructures, or regulated and chaotic systems mixed up as dynamically embedded globalizations, including among them all these commercializations of culture, learning, and entertainment amid restructurings of knowledge work. Together these enable our training sessions at whole other levels of distributed cognition and being. And this, then, is where one version of our posthumanity works out, beyond human exceptionalism, beyond agencies of control, in bits of consciousness characterizing worldly processes in which we play roles that matter, but not roles in which we own the action. This is no heuristic tension drawn between agency and structure, but rather a neurologically activated or *effectuated*, engaged and progressive learning in assemblage—learning in a strange "sort of" companionship with "kits" it turns out we too are bits of. In this learning we work out and *feel how it is that* we all move around among various networks, together or in spots emergently self-organizing.

Proprioceptive cognitive sensations of travel, googling among layers of locals and globals at varying degrees of resolution or grain of detail, are sometimes explicitly experienced and shared, other times perpendicularly demonstrated among these learnings amid media technologies. After all, first shown this way, and then shown that way, a posthumanities allows us to care for and about knowledges not fully available to consciousness or open for elegant management. To enable such learning, Latour shares an understanding of bodies as that "interface that becomes more and more describable when it learns to be affected by many more elements."[2] Learning to be affected is what this book is all about. And reenactments, understood extensively and intensively, are all about this too.

And we all need—with Latour and with the Belgian psychologist Vinciane Despret, whose philosophical work on emotion he draws upon—"to learn to be affected, meaning 'effectuated,' moved, put into motion by other entities, humans or nonhumans. If you are not engaged in this learning you become insensitive, dumb, you drop dead."[3] And the range—both scoping and scaling—across layered infrastructures itself adds aliveness, which is not the opposite of, say, artificiality. Indeed, says Latour, "the more artificiality, the more sensorium, the more bodies, the more affections, the more realities will be registered. . . . Reality and artificiality are synonyms not antonyms. Learning to be affected means exactly that: the more you learn, the more differences there exist."[4] "Articulation" is the word Latour—and other science studies folks—use to register material assemblages rather than affiliative authenticities:

> The decisive advantage of articulation over accuracy of reference is that there is no end to articulation whereas there is an end to accuracy. Once the correspondence between the statement and the state of affair, has been validated, it is the end of the story—except if a gnawing doubt about faithfulness is introduced to corrupt the quality of the correspondence. Articulations, on the other hand, may easily proliferate without stopping registering differences. On the contrary, the more contrast you add, the more differences and mediations you become sensible to. . . . [Indeed, say,] if you add the weight of commercial and industrial strategies trying to corner markets. . . . The more mediations the better to acquire a body, that is, to become sensitive to the effects on more different entities. . . . The more you articulate controversies, the wider the world becomes.[5]

So, I wish to notice myself and others learning to be affected and wish not to take the *thing* for everything it is about. These hopes move along with additional concerns shared between reenactments and a feminist transdisciplinary posthumanities. They outline risk, commercialization, timing, and convergences across old and new media. They involve often forced entry into environments with mandates to do work that make only too explicit inequities, limitations, inadequacies and fears. All this being one form, for better and worse, of feeling alive to more, and more, and more. (This is how I register the "posthuman.")

"LET SOMEONE ELSE TAKE THE RISKS"

Multiple commercial media distributed across platforms and delivery systems work to enable a practice the University of Southern California (USC) media scholar Henry Jenkins first called "transmedia storytelling." It is the topic of the third chapter of his book *Convergence Culture: Where Old and New Media Collide* (2006). Jenkins's early work was on the participatory fan cultures of science fiction television, similar to those I refer to in chapter 1 on *Highlander* and *Xena*.[6] Since then, Jenkins has become an amazing networker among knowledge cultures and worlds, studying gaming, comics, movies, computer art, and much more. So not surprisingly he knows folks who also traverse these media fandoms, scholarships, arts, and industries. Transmedia storytelling, then, involves the deliberative cultivation of the commercial enterprises that Bolter and Grusin examined for "repurposing" in their studies of remediation.[7] In an extensive form I tell my own transmedia story about reenactment in this book, and, more intensively, reenactments are also displayed among the genres of such transmedia storytelling as Jenkins describes:

> A transmedia story unfolds across multiple media platforms, with each new text making a distinctive and valuable contribution to the whole. In the ideal form of transmedia storytelling, each medium does what it does best—so that a story might be introduced in a film, expanded through television, novels, and comics; its world might be explored through game play or experienced as an amusement park attraction. Each franchise entry needs to be self-contained so you don't need to have seen the film to enjoy the game, and vice versa. Any given product is a point of entry into the franchise as a whole. Reading across the media sustains a depth of experience that motivates more consumption. . . . The economic logic of a horizontally integrated entertainment industry—that is, one where a single company may have roots across all of the different media sectors—dictates the flow of content across media. Different media attract different market niches. Films and television will probably have the most diverse audiences; comics and games the narrowest. A good transmedia franchise works to attract multiple constituencies by pitching the content somewhat differently in the different media. If there is, however, enough to sustain those different constituencies—and if each work offers fresh experiences—then you can count on a crossover market that will expand the potential gross.[8]

Jenkins locates the franchise created out of the film *The Matrix* (1999) as a premier example of such transmedia storytelling. He calls those who co-create as participants in transmedia "hunters and gatherers" as they hypertext across knowledge communities and variant media realities. He predicts that media-mix culture will inspire not only experimental artists and television directors (and I would include reenactors and also reenactment scholars), but will become intuitive for those growing up amid converging media, who learn how to play with media, information, visualization, and who live among and produce hypertexted or relational and relative materialities.[9]

And so does he, that is, live among and produce hypertexted and relational materialities, comparatively relative. And so do we—all those networked by the materialities presented here in this book, in knowledge industries and among reenactment interests. Media, eh? Well, transmedia and transdisciplinary knowledge worlds come to register and index each other in particular sensitivities over the course of the nineties. Media technologies and their products come to matter, come into matter—and they continue to matter, to create, to make material, to literalize, to solidify those relationalities. Globally restructuring academies, repositioned within and among enterprise and heritage culture industries and national economies of image, history, and science as well as money, are also working out their own versions of transmedia, transdisciplinary storytelling. I think of the activities at the Australian National University for the Fenner conferences as I say this, and of Julie Thompson Klein's transmedia, transdisciplinary storytelling there about disciplinary knowledges and interdisciplinary integration, as I describe in chapter 4, as well as the culture wars polarities drawn across political venues as I narrate them myself in chapter 2.

Jenkins himself is another amazing intellectual entrepreneur who surfs the tides of commerce, education, industry, and scholarship. His faculty website from his days at MIT transmediates for us his networked cognitions, like those across television and the web in my chapter 3.[10] His name, e-mail address, and blog link from the nineties and a bit after entitle this highly visual website, where, below them, a human brain is pictured, colored in sections with lines drawn from parts on the left and right sides to areas of Jenkins's work. From left brain to right brain are connected:

— comparative media studies → Comparative Media Studies—
  Program Head
— media convergence → Virtual Screening Room—Executive Producer
— media consumption → Women's Studies—Steering Committee
  Member
— children's culture → MIT Press—Media Studies Advisor
— gender and sexuality → Senior House—Housemaster
— media and democracy → Media in Transition—Co-Director
— genres of entertainment → Corporate Consultant

At the bottom are links to his curriculum vitae, his publications, his course syllabi, to press coverage about him or to which he has contributed,

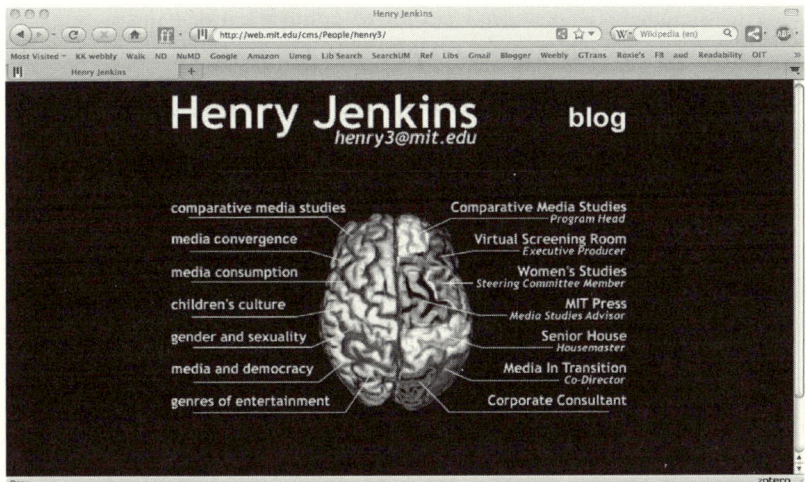

Henry Jenkins's MIT home page, a *timespot*.

and updates on his activities, the site, and other projects. Jenkins's own transdisciplinary storytelling is arrayed here archaeologically among these "platforms" for global academic restructuring amid more and less local and global campus and academy agencies. His highly distributed academic responsibilities and enterprises were energized as administrator, innovator (the Virtual Screen Room was an interactive textbook project), academic citizen, professional reviewer, campus housemaster, collaborative projects coordinator, industry consultant, teacher, newsworthy commentator, and own website manager.

This website was a particularly sophisticated one, as well as one now superseded by Jenkins's move to USC. Academics more and more find themselves needing and using such sites, and they are both specific and relative—undated often, but offering layers of time and technology— timespots. Those with the technical and design skills, or the money and support services, may have ones of great ingenuity and sometimes beauty. Many such sites are visually datable: the design features can place them within web-archaeologies of software or server "strata" among shrewd guesses about how long it has been since the faculty member personally worked with them or, perhaps, had professional help, or how long since their institution altered its server architecture, together with whatever attention and thought specific departments and universities give to these.

Jenkins's suggests that 2006, the year of publication of *Convergence Culture*, was a professional turning point that redirected his energies from explaining and marketing what he does to opening up participatory social media at the site itself: by 2008 it was his blog that energized the most current features alive on the site and became the vehicle that carried his web work from MIT to USC in 2009.

My point here is that the materialities of transmedia storytelling are very much intertwined with academic technology infrastructures amid transdisciplinary scholarship amid academic entrepreneurships, some mandated and some enthusiastic or "evangelizing" in technology-specific ways. And that the analyses Jenkins offers of each are properly mixed-in too with the material experiences of the others. Transdisciplinary work also networks worlds and genres, it too unfolds across multiple platforms —those "disciplines" and their institutional and conceptual apparatuses— with the claim that each bit makes its distinctive contribution to some whole. Supposedly each "medium" or knowledge world does what it does best: offering its special *things* for the edification of others. Still, as we have noted, everyone's special *things* tend to belong also to others, who inspect them in ways often quite alternative, and we have to relearn or unlearn stuff about our own *things* all the time too.

So, as Julie Thompson Klein teaches us, in transdisciplinary project-oriented research the ideal is that "story" and "medium" are especially suited and that collaborations explicitly work hard at the metalevel to create a similar joining—that these indeed are optimal when language, method, and practices are negotiable, provisional, and self-limiting. This is the "rigor" of learning to be affected, that is, learning that exquisite sensitivity to each momentary horizon of possible resources and infrastructures, local exigencies, and differential memberships.

All this is what allows such "franchise entries" to have points of self-containment (academically, that intensive disciplining), precisely when they extensively open up these as points of entry into the whole enterprise from many angles of value; in other words, open up to peripheral participation as well as to expertise. "Reading across the media" in transdisciplinary practice means engaging in collaborations in which peripheral participation even has its special advantages, not at all second best or reduced simply to an initiation into membership, as authoritative and alternative knowledges are over and over repositioned relationally, differentially. The "horizontally integrated entertainment industry" will soon have nothing on a globally restructured academy, sewn *now* into the projects of nation-states and re-commercialized along axes impossible to predict. Or maybe even altering what commercialization means. Maybe (wistfully) democratizing some forms of commercialization—maybe, maybe, maybe.

All the possibilities of artful participation are only too unclear, only too full of terror and possibility. Jenkins talks about the consumers of media who want to take these options to travel across media and "go in deep" or pull back and "just watch."[11] (Yes, let's keep laughing appreciatively with the wonderfully phallic sexualities of television studies.) Says Jenkins: "Relatively few, if any, franchises achieve the full aesthetic potential of transmedia story-telling—yet. Media makers are still finding the way and are more than willing to let someone else take the risks."[12]

So, let someone else take the risks. Latour quips: "Knowing interestingly is always a risky business."[13] For many feminisms one risk here is somehow turning out on the wrong "side." The side I do not want to be on is the one that substitutes metric accountability for messy reworked "mature" trust, or substitutes standardized policies for contingent practices worked out in good faith. (Surprisingly to some of us, the knowledge engineer Sue Stafford points out that so-called commercialization may provide positive occasions for having to learn to be affected in these very ways.[14]) The redress or amelioration of unanticipated consequences is, I think, a public good to be made as carefully detailed and technically practical as any metric for assessment. Indeed, I long for more and better grained "data" shared among nations and academies on the outcomes of global academic restructuring, used then to reposition already assumed and ideological predictions, valorizations, or justifications relying on what amounts to market research or other evangelizations—although I am aware wryly of naïveté here. Nor do I, generally speaking, wish to practice debunking, even though sometimes, as just now, practicing such essentializing does seem the only responsible way to make my sides clear and (vainly I fear) distance myself from unintended approval or allegiances. Actually, what I truly wish is to engage in the kinds of critique that *include* myself in noninnocent complicity *without overvaluing abjection*, registering in good faith the frightful *and* the ordinary, the confusion about what is terror and what is possibility.

Mostly I want *play*. I want that double consciousness that can posit the edge of what we do and do not want, trying it and reacting, "not." Or reacting, "yes." Valuing the labors of trial and error learning, responsiveness, and affectivity. How to do this at ranges of institution and infrastructure that cross many knowledge worlds, that tend to dynamite quickly and follow up slowly, accreting incrementally, and costing a lot? This is exactly where the technologies of just in time production and the innovations of "flexible" capital ought to serve us, rather than drive us. They are exactly technologies to enhance learnings to be affected and maybe could be used to react to unanticipated consequences and to further social goods and public necessities, not only to maximize profit.[15] And yet we also know them to be tied to forms of global inequality in ways not to overlooked. How do we reuse tools of "flexible" capital to sensitize worlds to the affects/effects of terror and possibility? Where are affective economies of effectuation, moved by other entities and their suffering and joy?[16]

Play between the extensive and intensive is another piece in any "rigor" of scholarships that prize knowledges in active making and alive revision, in relational shifts between exquisitely sensitized mappings of authority and much scaling and scoping among alternatives and between territories. (This is how I register "transdisciplinary.")

TERROR AND POSSIBILITY

The Chicana feminist and media theorist Chela Sandoval's notion of "differential consciousness" is useful here.[17] In the book Sandoval spent the nineties writing, *Methodology of the Oppressed*, she suggests that globalization processes today are producing simultaneously both a new (ironically spoken) "democratization of oppression" (what others have in properly urgent critiques unintentionally essentialized as "hyperoppression") and a new "global citizen" with emergent forms of subjectivity, that is, agency created within and by new forms of subjection and resistance.[18] Such emergent subjectivities create, require, and hone cognitive and other skills. Distributed being and distributed cognition are faceted angles onto and within such subjectivities. Unevenly distributed and suffered inequalities are others.

When Steven Johnson attempts to describe positively an *affected* relationality with the increasing complexity and intellectual challenges of contemporary popular culture honed in games, television, Internet, and films, he is opening one kind of transmedia storytelling path among such *things* and their globalized infrastructures.[19] He challenges assumptions and critiques that presume these *things* have relatively plain negative consequences rather than are a complicated soup of terror and possibility. He especially challenges the assumption that they are only "about" their "contents" rather than also, perhaps mostly, about the intensely individual and collective affective and cognitive experiences in which they participate. Trying to keep this complicated soup as elegant as possible in his book pitched to a broad popular audience, and assuming that negative analyses already widely known and *now* even folklored and stereotyped can often be taken tacitly for granted, Johnson persuasively emphasizes instead their positive opposite.

But Sandoval's methodology of the oppressed, a project in semiology and cognitive media too, is doing something both related *and* different. It is something especially attuned to that which Johnson himself terms "telescoping" and "probing"—that is, engaging dynamically simultaneous specificity and abstraction, elegance and complexity, accessibility and multilayered and suffered realities, in order to find their edges, powers, and unexpected agencies beyond essentialized critique. Sandoval responds to whole ranges of such tricky mapping problems by working out specifically for feminisms dynamic multidimensional visualizations and transmedia theories through an ethically augmented and *affected* cognitive sensorium. She also demonstrates persuasively that all these involve continuities built upon and with "US third world feminisms" of the seventies and eighties, upon and with situated knowledges recast during the nineties as a transformative politics of and about globalization. Sandoval's work is preemptive and proleptic, sometimes prophetic. Sandoval's conceptual medium itself is *media in pastpresents*, a literal infrastructure out of which her analysis of feminist politics emerged.

Sandoval synthesizes these in her own terms in an essay in 2002, foregrounding *how they cocreate and participate* in

> an apparatus comprised of five different *applications*, or technologies. These technologies connect and transmit through one another until they are recognizable as a singular method. This method provides cognitive and emotional maps necessary for guiding internal and collective action. Briefly put, the five technologies of this method are: (1) reading power as in radical semiotics, la facultad, or "signifyin'"; (2) deconstruction, or coatlicue; (3) meta-ideologizing; (4) differential perception, or

népantla; and (5) democratics, the ethical or moral technology that permits the previous four to be driven, mobilized, and organized into a singular methodology for emancipation.[20]

The vocabulary Sandoval gathers here—"la facultad," "signifyin,'" "coatlicue," "népantla," "meta-ideologizing," "differential perception," "democratics"—lattices a history between 1981 and 2002, the years between the publication of the groundbreaking collection, *This Bridge Called My Back: Writings by Radical Women of Color*, and the self-consciously interconnected later volume, *This Bridge We Call Home: Radical Visions for Transformation* (for which this particular Sandoval essay provides a foreword, "AfterBridge: Technologies of Crossing").[21] All this vocabulary lives *now* on the web, in links to scholarship, on blogs, and in online reference sites and travels within and among knowledge worlds and feminist identity politics.[22] Terms like "la facultad," "coatlicue," and "népantla" are often associated with the work of Gloria Anzaldúa and with theories of the quite literal geographical, cultural, and knowledge borderlands she inhabited, theorized, and shared in work scholarly, literary and artistic, pedagogical, activist and spiritual, technoscientific, and epistemological.[23] Quite properly this theorization of borderlands has become taken for granted, that is to say used directly and indirectly, as it has moved along feminist networks, including scholarship on knowledge engineering, such as that of Julie Thompson Klein, or on knowledge management and classification, such as that of Susan Leigh Star and Geof Bowker.[24]

The term "signifyin'" is often associated with early scholarly work by that other intellectual entrepreneur, Henry Louis Gates Jr., and it traces out additional networks of influence that interconnect transnational African diasporas with black politics and histories in the United States.[25] Signifyin' registers a playful, edgy, agonistic gaming practice of "the dozens," a kind of contest in insults that are pretty much always not *only* that and that has new registers in contemporary cultural performance, spoken word displays, and rap music.[26] Gates's intentions were to synthesize particular and specific African and African American traditions with poststructuralist versions of semiology in what one might call a kind of theory "*glocalization*" that pressured both the local and the global.[27] Gates's television work does this as well, working out and among transnational black journeys, knowledges, and oppressions, to energize and perform histories of black pasts from every possible source of evidence and knowledge world.[28]

The terms "meta-ideologizing," "differential perception," and "democratics" come from Sandoval's own synthesis of poststructuralisms and activist media politics of the seventies and eighties. Sandoval briefly studied with Gregory Bateson in graduate school in the History of Consciousness program at University of California, Santa Cruz, in the mid-seventies. She was already a film and video activist at that time, collaborating in a variety of feminist media projects. She also studied with the historiographer Hayden White, the feminist technoscience theorist Donna Haraway, the transnational anthropologist James Clifford, and the psychoanalytic film theorist Teresa de Lauretis. Her *Methodology of the Oppressed* includes a foreword by the philosopher and activist Angela Davis. Sandoval often explains her variously semiological terminology in *Methodology* with reference to Roland Barthes, whose work she studied with Hayden White, and who, together with Jacques Derrida, she identified with the anticolonial movements of the sixties. As with Henry Louis Gates Jr., her intellectual imaginations are drawn across transnational histories of decolonization and racial and cultural diasporas.

Sandoval works out with and among the sort of levels of abstraction, formalization, and recursion that can be found in Bateson's and Barthes's structuralisms. For example, "meta-ideologizing" is the term Sandoval uses in a synthesis of Barthes's notion of "exnomination" together with her understanding of the revolutionary politics of US radical activism in the late sixties and early seventies. She describes it as "a third level" ideological system, or "the ideologization of ideology itself," a paradoxical recursion both visionary and literal, an agency edged among language and signs:[29]

Zero level, a *zero degree of language*: social cognition at this level allows one to make meaning underlying the terms set by ideology but is preformed by and limits communication, especially at the edges, since poststructuralists consider that the acquisition and internalization of referential epistemology and of dominant ideology together make up what we call "language."

First and second levels, *simultaneous expressions of and resistances to ideology in and against language and signification, and noting all of these as expressions of power*: both forms of radical semiotics (as in la facultad or signifyin') and of deconstruction, says Sandoval, or coatlicue (which Anzaldúa understood as an unlooked for crisis of spirit, reason, passion, and reality itself)[30] in agencies of a language of revolution that performs a simultaneous destruction and remaking of worlds constituted within language; and/or Barthes's semiotic-mythology, with which one learns to read power and self-consciously to practice deconstruction; and/or an antilanguage of silence that refuses to engage with ideology; and/or an antilanguage of poetry that extends longing or abjection beyond language.

Third level, *the ideologizing of ideology* or meta-ideologizing: What Barthes called exnomination, and that, Sandoval says, "functions both within and against ideology." It "serves to display the original dominant ideology as naïve—and no longer natural—or to reveal, transform, or disempower its signification. . . . This manipulation of one's own consciousness through stratified zones of form and meaning requires the desire and the ability to move through one layer of [the signifier/signified/Sign] relationship and into another, 'artificial,' or self-consciously manufactured ideology and back again."[31] All this requires differential perception or movement or népantla.

"Népantla" is a term of transculturation, used by a range of Chicana and Chicano authors to describe the multiple consciousness created among the traumas of colonization, after that rending of reality Anzaldúa describes as coatlicue.[32] Both collective and individual, it is a form of what I have been referencing in "play" or "learning"—but the affects here are of greater range across trauma and change and closer to the cognitive affects and effects in several layers of individual and social organization that Bateson tags as a "profound reorganization of character."[33] Indeed, Bateson and Sandoval both register the miracle of individual and collective survival beyond coatlicue that népantla, or as Bateson puts it, the "transcontextual," builds upon.[34] Sandoval talks about this in terms of "differential" movement or perception or consciousness, and she sees its materializations in a range of forms and at several levels of scale, as forms of representation and signification, in choices among political movements and strategies, as liberatory practice immanent in shifting forms of power and social organization, and in an intersectional subjectivity of grace: "enough strength to confidently commit to a well-defined structure of identity for one hour, day, week, month, year; enough flexibility to self-consciously transform that identity according to the requisites of another oppositional ideological tactic if readings of power's formation require it; enough grace to recognize alliance with others committed to egalitarian social relations and race, gender, sex, class, and social justice, when their readings of power call for alternative oppositional stands."[35]

Differential or transcontextual perception or népantla is possible after the reorganization of character—individual or collective or some imbrications with both—that characterizes differential consciousness. And differential movement is a sort of cycling through possibility, through sets of interactive contexts and actions, which Sandoval names as the variable and sensitized tactics and ethics of democratics:

> This method asks practitioners to collectively and strategically distinguish, evaluate, and select tactics, among which may include integrationism, revolutionary action, supremacism, separatism, anarchism, political defense or redefinition of the human, or complete defiance of that category. However different, each tactic is strategically accomplished in order to intervene in and democratically refocus social and psychic powers through identifying "situated knowledges" (Haraway) that can understand and match globalizing psychic, cultural, and national sites (Spivak, "In a Word"). This methodology of emancipation functions as a place-based ecological activism—it works through self-consciously identifying and producing invigorating political and cultural planetary geographies.[36]

The purpose of the automobile part called a differential is to allow the wheels to move independently when necessary, each in sensitized differences of speed and distance as the motor directs energy to these points of environmental contact. Notice that this sort of differential is a piece within a mechanics of distributed adaptations that, as we promiscuously attach to it the poststructuralist valences between "difference" and "différance," work for Sandoval to multiply forms of recursion. Such a tensely held unity of movement is never entirely "synthesized" and, thus, deferred, operates at more than one level of structure and signification at the same time. In other words, it operates independently at particular material points but is never entirely uncoupled or disarticulated; in fact, the term itself moves among transdisciplinarities.

And Sandoval's politics works out among also articulated liberatory potentials, neither celebratory nor easily addressed within the too often inadvertently essentializing terms of negative critique: it is about wringing edgy possibilities out of the terrors of mandates for particular skills and survivals under globalization. Nonetheless, for some feminists and progressives such hybridity of critique and visionary longing remains essentialized as objectionably utopian, no matter its criticality and despite its distinct divergence from commercial evangelizations of technology, capitalism, and progress.[37] Any politics not continually re-registering its intentions to refuse complicity in new capital formations embedded within systems of hyperoppression, and not continually re-registering alliances made sharply clear in practices of critique or debunking, is, for some progressives, politically suspect as itself only another form of neoliberalism.

Nonetheless, Sandoval's hollowly ironic yet strangely oracular phrase "democratization of oppression" intends a "third path" through polarizations, another path also invoked in her descriptions of and alliances with historic agencies of "US third world feminism."[38] It assumes that time-specific political statements in urgent renunciation cannot capture messier long-term immanent realities in the lives of many unprivileged, migrant, or *glocalizing* peoples, whose abilities to maneuver in time among the territories of globalizing worlds are the very condition for their/our survival. Where the "they" and the "our" disaggregate or conflate messily moves around here, but collective survival eventually depends on all. Careful renunciation in these contexts may at times only be possible in forms of unexamined privilege or as only too understandable limitations on self-knowledge: always relative and relational. Nor is Sandoval's sort of immanent liberatory possibility tied to an end point of liberation, just as coatlicue, however shattering, is not (or not always) the end time of apocalypse. Instead immanent openings and coatlicue each index punctuated moments across nonlinear coincidence and among violated powers.

Mapping out and telescoping layers of locals and globals is necessary then in a liberatory politics of meta-ideologizing that understands itself as working within, constituted by, and in resistance to processes of globalization, not apart from them. This does not mean in some straightforward way that we are all inside globalization, contained and imprisoned by it, as the determinative structure that foils our agency, or even that we *are* globalization, although that is important to register too. What it means is that implication within globalization is *also* more properly indexed at different grains of detail, at different resolutions or densities of information, among layerings of locals and globals. And, thinking about and moving among *layers of locals and globals*—that is, in a revision of the so-called local and global, now to be understood as nondyadic and multiple, as telescoping and cascading layerings of maps and territories both relative and relational—is a feature alive to the affected and differential consciousness of Sandoval's (again hollowly ironic) new global citizen, whose consciousness is co-sensitizing worlds.

And, in a specific register for reenactment, these are also the resources and skills out of which today we create our shifting sensitizations for whole sets of punctuated moments or pastpresents, skills honed, exploited, and commercialized in contemporary and transnational popular culture. Indeed, sensitizing to globalization processes—while intensified today in historically specific forms, unique to our time periods—also calls to mind that globalization marks out historically discontinuous spacetime punctuations of intensity, as well as mutating continuities across colonialisms, neocolonialisms, and postcolonialisms that transnationally exist in long historic time frames. Any "pasts," now necessarily rethought among and with contemporary transmedia, are inevitably always also located in our "presents."

Such dynamic pastpresents are not failures in some structure of chronology, nor evidence of a disregard for objectivity or empirical method, or betrayals of an ethical and honorable "alterity"—but rather a condition of distributed being and production. Just as, traveling among eras, Hopkins playfully engages various economies of knowledge, or as, pouring through letters, Dinshaw reworks Boswell's professional archive—the forms of work perhaps essentialized in critique as "transhistorical" sometimes also are articulated among lively partialities that affectively alter and dynamically remix many kinds of sensitizing interactivities with pasts. *Reenactments have their special place here as transmedia knowledges that activate these forms of cognitive sensation.*

In inclusive solidarity within and adding to many politics of identity Sandoval *transfers* the knowledges of many social movements and their tactics and theories of social change: naming them abstractly enough to gracefully register alliance, while honoring the historical and political specificities they also recall, as she carefully characterizes core practices. These practices are not set against each other in some taxonomy of mutual critique. Instead, with mindful sensitivity, Sandoval pivots, networks, and decenters all these tactics as she calls out to them and their variously centered identity formations in differential movement: "integrationism, revolutionary action, supremacism, separatism, anarchism, political defense or redefinition of the human, or complete defiance of that category." "Democratics," as Sandoval drives it, needs the environmental touchdown of all and each of these wheels. Bits in political training kits in which activists and others learn to be affected within transnational webs of power, they aid actively distributing embodiments and beings to become alive to more and more in sensitized worlds, among them those of feminist identity politics.

So, as expressions of and within a range of trans knowledges these tactics are a *feminist* feature of the differential consciousness Sandoval enjoins. Transnational, transgenic, transgender, transmedia, transdisciplinary: these emerge out of the conditions of postmodernity, and feminisms find them to be daunting companion species, always too much and not enough. But however we work it, in terror and possibility, the default is transformation.[39] (This is how I register "feminist.")

"CLARITY HERE WOULD BE MISLEADING"[40]

Why call that something the humanities are turning into and out of a "posthumanities"? Is it only a terminology of place holding until we have a better sort of nomenclature to register this transformation instead? Maybe. I am not totally committed to this term. I find it uncomfortable just as I find the term "posthuman" rather uncanny. (I cannot imagine justifying that term to, say, Gregory Bateson. And to me that matters.) Nonetheless over the nineties and after I have discovered myself increasingly in alliance with others indexing as "posthuman" a set of issues opening up and adding to what I understand makes a difference in knowledge making and sharing. And although a "posthumanities" feels a bit more comfortable than something "posthuman," I am fairly sure that comfort is not the point. Maybe both terms are valuable precisely because they continue to be unsettling and disconcerting and precisely because it is not easy to register a "side" to be on. Clarity here would be misleading.

Yet posthuman does also index my own desire to understand and engage with emergent processes in ways that keep sharpening our understanding of systems, of emergence itself, of distributed cognition and distributed being. Some of those I would ally with are especially concerned with animals and work to create the field of animal studies, ingeniously using both of these concerns sometimes together with the notion of the posthuman as intensive entry points to extensive concerns they properly critique as human exceptionalism. Donna Haraway's work and her own stated ambivalences here I find pivotal in this regard, especially because they also demonstrate, sometimes perpendicularly, how all these are also feminist issues, a point that can feel, sometimes, counterintuitive.[41]

And, as I understand it, the term "posthumanities" also names an institutional infrastructure only too troubled under global academic restructuring, and in terms that re-form institutional powers as well as pressure conceptual territories. Such reorganizations of knowledge classifications and knowledge institutions are happening at all levels of infrastructure, and whether we like it or not. The term "posthumanities" indicates that these are material trends in emergent formation, and that we cannot clearly predict what is coming into being. Nor should we be too quick to do such prediction, even as we acknowledge the edge of terror and possibility these moments in a posthumanities bring us to, or their unevenly experienced forms of suffering and advantage. We need "posthumanities" resources that come from hunting and gathering many transmedia, transdisciplinary story lines and assessments of what is happening, punctuated across pastpresents. Manipulating our own consciousness, as Sandoval might say, or, maybe better, also working with what we are finding out about consciousness and its material structures, neurological as well as, say, systemically economic, technological as well as, say, nationalistic, we "re-cognize" and work around the hypnotic rewards or addictions of control. Such simultaneously cognitive and ethical practices are something Bateson felt cybernetics required too.

As someone, like thousands (millions?) of others, grappling with the local, departmental, college, campus, and university system, indeed national and international conditions of global academic restructuring, I find myself longing to work on restructuring *in good faith*. Maybe, say, a good faith cocreation among faculties, staffs, administrators, students, and state publics, informed by a savvy behaviorist kindliness—what Donna Haraway calls "positive reinforcement properly done," a contribution from an animal studies inflected posthumanities.[42] Somewhat ruefully, somewhat playfully, often ironically, perhaps despairingly, I imagine many intransitive forms of infrastructural power deviled by the details of the learning to be affected Donna Haraway describes in her accounts of "training in the contact zone."

In her book *When Species Meet* (one in the University of Minnesota's "Posthumanities" book series), Haraway says the learning, training, and playing together of dog and human companion species, provokes "strong and unexpected emotions and preconception-breaking thinking about power, status, failure, skill, achievement, shame, risk, injury, control, companionship, body, memory, joy, and much else."[43] Joking around myself (yet not so secretly serious too) and working from Haraway's list of the deviling details of agility training, I imagine an outrageous (and courageous?) partnership in an alternate epistemological melodrama of campus governance, amid institutional and personal structures of reward and (increasingly mobilized punitively) assessment. Some deviling details, recounted by Haraway, of positive reinforcement properly done, might well have something to teach us here.

For example, Haraway starts off her list of the insightful "demons" that drive her attempts at "positive reinforcement well done," with: "learning how to mark what one thinks one is marking (say, with a click of a little tin cricket or, less accurately, a word like 'yes!')."[44] The very behavior to be reinforced or elicited is indicated *as particularly mindful* of one's partners, *by the reward* that *marks* it. What are some of the broad concerns that need particular mindful markings in the academic context? Which are the restructured institutional behaviors to be mindfully recognized, what are the new units of campus agency to address and (fairly) to empower? What *rewards* mark alternate sources of revenue, consolidations of service? How can cuts in resources and people be *ameliorated and redressed*, rather than felt directly as the punitive effects of so-called assessment? In what forms can assessments of students, professors, curricula, and institutions be worked ethically in terms of positive reinforcement? And how can such so-called assessment data be collected together with (rather than instead of) *data on the consequences of restructuring itself*? How might good faith deterritorialization in and among knowledge worlds be properly *marked by new agency*? How is faculty and campus governance properly figured as "contact in the training zone"?

Coming up with an imaginative set of psychic as well as material rewards might well elicit a broader range of innovative behaviors than does a punitively registered and negatively reinforced feedback based on so-called assessment. It is impossible to engage in good faith an assessment that we all collectively fear and occasionally observe is an attempt to trick us into doing ourselves harm. Such abusive "training" needs to be interrupted, its victims redressed, and new partnerships redrawn as "an intra-acting crowd of players that include people, organisms, and apparatuses all coming together. . . . Strong negative words like 'no!' . . . are rationed severely, kept for dangerous situations and emergencies, and not used as training tools."[45]

Some of the other demons Haraway shares with us, in that joking form that allows for the double consciousness of play and that here might allow us to think in a more playful yet rigorous creativity (violence, not!), are:

— timing (i.e., knowing how long after a mark one has to deliver a reward and delivering it in that window; otherwise whatever just last happened is what's being rewarded)
— working and playing in such a way that dogs (and people) offer interesting things that can be positively reinforced (Luring can help show what's wanted in early training of something new, but luring does not reinforce and quickly gets in the way)
— knowing what is really rewarding and interesting to one's partner
— correctly seeing what actually just happened
— understanding what one's partner is in fact paying attention to
— learning how to break complex patterns down into technical bits or behaviors that can be marked and rewarded
— knowing how to link behaviors into chains that add up to something useful
— knowing how to teach chains of behavior from the last part to the first (backchaining), by using bits of a behavior chain that a dog already understands as a reward for a bit that comes right before
— knowing how many repetitions are informative and effective and how many shut everybody down with stress and boredom
— knowing how to identify and reward approximations to the end-goal behavior (Trying to teach left and right turns? Start by marking and rewarding spontaneous glances in the desired direction, don't rush over steps, don't go so slow that your dog dies of old age or boredom.)
— knowing when—and how—to stop if something is not working
— keeping accurate count of the actual frequency of correct responses in a given task instead of imagining what they are, whether one is in an inflationary or deflationary mood
— keeping learning situations fun and cognitively interesting for one's partner

— evaluating whether or not the dog, the human, and the team actually do know how to do something in all the circumstances in which they will need to perform the "behavior" (Chances are high that the relevant variable in a real agility trial was left out of training, and so what was the variable that caused a dog who knew her job, or so one thought, to blow an obstacle? or caused the human to become un-readable? Go back and train.)

— avoiding tripping on one's dog or the equipment

— perceiving the difference between a lure, a reward, and a tug rope

— crashing into one's unsuspecting dog's head because the handler can't throw accurately

— not dropping food treats and clickers all over the practice field

— figuring out how to reward oneself and one's partner when every-thing seems to be falling apart[46]

Trust in individuals once replaced, perhaps functionally, by trust in institutional processes or policies, has been continually re-eroded in the exigencies of restructuring. What are the conditions required for the "mature trust" that the philosopher and knowledge engineer Sue Stafford discusses are needed in knowledge *management* as well as in any standards for *validity*? Stafford says of trust:

> The nature of trust and trustworthiness as they function in creating, using, and sharing knowledge is complex. . . . Mature trust is trust that is articulated and reflected upon. . . . not taken for granted, [it] is gener-ated dynamically by the explicit and implicit understandings, demands, promises, expectations and dependencies that characterize knowledge enterprises . . . as knowers come to know which people and which institutions to trust about what. . . . The relationship that is mature trust is dynamic and ongoing, and continually requires renegotiation and renewal that may be implicit rather than explicit.[47]

Stafford links such trust to what she and others call "intellectual virtue." In professions that prize autonomy, recognition, and respect, often above (eroded but still relatively privileged levels of) income, intellectual virtues are goods in themselves as well as ethical practices:

> The concepts of intellectual virtue, epistemic responsibility, and per-sonal "care-abouts" demonstrate the link between knowledge and val-ues. . . . Intellectual virtues are character traits . . . that work in com-

bination with knowledge . . . [and] have a motivational component. . . . [And because they are] so difficult to develop . . . consequently develop gradually over time. . . . [Indeed] knowers are responsible for their knowledge and responsible for knowing well. [Lorraine] Code has called this responsibility epistemic responsibility. . . . Care-abouts are personal character traits that motivate knowers to create, maintain and share knowledge.[48]

The psychic investments of intellectual virtue, epistemic responsibility, and personal "care-abouts" make them all goods in themselves, as well as proper actions and practices and even complex cocreated "rewards" in mindful contexts of distributed production and being. *Opportunities for practicing intellectual virtues in contexts of good faith are far better and much less addicting rewards than intensified and increasingly differentiated forms of discipline and control.*

And what do we do with all that overloading affect that arises with new demands and possibilities, or that we numb out in overwork to get through changes we often cannot even discriminate as constructive or abusive? Although Haraway was describing the panoply of emotions encountered in agility training, they deserve to be re-registered here too: "strong and unexpected emotions and preconception-breaking thinking about power, status, failure, skill, achievement, shame, risk, injury, control, companionship, body, memory, joy, and much else."[49] Honoring these, how far can we go in properly figuring faculty and campus governance as "contact in the training zone"?

How do we open up an ethical "training kit" for restructuring across the commercial and academic (and more?) in which everyone learns to be affected? Julie Thompson Klein offered the 2004 Fenner Conference a protocol for project-driven interdisciplinary integration, intended to create "robust knowledge." She described knowledge that spans not only academic disciplines but also includes lay knowledges and, for this environmental conference, also indigenous knowledges. For creating robust knowledges aiding academic restructuring, collaborations might also include commercial, policy, professional, and legislative knowledges in various combinations. And, says Klein, "If we are going to create robust knowledge, we need to be engaged in a process of negotiating, brokering and leveraging knowledge." She lists twenty-eight actions in a five-step process disciplinary, interdisciplinary, and transdisciplinary:

A: INITIAL PHASE

   1 Define the problem and project or initiative collaboratively.

   2 Determine goals, objectives, research questions, and variables jointly.

   3 Envision a spectrum that is neither too narrow nor too broad for the task at hand.

   4 Identify relevant approaches, tools, and partners together.

B: ORGANISATIONAL AND CONCEPTUAL FRAMEWORK

   5 Devise a mutual plan that is both significant and comprehensive yet feasible.

   6 Incorporate state-of-the-art knowledges in pertinent disciplines, professions, interdisciplinary fields, and sectors of society.

   7 Allow for flexibility in shifting groupings of individuals and approaches.

C: SOCIAL LEARNING AND COMMUNICATION

   8 Use role clarification to find out what partners need and expect from each other.

   9 Clarify differences in language, methods, tools, concepts, theories, and worldviews.

  10 Provide time for mutual learning.

  11 Insure ongoing communication and exchange, both face-to-face and electronically.

  12 Craft a hybrid interlanguage.

  13 Use conflicts creatively to refine and advance the work.

  14 Capture the knowledge produced throughout the work process in tangible forms.

  15 Communicate with counterpart teams, projects, and initiatives at regional, national, and international levels to share ideas, approaches, and results.

D: COLLABORATION AND INTEGRATION

  16 Provide for sustained interaction and coordinated tasks in structure and work plan.

  17 Engage in ongoing integration, joint activities, and iteration.

  18 Use known techniques for integration and collaboration.

  19 Strive for interdependence, "teamness," and equal power sharing.

20 Move from a multidisciplinary contracting mode to consulting and partnering modes.

21 Triangulate depth, breadth, and synthesis to achieve an interdependent, collaborative outcome rather than a multidisciplinary compilation of separate inputs.

22 Reflect explicitly and collectively on interdisciplinary and collaborative components.

E: EVALUATION AND DISSEMINATION

23 Evaluate interdisciplinary and collaborative aspects.

24 Implement new knowledge, models of research and education, and action plans.

25 Bridge academic, non-academic, and public discourses.

26 Forge integrative partnerships with stakeholders outside the university.

27 Articulate findings and recommendations in the public sphere, using all appropriate media from electronic means to informal community-based networks.

28 Disseminate findings, recommendations, and results in pertinent disciplines, professions, and interdisciplinary fields.[50]

What sort of a transdisciplinary *knowledge* project is global academic restructuring? My understanding of a posthumanities is as that very knowledge project. Restructuring is not just the stage set or context for this book on networked reenactments, but actually their companion species. These changes over the nineties across knowledge work, culture crafts and industries, and academic capitalism are something I ambivalently engage as the condition for my own continuing.

While the changes occurring in academic restructuring are often supposed to be drawn from commercial practices and corporate management, such a genealogy can work to either justify or demonize the worst of such practices, not necessarily to open up to the best of them and others in wide ranges of experience and innovation. Commercialization and privatization are indisputably linked but not simply equivalent. Privatization is about the transfer of public goods into private hands. Marking public goods carefully is an ethical economic practice too.[51] No progressive antiglobalization movement can operate without engagement in and with globalization. No progressive anticorporate movement can operate without engagement in and with corporations. An exceptionalism of the academy or of the humanities works as a line too simply drawn in a resistance to so-called commercialization. That battle was lost before it began: representations of a "before" here overflow with nostalgic idealization, not with historical complexity.

And the deeply colonial project that once was the humanities should not be recuperated as relatively innocent now, instead of being clear that a not yet finished project of accountability and redress for roles played in that colonialism is being only too easily erased in the exigencies of restructuring. A struggled after "posthumanities" tasks itself, from the very depths of restructuring, to refocus on many projects of decolonization, antiracist politics, feminist transformation, and sensitized transmedia knowledge practices. This is how I register a feminist transdisciplinary posthumanities.

REENACTMENT R AND D

So what is the R and D—a research and development phase of a feminist transdisciplinary posthumanities—offered by the nineties reenactment television practices extensively described in this book, and by a reenactment studies intensively coming into being? Both *the work of reenaction* and *the work of affectivity* are key here. These are agencies dependent on *how* we learn to acquire new body parts for distributed bodies. They allow us to inhabit knowledge worlds sensitized by neurosensory specificities.

A scholar of cinema, critical studies, and African American studies at USC, Kara Keeling points out that film and television are able to "make sense(s) common" to both "surplus" markets (usually un-valorized as not commercially profitable, but in conditions of economic extremity re-valorized in appeals to limited but meaningful commercial advantages) and broad mainstream markets, but "not because film or television 're-flects' reality or imposes itself on 'real life.' It is because the labor (affectivity) required to make sense of the images that cinematic machines select, cut, frame, and circulate is the same kind of labor required to live in and make sense of the world organized by the cinematic."[52] Although *the work of affectivity*, according to Keeling, together with the cinematic, trains us to accommodate to current conditions of life, indeed numbs our neurological systems to absorb shock as clichés, it also "retains the potential to manifest an alternate perceptual schema that could perfect a different social reality." "In order to enter into a relation with thinking, cinema's images have to confront that state to which they constantly sink: cliché. . . . That clichés are what 'we' normally perceive is the outcome of adaptation and survival. . . . We have schemata for turning away when it is too unpleasant, for prompting resignation when it is terrible and for assimilating when it is too beautiful."[53] Kinds of "surplus" markets Keeling considers are, say, those of disaffected urban black youth in the sixties addressed by so-called blaxploitation films *then*, and, say, those appealed to as "lesbians," together with those of adolescent and adult heterosexual males, oddly jointly addressed by such serial dramas on cable-television channels as *The L Word* later on and closer to *now*. As representative and representation the person and image of actor Pam Grier queerly link these by 2007: "Pam Grier's presence in *The L Word* might introject into the series some of blaxploitation's surplus value and its surplus populations (and with them the potential for a critique of normative ideals of race, gender, class, and sexuality)."[54]

For Keeling, "common sense" consists both of common ways bodies neurologically connect sensory perception as emotion and also a common "set of memory-images that includes experiences, knowledges, traditions, and so on and that are available to memory during perception."[55] "By claiming that common sense is a shared set of memory-images and a set of commonly habituated sensory-motor movements with the capacity to enable alternative perceptions and, hence, alternative knowledges, I am challenging narratives of political struggle that reify Reason . . . [including] political organizing based on consciousness raising more generally. I am also insisting on a conceptualization of common sense in which shared conceptions of the world are inseparable from sensory-motor functions."[56]

Reenaction and reenactment also entail the work of affectivity disquieting the "Reason" that Keeling analyzes, with the help of those theorists, activists, artists, devices, and genealogies she demonstrates for us, her personal "careabouts" that we learn in her demonstrations also to find affecting, to be effectuated by. The complex and sometimes idiosyncratic archive she shares with us spans knowledge worlds emblematized by appeals to Walter Benjamin that overflow any critique essentialized as "the Frankfort School," Gayatri Chakravorty Spivak and the conflicts of feminist deconstruction, W. E. B. Du Bois and a doubly conscious Pan Africanism, women of the Black Panther Party figuring in Pam Grier's blaxsploitations, the transformative abjections in a psychiatry of colonialism of Franz Fanon, as well as the canny commercialisms that raise but cannot open up its black femme function of Kasi Lemmons's *Eve's Bayou*; all that and much more. This is one sort of transdisciplinary R and D: making use of what you have on hand and seeing what you can put together with it. Like reenactment authenticities it is sensitive to what is available for use. Thus, it is not a kind of scholarship that works first to design and control its research model, to lay out a menu of research methods and choose the proper ones, to carefully investigate subject matters that can be seen finally to be integrated at some point of intersecting convergence. Its forms of robust knowledge are clearly contingent and primarily suggestive —in other words pointing beyond itself. Such robust knowledge making appeals to transmedia hunting and gathering practices across knowledge worlds. It rewards a telescoped and scaling un-black-boxing set of meanings, yet still tantalizes and truly shares its work also with more intensively hailed but widely distributed communities of practice and identity.

Keeling's is not an elegant argument, in original intention or in a retrospective parsimony of explanation, but instead, as with Despret's retelling of the clever Hans story, it furthers a multiplication of entities— enlarging sensoria and sensitizing worlds. To greet a book of this sort and its transdisciplinary projects means to engage in significant othernesses: of method, identity, knowledge. It connects across, through, and beyond archives or legibilities among particular memberships, and models how to learn and unlearn in an increasingly enlarged world.

What the reenactments, reenactors, and reenactions described and analyzed here index, together with what the materialities of reenactment studies in its own creation might offer us, are entry points into various "rigors" of learning to be affected. By scoping and scaling among their various "kits" we come across opportunities for becoming progressively more alive, and, through each new exquisite sensitivity to each already existing but yet momentary horizon of possible resources and infrastructures, local exigencies, and differential memberships, we *add* these to our worldly territories. And we learn to do that without taking each one as all and for *everything* it might also turn out to be about.

NOTES

FOREWORD

1 Katie King, *Epistemology: Stories Knowledges Tell*, http://wmst601fall10.blog spot.com.
2 For example, see Talal Asad, Wendy Brown, Judith Butler, and Saba Mahmood, "Is Critique Secular? Blasphemy, Injury and Free Speech," Townsend Center for the Humanities, 2009, http://escholarship.org/uc/item/84q9c 6ft; Bruno Latour, "Why Has Critique Run out of Steam? From Matters of Fact to Matters of Concern," *Critical Inquiry* 30 (Winter 2004): 225–48; and Maria Puig, "Matters of Care in Technoscience: Assembling Neglected Things," *Social Studies of Science* 41, no. 1 (February 2011).
3 Jacques Derrida, *Specters of Marx: The State of the Debt, the Work of Mourning, and the New International*, trans. Peggy Kamuf (New York and London: Routledge, 1994), 54.
4 Katie King, "'Knowledge-weaving': Befriending Transdisciplinarity under the Urgencies of Global Academic Restructuring," *Knowledges Weaving Stories*, http://weaveknowledge.blogspot.com/.
5 Ibid.

PREFACE

1 Exemplified by the wonderful work of Jenny Thompson. See her "What Are the People Who Re-Enact 20th Century Wars up To?," University of York, http://www.york.ac.uk/ipup/projects/reenactment/discussion/thompson .html. See also her *War Games*.
2 A lively intensively understood version is Taylor, *Play between Worlds*.
3 Spigel and Mann, eds., *Private Screenings*; Gitelman, *Always Already New*; Sobchack, *Meta-Morphing*.
4 For example, Juul, *Half-Real*.
5 Especially Bolter and Grusin, *Remediation*.

1 "Other globalizations" used here in solidarity with activists around the world that, as Donna Haraway says, "stress that their approaches to militarized neoliberal models of world building are not about antiglobalizations but about nurturing a more just and peaceful other-globalization" (Haraway, *When Species Meet*, 3).

2 For one discussion, see Wikipedia, "Don't Be Evil," http://en.wikipedia.org/wiki/Don't_be_evil.

3 For an example of the many popular histories of Google, see Vise and Malseed, *The Google Story*.

4 Valuable materials opening onto these domains are: Star, ed., *Ecologies of Knowledge*; Suchman, "Located Accountabilities in Technology Production"; Gieryn, "Policing S.T.S."; and Slaughter and Rhoades, *Academic Capitalism and the New Economy*.

5 For more information on *ITN Factual*, see their website at http://corporate.itn.co.uk/itn-factual.aspx.

6 See either the trailer on YouTube via Paul Sapin's channel, xraysapin, *Leonardo's Dream Machines*, http://www.youtube.com/user/xraysapin#p/u/8/6y4bgibiRdg; or at Sapin online, *X-ray Spex Ltd.*, http://www.sapinxray.com. You can also buy the documentary on DVD from PBS Home Video, http://www.shoppbs.org.

7 See the official website of the Woodvilles, http://woodvilles.org.uk.

8 King, "Pastpresents: Playing Cat's Cradle with Donna Haraway."

9 Bowker and Star, *Sorting Things Out*.

10 You can see this sequence in the trailer mentioned in note 6.

11 For an argument that makes such shorthand possible, see Johnson, *Everything Bad Is Good for You*. There is an extensive scholarly and industrial literature on gaming now. One example from this wide-open research and commercial area I discuss in chapter 4 is Salen and Zimmerman, *Rules of Play*.

12 One influential strand of pioneering work in these analyses emerges from collaborations in several conferences and the special issue of at least one journal. See Agnew and Lamb, eds., "Extreme and Sentimental History," special issue, *Criticism* 46, no. 3. I discuss these in more depth in chapter 4.

13 Klein, "Disciplinary Origins and Differences." (She is citing Clark, *Places of inquiry*, 193.) See also Klein, "Interdisciplinary Needs."

14 For a tantalizing discussion concerning such travel and contextualization, see Vann and Bowker, "Instrumentalizing the Truth of Practice." Also Stafford, "Epistemology for Sale." Whole realms of practice and educational theory work out among such experimental forms of learning: for example, the MIT Media Lab's Future of Learning Group, http://learning.media.mit.edu/, and analysis emerging from it such as E. Ackerman, "Piaget's Constructivism, Papert's Constructionism: What's the Difference?," MIT Media Lab, http://learning.media.mit.edu/content/publications/EA.Piaget%20_%20Papert.pdf.

15 I learned to use the term "complex personhood" from Gordon, *Ghostly Matters*.

16 A wonderful example is Hayward, "FingeryEyes."

17 For a similar argument, see G. Bateson, "Effects of Conscious Purpose on Human Adaptation" and "Ecology and Flexibility in Urban Civilization," in *Steps to an Ecology of Mind*; G. Bateson, *Mind and Nature*; M. C. Bateson, *Our Own Metaphor*. See also Hayles, *How We Became Posthuman*.

1. NATIONALITIES, SEXUALITIES, GLOBAL TV

1 For example, see the discussion in Sardar, Nandy, Davies, and Alvares, *The Blinded Eye*.

2 Fréches, *La Guerre Des Images* is quoted by Morley and Robins in *Spaces of Identity*, 34.

3 See Sherwood, "Historic Agreements: Like Its Mythic Hero, 'Highlander' Has a Distinctly International Flair," in *"Highlander,"* special issue, *Hollywood Reporter* (December 3, 1996), S6, S30–S42. See also the complete collection of the *Highlander* TV series, *Highlander—The Complete Series* (*Seasons 1–6*), Peter Davis and Bill Panzer (Anchor Bay Entertainment, 2005), DVD.

4 Closed at the original site during World War II the current bookstore is today located on the Seine, at 37, Rue de la Bucherie. See Ian C. Mills, "Shakespeare and Company: 12, Rue de l'Odéon," DiscoverFrance.net, December 6, 2002, http://www.discoverfrance.net/France/Paris/Paris_Hemingway3.shtml; and Fitch, "Shakespeare and Company." See also Fitch, *Sylvia Beach and the Lost Generation*.

5 Jeffrey Ressner, "Freddie Mercury, 1946–1991: *Queen* Singer Is Rock's First Major AIDS Casualty," *Rolling Stone* (January 9, 1992), 13. Adam Block and R. Laermer, "Freddie Mercury and the AIDS closet," *Advocate* (December 31, 1991), 74. J. Clark-Meads, "Queen Sales Soar in Wake of Freddie Mercury Death," *Billboard* (December 21, 1991), 14.

6 Jess Cagle, "America Sees Shades of Gay," *Entertainment Weekly* (September 8, 1995), 22, 24, 31.

7 Hennessy, "Queer Visibility in Commodity Culture," 164–65, 177.

8 *Ellen*, 1994–1998, TV series, created by Carol Black, Neal Martins, and David S. Rosenthal, starring Ellen DeGeneres, David Anthony Higgins, and Joely Fisher. For lesbian and gay commentary on the teasing period before the coming out episode, see Anne Stockwell, *"Ellen's Gay Games," Advocate* (November, 12, 1996), 59–61. The coming out episode aired in April 1997. It was celebrated on the famous "Yep, I'm Gay" *Time* magazine cover, April 14, 1997, which is archived at GLADD online, "Ellen: 10 Years Out—A Timeline," http://archive.glaad.org/media/resource_kit_detail.php?id=4000. See also Bruce Handy, Elizabeth Bland, William Tynan, and Jeffrey Ressner, "Roll over, Ward Cleaver," *Time* (April 14, 1997), 78–83; and Bruce Handy, "He Called Me Ellen Degenerate?" *Time* (April 14, 1997), 86. For retrospective discussion, see Hilary De Vries, "Out & About: Ellen DeGeneres," *TV Guide*

(October 11, 1997), 20; and Hubert, "What's Wrong with This Picture?" For discussion of inside jokes in "encrypted ads" intended to appeal to gay markets without alienating straight audiences, especially one premiering on the coming out episode, see Ronald Alsop, "Cracking the Gay Market Code," *Wall Street Journal* (June 29, 1999), B1.

9 *Xena: Warrior Princess*, TV series, created by John Schulian and Robert G. Tapert, starring Lucy Lawless, Renée O'Connor, and Ted Raimi (MCA Television, 1995–2001). See Elizabeth Kastor, "Woman of Steel: Television's Warrior Xena Is a Superheroine With Broad Appeal," *Washington Post* (September 21, 1996), C1, C5; Freeman, "Mything in Action"; Hayes, "Lucy Lawless: Xena." See also Michele Kort, "Xena Cyberprincess," *Advocate* (March 2, 1999), 24–30; and Pullen, "I-Love-Xena.Com."

10 See the website for Highlander Worldwide, the Official Highlander Fan Club, http://www.highlanderworldwide.com.

11 Sandoval, *Methodology of the Oppressed*.

12 Haraway, *Modest_Witness*, 16, 273. Latour, *We Have Never Been Modern*, 144–45.

13 Johnson, *Everything Bad Is Good for You*.

14 *Highlander*, TV series, starring Adrian Paul, Stan Kirsch, and Jim Byrnes (Davis-Panzer Productions, 1992–1998). See Turman, "Gaumont," 22.

15 See "Interview with Peter Davis and William Panzer, Producers of *Highlander: The TV Series*," in "*Highlander*," special issue, *Hollywood Reporter* (December 3, 1996), S20.

16 Sherwood, "Historic Agreements," S40; and Sherwood, "Fantastic Voyages: As It Reaches the Century Mark 'Highlander' Looks to the Future while Embracing the Past," in "*Highlander*," special issue, *Hollywood Reporter* (December 3, 1996), S1.

17 Sherwood, "Historic Agreements," S32.

18 *Highlander: The Raven*, TV series, starring Paul Johansson, Elizabeth Gracen, and Patricia Gage (Davis-Panzer Productions, 1998–1999). See also *Highlander: The Animated Series*, 1994, TV series, created by Serge Rosenzweig, starring Miklos Perlus, Lawrence Bayne, and Tracey Moore.

19 *Highlander IV: Endgame*, directed by Douglas Aarniokoski (Davis-Panzer Productions and Miramax, 2000). See also *Highlander V: The Source*, directed by Brett Leonard (Davis-Panzer Productions and Lions Gate, 2007). See also Peter Davis, "Re: *Highlander: The Source*," available via the Internet Archive's Wayback Machine.

20 *Highlander*, directed by Russell Mulcahy (Thorn EMI and Twentieth Century Fox, 1986); *Highlander II: The Quickening*, directed by Russell Mulcahy (Lamb Bear Entertainment and Interstar, 1991); and *Highlander III: The Final Dimension*, directed by Andrew Morahan (Fallingcloud and Miramax, 1994).

21 Turman, "Gaumont," 22, 23; Millar, "Alice Guy," 229.

22 Diversification table in Wasko, *Hollywood in the Information Age*, 43, 63–65; adapted from *Standard & Poor's Industry Surveys* (11 March 1993), L17.

23 See Vivendi Universal, "Company History," http://www.vivendi.com/vivendi/ Company-history; Bates, "Lew R. Wasserman"; Sandow, "In the Fray"; "Bronfman Family Holdings," *Los Angeles Times* (October 8, 2002), http:// articles.latimes.com/2002/oct/08/business/fi-bronfgraphic8. These corporations have morphed considerably since I began my research as I have tried to indicate here.

24 NBC Universal, "Company Overview" (June 2, 2007), http://www.nbcuni .com/About_NBC_Universal/Company_Overview; this information has obviously also altered since I began my research, and for current NBC Universal company information, see http://www.nbcuni.com/about-us/. Sci Fi changed its brand name to Syfy in July 2009. The History Channel changed its brand name to History in February 2008.

25 Sassen, ed., *Global Networks, Linked Cities.*

26 "Gaumont Topper Thinks 'Upgrade,'" *Variety* (December 12–18, 1994), 58.

27 Lisa Gubernick, "No Trade War Here," *Forbes* (February 28, 1994), 118.

28 "Gaumont Topper Thinks 'Upgrade,'" 58.

29 Sherwood, "Historic Agreements," S34.

30 I have borrowed the term "recombinant subgenre" from Sanjek, "Home Alone."

31 Sherwood, "Historic Agreements," S38.

32 Both the *Highlander* and *Xena* catalogs are, as of 2010, online together; see Davis Merchandising Corporation, "Legendary Heroes," http://www.digicap sule.com/LegendaryHeroes/index.html. Interestingly enough, Panzer and Davis have been involved in the merchandizing of both shows (presumably because they share overlapping fandoms).

33 The demographic research I am quoting from here has only been done within the United States and does not contain information about distribution of nationalities, or about the race, class, and gender composition of these audiences in countries other than the United States, although it may be roughly comparable. Bacon-Smith, "Who Are Fanziners? Demographics."

34 David Denby, "The Quick and the Dead," *New York Magazine* (February 27, 1995), 108.

35 All assembled in the Xena Media Review Archives, 1996–1998, edited by Kym Masera Taborn, http://www.xenafan.com/xmr/, "XMR/TWXN Online ReadingArea," xmr02ob.txt, annotation #149.5 (1/28/96), Auckland *Sunday News*, "Legendary Stuff," 31; annotation #144.5 (01/27/96), Wellington *Dominion*, "Pilot to Kick Off Hercules' NZ Run," 23; and annotation #267 (05/12/96), Brennan, "MCA's Dynamic Duo Goes Int'l: 'Hercules' and 'Xena' Wrap Up Virtually Every Major Market," *Hollywood Reporter.*

36 Morley and Robins, *Spaces of Identity*, 33, 36.

37 Fréches, *La Guerre Des Images* ("image superpowers") is quoted by Morley and Robins in *Spaces of Identity*, 34.

38 Sassen, "Introduction: Locating Cities on Global Circuits," 20; and Morley and Robins, *Spaces of Identity*, 36.

39 For example see Sassen, *Global City*; Sassen, *Cities in a World Economy*; Sassen, *Globalization and Its Discontents*; and Sassen, "Economic Globalization."

40 Sassen, "Introduction: Locating Cities on Global Circuits," 16–17.

41 Johnson, *Everything Bad Is Good for You*, 46.

42 Ibid., 54 (emphasis mine).

43 Collins, "National Culture: A Contradiction in Terms?," quoted in Morley and Robins, *Spaces of Identity*, 43.

44 The creation of and contests for what counts as a "gay market" can be traced in materials such as Ronald Alsop, "Cracking the Gay Market Code"; Alsop, "Are Gay People More Affluent Than Others?" *Wall Street Journal* (December 30, 1999), B1; and Alsop, "In Marketing to Gays, Lesbians Are Often Left Out," *Wall Street Journal* (October 11, 1999), B1. See especially Badgett, *Money, Myths, and Change*.

45 Morley and Robins, *Spaces of Identity*, 117.

46 Hogan, *Complete Guide to the Music of Queen*. Note especially the pictures showing how Mercury's image morphed over decades.

47 Block and Laermer, "Freddie Mercury and the AIDS Closet"; Ressner, "Freddie Mercury, 1946–1991"; Clark-Meads, "Queen Sales Soar in Wake of Freddie Mercury Death."

48 Hogan, *Complete Guide to the Music of Queen*, 96. See also, EMI online, "*Queen*—the Ultimate Biography," http://fly.cc.fer.hr/~mvidacek/history.htm. See also Queen, *A Kind of Magic* (EMI Records, 1986).

49 "Princes of the Universe" (theme from *Highlander*), music video directed by Russell Mulcahy (1986). See also QueenZone, "Queen Biography for 1986," http://www.queenzone.com/biography/queen-biography-for-1986.aspx.

50 See Benetton Group, "What We Say | About Our Past Campaigns | AIDS and Safer Sex," available via the Internet Archive's Wayback Machine; Musée de la Publicité, "United Colors of Benetton Advertising History," available via the Internet Archive's Wayback Machine. See also The Commercial Closet, http://www.commercialcloset.org.

51 Ang, *Living Room Wars*, 146.

52 *Highlander*, "Chivalry," production number 95410–76, season 4, episode 10, 1995.

53 *Highlander*, "Timeless," production number 95411–77, season 4, episode 11, 1995.

54 Bacon-Smith, *Enterprising Women*; Jenkins, *Textual Poachers*; Penley, *Nasa/Trek*; Penley, "Brownian Motion"; Penley, ed., *Close Encounters*.

55 *Boston Legal*, 2004–2008, TV series, created by David E. Kelley, starring James Spader, William Shatnet, and Candice Bergen.

56 Russ, "Pornography By Women For Women, With Love." See also Penley, *Nasa/Trek*.

57 For example, Karen Nicholas, "Slash Fan Fiction on the Net," available via the Internet Archive's Wayback Machine; Trekscribe, "*Crossing the Nebula*: Home of the *Voyager* Alternative/Slash Fan Fiction Series *The Delta Quadrant Chron-*

icles," http://www.crossingthenebula.com/index.htm. For examples of *Highlander* slash in particular online, see Novik, "The Unthinkable Alternative: A Duncan/Methos Archive," available via the Internet Archive's Wayback Machine; and AnnF, "The Seventh Dimension: Highlander Fan Fiction Archive," http://www.seventh-dimension.org.

58 For examples of *Xena* slash online, see "Hergerbabe's Parlour," available via the Internet Archive's Wayback Machine; and Xenite.org, "Worlds of Imagination on the Web," http://www.xenite.org. "Slash Xena Fan Fiction Review Plus," http://slashxenafanficreview.com, is unfortunately no longer available.

59 Cynthia Cooper, Debbie Cassetta, Ted Turocy, and K. Wieczerza, "The Xena: Warrior Princess FAQ: The Sapphic Subtext," Whoosh!, http://www.whoosh .org/faq/faq.html. See also Diane Silver, "Xena: Warrior Princess, A FAQ for Subtext Fans and the Loyal Opposition," available via the Internet Archive's Wayback Machine.

60 Internet Movie Database (IMDb), "Lucy Lawless Filmography," http://www .imdb.com/name/nm0005128. See also Diane Silver, "A Cyber History of the Online Xena Community." Whoosh!, http://www.whoosh.org/issue13/sil ver2.html.

61 For example, Alex Tresniowski and Craig Tomashoff, "Lawfully Wedded," *People* (April 13, 1998), 151–52, http://www.people.com/people/archive/ar ticle/0,,20124979,00.html.

62 See history of XenaVerse in Silver, "A Cyber History of the Online Xena Community."

63 Cooper, Cassetta, Turocy and Wieczerza, "The Xena: Warrior Princess FAQ."

64 Morley and Robins, *Spaces of Identity*, 34.

65 For example, Hadden, *The Civil War Reenactor's Handbook*; and "Lance and Liz's Reenacting Page," available via the Internet Archive's Wayback Machine.

66 Spigel, "Installing the Television Set," 16, 18. See also *George Burns and Gracie Allen Show*, 1950–1958, TV series; *I Love Lucy*, 1951–1957, TV series.

67 *Xena*, "Destiny," season 2, episode 12, 1997.

68 Frozina, "Humorous Disclaimers Summary," Logomancy *Xena*, http://www .klio.net/XENA/EPIsoDES/xenadishum.html.

69 *Xena*, "Altared States," season 1, episode 19, 1996.

70 From Frozina, "Humorous Disclaimers Summary": "Season 1, used in: 'Hooves & Harlots': No Males, Centaurs or Amazons were harmed / during the production of this motion picture." "Season 1, used in: 'The Royal Couple Of Thieves': No Ancient and Inflexible Rules governing / moral behavior were harmed during the / production of this motion picture." "Season 1, used in: 'Altared States': No Unrelenting or Severely Punishing Deities were / harmed during the production of this motion picture." "Season 1, used in: 'Ties That Bind': No Fathers, Spiritual or Biological, were harmed / during the production of this motion picture."

71 From Frozina, "Humorous Disclaimers Summary": "Season 2, used in: 'Destiny': Julius Caesar was not harmed during the / production of this motion

picture. / However, the Producers deny responsibility for any / unfortunate acts of betrayal occurring soon thereafter." And "Season 2, used in: 'The Quest': Xena's body was not harmed during the production / of this motion picture. However, it took weeks for / Autolycus to get his swagger back."

72 Whoosh, "Destiny Episode Summary," http://www.whoosh.org/epguide/ destiny.html.

73 My thanks to Bill Pietz for long discussions about the psychology of reception and for making this particular point.

74 *Highlander*, "Valkyrie," production number 96510–98, season 5, episode 11, 1996.

75 Charles Trueheart, "Thousands of Protesters March as French Far-Right Group Meets," *Washington Post* (March 30, 1997), A17.

76 Footage edited together from several episodes in which Duncan's involvement in the American Civil War and civil rights movement is depicted can be viewed on the video *Life and Times of Duncan MacLeod* (Davis-Panzer Productions, 1995), videocassette. See for example *Highlander*, "Run for Your Life," production number 93209–31, season 2, episode 9, 1993.

77 Sherwood, "Fantastic Voyages," S3; see the Official Adrian Paul Website, http://adrianpaul.net, which includes the Peace Fund, http://www.thepeace fund.org, on the "Charity" tab on Paul's homepage.

78 Morley and Robins, *Spaces of Identity*, 50.

79 See for example *Highlander*, "For Tomorrow We Die," production number 92116–15, season 1, episode 15, 1993. See also Edge, *Fine Young Cannibals' Story*.

80 Baun, "The Maastricht Treaty as High Politics," 605. Also Cere, *European and National Identities in Britain and Italy*.

81 *Disclosure*, directed by Barry Levinson (Warner Brothers Pictures, 1994). And see Crichton, *Disclosure: A Novel*.

82 *Fatal Attraction*, directed by Adrian Lyne (Paramount Pictures, 1987).

83 Examples of available products are at Amazon.com or Toys'R'Us. See also Davis Merchandising Corporation, "Legendary Heroes," http://www.digicap sule.com/LegendaryHeroes/index.html. For examples of stories of production, listing episodes and their writers, and offering critical discussions, from fans, from journalists, and from academics, see Weisbrot, *Xena, Warrior Princess*; Crenshaw, *Xena X-Posed*; or Pullen, "I-Love-Xena.Com."

84 Bolter and Grusin, *Remediation*, 68.

85 Davis Merchandising Corporation, "Legendary Heroes," http://www.digicap sule.com/LegendaryHeroes/index.html.

86 See Davis Merchandising Corporation and David Panzer Productions, "*Xena* Store," http://www.legendaryheroes.com/indexXena.asp.

87 *Highlander* Official online, "The Immortals Live On as *Highlander: The Source* prepares to film," exact target e-mail redirected online, August 4, 2005, from http://view.exacttarget.com/?ffcc17-fe8e15757365027b7d-fe33157176660 d7d711173, no longer available.

88 Sci Fi Wire, "New *Highlander* to Shoot," August 4, 2005, http://www.scifi .com/scifiwire2005/index.php?id=31891, no longer available.

89 Cooper, Cassetta, Turocy, and Wieczerza, "The Xena: Warrior Princess FAQ."

90 *Xena*, "Destiny"; *Xena*, "The Quest," season 2, episode 13, 1997.

91 *Xena*, "The Bitter Suite," season 3, episode 12, 1998.

92 *From Here to Eternity*, directed by Fred Zinnemann (Columbia Pictures Corporation, 1953).

93 See also Joseph, "The Performance of Production and Consumption."

2. SCIENCE IN AMERICAN LIFE

1 And to be visited as such by creationist students learning how to respond to evolution-based arguments. See Steve Hendrix, "The Genesis of a Debate: Creationist Students Take Field Trip to Hotbed of Evolution: The Smithsonian," *Washington Post* (March 11, 2009), A1, A12.

2 Jacqueline Trescott, "No Shortage of Names for Smithsonian Successor," *Washington Post* (March 28, 2007), C01; and Jaqueline Trescott and James V. Grimaldi, "Smithsonian's Small Quits in Wake of Inquiry," *Washington Post* (March 27, 2007), A1.

3 Robert Sullivan, "Castle in Disrepair; It's Been Politicized and Kitschified, and Its Luster Is Gone," *Washington Post* (April 1, 2007), B1.

4 Smithsonian Institution, *Science in American Life*, exhibition (National Museum of American History, Kenneth E. Behring Center, 1994–), http://ameri canhistory.si.edu/exhibitions/exhibition.cfm?key=38&exkey=57.

5 Rhees, "The Chemists' Crusade." Rhees had been a predoctoral fellow at the Smithsonian's NMAH and his advisor there was *SAL*'s chief curator, Arthur P. Molella, in 1984–1985.

6 Smithsonian American Art Museum, William Truettner, *The West as America: Reinterpreting Images of the Frontier, 1820–1920*, exhibition (Smithsonian American Art Museum, 1991); Truettner and Anderson, eds., *The West as America*; and Robert Hughes, "How the West Was Spun," *Time* (May 13, 1991), 79–80. See also Perkins, "Museum War Exhibits."

7 Smithsonian Institution, National Air and Space Museum, *Enola Gay*, exhibition (National Air and Space Museum, 1995–1998; 2003–), http://www .nasm.si.edu/exhibitions/gal103/enolagay; Linenthal and Engelhardt, eds., *History Wars*; Perkins, "Museum War Exhibits."

8 Nobile, ed., *Judgment at the Smithsonian*; Harwit, *An Exhibit Denied*.

9 Lubar, "Exhibiting Memories"; Dubin, *Displays of Power*.

10 Republican Study Committee, "Policy Brief National Endowment for the Arts," July 19, 2002, available via the Internet Archive's Wayback Machine. Under the second Bush administration proposals to privatize professional jobs in, for example, the National Park Service, also worked to punish progressive cultural efforts; see Julie Cart, "70% of Jobs in Park Service Marked

Ripe for Privatizing," *Los Angeles Times* (January 26, 2003); Christopher Lee, "Park Service Plans Outsourcing," *Washington Post* (April 19, 2003), A4.

11 Park, "Is Science the God That Failed?," 207.

12 Latour and Weibel, eds., *Iconoclash*.

13 Latour, *War of the Worlds*, 21.

14 Bowker and Star, *Sorting Things Out*, esp. 294–300.

15 Latour, *We Have Never Been Modern*, 114–29.

16 Ibid., 39.

17 Ibid., 40.

18 Latour, "The Promises of Constructivism," 32.

19 Gieryn, "Preface to the Deconstruction," 52–53 (emphasis mine).

20 Ibid., 54.

21 Star, "Introduction to *Ecologies of Knowledge*," 22.

22 Latour, "Iconoclash or Is There a World Beyond the Image Wars?," http://www.bruno-latour.fr/articles/2002.html.

23 Latour, "Iconoclash."

24 The dummy scientists are named, representing specific people. They are, in rough order of appearance (the asterisk indicates which ones appear in later parts of the exhibit):

> Vijaya L. Melnick, biology (South Asian woman)*
> Cynthia Friend, chemist (white woman)*
> Matthew George, evolutionary biology (black man)*
> S.B. Woo, physicist (Asian man)*
> Jo Anne V. Simson, cell biologist (white woman)
> Jonathan A. Coddington, arachnologist (young white man)
> Samuel T. Durrance, astronomer and astronaut (white man)
> Rita R. Colwell, microbiologist (older white woman)
> Susan Solomon, atmospheric chemist (white woman)*
> Jose V. Martinez, chemical physicist (Hispanic man)*

The children are:

> Mitzuki Tanabe, 8th grade (Asian girl; interest in genetic engineering)
> Kyle Connor, 6th grade (black boy; interest in chemical science)

The laminated book, which describes all of them, not in any obvious order, uses these categories for adult scientists: name, position, photo, quote; most exciting thing about your work, proudest moments, most important [lost word?]; spare time pursuits, another photo. For the children the categories are: name, grade, photo, quote; science interest, photo, hobbies.

25 For Lynn Mulkey and William Dougan's outline, see Mulkey and Dougan, "The Smithsonian Institution Exhibition of 'Science in American Life': Science as It Consists of Normalized Practices," *American Sociologist* 27, no. 2 (1996): 69; for Gieryn's notes, see Thomas Gieryn, "Policing STS: A Boundary-Work Souvenir from the Smithsonian Exhibition on 'Science in American Life,'" *Science, Technology, and Human Values* 21, no. 1 (1996): 100–15.

26 Dioramas at various scales produce reenactment effects throughout *SAL*. I

argue in this chapter that these *SAL* reenactment effects offer forms of scaled identifications and disidentifications (shadowing and witnessing) that link it to other reenactment effects described elsewhere in this book. Donna Haraway argues that the effects of some past dioramas, such as those of Carl Akeley in the African Hall of the American Museum of Natural History in New York City, create moments of communion at which the sacred and secular meet. See Haraway, *Primate Visions*, 29–32.

27 Mulkey and Dougan, "Smithsonian Institution Exhibition of 'Science in American Life,'" 69.

28 Ibid.

29 Gieryn, "Policing STS," 103.

30 Mulkey and Dougan, "Smithsonian Institution Exhibition of 'Science in American Life,'" 69.

31 Ibid.

32 Gieryn, "Policing STS," 103.

33 Mulkey and Dougan, "Smithsonian Institution Exhibition of 'Science in American Life,'" 69.

34 Ibid.

35 Ibid.

36 Ibid.

37 Gieryn, "Policing STS," 103.

38 Mulkey and Dougan, "Smithsonian Institution Exhibition of 'Science in American Life,'" 69.

39 Ibid.

40 Ibid.

41 Gieryn, "Policing STS," 104.

42 Mulkey and Dougan, "Smithsonian Institution Exhibition of 'Science in American Life,'" 69.

43 Ibid.

44 Ibid.

45 Ibid.

46 Gieryn, "Policing STS," 104.

47 Ibid. (emphasis mine).

48 Singleton and Michael, "Actor-Networks and Ambivalence," 228.

49 See Latour, *Science in Action*.

50 Singleton and Michael, "Actor-Networks and Ambivalence," 230 (emphasis mine). See also Callon, "The Sociology of an Actor-Network."

51 Gross, "Reply to Tom Gieryn," 119.

52 Gieryn, "Policing STS," 107.

53 Pekarik, Doering, and Bickford, "Visitors' Role in an Exhibition Debate," 117, 127, 126 (emphasis mine).

54 Ibid., 121.

55 Molella, "Science in American Life, National Identity, and the Science Wars," 113.

56 Mulkey and Dougan, "Smithsonian Institution Exhibition of 'Science in American Life,'" 77 (emphasis mine).

57 Gieryn, "Policing STS," 114n4.

58 Latour's phrase, "Promises of Constructivism."

59 Haraway's phrase, *Companion Species Manifesto*, 6.

60 Latour, *We Have Never Been Modern*, 125.

61 Mulkey and Dougan, "Smithsonian Institution Exhibition of 'Science in American Life,'" 73 (emphasis mine).

62 Haraway, "Situated Knowledges."

63 Mulkey and Dougan, "Smithsonian Institution Exhibition of 'Science in American Life,'" 73 (emphasis mine).

64 Haraway, *Modest_Witness*, 267, 70. Note that the second paragraph of the extracted quote is from an earlier section of Haraway's book.

65 Mulkey and Dougan, "Smithsonian Institution Exhibition of 'Science in American Life,'" 74, 76.

66 Noah Adams, "Timeline: Remembering the Scopes Monkey Trial," NPR (July 5, 2005); Doug Gross, "Challenge to Evolution Dropped in Georgia," MSNBC.com (December 19, 2006).

67 Weston, *Gender in Real Time*, 122 (emphasis mine).

68 Ibid., 124, 35.

69 Ibid., 138 (emphasis mine).

70 Latour, *War of the Worlds*, 40.

71 Haraway, *Modest_Witness*, 268.

72 Haraway and Goodeve, *How Like a Leaf*, 107.

73 Star, "Introduction to *Ecologies of Knowledge*," 22.

74 Haraway elaborates and animates theories of Alfred North Whitehead: "Reality is an active verb, and the nouns all seem to be gerunds with more appendages than an octopus. Through their reaching into each other, through their 'prehensions' or graspings, beings constitute each other and themselves. Beings do not preexist their relatings. 'Prehensions' have consequences. The world is a knot in motion" (*Companion Species Manifesto*, 6–7).

75 Pekarik, Doering, and Bickford, "Visitors' Role in an Exhibition Debate," 126.

76 For an insightfully critical analysis, see, for example, Poovey, "The Twenty-First-Century University and the Market."

77 Slaughter and Leslie, *Academic Capitalism*, 5–11.

78 Vann and Bowker, "Instrumentalizing the Truth of Practice," 248 (emphasis mine). See also, Lave, *Cognition in Practice*; Lave and Wenger, *Situated Learning*; and Wenger, *Communities of Practice*.

79 Bowker and Star, *Sorting Things Out*, 297.

80 Simmons College, "Simmons College: Character," available via the Internet Archive's Wayback Machine.

81 Stafford, "Epistemology for Sale," 215, 215–16.

82 Lewenstein, "An American Historical Perspective on Public Communication of Science," n.p. (emphasis mine).

83 Ibid., n.p. (emphasis mine).

84 Smithsonian, Newsdesk, "Facts Sheet: Secretaries of the Smithsonian Institution," http://newsdesk.si.edu/factsheets/secretaries-smithsonian-institution.

85 Smithsonian, Newsdesk, "Press Biography of Lawrence M. Small," available via the Internet Archive's Wayback Machine.

86 The first phrase is from Secretary Small's testimony before the Senate Rules Committee, "Testimony of Lawrence M. Small," US Senate Committee on Rules and Administration, June 27, 2000. The second is from Mokhiber and Weissman, "Blue Light Special at the Smithsonian," Common Dreams (February 17, 2001), http://www.commondreams.org/views01/0217-07.htm. For the "crisis," see also Penrice, "Can This Museum Be Saved?"; Jasmin Chua, "Crisis at the Smithsonian." *Archaeology* (September 19, 2002), http://www.archaeology.org/online/features/smithsonian/index.html; Jacqueline Trescott, "Display Care Courting Cash, Museums Told," *Washington Post* (November 22, 2002), C12; and Patricia Nelson Limerick, "The Smithsonian Scandal That Wasn't," History News Network (May 22, 2002), http://hnn.us/articles/748.html.

87 John Johnston, "Meet the Freedom Center's Executive Director, Crew's Opportunity: Bringing History to Life," *Cincinnati Enquirer* (November 15, 2001), http://www.enquirer.com/editions/2001/11/15/loc_meet_freedom _centers.html. See also Smithsonian Institution, National Museum of American History, *Field to Factory: Afro-American Migration 1915–1940*, exhibition (National Museum of American History, 1987–2006), http://www.si.edu/ Exhibitions/Details/Field-to-Factory-Afro-American-Migration-1915–1940 -3994.

88 Smithsonian, "Brent D. Glass Named Director of the Smithsonian's National Museum of American History," National Museum of American History (October 17, 2002), http://americanhistory.si.edu/news/pressrelease.cfm?key= 29&newskey=76.

89 Smithsonian, "Smithsonian Institution Announces Biggest Single Donation in its 154-year History," National Museum of American History (September 19, 2000), http://americanhistory.si.edu/news/pressrelease.cfm?key= 29&newskey=93; Smithsonian, "Engaging America: Let the Campaign Begin —Report of the Office of Capital Campaign," External Relation and Board Liaison (2000), no longer available online; and Smithsonian, "Smithsonian Year 2000: Annual Report," Office of the Secretary (September 2000), http:// www.si.edu/opanda/docs/RegentsReports/RRFY2000Q4.pdf.

90 Although some claim Small had a hand in the further gift and how it was going to be used. See Penrice, "Can This Museum Be Saved?"

91 Smithsonian Institution Archives, "National Museum of American History— Agency History," Smithsonian (August 29, 2002), http://siarchives.si.edu/ research/ahoo005nmah.html.

92 See, for example, Organization of American Historians, "Smithsonian Institution: Control over Exhibit Design and Content," *OHA Newsletter* 29 (August

2001), http://www.oah.org/pubs/nl/2001aug/smithsonian.html; Lawrence Small, "Generosity and Standards," *Smithsonian* (July 2001), http://www.smithsonianmag.com/history-archaeology/small_jul01.html; National Museum of American History, "Messages from the Director," "From the Acting Director," and "From the Chairman," Annual Report 2001 (2001), http://americanhistory.si.edu/reports/2001annualreport/messages1.html; BBC News, "Smithsonian Cash 'Withdrawn,'" (February 5, 2002), http://news.bbc.co.uk/1/hi/entertainment/arts/1801974.stm; Bruce Craig, "Reynolds Foundation Withdraws Support to the Smithsonian Institution," *Perspectives* 40, no. 3 (March 2002), http://www.historians.org/perspectives/issues/2002/0203/0203news1.cfm; Limerick, "Smithsonian Scandal That Wasn't"; Marketplace: News Archive, "Business and the Arts," http://marketplace.publicradio.org/shows/2002/02/05_mpp.html: "The Smithsonian Institution Dodged the Bush Administration Budget Ax but Took a Hit from the Private Sector"; Penrice, "Can This Museum Be Saved?"; Chua, "Crisis at the Smithsonian"; *"60 Minutes* Interview with Catherine Reynolds," History News Network (December 5, 2002), http://hnn.us/comments/5881.html. Reynolds has since given $100 million to the Kennedy Center.

93 On June 29, 2001, the Smithsonian Board of Regents, chaired by the chief justice of the Supreme Court, William H. Rehnquist, appointed a Blue Ribbon Commission on the National Museum of American History. They were asked to advise the Regents on "the most timely and relevant themes and methods of presentation for the Museum in the 21st. Century." The twenty-three members of the commission submitting this Report in 2002 were (as identified in the report): Richard Darman (commission chair and partner of the Carlyle Group, a global private equity firm); Tom Brokaw (anchor and managing editor of "NBC Nightly News with Tom Brokaw"); Ellsworth Brown (president and CEO of Carnegie Museums of Pittsburgh); Sheila P. Burke (ex officio member as the Smithsonian's undersecretary for American Museums and National Programs); Spencer R. Crew (executive director and CEO for the National Underground Railroad Freedom Center); Loni Ding (Asian American independent filmmaker, television producer, and university instructor); David Herbert Donald (Charles Warren Professor of American History and professor of American Civilization Emeritus at Harvard University); Eric Foner (DeWitt Clinton Professor of History at Columbia University); Diane Frankel (program director for children, youth, and families at the James Irvine Foundation); Ramón A. Gutiérrez (professor of ethnic studies and history, founder and director of the Center for the Study of Race and Ethnicity, and founding chair of the Ethnic Studies Department at the University of California, San Diego); Neil Harris (Preston and Sterling Morton Professor of History at the University of Chicago); K. Tsianina Lomawaima (professor of American Indian studies at the University of Arizona); Roger Mudd (journalist associated with CBS News, NBC News, and the Lehrer Newshour on PBS, as well as the History Channel); Don T. Nakanishi (director and pro-

fessor of the UCLA Asian American Studies Center); Chet Orloff (director emeritus of the Oregon Historical Society); Marc Pachter (ex-officio member as director of the National Portrait Gallery, and acting director of the National Museum of American History, Behring Center); William F. Russell (a former NBA MVP, now a motivational speaker, a sports commentator, an advocate for mentoring, and an author); Richard Norton Smith (presidential historian and award-winning author associated with the Ford, Reagan, Hoover, and Eisenhower presidential libraries); John Kuo Wei Tchen (historian and cultural activist associated with Asian Pacific American studies); Charles H. Townes (staff member of Bell Laboratories from 1939–47, later professor and chairman of the Physics Department at Columbia University. He received the Nobel Prize in 1964); Laurel Thatcher Ulrich (historian of early America and pioneer in the field of women's history); G. Edward White (the E. James Kelly Research Professor of the Virginia Law Faculty); Don Wilson (archivist of the United States until 1993, then executive director of the George Bush Presidential Library Center at Texas A&M University, now president of Don W. Wilson and Associates, a consulting firm specializing in the management of nonprofit institutions).

94 Smithsonian Institution, "Report of the Blue Ribbon Commission on the National Museum of American History" (March 2002), http://americanhistory.si.edu/reports/brc/1a.htm (emphasis mine).

95 "60 Minutes Interview with Catherine Reynolds."

96 Limerick, "Smithsonian Scandal That Wasn't."

97 Smithsonian Institution, "Report of the Blue Ribbon Commission."

98 Bowker and Star, Sorting Things Out, 297.

99 Small, "Generosity and Standards."

100 Organization of American Historians, "Smithsonian Institution."

101 Craig, "Reynolds Foundation Withdraws Support to the Smithsonian Institution."

102 Bowker and Star, Sorting Things Out, 297.

103 Smithsonian Institution, "Report of the Blue Ribbon Commission" (emphasis mine).

104 Smithsonian Institution, "Arctic National Wildlife Refuge: Seasons of Life and Land, Photographic Journey by Subhankar Banerjee," New and Upcoming Exhibitions at the Natural History Museum (2003); Subhankar Banerjee, The Arctic Project, http://www.subhankarbanerjee.org/arcticproject.html.

105 Jacqueline Trescott, "Smithsonian's Arctic Refuge Exhibit Draws Senate Scrutiny," Washington Post (May 21, 2003), C1.

106 Jacqueline Trescott, "Museums and Galleries, Museum's Shift of Arctic Refuge Exhibit Gets Cold Reception: Officials Deny Politics Forced Move, New Text," Washington Post (April 29, 2003), C1. See also Matthew Daly, "Dems: Smithsonian Self-Censored Exhibit," AP (May 21, 2003); Senate Office of Senator Ted Stevens, "Stevens Defends Smithsonian Institution on ANWR Exhibit," (2003).

107 Mokhiber and Weissman, "Blue Light Special at the Smithsonian."
108 Mokhiber and Weissman, *Corporate Predators*.
109 Vincent P. Bzdek, "The Ad Subtractors, Making a Difference," *Washington Post* (July 29, 2003), C9. See also Commercial Alert, "Home Page," http://www.commercialalert.org.
110 Latour, "Iconoclash."
111 Lucy Suchman and Claus Otto Scharmer, "I have, more than ever, a sense of the immovability of these institutions: An Interview with Lucy Suchman" (August 13, 1999), http://www.dialogonleadership.org/interviews/Suchman.shtml (emphasis mine).
112 Lucy Suchman, "Anthropology as 'Brand': Reflections on Corporate Anthropology," paper presented at the Colloquium on Interdisciplinarity and Society, Oxford University, Febraury 24, 2007 (published by the Department of Sociology, Lancaster University), 8. Suchman quotes Klein, *No Space, No Choice, No Jobs, No Logo*, 3.
113 Suchman, "Anthropology as 'Brand,'" 8, 12. Suchman quotes Klein, *No Space, No Choice, No Jobs, No Logo*, xx (emphasis mine).
114 Suchman, "Anthropology as 'Brand,'" 13, 14, (emphasis mine). Suchman quotes Miller, *A Theory of Shopping*, 9.
115 Joyce Appleby, "Should We All Become Public Historians?" American Historical Association, *Perspectives Online* 35, no. 3 (March 1997).
116 Linda Shopes, "AHA Establishes Task Force on Public History" American Historical Association, *Perspectives Online* 39, no. 6 (September 2001).
117 Lee, "Park Service Plans Outsourcing."
118 Cart, "70% of Jobs in Park Service Marked Ripe for Privatizing."
119 Guy Gugliotta, "House Votes to Save Jobs of Park Service Archaeologists," *Washington Post* (July 19, 2003), A4.
120 Stafford, "Epistemology for Sale," 221.

3. TV AND THE WEB COME TOGETHER

1 The History Channel, "Discover the 'True' Purpose of Machu Picchu!" e-mail to author (March 2007).
2 Throughout the book I will continue using the name the History Channel. However, in March 2008, this international satellite and cable television company owned by the joint venture A&E Television Networks (AETN), changed its name to History. See Associated Press, "Television's the History Channel Drops 'The' and 'Channel' from Its Name, Keeps History," *International Herald Tribune* (March 20, 2008). See also A&E Television Networks, "About AETN," http://www.aetn.com/about.html.
3 *Digging for the Truth*, TV series, starring Josh Bernstein (A&E Television Networks, 2005–2007); *Engineering an Empire*, TV series (KPI Productions, 2006–); *Cities of the Underworld*, TV series, starring Don Wildman (Authentic

Entertainment, 2007–9); *Ancient Discoveries*, TV series (Wild Dream Film, 2003–9).

4 Latour, *We Have Never Been Modern*, 119.

5 *Secrets of Lost Empires I*, TV series (PBS *Nova*/WGBH, 1992–97).

6 *Secrets of Lost Empires II*, TV series (PBS *Nova*/WGBH, 1999–2000).

7 Barnes, *Secrets of Lost Empires*; Fisher and Fisher, *Mysteries of Lost Empires*.

8 See the second series website, *Nova*, "Secrets of Lost Empires," http://www.pbs .org/wgbh/nova/lostempires.

9 Lewenstein, "An American Historical Perspective on Public Communication of Science."

10 Stewart, "Ambrosino and *Nova*: Making Stories that Go 'Bang,'" *Current* (May 4, 1998), http://www.current.org/doc/doc808nova.html.

11 The first quotation is from Ray Wilding-White, Excerpts from "One Way to Run a Railroad (1946–59)," WGBH Alumni (January 1, 2000), http://wgb halumni.org/2000/01/01/run-a-railroad/. The second quote is from American Association for the Advancement of Science (AAAS), "About AAAS: History and Archives," "150 Years of Advancing Science" (2010), http://archives .aaas.org/exhibit/change4.php.

12 For more information, see Wikipedia, "Lowell Institute," http://en.wikipedia .org/wiki/Lowell_Institute (accessed August 2007).

13 See Don Hollock, "WGBH Timeline (1946–1978)," WGBH Alumni (January 1, 2007), http://wgbhalumni.org/2007/01/01/wgbh-timeline-1946–1978.

14 Stewart, "Ambrosino and *Nova*."

15 Ibid. (emphasis mine).

16 Ibid.

17 Ibid. See also Michael Ambrosino, "Profiles, Michael Ambrosino," WGBH Alumni (2007), http://wgbhalumni.org/profiles/a/ambrosino-michael; Ben Shedd, "*Nova*: From the Beginning (1970s)" (March 25, 2000), http://wgb halumni.org/2000/03/25/nova; and Stewart, *PBS Companion*.

18 Bolter and Grusin, *Remediation*, 45, 68.

19 Edelman, "Reuse, Repurposing, and Recapture." See also Take One, "Repurposing: What Is It?," available via the Internet Archive's Wayback Machine.

20 Linda Moss, "Repurposing Permutations Yield Varied Returns," Multichannel News (October 13, 2002), http://www.multichannel.com; Linda Moss, "TNN, ABC Family Try New Fixes," Multichannel News (April 20, 2003), http://www.multichannel.com; Valerie Milano, "Debate over Repurposing: But What the Heck Is It?," *Video Age International* 21, no. 6 (October 2001); and R. Thomas Umstead, "Repurposing's Still the Rave for Nets," Multichannel News (May 12, 2002), http://www.multichannel.com.

21 See *Surviving the Iron Age*, TV series (BBC, 2000). *The Ship: Retracing Cook's Endeavour Voyage*, TV series (BBC, 2002). See Wall to Wall, "Wall to Wall Highlights," http://www.walltowall.co.uk/highlights.aspx; *The 1900 House*, TV series (Wall to Wall TV, Channel 4/WNET Thirteen, 2000); *Frontier House*,

TV series (Channel 4, PBS/WNET Thirteen, 2002). For more about *Secrets of Lost Empires*, see *Nova*, "Secrets of Lost Empires," http://www.pbs.org/wgbh/nova/lostempires. See also History, *Ancient Discoveries*, http://www.history.com/shows/ancient-discoveries.

22 Latour, *We Have Never Been Modern*, 144–45.

23 See Barnes, "Introduction" in *Mysteries of Lost Empires*; *Nova*, "Transcripts; *Secrets of Lost Empires*: Roman Bath," http://www.pbs.org/wgbh/nova/transcripts/27rbroman.html; *Nova*, "*Secrets of Lost Empires*: 'Roman Bath,'" http://www.pbs.org/wgbh/nova/lostempires/roman. I am also indebted to Nancy Linde at WGBH who went over details of the production process with me, shared some wonderful stories about these folks, and corrected my understandings of what had happened in a lively telephone conversation on March 31, 2009. Linde worked for *Horizon* in the UK in the eighties and for *Nova* in the United States in the nineties. As well as being writer, director, and producer for "Roman Bath," she also developed *Nova* ScienceNOW. See also, Linde, "*Nova*: The Leading Edge" and "A Burger, a Beer . . . and a Side of Science."

24 See Yegül, Bolgil, and Foss, *The Bath-Gymnasium Complex at Sardis*; Yegül, *Baths and Bathing in Classical Antiquity* and "The Marble Court of Sardis and Historical Reconstruction."

25 See Fagan, *Archaeological Fantasies* and *Bathing in Public in the Roman World*.

26 See Aicher, *Guide to the Aqueducts of Ancient Rome* and *Rome Alive*.

27 See the home page of Max Fordham, "Max Fordham: Whole Building Engineers," http://www.maxfordham.com/index.php.

28 *Secrets of Lost Empires II*, "Roman Bath," episode 4 (February 22, 2000).

29 Brightwell, "Introduction."

30 *Deadliest Catch*, TV series (Discovery Network, 2005–); *Ice Road Truckers*, TV series (Original Productions, 2007–); *MythBusters*, TV series (Beyond Entertainment, 2003–); *CSI: Crime Scene Investigation*, TV series (CBS, 2000–). The *CSI* exhibition was at Chicago's Museum of Science and Industry in 2007. Franchise description of *CSI* can be found on Wikipedia, "*CSI* (franchise)," http://en.wikipedia.org/wiki/CSI_%28franchise%29 (accessed April 2011).

31 Latour, "The Promises of Constructivism," 32–33. See also *Secrets of Lost Empires II*, "Roman Bath"; and Fisher and Fisher, "Roman Bath"; *Nova*, "Transcripts; *Secrets of Lost Empires*: Roman Bath"; and *Nova*, "*Secrets of Lost Empires*: 'Roman Bath.'"

32 *Living in the Past*, TV series (BBC, 1978).

33 See Pembrokeshire Coast Nation Park, "Castell Henllys Iron Age Hill Fort," http://www.pembrokeshirecoast.org.uk/default.asp?PID=397. See also Firstbrook, *Surviving the Iron Age*, 54.

34 By 2003 this page was no longer on the web. The Castell Henllys link to it was redirected to a less TV show-specific and more historically pedagogical page. See BBC, "Ancient History: British Prehistory," http://www.bbc.co.uk/history/ancient/british_prehistory.

35 Firstbrook, *Surviving the Iron Age*, 60 (emphasis mine).

36 Definition of "thing" via *Oxford English Dictionary Online*, http://www.oed .com (requires subscription).

37 Firstbrook, *Surviving the Iron Age*, 21.

38 Ibid., 15, 27, 28 (emphasis mine).

39 Ibid., 35.

40 Ibid., 127, 58, 80 (emphasis mine).

41 Ibid., 133.

42 For example, see Piccini, "Filming through the Mists of Time."

43 See James Appleyard, "The Celts, the Iron Age, and the European Community," About.com (October 9, 2000), available via the Internet Archive's Wayback Machine. Compare with Spector, *What This Awl Means*.

44 Dietler, "Our Ancestors the Gauls," 597.

45 Piccini, "Filming through the Mists of Time," S90; and Piccini, "Commentary on James F. Weiner's Televisualist Anthropology," 221.

46 Dietler, "Our Ancestors the Gauls," 584 (emphasis mine).

47 Piccini, "Filming through the Mists of Time," S93, S91.

48 Heather Perkins, "The Music and Sound Design of *Xena: Warrior Princess*," Whoosh! (1998), http://www.whoosh.org/issue23/perkins1.html.

49 Piccini, "Filming through the Mists of Time," S95, S91, S97 (emphasis mine).

50 Dietler, "Our Ancestors the Gauls," 585.

51 Firstbrook, *Surviving the Iron Age*, 44–45.

52 Ibid.

53 Johnson, *Everything Bad Is Good for You*, 77–78.

54 Weston, *Gender in Real Time*, 13.

55 Firstbrook, *Surviving the Iron Age*, 57, 57–59.

56 Firstbrook, *Surviving the Iron Age*, 139 (emphasis mine).

57 Handler and Gable, *New History in an Old Museum*, esp. 174–219.

58 See Suissa, Brown, and Graham, "Reality Check." Also Veverka, *Interpretive Master Planning*; Tilden, *Interpreting Our Heritage*; *Costumed History Performers*; home page of Sally Roesch, "Sally Roesch Wagner: Liberty, Freedom, and Justice through History," http://www.sallyroeschwagner.com; Ron Tomson and Marilyn Harper, "Telling the Stories: Planning Effective Interpretive Programs for Properties Listed in the National Register of Historic Places," US Department of the Interior, National Park Service (2000), http://www.cr .nps.gov/nr/publications/bulletins/interp/index.htm; Mackintosh, *Interpretation in the National Park Service*; Miller et al., "Exploring a Common Past: Researching and Interpreting Women's History for Historic Sites," US Department of the Interior, National Park Service (2003), http://www.nps.gov/ history/history/hisnps/NPSHistory/womenshistory.pdf. See also Lance & Liz's Reenacting Page," available via the Internet Archive's Wayback Machine; Ronald Luckenbill online, "Recreating History," http://www.recreatinghis tory.com; Luke E. Pearson online, "17th Century Reenacting and Living History Resources," http://www.lukehistory.com/resources/index.html; Twisted

Spinsters, "Beaver Vous 2002 . . . Historian/Re-Enactors Emersion Rendezvous for Women," available via the Internet Archive's Wayback Machine.

59 Pembrokeshire Coast Nation Park, "Castell Henllys Iron Age Hill Fort"; A. M. A. de Quesada online, "Volkssturm Living Historian's Resources," available via the Internet Archive's Wayback Machine; Woodward, "Attack of the Clones."

60 I emblemize these manifold literatures by referencing two somewhat different edges of science studies literatures: Star, "Introduction" and Hayles, *How We Became Posthuman*.

61 Star, "Introduction," 18–19.

62 G. Bateson, *Steps to an Ecology of Mind*.

63 Hayles, *How We Became Posthuman*, 290.

64 I first encountered this phrase and some of these meanings at a talk by the queer literary historian and theorist Michael Moon, working from a book in progress: "Weird Flesh and Drives: Darger and the Pulps."

65 See, for example, the preface and foreword to the two editions of *Steps to an Ecology of Mind*: M. C. Bateson, "Foreword to the New University of Chicago Edition of *Steps to an Ecology of Mind* by Gregory Bateson"; and Engel, "Preface."

66 G. Bateson, *Steps to an Ecology of Mind*, 1.

67 G. Bateson, "Metalogue: Why a Swan," 36–37.

68 Cooper, ed., *To Free a Generation*, 7. See also Carolee Schneemann online, "Performance Chronology," http://www.caroleeschneemann.com/performance chron.html.

69 M. C. Bateson, *Our Own Metaphor*; Hayles, *How We Became Posthuman*.

70 G. Bateson, "Conscious Purpose Versus Nature" and "Effects of Conscious Purpose on Human Adaptation"; G. Bateson, Goodman, and Vinkenoog, *Dialectics of Liberation* (Intersound Records Ltd., 1967), audio recordings. See also Turner, *From Counterculture to Cyberculture*.

71 Bowker and Star, *Sorting Things Out*, 293.

72 Handler and Gable, *New History in an Old Museum*, 198, 96, 201.

73 Ibid., 202, 205.

74 Ibid., 206, 207.

75 Ibid., 217–19.

76 Zoidis, "The New History in an Old Museum (Book Review)."

77 Woodward, "Attack of the Clones," W08–W11, W21–23, W26.

78 Joan Jett in *Highlander*, "Free Fall," production number 92101–5, episode 5, season 1, 1992. Vanity in *Highlander*, "Revenge Is Sweet," production number 92109–10, episode 10, season 1, 1992. More successful was Sheena Easton in *Highlander*, "An Eye for an Eye," production number 93205–27, episode 5, season 2, 1993.

79 *Highlander*, "The Lady and the Tiger," production number 92121–18, episode 18, season 1, 1993.

80 *Highlander*, "The Return of Amanda," production number 93207–29, episode 7, season 2, 1993; and *Highlander*, "Legacy," production number 93219–41, episode 19, season 2, 1994.

81 Salmonson and Shultz, *Tomoe Gozen*; Salmonson, Clavette, and Shultz, *Swordswoman*; Salmonson, Wees, and Craft, *Thousand Shrine Warrior*. See also Salmonson, *Encyclopedia of Amazons*.

82 For example Dugaw, *Warrior Women and Popular Balladry*; Fraser, *Warrior Queens*; Newark, *Women Warlords*; Wheelwright, *Amazons and Military Maids*; Blanton, "Women Soldiers of the Civil War"; Burgess and Wakeman, eds., *An Uncommon Soldier*. For later examples, see Stanley et al., eds., *Bold in Her Breeches*; Creighton and Norling, eds., *Iron Men, Wooden Women*; Druett, *She Captains*; Davis-Kimball and Behan, *Warrior Women*; Howe, "Covert Force; Hundreds of Women Fought in the Civil War Disguised as Men"; Lorimer and Synarski, *Booty: Girl Pirates on the High Seas*.

83 Goldman, ed., *Female Soldiers*. See also Enloe, *Does Khaki Become You?*; *Bananas, Beaches & Bases*; and *Morning After*. For changing numbers and career paths, see Department of Defense, "Population Representation in the Military Services, Fiscal Year 2000," Twenty-Seventh Annual Department of Defense Report on Social Representation in the US Military Services (February 2002), http://prhome.defense.gov. For women soldier reenactor sites see W. A. King, "Women Soldiers Reenactors Page," available via the Internet Archive's Wayback Machine; American Military Impressions, "Living History, 1776–1991," http://www.freewebs.com/americanmilitaryimpressions. For discussions of women in the US military since, see Kathline T. Rhem, "Congresswomen, Military Leaders Honor Women Troops, Vets," US Department of Defense, News, American Forces Press Service (May 22, 2002), http://www.defense.gov; Feinman, *Citizenship Rites*; Francke, *Ground Zero*; Herbert, *Camouflage Isn't Only for Combat*.

84 See, for example, the extraordinary work of Judith Jack Halberstam, both instantiating these emergent interests and commenting on them. Halberstam, *Skin Shows*, *Female Masculinity*, *In a Queer Time and Place* and Halberstam and Livingston, *Posthuman Bodies*.

85 *Highlander*, "Take Back the Night," production number 92101–5, episode 18, season 3, 1995.

86 *Xena: Warrior Princess*, TV series, created by John Schulian and Robert G. Tapert, starring Lucy Lawless, Renée O'Connor, and Ted Raimi (MCA Television, 1995–2001).

87 Joyce Appleby, "Should We All Become Public Historians?," American Historical Association, *Perspectives Online* 35, no. 3 (March 1997), http://www.historians.org/perspectives/issues/1997/9703/9703pre.cfm.

88 *Gladiatrix*, TV documentary (Discovery, 2002). See also the earlier *Discover* magazine article by Heather Pringle, "Gladiatrix," *Discover* (December 1, 2001), http://discovermagazine.com/2001/dec/featglad.

89 Amy Zoll, *Gladiatrix*; Trihn Tran, "Amy Zoll Has Written a New Book on a Female Warrior," Penn Current online, http://www.upenn.edu/pennnews/current/2002/120502/staff.html.

90 See commercial education websites such as Ablemedia's Classics Technology Center, "The Roman Gladiator: Female Gladiators," http://ablemedia.com/ctcweb/consortium/gladiator6.html.

91 Museum of London, Archaeology, "Commercial Services," http://www.museumoflondonarchaeology.org.uk/English/SkillsServices.

92 D. Williams, "Rome Puts Modern-Day Gladiators (and Caesars) under Its Thumb [Female Gladiator Re-Enactors]," *Washington Post* (September 9, 2002), A14.

93 PBS, *Secrets of the Dead* online, "Amazon Warrior Women: Interview with Jeannine Davis-Kimball," http://www.pbs.org/wnet/secrets/previous_seasons/case_amazon/interview.html.

94 *Secrets of the Pharaohs*, TV series (PBS and Thirteen/WNET, 2001). See the PBS website for the series, http://www.pbs.org/wnet/pharaohs/index.html.

95 Tigress Productions Limited, "Company Details," http://www.tigressproductions.co.uk/company.asp.

96 KunhardtMcGee Productions, "Our Films," http://www.kunhardtmcgee.com.

97 See the Wikipedia entry, "Peter Kunhardt," http://en.wikipedia.org/wiki/Peter_Kunhardt.

98 National Geographic Society, "The Genographic Project," https://genographic.nationalgeographic.com/genographic/index.html.

99 Gates, "Dr. Entrepreneur."

100 *African American Lives*, TV series (Kunhardt and PBS, 2006–8).

101 *Oprah's Roots: An African American Lives Special*, TV documentary (Kunhardt and PBS, 2007).

102 Oprah, "Building a Dream: The Oprah Winfrey Leadership Academy," http://www.oprah.com/entertainment/Oprah-Winfrey-Leadership-Academy-for-Girls.

103 See the website of *African American Lives*, http://www.pbs.org/wnet/aalives.

104 Ibid.

105 See discussions of these terms on Wikipedia, "Phylogeography," http://en.wikipedia.org/wiki/Phylogeographic and "Archaeogenetics," http://en.wikipedia.org/wiki/Archaeogenetic.

106 *Secrets of the Dead*, "Amazon Warrior Women," episode 5, season 1, 2004. See ZDF online, "English Information about ZDF: Welcome to ZDF German Television!," http://www.zdf.com.

107 Jeannine Davis-Kimball, "Center for the Study of Eurasian Nomads," http://www.csen.org.

108 Davis-Kimball and Behan, *Warrior Women*.

109 PBS, *Secrets of the Dead* online, "Amazon Warrior Women: Interview with Jeannine Davis-Kimball."

110 One starting place in a tentative mapping of the multiple (inter)interdis-

ciplinary and nonacademic uses of Gimbutas's work as well as her person and figuration are the talk pages of Wikipedia, "Marija Gimbutas," http://en.wiki pedia.org/wiki/Gimbutas; and "Kurgan Hypothesis," http://en.wikipedia.org/ wiki/Kurgan_hypothesis. The pressure at Wikipedia to resolve "noise," to generalize, and to present knowledge as neutral is put to the test when users attempt to describe Gimbutas as if she herself and her work are not substantially "different" in different communities of practice. Even what counts as "the kurgan hypothesis" is drawn variantly. A tiny sampling of academic subspecialities and recombinant knowledges: Gimbutas, "Comment" together with Anthony et. al., "The 'Kurgan Culture.'" See also Piazza et al., "Genetics and the Origin of European Languages"; Eichenlaub, "Marija Gimbutas and the Future of a Legacy"; Berggren and Harrod, "Understanding Marija Gimbutas." A side note: Kurgan culture is a point of imagination in *Highlander* conceptualizations and community in historical assumptions that anchor a range of representations from origins of the show itself to costuming and other low budget mimetic realisms.

111 See also Davis-Kimball, *Kurgans, Ritual Sites, and Settlements* and *Kurgans on the Left Bank of the Ilek*.

112 Lively discussion of this justification and other questions of generalizability and "neutrality" are evident in the talk section of Wikipedia, "Craniofacial Anthropometry," http://en.wikipedia.org/wiki/Craniofacial_anthropometry.

113 Fionn, "Yes, indeed. . . . Meiramgul, die kleine Amazone!," online discussion thread via Pan Aryan Alliance (August 20, 2007), http://panaryan.com/ forum (thread no longer available).

114 See the website of the International HapMap Project, http://www.hapmap .org. Consider comparisons with, for example, Wikipedia's entry for "Phylogeography," http://en.wikipedia.org/wiki/Phylogeographic (accessed August 2007) and Joseph L. Graves, "What We Know and What We Don't Know: Human Genetic Variation and the Social Construction of Race," Social Science Research Council, "Is Race 'Real'?" SSRC.org, http://raceandgenomics .ssrc.org/Graves.

115 For example, see Social Science Research Council, "Is Race 'Real'?" SSRC.org, http://raceandgenomics.ssrc.org.

4. SCHOLARS AND ENTREPRENEURS

1 Hopkins, *A World Full of Gods*, 2.

2 Dinshaw, *Getting Medieval*, 1, 22–34. Boswell, *Christianity, Social Tolerance, and Homosexuality*.

3 Dinshaw, *Getting Medieval*, 14 (invoking Haraway, "Situated Knowledges," 193).

4 Ibid., 16.

5 Biddick, "Bede's Blush," 83–101, 623–35.

6 Ibid., 83.

7 Ibid., 98.

8 Ibid., 100.

9 Ibid., 101.

10 Talking with and reading the work of the Chicana theorist Chela Sandoval over the last thirty years has taught me this kind of analysis. See especially Sandoval, *Methodology of the Oppressed*.

11 Moraga, *Waiting in the Wings* and *Loving in the War Years*; Alfaro et al., *Plays from South Coast Repertory*.

12 For more analysis of Anzaldúa's complex career and work, as well as the autobiography, poetry, and plays of Moraga, see Bost, *Encarnación*.

13 See Katie King, "Theorizing Structures in Women's Studies" (working paper, Women's Studies Research Works, Digital Repository at the University of Maryland, May 2002), http://hdl.handle.net/1903/3029.

14 *You Are There*, TV series (CBS, 1953–57); see also Walter Cronkite, "Remembering *You Are There*," National Public Radio (October 27, 2003), audio recording, http://www.npr.org/templates/story/story.php?storyId=1480691. *Meeting of Minds*, TV series (PBS, 1977–81).

15 See Cronkite, "Remembering *You Are There*."

16 See Steve Allen's website, "*Meeting of Minds*," http://www.steveallenonline.com/television_pioneer/meeting_of_minds.htm.

17 Hopkins, *A World Full of Gods*, 2.

18 Graham Burton, "Keith Hopkins, Historian Who Revolutionised the Approach to Ancient History," *Guardian* (March 29, 2004).

19 Hopkins, *A World Full of Gods*, 19–20.

20 Ibid., xi.

21 British Council, Arts Group of the British Council, "Ben Hopkins," British Film Directors, a Serachable Directory, http://www.britfilms.com/; Tom Fogg, "The Nine Lives of Ben Hopkins," *Netribution* (2001), http://www.netribution.co.uk/features/interviews/2001/tomas_katz/1.html; Ben Hopkins's films include: *Simon Magus*, 1998; *37 Uses for a Dead Sheep*, 2005; *The Nine Lives of Tomas Katz*, 1999; and his television documentary: *Footprints*, 2003.

22 Internet Movie Database, "Biography for Professor Keith Hopkins," http://www.imdb.com/name/nm1582345/bio. *I, Caesar*, TV series (BBC, 1997). *Hidden History of Rome, with Terry Jones*, TV documentary (BBC, 2001). See also the website of Seventh Arts Productions, http://www.seventh-art.com. *Colosseum, A Gladiator's Story*, TV documentary (BBC, 2003).

23 Finley, *Ancient Economy*.

24 See the Institute of Historical Research's Interviews with Historians Series, *Moses Finley Interviewed by Keith Hopkins* (1985), video.

25 Burton, "Keith Hopkins"; Robertson, "Keith Hopkins, 69, Historian with an Unusual Approach," *New York Times* (March 15, 2004), B7. Hopkins, *Conquerors and Slaves* and *Death and Renewal*.

26 Hopkins, *A World Full of Gods*, 2, 6 (emphasis mine).

27 Etzkowitz and Leydesdorff, "The Triple Helix of University-Industry-

Government Relations." Etzkowitz and Leydesdorff, eds., *Universities and the Global Knowledge Economy*.

28 Steve Lawson, "The Triple Helix," Linus Pauling Institute Research Report (May 2003), http://lpi.oregonstate.edu/ss03/triplehelix.html.

29 For a popular account highlighting private capital adventures, see Shreeve, *Genome War*.

30 Lewontin, *Triple Helix*; Etzkowitz and Viale, "Third Academic Revolution."

31 Hopkins, *A World Full of Gods*, 7–9.

32 Ibid., 53–54.

33 See the Leverhulme Trust, "About the Leverhulme Trust," http://www.lever hulme.ac.uk/about/about.cfm; Unilever online, "About Us: Our History," http://www.unilever.com/aboutus/ourhistory; Wikipedia's entry "Unilever," http://en.wikipedia.org/wiki/Unilever; Faculty of Classics, "Ancient History at Cambridge, Arts and Humanities Research Council (AHRC)," available via the Internet Archive's Wayback Machine.

34 Slaughter and Leslie, *Academic Capitalism*, 208–10. Slaughter and Metcalfe, "Differential Effects," 31.

35 Slaughter and Metcalfe, "Differential Effects," 29.

36 Lucy Suchman, "Located Accountabilities in Technology Production."

37 Slaughter and Metcalfe, "Differential Effects," 36.

38 Ghamari-Tabrizi, *The Worlds of Herman Kahn*.

39 Geiger, *Knowledge and Money*; Lattuca, *Creating Interdisciplinarity*; Strathern, *Audit Cultures*; Vickers, " '[U]Framed in Open, Unmapped Fields,' " 11–42.

40 Ghamari-Tabrizi, *The Worlds of Herman Kahn*.

41 Ibid., 149.

42 Ibid., 161, 64, 65–66.

43 Ibid., 179, 66.

44 Ibid., 155, 59, 60, 59.

45 Such analysis is exemplified in wonderful examples by Jenny Thompson. See her "What Are the People Who Re-Enact 20th Century Wars up To?," University of York, http://www.york.ac.uk/ipup/projects/reenactment/discussion/thompson.html. See also her *War Games*.

46 An intensive analysis is Taylor, *Play between Worlds*.

47 Spigel and Mann, eds., *Private Screenings*. Gitelman, *Always Already New*. Sobchack, *Meta-Morphing*.

48 See Juul, *Half-Real*.

49 Especially Bolter and Grusin, *Remediation*.

50 For example Haraway, *Primate Visions*.

51 Latour, *We Have Never Been Modern*, 119.

52 See especially G. Bateson, "Part III: Form and Pathology in Relationship."

53 Salen and Zimmerman, *Rules of Play*.

54 Slaughter and Leslie, *Academic Capitalism*, 208–10. Slaughter and Metcalfe, "Differential Effects," 31.

55 Institute of Play, "Work: Quest to Learn," http://www.instituteofplay.org/

work/projects/quest-to-learn; the New Scool, Katie Salen, "Faculty List: Katie Salen," http://www.newschool.edu/facultyexperts/faculty.aspx?id=23746; Eric Zimmerman home page,http://www.ericzimmerman.com.

56 Slaughter and Leslie, *Academic Capitalism*.

57 Salen and Zimmerman, *Rules of Play*, 450, 451. Ryan, *Narrative as Virtual Reality*, 2.

58 Salen and Zimmerman, *Rules of Play*, 451.

59 This is my own synthesis of Gregory Bateson's claims throughout *Steps to an Ecology of Mind*, with especial attention to "A Theory of Play and Fantasy" (177–94) and Bateson's insights from *Men Are Grass*.

60 Salen and Zimmerman, *Rules of Play*, 440, 50.

61 Ibid., 452.

62 See, for example, as interconnecting arguments across several books, Johnson, *Everything Bad Is Good for You*, *Mind Wide Open*, and *Emergence*.

63 G. Bateson, "Form, Substance, and Difference," 454–71.

64 Following Whitehead and Russell, *Principia Mathematica*. For the kinds of "errors" with worldly implications as Bateson saw them, see "Steps: Part II: Form and Pattern in Anthropology" and *Mind and Nature*.

65 G. Bateson, *Mind and Nature*, 15.

66 Intentions and hopes narrated in many forms in Haraway, *When Species Meet*.

67 G. Bateson, *Mind and Nature*, 4 (emphasis in original).

68 G. Bateson, "Afterword," 237, 45–46.

69 G. Bateson, "Cybernetic Explanation," 416 (emphasis in original).

70 G. Bateson, *Mind and Nature*, 26–27.

71 G. Bateson, "The Logical Categories of Learning and Communication," 280–81.

72 G. Bateson, *Mind and Nature*, 185.

73 Ibid., 116.

74 G. Bateson, "The Logical Categories of Learning and Communication," 308 (emphasis mine).

75 G. Bateson, *Mind and Nature*, 21–22.

76 G. Bateson, "The Logical Categories of Learning and Communication," 288.

77 Ibid., 289.

78 Ibid., 287.

79 Ibid., 293 (emphasis mine).

80 See, for example, his discussion of the blind man and his stick in "Cybernetics of 'Self,'" 318.

81 G. Bateson, "The Logical Categories of Learning and Communication," 293.

82 Ibid., 297–301.

83 Ibid., 298.

84 Ibid., 301.

85 Ibid., 302–6.

86 G. Bateson, "Double Bind, 1969," 272.

87 See, for example, Hayles, *How We Became Posthuman*; Gee, *What Video Games*

Have to Teach Us About Learning and Literacy; Turner, *From Counterculture to Cyberculture*; and Klein, *Crossing Boundaries*.

88 Kesey, *One Flew Over the Cuckoo's Nest*.

89 Citing the Macy Conferences in Cybernetics is complicated. As the American Society for Cybernetics notes "there is a lack of comprehensive documentation on the Macy Conferences. Part of this derives from the fact that the first five conferences—by all accounts the most lively and energizing—were never formally documented with published proceedings. Part of this derives from the fact that it was not until Steve Joshua Heims undertook his massive research decades after the fact that anyone addressed the Macy Conferences as a historical subject. Even Heims's work, impressive though it is, doesn't bother to give a uniformly detailed historical account of the conferences." (Citations are necessarily often a bit made up—the conferences occurred over the period 1946–53.) See the American Society for Cybernetics, "Foundations: The Macy Conferences Summary," http://www.asc-cybernetics.org/foundations/history/MacySummary.htm. See also Heims, *Cybernetics Group*; and Hayles, *How We Became Posthuman*.

90 Brockman, ed., *About Bateson*, 248–49.

91 Greenberg, *I Never Promised You a Rose Garden*.

92 G. Bateson, "Language and Psychotherapy: Frieda Fromm-Reichmann's Last Project." I am indebted to Mark Engel, Bateson's research assistant and editorial collaborator for *Steps* during the late sixties and early seventies, for sharing the eulogy and other details of these associations.

93 G. Bateson, "Epidemiology of a Schizophrenia," 194.

94 Ibid., 199.

95 G. Bateson, "Toward a Theory of Schizophrenia," 206–7.

96 Kesey, *One Flew Over the Cuckoo's Nest*.

97 Doherty, *Cold War, Cool Medium*. Marmor, Bernard, and Ottenberg, "Psychodynamics of Group Opposition to Mental Health Programs." See also Wikipedia's entry for "McCarthyism," http://en.wikipedia.org/wiki/Macarthyism.

98 McCalman, "The Little Ship of Horrors," 478.

99 Chris Terrill, "The Making of *The Ship*," BBC History TV and Radio Programmes, Programme Archives (August 1, 2002), http://www.bbc.co.uk/history/programmes/programme_archive/theship_about_01.shtml. Meg Carter, "History Is Updated: A New BBC Series Has Re-enacted Captain Cook's Voyage of Discovery," *Independent* (August 20, 2002). See also Baker, *The Ship*.

100 McCalman, "The Little Ship of Horrors," 478–81.

101 BBC, Press Office, "*The Ship* Press Pack," http://www.bbc.co.uk/pressoffice/pressreleases/stories/2002/07_july/31/theshippack.PDF; see the home page of Laurence Rees, http://www.rhgdigital2.co.uk/minisites/laurence rees/index.html; the Internet Movie Database, "Laurence Rees," http://www.imdb.com/name/nm0715931; and Wikipedia's entries for both "Laurence Rees,"

http://en.wikipedia.org/wiki/Laurence_Rees, and "*The Ship* (TV series)," http://en.wikipedia.org/wiki/The_Ship_%282002%29. See also, Baker, *The Ship*; and Baker, *Ancient Rome.*

102 A partial listing of such shows follows, with information drawn from Wikipedia's, "*The 1900 House*," http://en.wikipedia.org/wiki/The_1900_House 1) and dates and production information drawn from the Internet Movie Database: *The 1900 House* (Channel 4, 1999); *1940s House* (Channel 4, 2001); *Black Forest House 1902*—a family "living" without electricity (SWR, 2001); *Treats from the Edwardian Country House* (Channel 4, 2002); *The Edwardian Country House* (Channel 4, 2002); *Frontier House* (Channel 4/WNET, 2004); *Pioneer House* (Channel 4, 2004); *Colonial House* (WNET, 2004); *The Regency House Party* (Channel 4/WNET, 2004); *The 1900 Adventure*—family and their servants in manor near Berlin (Degeto/ARD, 2004); *Outback House*—a family running a sheep station in 1861 Outback Australia (ABC, 2005); *The Colony*—life in New South Wales of 1800, (SBS, 2005); *Das Auswandererschiff 1855*—an emigration ship to the United States (Caligari, 2005); *The 1927 Adventure*—life in the manor from 1900, but in the Roaring Twenties (Zero, 2005); *Difficult 1950's School*—teachers and students in a boarding school (Tresor, 2005); *The Medieval Adventure*—people living in a fifteenth-century castle (Doc.station/ARD, 2005); *Texas Ranch House* (PBS, 2006); *The Stone Age Experiment*—life under conditions of the stone age (SWR, 2007); *Die Bräuteschule 1958*—teenage girls attending a domestic science school (ARD, 2007); and *Coal House*—a 1920s Welsh mining community (Indus Films for BBC Wales, 2007).

103 Barclay and Turner, *Humanities Research Centre*, 232, Australian National University, Humanities Research Centre, "HRC Research Platform: Historical Re-Enactment and Public Memory," http://www.anu.edu.au/hrc/research _platforms/Historical_Re-enactment.php. University of York, Institute for the Public Understanding of the Past, http://www.york.ac.uk/ipup/index .html.

104 Agnew et al., conference, "Extreme and Sentimental History: On the Re-Enactment of Historical Events" (Vanderbilt University, Nashville, April 2–3, 2004); Agnew and Lamb, eds., "Extreme and Sentimental History," special issue, *Criticism*; King, "Historiography as Reenactment," 459–75.

105 Two others (not represented in the journal and apparently not participants in any of the reenactment conferences) were Mereta Kawharu and Andrew Lambert, according to Lambert's account in "Retracing the Captain: 'Extreme History,' Hard Tack and Scurvy," 247. Lambert did not complete the voyage but was airlifted out with pneumonia the day before 9/11. Kawharu and Lambert are referred to in the BBC's "*Ship* Press Pack" specialists list as, "Andrew, Naval Historian (British)" and "Merata, Anthropologist (New Zealander)."

106 BBC, "*The Ship* Press Pack."

107 McCalman, "Criticism," 479. Lambert says he was clued in earlier than this by

friends "anxious I should be under no illusions," and that he had all along understood "extreme history" to mean "learn by suffering." Lambert, "Retracing the Captain," 247, 46.

108 Agnew et al., conference, "Extreme and Sentimental History: On the Re-Enactment of Historical Events."

109 See McCalman, "Telstra Address: Making Culture Bloom." The speech was broadcast live to a large national audience on the Australian Broadcasting Corporation's television network.

110 See, for example, Landon Thomas, "The Irish Economy's Rise Was Steep, and the Fall Was Fast," *New York Times* (January 4, 2009), BU1.

111 For more information about the term "technology evangelist," see Wikipedia's entry for "Technology Evangelist," http://en.wikipedia.org/wiki/Technology_evangelist.

112 Morley and Robins, *Spaces of Identity.*

113 A Google timeline search conducted in 2009 suggests that the term has been useful to those archived on the web to describe cultural activities sporadically and intermittently beginning in the mid-nineteenth century, with more densely described practices in the mid- to late sixties, and then taken up in more concentration from the mid-eighties until now. The earliest self-description as "intellectual entrepreneur" that I have found so far comes from Henry Louis Gates Jr.'s own use; see his "Dr. Entrepreneur." See also *African American Lives*, TV series (Kunhardt and PBS, 2006–8) and *Oprah's Roots: An African American Lives Special*, TV documentary (Kunhardt and PBS, 2007).

114 See Australian Academy of Science, "Understanding the Population-Environment Debate: Bridging Disciplinary Divides," 2004 Fenner Environmental Conference (Shine Dome, Canberra, May 24–25, 2004), http://www.science.org.au/events/fenner/fenner2004.

115 Klein, "Integration Panel Report to Floor"; Monk, "Enhancing Our Grasp of Complex Arguments."

116 Austhink, Rationale, "Learn: Argument Mapping," http://rationale.austhink.com/learn/argument-mapping.

117 Klein, "Disciplinary Origins and Differences."

118 Monk and Gelder, "Enhancing Our Grasp of Complex Arguments."

119 Austhink, Rationale, "Learn: Research on Argument Mapping," http://rationale.austhink.com/learn/research.

120 Klein, *Interdisciplinarity, Crossing Boundaries*, and *Transdisciplinarity.*

121 Klein, "Disciplinary Origins and Differences."

122 Ibid.

123 Klein, "Prospects for Transdisciplinarity." She refers to Ramadier, "Transdisciplinarity and Its Challenges"; Nicolescu, *Manifesto of Transdisciplinarity*; CIRET, see CIRET: International Center for Transdisciplinary Research, http://basarab.nicolescu.perso.sfr.fr/ciret (French website with some English translation available); and Lawrence and Despres, "Introduction: Futures of Transdisciplinarity."

124 Australian Government, Department of Education, Science and Training (DEST), *Knowledge Transfer and Australian Universities and Publicly Funded Research Agencies* (March 2006), http://www.dest.gov.aulace Relations. See the website of the Department of Education, Employment and Workplace Relations (DEEWR), http://www.deewr.gov.au/Pages/Default.aspx.

125 Slaughter and Metcalfe, "The Differential Effects," 29.

126 DEST, *Knowledge Transfer*, 43, 40.

127 DEST, *Knowledge Transfer*, 49.

128 Stafford, "Epistemology for Sale," 221.

129 Hayles, *How We Became Posthuman*, 290. See also M. C. Bateson, *Our Own Metaphor*; and Hutchins, *Cognition in the Wild*, 316.

130 University of York, Institute for the Public Understanding of the Past, http://www.york.ac.uk/ipup/index.html.

131 *African American Lives*, TV series (Kunhardt and PBS, 2006–8).

132 Rosenzweig and Thelen, *Presence of the Past*, 210.

133 Ibid., 21–22, 34, 186.

134 Ibid., 178–79, 81. Rosenzweig is also summarizing here the findings of historian Michael Frisch, esp. *A Shared Authority*, xx, xxii.

135 King, "Historiography as Reenactment."

136 Mulkey and Dougan, "The Smithsonian Institution Exhibition of 'Science in American Life,'" 61–78.

137 The six conferences were: "Extreme and Sentimental History: A Conference on the Re-Enactment of Historical Events" (Vanderbilt University, Nashville, April 2–3, 2004); "Re-Enactment and the Question of Realism: Second Re-Enactment Conference and Series of Graduate Workshops" (Huntington Library, San Marino, California, May 14 [workshops May 9–10 at CalTech, Pasadena, August 5, Humanities Research Centre, Canberra, August 8–9, ANU House, Melbourne], 2005); "Settlers, Creoles, and the Re-Enactment of History" (Vanderbilt University, Nashville, November 11–12, 2005); "Re-Enactment History and Affective Knowing" (Centre for Research in the Arts, Social Sciences, and Humanities [CRASSH], Cambridge, England, March 21, 2007); "Art and Re-Enactment Conference: One in a Series of Conferences and Workshops. Related to the Humanities Research Centre Research Theme of Historical Re-Enactment and Public Memory" (Australian National University, Canberra, June 5–7, 2007); and "Once More with Feeling: Re-Enactment and the Capture of the Past Conference" (Shandy Hall, Yorkshire, England, October 17–18, 2008). For more about the research platform theme at the ANU's Humanities Research Centre, see Australian National University, Humanities Research Centre, "HRC Research Platform: Historical Re-Enactment and Public Memory," http://www.anu.edu.au/hrc/research_plat forms/Historical_Re-enactment.php.

138 For the two edited volumes, see Lamb and Agnew, eds., *Settler and Creole Reenactment*; and McCalman and Pickering, eds., *Historical Re-Enactment*. For

the special issue, see Agnew and Lamb, eds., "Extreme and Sentimental History," special issue, *Criticism*.

139 See the University of York, Institute for the Public Understanding of the Past, http://www.york.ac.uk/ipup/index.html. For more about the Evliya Çelebi Ride, see the University of Kent, School of English, "The Evliya Çelebi Way," http://www.kent.ac.uk/english/evliya/index.html; the University of Kent, School of English, "People: Professor Donna Landry," http://www.kent.ac.uk/english/people/profiles/landry.htm; and Donna Landry and the University of Kent, "Hoofprinting with Evliya," http://www.hoofprinting.blogspot.com.

140 Dinshaw, *Getting Medieval*, 173–82. Boswell, *Christianity, Social Tolerance, and Homosexuality*.

141 Carries Johnson, "Obama Says Marriage Law Should Be Repealed," *Washington Post* (August 18, 2009), A2.

142 Boswell, *Same-Sex Unions in Premodern Europe*.

143 See "Coda" in Dinshaw, *Getting Medieval*, 183–206.

144 Dinshaw, *Getting Medieval*, 35.

145 Ibid., 32.

146 Ibid., 28, 27.

147 Ibid., 27.

148 Ibid., 59.

149 Singleton and Michael, "Actor-Networks and Ambivalence," 230 (emphasis mine). See also Callon, "The Sociology of an Actor-Network."

CONCLUSION

1 Latour, "How to Talk about the Body?," 207.

2 Ibid., 206.

3 Ibid., 205. See Despret, "The Becomings of Subjectivity in Animal Worlds," 123–39, and "The Body We Care For," 111–34.

4 Latour, "How to Talk about the Body?," 213.

5 Ibid., 210–11.

6 One example is Jenkins, *Textual Poachers*.

7 Bolter and Grusin, *Remediation*.

8 Jenkins, *Convergence Culture*, 95–96.

9 Ibid., 129–30.

10 MIT, Comparative Media Studies, "People: Henry Jenkins," http://web.mit.edu/cms/People/henry3.

11 Jenkins, *Convergence Culture*, 130.

12 Ibid., 97.

13 Latour, "How to Talk about the Body?," 215.

14 Stafford, "Epistemology for Sale," 215–30.

15 I wonder here about the work of the Nobel Prize winner Elinor Ostrum; see

for example: *Governing the Commons*; *Understanding Institutional Diversity*; Ostrom, Gardner, and Walker, *Rules, Games, and Common-Pool Resources*; and Ostrom and Walker, *Trust and Reciprocity*.

16 I am thinking here of the theoretical apparatus used in an amazing project, Keeling, *Witch's Flight*. More below.

17 Sandoval, *Methodology of the Oppressed*.

18 Ibid. Compare with Hennessy, *Profit and Pleasure*. See also Falk, "The Making of Global Citizenship."

19 Johnson, *Everything Bad Is Good for You* and *Mind Wide Open*.

20 Sandoval, *Methodology of the Oppressed*, 24.

21 Sandoval, "Foreword: Afterbridge: Technologies of Crossing," 24.

22 For example, of "la facultad," see Net Industries' JRank Science and Philosophy online, "Multiple Identity—New Philosophical Challenges," http://science.jrank.org/pages/9750/Multiple-Identity-New-Philosophical-Challenges.html; Tamdgidi, "Proceedings of the Third Annual Social Theory Forum, March 27–28, University of Massachusetts, Boston"; and Graduate Authors in Composition and Cultural Rhetoric blogging at Syracuse University, "Gloria Anzaldua Borderlands/La Frontera: The New Mestiza," *thoughtjam* (January 2, 2009), http://thoughtjam.wordpress.com.

23 Such as Anzaldúa, *Borderlands / La Frontera*; "La Conciencia De La Mestiza"; "Now Let Us Shift . . . The Path of Conocimiento." See also Bost, *Encarnación*.

24 For example, not only in one of Klein's titles and book structure itself, but also throughout its chapter 4 on interdisciplinary studies, including women's studies, in Klein, *Crossing Boundaries*, especially for example, 130–32. For another example, see also, the section titled "Borderlands and Monsters" in Bowker and Star, *Sorting Things Out*, 302–305.

25 See Gates, *Signifying Monkey*.

26 Rose, *Black Noise* and *Hip Hop Wars*; An, "The Spoken Word in within Our Gates"; Hume, "Improvisational Insurrection."

27 For example, Appiah and Gates, *Africana: The Encyclopedia*; Appiah, Gates, and Microsoft, "Microsoft Encarta Africana 2000"; Appiah, Gates, and Vazquez, *Dictionary of Global Culture*.

28 *African American Lives*, TV series (Kunhardt and PBS, 2006–8).

29 Sandoval, *Methodology of the Oppressed*, especially 107–14.

30 Anzaldúa, *Borderlands / La Frontera*, for example, 41–51.

31 Sandoval, *Methodology of the Oppressed*, 110.

32 Among them Gloria Anzaldúa, Pat Mora, Yreina Cervantez, and Miguel Leon Portilla, as described by Sybil Venegas, "Nepantla Aesthetics," Chicanoart.org, http://www.chicanoart.org/nepantla.html. See also Pérez, *Chicana Art*.

33 G. Bateson, "The Logical Categories of Learning and Communication," 301.

34 G. Bateson, "Double Bind, 1969," 272.

35 Sandoval, *Methodology of the Oppressed*, 59. See also Haraway, "Situated Knowledges"; and Spivak and Rooney, "In a Word, Interview."

36 Sandoval, "Foreword: Afterbridge: Technologies of Crossing," 20.

37 Perhaps Ebert, *Ludic Feminism and After*.

38 A "third path" that significantly predates and preempts any neoconservative claims using this or similar phrasing, and which also differs from some associations with the so-called third wave in histories of feminist ideology.

39 For thinking that has utterly altered my understanding of these issues, and that permeates this book even when not specific to citation, I think thankfully of the work of Eva Hayward and Bailey Kier, including but not limited to their articles "FingeryEyes" and "Spider City Sex" (Hayward) and "Interdependent Ecological Transsex" (Kier).

40 Latour, "How to Talk about the Body?," 209.

41 See Haraway, "Animal Sociology and a Natural Economy of the Body Politic" (parts I and II); *Primate Visions*; *Simians, Cyborgs, and Women*; *Modest_Witness*; *Haraway Reader*; *When Species Meet*; and Haraway and Goodeve, *How Like a Leaf*.

42 Haraway, *When Species Meet*, 212.

43 Ibid., 213–14.

44 Ibid., 212–13.

45 Ibid., 211.

46 Ibid., 212–13.

47 Stafford, "Epistemology for Sale," 221.

48 Ibid., 222. See also Code, *Epistemic Responsibility*.

49 Haraway, *When Species Meet*, 213–14.

50 Klein, "Disciplinary Origins and Differences."

51 Again, considering Ostrom, *Governing the Commons*; *Understanding Institutional Diversity*; Ostrom, Gardner, and Walker, *Rules, Games, and Common-Pool Resources*; and Ostrom and Walker, *Trust and Reciprocity*.

52 Keeling, *Witch's Flight*, 42–43.

53 Ibid., 14, 15, 16.

54 Ibid., 116.

55 Ibid., 14.

56 Ibid., 20.

Agnew, V., and J. Lamb, eds. 2004. "Extreme and Sentimental History." Special issue, *Criticism* 46, no. 3.

Aicher, P. J. 1995. *Guide to the Aqueducts of Ancient Rome*. Wauconda, Ill.: Bolchazy-Carducci.

———. 2004. *Rome Alive: A Source-Guide to the Ancient City*. Wauconda, Ill.: Bolchazy-Carducci.

Alfaro, L., J. Farías, R. Martinez, C. Cram, O. Solis, J. Rivera et al. 2000. *Plays from South Coast Repertory: Hispanic Playwrights Project Anthology*. New York: Broadway Play.

An, G. 2006. "The Spoken Word in *Within Our Gates*: Revisited and Remixed." *Moving Image* 6, no. 2: 128–32.

Ang, I. 1996. *Living Room Wars: Rethinking Media Audiences for a Postmodern World*. London and New York: Routledge.

Anzaldúa, G. 1987. *Borderlands / La frontera: The New Mestiza*. San Francisco: Spinsters/Aunt Lute.

———. 1990. "La conciencia de la mestiza: Towards a New Consciousness." In *Making Face, Making Soul / Haciendo caras: Creative and Critical Perspectives by Feminists of Color*, edited by G. Anzaldúa, 377–89). San Francisco: Aunt Lute.

———. 2002. "Now Let Us Shift . . . the Path of Conocimiento . . . Inner Work, Public Acts." In *This Bridge We Call Home: Radical Visions for Transformation*, edited by G. Anzaldúa and A. Keating, 540–78. New York: Routledge.

Appiah, A., and H. L. Gates. 1999. *Africana: The Encyclopedia of the African and African American Experience*. New York: BasicCivitas.

Appiah, A., H. L. Gates, and M. C. Vazquez. 1997. *The Dictionary of Global Culture*. New York: Knopf and Random House.

Bacon-Smith, C. 1992. *Enterprising Women: Television Fandom and the Creation of Popular Myth*. Philadelphia: University of Pennsylvania Press.

———. 1992. "Who Are Fanziners? Demographics." In *Enterprising Women: Television Fandom and the Creation of Popular Myth*, 319–23. Philadelphia: University of Pennsylvania Press.

Badgett, M. V. L. 2001. *Money, Myths, and Change: The Economic Lives of Lesbians and Gay Men*. Chicago: University of Chicago Press.

Baker, S. 2002. *The Ship: Retracing Cook's Endeavour Voyage*. London: BBC Worldwide.

——. 2006. *Ancient Rome: The Rise and Fall of an Empire*. London: BBC.

Barclay, G. S. J., and C. Turner. 2004. *Humanities Research Centre: A History of the First 30 Years of the HRC at the Australian National University*. Canberra, Australia: Humanities Research Centre, 2004. http://epress.anu.edu.au/hrc/frames.php.

Barnes, M. 1996. *Secrets of Lost Empires: Reconstructing the Glories of Ages Past*. New York: Sterling.

——. 2000. "Introduction." In *Mysteries of Lost Empires*, edited by M. Fisher and D. E. Fisher, 6–19. London: Channel 4.

Bateson, G. 1957. "Language and Psychotherapy: Frieda Fromm-Reichmann's Last Project." *Psychiatry* 21, no. 1: 96–100.

——. 1972 [1954]. "Metalogue: Why a Swan." In *Steps to an Ecology of Mind: Collected Essays in Anthropology, Psychiatry, Evolution, and Epistemology*. San Francisco: Chandler, 33–37.

——. 1972 [1954]. "A Theory of Play and Fantasy." In *Steps to an Ecology of Mind: Collected Essays in Anthropology, Psychiatry, Evolution, and Epistemology*. San Francisco: Chandler, 177–94.

——. 1972 [1955]. "Epidemiology of a Schizophrenia," In *Steps to an Ecology of Mind: Collected Essays in Anthropology, Psychiatry, Evolution, and Epistemology*. San Francisco: Chandler, 194–200.

——. 1972 [1956]. "Toward a Theory of Schizophrenia." In *Steps to an Ecology of Mind: Collected Essays in Anthropology, Psychiatry, Evolution, and Epistemology*. San Francisco: Chandler, 201–27.

——. 1972 [1967]. "Conscious Purpose versus Nature." In *Steps to an Ecology of Mind: Collected Essays in Anthropology, Psychiatry, Evolution, and Epistemology*. San Francisco: Chandler, 432–45.

——. 1972 [1967]. "Cybernetic Explanation." In *Steps to an Ecology of Mind: Collected Essays in Anthropology, Psychiatry, Evolution, and Epistemology*. San Francisco: Chandler, 405–16.

——. 1972 [1968]. "Effects of Conscious Purpose on Human Adaptation." In *Steps to an Ecology of Mind: Collected Essays in Anthropology, Psychiatry, Evolution, and Epistemology*. San Francisco: Chandler, 446–53.

——. 1972 [1968–1971]. "The Logical Categories of Learning and Communication." In *Steps to an Ecology of Mind: Collected Essays in Anthropology, Psychiatry, Evolution, and Epistemology*. San Francisco: Chandler, 279–308.

——. 1972 [1969]. "Double Bind, 1969." In *Steps to an Ecology of Mind: Collected Essays in Anthropology, Psychiatry, Evolution, and Epistemology*. San Francisco: Chandler, 271–78.

——. 1972 [1970]. "Ecology and Flexibility in Urban Civilization." In *Steps to an*

Ecology of Mind: Collected Essays in Anthropology, Psychiatry, Evolution, and Epis-temology. San Francisco: Chandler, 502–13.

——. 1972 [1970]. "Form, Substance, and Difference." In *Steps to an Ecology of Mind: Collected Essays in Anthropology, Psychiatry, Evolution, and Epistemology.* San Francisco: Chandler, 454–71.

——. 1972 [1971]. "The Cybernetics of 'Self': A Theory of Alcoholism." In *Steps to an Ecology of Mind: Collected Essays in Anthropology, Psychiatry, Evolution, and Epistemology.* San Francisco: Chandler, 309–37.

——. 1972. "Part II: Form and Pattern in Anthropology." In *Steps to an Ecology of Mind: Collected Essays in Anthropology, Psychiatry, Evolution, and Epistemology.* San Francisco: Chandler, 59–156.

——. 1972. "Part III: Form and Pathology in Relationship." In *Steps to an Ecology of Mind: Collected Essays in Anthropology, Psychiatry, Evolution, and Epistemology.* San Francisco: Chandler, 159–339.

——. 1972. *Steps to an Ecology of Mind: Collected Essays in Anthropology, Psychiatry, Evolution, and Epistemology.* San Francisco: Chandler.

——. 1977. "Afterword." In *About Bateson: Essays on Gregory Bateson*, edited by J. Brockman, 233–47.

——. 1979. *Mind and Nature: A Necessary Unity.* New York: Dutton.

——. 1980. *Men Are Grass: Metaphor and the World of Mental Process.* West Stock-bridge: Lindisfarne.

Bateson, M. C. 1972. *Our Own Metaphor: A Personal Account of a Conference on the Effects of Conscious Purpose on Human Adaptation.* New York: Knopf and Random House.

——. 2000. *"Foreword* by Mary Catherine Bateson, 1999." In *Steps to an Ecology of Mind*, by G. Bateson, vi–xvii. Chicago: University of Chicago Press.

Baun, M. J. 1995–96. "The Maastricht Treaty as High Politics: Germany, France, and European Integration." *Political Science Quarterly* 110, no. 4: 605–24.

Berggren, K., and J. B. Harrod. 1996. "Understanding Marija Gimbutas." *Journal of Prehistoric Religion* 10:70–73.

Biddick, K. 1998. "Bede's Blush: Postcards from Bali, Bombay, Palo Alto." In *The Shock of Medievalism*, 83–101. Durham: Duke University Press. Reprinted from J. V. Engen, ed. 1992. *The Past and Future of Medieval Studies*, 623–35. Notre Dame: Notre Dame.

Blanton, D. 1993. "Women Soldiers of the Civil War." *Prologue: A Quarterly Publication of the National Archives and Records Administration* 25, no. 1. http://www.archives.gov/publications/prologue/1993/spring/women-in-the-civil-war-1.html.

Bolter, J. D., and R. Grusin. 1999. *Remediation: Understanding New Media.* Cambridge: MIT Press.

Bost, S. 2010. *Encarnación: Illness and Body Politics in Chicana Feminist Literature.* New York: Fordham.

Boswell, J. 1980. *Christianity, Social Tolerance, and Homosexuality: Gay People in*

Western Europe from the Beginning of the Christian Era to the Fourteenth Century. Chicago: University of Chicago Press.

——. 1994. *Same-Sex Unions in Premodern Europe*. New York: Villard.

Bowker, G. C., and S. L. Star. 1999. *Sorting Things Out: Classification and Its Consequences*. Cambridge: MIT Press.

Brightwell, R. 1997. "Introduction." In *Secrets of Lost Empires*, edited by M. Barnes.

Brockman, J., ed. 1977. *About Bateson: Essays on Gregory Bateson*. New York: Dutton.

Burgess, L. C., and S. R. Wakeman, ed. 1994. *An Uncommon Soldier: The Civil War Letters of Sarah Rosetta Wakeman*. Pasadena: Minerva Center.

Callon, M. 1986. "The Sociology of an Actor-Network: The Case of the Electric Vehicle." In *Mapping the Dynamics of Science and Technology: Sociology of Science in the Real World*, edited by M. Callon, A. Rip, and J. E. Law, 19–34. London: Macmillan.

Cere, R. 2000. *European and National Identities in Britain and Italy: Maastricht on Television*. Lewiston: Edwin Mellen.

Code, L. 1987. *Epistemic Responsibility*. Hanover: Brown University; University of New England Press.

Collins, R. 1991. "National Culture: A Contradiction in Terms?" *Canadian Journal of Communication* 16, no. 2: 207–24.

Cooper, D. G., ed. 1969. *To Free a Generation: The Dialectics of Liberation*. New York: Collier.

Creighton, M. S., and L. Norling, ed. 1996. *Iron Men, Wooden Women: Gender and Seafaring in the Atlantic World, 1700–1920*. Baltimore: Johns Hopkins University Press.

Crenshaw, N. 1997. *Xena X-Posed: The Unauthorized Biography of Lucy Lawless and Her On-screen Character*. Rocklin: Prima.

Crichton, M. 1994. *Disclosure: A Novel*. New York: Knopf.

Davis-Kimball, J. 1995. *Kurgans on the Left Bank of the Ilek: Excavations at Pokrovka, 1994*. Berkeley: Zinat Press.

——. 2000. *Kurgans, Ritual Sites, and Settlements: Eurasian Bronze and Iron Age*. Oxford: Archaeopress.

Davis-Kimball, J., and M. Behan. 2002. *Warrior Women: An Archaeologist's Search for History's Hidden Heroines*. New York: Warner.

Despret, V. 2004. "The Body We Care for: Figures of Anthropo-zoo-genesis." In "Bodies on Trial," edited by M. Akrich and M. Berg. Special issue, *Body and Society*, 10, nos. 2–3: 111–34.

——. 2004. *Our Emotional Makeup: Ethnopsychology and Selfhood*. New York: Other Press.

——. 2008. "The Becomings of Subjectivity in Animal Worlds." *Subjectivity* 23:123–39.

Dietler, M. 1994. "'Our Ancestors the Gauls': Archaeology, Ethnic Nationalism, and the Manipulation of Celtic Identity in Modern Europe." *American Anthropologist* 96, no. 3: 584–605.

Dinshaw, C. 1999. *Getting Medieval: Sexualities and Communities, Pre- and Post-modern*. Durham: Duke University Press.

Doherty, T. P. 2003. *Cold War, Cool Medium: Television, McCarthyism, and American Culture*. New York: Columbia University Press.

Druett, J. 2000. *She Captains: Heroines and Hellions of the Sea*. New York: Simon and Schuster.

Dubin, S. C. 1999. *Displays of Power: Memory and Amnesia in the American Museum*. New York: NYU Press.

Dugaw, D. 1989. *Warrior Women and Popular Balladry, 1650–1850*. Cambridge; New York: Cambridge University Press.

Ebert, T. L. 1996. *Ludic Feminism and After: Postmodernism, Desire, and Labor in Late Capitalism*. Ann Arbor: University of Michigan Press.

Edelman, I. 2002. "Reuse, Repurposing and Recapture." Paper presented at the Common Threads MDA Conference, Birmingham Botanical Gardens, September 4–6.

Edge, B. 1991. *The Fine Young Cannibals' Story: The Sweet and the Sour*. London: Omnibus.

Eichenlaub, C. 2000. "Marija Gimbutas and the Future of a Legacy." *European Legacy* 5, no. 5: 733–35.

Engel, M. 1972. "Preface." In *Steps to an Ecology of Mind: Collected Essays in Anthropology, Psychiatry, Evolution, and Epistemology*, by G. Bateson, vii–ix. San Francisco: Chandler.

Enloe, C. H. 1983. *Does Khaki Become You? The Militarisation of Women's Lives*. Boston: South End Press.

——. 1990. *Bananas, Beaches, and Bases: Making Feminist Sense of International Politics*. Berkeley: University of California Press.

——. 1993. *The Morning After: Sexual Politics at the End of the Cold War*. Berkeley: University of California Press.

Etzkowitz, H., and L. A. Leydesdorff. 1995. "The Triple Helix of University-Industry-Government Relations: A Laboratory for Knowledge Based Economic Development." *EASST Review* 14, no. 1: 11–19.

——, eds. 1997. *Universities and the Global Knowledge Economy: A Triple Helix of University-Industry-Government Relations*. London and New York: Pinter Publishers.

Etzkowitz, H., and R. Viale. 2005. "Third Academic Revolution: Polyvalent Knowledge; the 'DNA' of the Triple Helix." Paper presented at "Triple Helix 5: The Capitalization of Knowledge," conference. http://citeseerx.ist.psu.edu/viewdoc/summary?doi=10.1.1.88.2728.

Fagan, G. G. 1999. *Bathing in Public in the Roman World*. Ann Arbor: University of Michigan Press.

——. 2003. "Far-Out Television." *Archaeology* 56, no. 3: 46–50.

——. 2006. *Archaeological Fantasies: How Pseudoarchaeology Misrepresents the Past and Misleads the Public*. London and New York: Routledge.

Falk, R. 1993. "The Making of Global Citizenship." In *Global Visions: Beyond the*

New World Order, edited by J. Brecher, J. B. Childs, and J. Cutler, 39–50. Boston: South End Press.

Feinman, I. R. 2000. *Citizenship Rites: Feminist Soldiers and Feminist Antimilitarists*. New York: NYU Press.

Finley, M. I. 1973. *The Ancient Economy*. Berkeley: University of California Press.

Firstbrook, P. 2001. *Surviving the Iron Age*. London: BBC Worldwide.

Fisher, M., and D. E. Fisher. 2000. *Mysteries of Lost Empires*. London: Channel 4.

———. 2000. "Roman Bath." In *Mysteries of Lost Empires*, 134–71.

Fitch, N. R. 1983. *Sylvia Beach and the Lost Generation: A History of Literary Paris in the Twenties and Thirties*. New York: Norton.

———. 1986. "Shakespeare and Company." *Journal of Library History* 21, no. 3: 600–603.

Francke, L. B. 1997. *Ground Zero: The Gender Wars in the Military*. New York: Simon and Schuster.

Fraser, A. 1989. *The Warrior Queens*. New York: Knopf.

Fréches, J. 1986. *La Guerre des Images*. Paris: Denoèel.

Freeman, M. 1996. "Mything in Action." *MediaWeek* 6, no. 18: 42.

Frisch, M. H. 1990. *A Shared Authority: Essays on the Craft and Meaning of Oral and Public History*. Albany: SUNY Press.

Gates, H. L. 1988. *The Signifying Monkey: A Theory of Afro-American Literary Criticism*. New York: Oxford University Press.

———. 1999. "Dr. Entrepreneur." *Black Issues in Higher Education* 15 (25), 18–23.

Gee, J. P. 2003. *What Video Games Have to Teach Us about Learning and Literacy*. New York: Palgrave Macmillan.

Geiger, R. L. 2004. *Knowledge and Money: Research Universities and the Paradox of the Marketplace*. Stanford: Stanford University Press.

Ghamari-Tabrizi, S. 2005. *The Worlds of Herman Kahn: The Intuitive Science of Thermonuclear War*. Cambridge: Harvard University Press.

Gieryn, T. 1996. "Policing STS: A Boundary-Work Souvenir from the Smithsonian Exhibition on 'Science in American Life.'" *Science, Technology, and Human Values* 21, no. 1: 100–115.

———. 1996. "Preface to the Deconstruction of an Exhibition on Science in American Life." *American Sociologist* 27, no. 2: 52–54.

Gimbutas, M. 1986. "Comment." In response to: "The 'Kurgan Culture,' Indo-European Origins, and the Domestication of the Horse: A Reconsideration" by D. W. Anthony. *Current Anthropology* 27, no. 4: 291–313.

Gitelman, L. 2006. *Always Already New: Media, History, and the Data of Culture*. Cambridge: MIT Press.

Goldman, N. L., ed. 1982. *Female Soldiers—Combatants or Noncombatants? Historical and Contemporary Perspectives*. Westport: Greenwood Publishing Group.

Gordon, A. 1997. *Ghostly Matters: Haunting and the Sociological Imagination*. Minneapolis: University of Minnesota Press.

Greenberg, J. 1964. *I Never Promised You a Rose Garden*. New York: Holt.

Gross, P. R. 1996. "Reply to Tom Gieryn." *Science, Technology, and Human Values* 21, no. 1: 116–20.

Hadden, R. L. 1990. *The Civil War Reenactor's Handbook: A Guide to Historical Interpretation, Teaching History, and Living History.* Greenville, N.C.: HadCo Associates.

Halberstam, J. 1995. *Skin Shows: Gothic Horror and the Technology of Monsters.* Durham: Duke University Press.

——. 1998. *Female Masculinity.* Durham: Duke University Press.

——. 2005. *In a Queer Time and Place: Transgender Bodies, Subcultural Lives.* New York: NYU Press.

Halberstam, J., and I. Livingston. 1995. *Posthuman Bodies.* Bloomington: University of Indiana Press.

Handler, R., and E. Gable. 1997. *The New History in an Old Museum: Creating the Past at Colonial Williamsburg.* Durham: Duke University Press.

Haraway, D. 1978. "Animal Sociology and a Natural Economy of the Body Politic, Part I: A Political Physiology of Dominance." *Signs* 4, no. 1: 21–36.

——. 1978. "Animal Sociology and a Natural Economy of the Body Politic, Part II: The Past Is the Contested Zone." *Signs* 4, no. 1: 37–60.

——. 1989. *Primate Visions: Gender, Race, and Nature in the World of Modern Science.* New York: Routledge.

——. 1991. "Situated Knowledges: The Science Question in Feminism and the Privilege of Partial Perspective." *Simians, Cyborgs, and Women: The Reinvention of Nature,* 183–201. New York: Routledge.

——. 1997. *Modest_Witness@Second_Millennium.FemaleMan©_Meets_Onco Mouse™: Feminism and Technoscience.* New York: Routledge.

——. 2003. *The Companion Species Manifesto: Dogs, People, and Significant Otherness.* Chicago: Prickly Paradigm Press.

——. 2008. *When Species Meet.* Minneapolis: University of Minnesota Press.

Haraway, D., and T. N. Goodeve. 2000. *How Like a Leaf: An Interview with Thyrza Nichols Goodeve.* New York: Routledge.

Harwit, M. 1996. *An Exhibit Denied: Lobbying the History of Enola Gay.* New York: Copernicus.

Hayes, E. 1997. "Lucy Lawless: Xena." *Lesbian News* 23, no. 4: 22–25.

Hayles, N. K. 1999. *How We Became Posthuman: Virtual Bodies in Cybernetics, Literature, and Informatics.* Chicago: University of Chicago Press.

Hayward, E. 2010. "FingeryEyes: Impressions of Cup Corals." *Cultural Anthropology* 25, no. 4: 577–99.

——. 2010. "Spider City Sex." *Women and Performance* 20, no. 3: 225–51.

Heims, S. J. 1991. *The Cybernetics Group.* Cambridge: MIT Press.

Hennessy, R. 1995. "Queer Visibility in Commodity Culture." In *Social Postmodernism: Beyond Identity Politics,* edited by L. J. Nicholson and S. Seidman, 142–84. Cambridge and New York: Cambridge University Press.

——. 2000. *Profit and Pleasure: Sexual Identities in Late Capitalism.* New York: Routledge.

Herbert, M. S. 1998. *Camouflage Isn't Only for Combat: Gender, Sexuality and Women in the Military*. New York: NYU Press.

Hogan, P. K. 1994. *The Complete Guide to the Music of Queen*. London: Omnibus.

Hopkins, K. 1978. *Conquerors and Slaves*. Cambridge and New York: Cambridge University Press.

———. 1983. *Death and Renewal*. Cambridge and New York: Cambridge University Press.

———. 1999. *A World Full of Gods: Pagans, Jews and Christians in the Roman Empire*. London: Weidenfeld and Nicolson.

Howe, R. F. 2002. "Covert Force; Hundreds of Women Fought in the Civil War Disguised as Men." *Smithsonian* 33 (October): 127–31.

Hubert, S. J. 1999. "What's Wrong with This Picture? The Politics of Ellen's Coming Out Party." *Journal of Popular Culture* 33, no. 2: 31–36.

Hume, C. 2006. "Improvisational Insurrection: The Sound Poetry of Tracie Morris." *Contemporary Literature* 47, no. 3: 415–39.

Hutchins, E. 1995. *Cognition in the Wild*. Cambridge: MIT Press.

Jenkins, H. 1992. *Textual Poachers: Television Fans and Participatory Culture*. New York: Routledge.

———. 2006. *Convergence Culture: Where Old and New Media Collide*. New York: NYU Press.

Johnson, S. 2001. *Emergence: The Connected Lives of Ants, Brains, Cities, and Software*. New York: Scribner.

———. 2004. *Mind Wide Open: Your Brain and the Neuroscience of Everyday Life*. New York: Scribner.

———. 2005. *Everything Bad Is Good for You: How Today's Popular Culture Is Actually Making Us Smarter*. New York: Riverhead Books.

Joseph, M. 1998. "The Performance of Production and Consumption." *Social Text* 16, no. 1: 25–61.

Juul, J. 2005. *Half-real: Video Games between Real Rules and Fictional Worlds*. Cambridge: MIT Press.

Keeling, K. 2007. *The Witch's Flight: The Cinematic, the Black Femme, and the Image of Common Sense*. Durham: Duke University Press.

Kesey, K. 1962. *One Flew Over the Cuckoo's Nest*. New York: Viking.

Kier, B. 2010. "Interdependent Ecological Transsex: Notes on Re/production, 'Transgender' Fish, and the Management of Populations, Species, and Resources." *Women and Performance* 20, no. 3: 299–19.

King, K. 2004. "Flexible Knowledges: Histories Under Globalization." Paper presented for the Women's, Gender, and Sexuality Studies Colloquia Series, Colby College, Waterville, Maine, March 4. http://www.womensstudies.umd.edu/wmstfac/kking/present/Colby04/colby1.html.

———. 2004. "Historiography as Reenactment: Metaphors and Literalizations of TV Documentaries." *Criticism* 46, no. 3: 459–75.

———. 2011. "Pastpresents: Playing Cat's Cradle with Donna Haraway." In "Party

Writing for Donna Haraway!," edited by K. King. Unpublished manuscript, available in part at http://partywriting.blogspot.com/.

Klein, J. T. 1990. *Interdisciplinarity: History, Theory, and Practice*. Detroit: Wayne State University Press.

——. 1996. *Crossing Boundaries: Knowledge, Disciplinarities, and Interdisciplinarities*. Charlottesville: University of Virginia Press.

——. 1996. "Interdisciplinary Needs." *Library Trends* 45, no. 2: 134–54.

——. 2001. *Transdisciplinarity: Joint Problem Solving among Science, Technology, and Society: An Effective Way for Managing Complexity*. Basel and Boston: Birkhäuser.

——. 2004. "Disciplinary Origins and Differences." Paper delivered at Fenner Conference on the Environment, "Bridging Disciplinary Divides," Canberra, May 24–25. http://www.science.org.au/events/fenner/fenner2004/klein.html.

——. 2004. "Integration Panel Report to Floor: Julie Thompson Klein's Remarks." Fenner Conference on the Environment, "Bridging Disciplinary Divides," Canberra, May 24–25. http://www.science.org.au/events/fenner/fenner2004/integration.html.

——. 2004. "Prospects for transdisciplinarity." *Futures* 36, no. 4: 515–26.

——. 2005. *Humanities, Culture, and Interdisciplinarity: The Changing American Academy*. Albany: SUNY Press.

Klein, N. 2000. *No Space, No Choice, No Jobs, No Logo: Taking Aim at the Brand Bullies*. New York: Picador USA.

Lamb, J., and V. Agnew, ed. 2010. *Settler and Creole Reenactment*. Basingstoke and New York: Palgrave Macmillan.

Lambert, A. 2004. "Retracing the Captain: 'Extreme History,' Hard Tack and Scurvy." In *Captain Cook: Explorations and Reassessments*, edited by G. Williams, 246–55. Woodbridge: Boydell Press.

Latour, B. 1987. *Science in Action: How to Follow Scientists and Engineers through Society*. Cambridge: Harvard University Press.

——. 1993 [1991]. *We Have Never Been Modern*. Translated by C. Porter. Cambridge: Harvard University Press.

——. 2002. "Iconoclash or Is There a World Beyond the Image Wars?" In *Iconoclash: Beyond the Image Wars in Science, Religion, and Art*, edited by B. Latour and P. Weibel. http://www.bruno-latour.fr/articles/2002.html.

——. 2002. "The Promises of Constructivism." In *Chasing Technoscience: Matrix of Materiality*, edited by D. Idhe and E. Selinger, 27–46. Bloomington: Indiana University Press. http://www.bruno-latour.fr/articles/2002.html.

——. 2002. *War of the Worlds: What About Peace?* Chicago: Prickly Paradigm Press.

——. 2004. "How to Talk About the Body? The Normative Dimension of Science Studies." In "Bodies on Trial," edited by M. Akrich and M. Berg. Special issue, *Body and Society* 10, nos. 2–3: 205–29.

Latour, B., and P. Weibel, ed. 2002. *Iconoclash: Beyond the Image Wars in Science, Religion, and Art*. Cambridge: MIT Press.

Lattuca, L. R. 2001. *Creating Interdisciplinarity: Interdisciplinary Research and Teaching among College and University Faculty*. Nashville: Vanderbilt University Press.

Lave, J. 1988. *Cognition in Practice: Mind, Mathematics, and Culture in Everyday Life*. Cambridge and New York: Cambridge University Press.

Lave, J., and E. Wenger. 1991. *Situated Learning: Legitimate Peripheral Participation*. Cambridge and New York: Cambridge University Press.

Lawrence, R. J., and C. Despres. 2004. "Introduction: Futures of Transdisciplinarity." *Futures* 36, no. 4: 397–405.

Lewenstein, B. V. 2000. "An American Historical Perspective on Public Communication of Science." Paper presented at the Science Communication, Education, and the History of Science Conference, British Society for the History of Science, the Royal Society, London, July 12–13.

Lewontin, R. C. 2000. *The Triple Helix: Gene, Organism, and Environment*. Cambridge: Harvard University Press.

Linde, N. 2004. "*Nova*: The Leading Edge." In *Creating Connections: Museums and the Public Understanding of Current Research*, edited by D. Chittenden, G. Farmelo, and B. V. Lewenstein, 311–17. Walnut Creek: AltaMira Press.

———. 2008. "A Burger, a Beer . . . and a Side of Science." In *Exemplary Science in Informal Education Settings: Standards-Based Success Stories*, edited by R. E. Yager and J. H. Falk, 1–13. Arlington: National Science Teachers Association.

Linenthal, E. T., and T. Engelhardt, ed. 1996. *History Wars: The Enola Gay and Other Battles for the American Past*. New York: Metropolitan Books.

Lorimer, S., and S. Synarski. 2002. *Booty: Girl Pirates on the High Seas*. San Francisco: Chronicle Books.

Lubar, S. 1996. "Exhibiting Memories." *Museum News* 75, no. 4: 60–72.

Mackintosh, B. 1986. *Interpretation in the National Park Service: A Historical Perspective*. History Division National Park Service, Department of the Interior. http://www.cr.nps.gov/history/online_books/mackintosh2/index.htm.

Marmor, J., V. W. Bernard, and P. Ottenberg. 1994. "Psychodynamics of Group Opposition to Mental Health Programs." In *Psychiatry in Transition*, edited by J. Marmor, 355–73. Piscataway: Transaction Publishers.

McCalman, I. 2004. "The Little Ship of Horrors." In "Extreme and Sentimental History." Special issue, *Criticism* 46, no. 3: 477–86.

———. 2004. "Telstra Address: Making Culture Bloom." Paper presented at the National Press Club. http://www.chass.org.au/speeches/SPE20040616IM.php.

McCalman, I., and P. A. Pickering, ed. 2010. *Historical Reenactment: From Realism to the Affective Turn*. Basingstoke: Palgrave Macmillan.

Millar, M. 1996. "Alice Guy: A Life in Motion." *French Cultural Studies* 7, no. 21: 229–45.

Miller, D. 1998. *A Theory of Shopping*. Ithaca: Cornell University Press.

Miller, P. P., G. Dubrow, S. Evans, D. A. Nelson, D. T. Pitcaithley, and S. Weber. 1996. *Exploring a Common Past: Interpreting Women's History in the National Park Service*. National Park Service and the Organization of American Histo-

rians. http://www.nps.gov/history/history/hisnps/NPSHistory/womens
history.pdf.

Mokhiber, R., and R. Weissman. 1999. *Corporate Predators: The Hunt for Mega-Profits and the Attack on Democracy*. Monroe: Common Courage Press.

Molella, A. P. 1999. "Science in American Life, National Identity, and the Science Wars: A Curator's View." *Curator* 42, no. 2: 108–16.

Monk, P., and T. V. Gelder. 2004. "Enhancing Our Grasp of Complex Arguments." Paper delivered at Fenner Conference on the Environment, "Bridging Disciplinary Divides," Canberra, May 24–25. http://www.science.org.au/events/fenner/fenner2004/monk.html.

Moraga, C. 1997. *Waiting in the Wings: Portrait of a Queer Motherhood*. Ithaca: Firebrand Books.

———. 2000. *Loving in the War Years: Lo que nunca pasó por sus labios*. Cambridge: South End Press.

Morley, D., and K. Robins. 1995. *Spaces of Identity: Global Media, Electronic Landscapes, and Cultural Boundaries*. London and New York: Routledge.

Mulkey, L. M., and W. Dougan. 1996. "The Smithsonian Institution Exhibition of 'Science in American Life': Science as It Consists of Normalized Practices." *American Sociologist* 27, no. 2: 61–78.

Newark, T. 1989. *Women Warlords: An Illustrated Military History of Female Warriors*. London and New York: Blandford; Sterling.

Nicolescu, B. 2002. *Manifesto of Transdisciplinarity*. Translated by K. C. Voss. Albany: SUNY Press.

Nobile, P., ed. 1995. *Judgment at the Smithsonian*. New York: Marlowe and Co.

Ostrom, E. 1990. *Governing the Commons: The Evolution of Institutions for Collective Action*. Cambridge and New York: Cambridge University Press.

———. 2005. *Understanding Institutional Diversity*. Princeton: Princeton University Press.

Ostrom, E., and J. Walker. 2003. *Trust and Reciprocity: Interdisciplinary Lessons from Experimental Research*. New York: Russell Sage.

Ostrom, E., R. Gardner, and J. Walker. 1994. *Rules, Games, and Common-Pool Resources*. Ann Arbor: University of Michigan Press.

Park, R. L. 1994. "Is Science the God that Failed?" *Science Communication* 16, no. 2: 206–11.

Pekarik, A. J., Z. D. Doering, and A. Bickford. 1999. "Visitors' Role in an Exhibition Debate: Science in American Life." *Curator* 42, no. 2: 117–29.

Penley, C. 1991. "Brownian Motion: Women, Tactics, and Technology." In *Technoculture*, edited by C. Penley and A. Ross. Minneapolis: University of Minnesota Press.

———, ed. 1991. *Close Encounters: Film, Feminism, and Science Fiction*. Minneapolis: University of Minnesota Press.

———. 1997. *NASA/TREK: Popular Science and Sex in America*. New York: Verso Press.

Penrice, D. 2002. "Can This Museum Be Saved?" *Common-Place* 3, no. 1 (October).

American Antiquarian Society and the University of Oklahoma. http://
www.common-place.org/vol-03/no-01/penrice/penrice-2.shtml.

Pérez, L. E. 2007. *Chicana Art: The Politics of Spiritual and Aesthetic Altarities*. Durham: Duke University Press.

Perkins, G. 1999. "Museum War Exhibits: Propaganda or Interpretation?" In "Sacred Places and Military History." Special issue, *Interpretation* 4, nos. 1 and 2.

Piazza, A., S. Rendine, E. Minch, P. Menozzi, J. Mountain, and L. L. Cavalli-Sforza. 1995. "Genetics and the Origin of European Languages." *Proceedings of the National Academy of Sciences of the United States of America* 92, no. 13: 5836–40.

Piccini, A. 1996. "Filming through the Mists of Time: Celtic Constructions and the Documentary." In "Anthropology in Public." Supplement and special issue, *Current Anthropology* 37, no. 1: S87–S111.

——. 1997. "Commentary on James F. Weiner's Televisualist Anthropology: Representation, Aesthetics, Politics." *Current Anthropology* 38, no. 2: 197–235.

Poovey, M. 2001. "The Twenty-First-Century University and the Market: What Price Economic Viability?" *differences* 12, no. 1: 1–16.

Pullen, K. 2000. "I-love-Xena.com: Creating Online Fan Communities." In *Web.studies: Rewiring Media Studies for the Digital Age*, edited by D. Gauntlett. London and New York: Arnold; Oxford University Press.

Ramadier, T. 2004. "Transdisciplinarity and Its Challenges: The Case of Urban Studies." *Futures* 36, no. 4: 423–39.

Rhees, D. J. 1987. "The Chemists' Crusade: The Rise of an Industrial Science in Modern America, 1907–1922." Unpublished dissertation, University of Pennsylvania.

Rose, T. 1994. *Black Noise: Rap Music and Black Culture in Contemporary America*. Hanover: University Press of New England.

——. 2008. *The Hip Hop Wars: What We Talk about When We Talk about Hip Hop—And Why It Matters*. New York: BasicCivitas.

Rosenzweig, R., and D. P. Thelen. 1998. *The Presence of the Past: Popular Uses of History in American Life*. New York: Columbia University Press.

Russ, J. 1985. "Pornography By Women For Women, With Love." In *Magic Mommas, Trembling Sisters, Puritans and Perverts: Feminist Essays*, 79–99. Trumansburg: Crossing Press.

Ryan, M. L. 2001. *Narrative as Virtual Reality: Immersion and Interactivity in Literature and Electronic Media*. Baltimore: Johns Hopkins University Press.

Salen, K., and E. Zimmerman. 2003. *Rules of Play: Game Design Fundamentals*. Cambridge: MIT Press.

Salmonson, J. A. 1991. *The Encyclopedia of Amazons: Women Warriors from Antiquity to the Modern Era*. New York: Paragon House.

Salmonson, J. A., D. Clavette, and W. A. Shultz. 1982. *The Swordswoman*. New York: Tom Doherty.

Salmonson, J. A., and W. A. Shultz. 1981. *Tomoe Gozen*. New York: Ace Books.

Salmonson, J. A., W. Wees, and K. Craft. 1984. *Thousand Shrine Warrior*. New York: Ace Books.

Sandoval, C. 2000. *Methodology of the Oppressed*. Minneapolis: University of Minnesota Press.

———. 2002. "Foreword: AfterBridge: Technologies of Crossing." In *This Bridge We Call Home: Radical Visions for Transformation,* edited by G. E. Anzaldúa and A. Keating, 21–26. New York: Routledge.

Sanjek, D. 1995. "Home Alone: The Phenomenon of Direct-to-Video." *Cineaste* 21, nos. 1 and 2: 98–99.

Sardar, Z., A. Nandy, M. W. Davies, and C. Alvares. 1993. *The Blinded Eye: 500 Years of Christopher Columbus*. Goa and New York: Other India; Apex.

Sassen, S. 1993. "Economic Globalization: A New Geography, Composition, and Institutional Framework." In *Global Visions: Beyond the New World Order,* edited by J. Brecher, J. B. Childs, and J. Cutler, 61–66. Boston: South End Press.

———. 1998. *Globalization and Its Discontents: Essays on the New Mobility of People and Money*. New York: New Press.

———. 2000. *Cities in a World Economy*. 2nd ed. Thousand Oaks, Calif.: Pine Forge.

———. 2001. *The Global City: New York, London, Tokyo*. 2nd ed. Princeton: Princeton University Press.

———, ed. 2002. *Global Networks, Linked Cities*. New York: Routledge.

———. 2002. "Introduction: Locating Cities on Global Circuits." In *Global Networks, Linked Cities,* edited by S. Sassen, 1–36. New York: Routledge.

Shreeve, J. 2004. *The Genome War: How Craig Venter Tried to Capture the Code of Life and Save the World*. New York: Knopf.

Singleton, V., and M. Michael. 1993. "Actor-Networks and Ambivalence: General Practitioners in the UK Cervical Screening Programme." *Social Studies of Science* 23, no. 2: 227–64.

Slaughter, S., and L. L. Leslie. 1997. *Academic Capitalism: Politics, Policies, and the Entrepreneurial University*. Baltimore: Johns Hopkins University Press.

Slaughter, S., and A. Metcalfe. 2007. "The Differential Effects of Academic Capitalism on Women in the Academy." Institute for Higher Education, University of Georgia. http://www.uga.edu/ihe/slaughter.html. In *Unfinished Agendas: New and Continuing Gender Challenges in Higher Education,* edited by J. Glazer-Raymo. 2008. Baltimore: Johns Hopkins University Press.

Slaughter, S., and G. Rhoades. 2004. *Academic Capitalism and the New Economy: Markets, State, and Higher Education*. Baltimore: Johns Hopkins University Press.

Sobchack, V. C. 2000. *Meta-morphing: Visual Transformation and the Culture of Quick-Change*. Minneapolis: University of Minnesota Press.

Spector, J. 1993. *What This Awl Means: Feminist Archaeology at a Wahpeton Dakota Village*. St. Paul: Minnesota Historical Society.

Spigel, L. 1992. "Installing the Television Set: Popular Discourses on Television and Domestic Space, 1948–1955." In *Private Screenings: Television and the Female Consumer*, edited by L. Spigel and D. Mann, 3–38.

Spigel, L., and D. Mann, ed. *Private Screenings: Television and the Female Consumer*. Minneapolis: University of Minnesota Press.

Spivak, G. C., and E. Rooney. 1989. "In a Word, Interview." *differences* 1, no. 2: 151–84.

Stafford, S. 2001. "Epistemology for Sale." *Social Epistemology* 15, no. 3: 215–30.

Stanley, J., A. Chambers, D. H. Murray, and J. Wheelwright, ed. 1995. *Bold in Her Breeches: Women Pirates across the Ages*. London and San Francisco: Pandora.

Star, S. L. 1995. "Introduction." *Ecologies of Knowledge: Work and Politics in Science and Technology*, 1–35. Albany: SUNY Press.

Stewart, D. C. 1999. *The PBS Companion: A History of Public Television*. New York: TV Books.

Strathern, M. 2000. *Audit Cultures: Anthropological Studies in Accountability, Ethics, and the Academy*. London and New York: Routledge.

Suchman, L. 2000. "Located Accountabilities in Technology Production." Paper presented at Sawyer Seminar on Heterarchies, Santa Fe Institute, October.

Suissa, S., J. Brown, and A. Graham. 2001. "Reality Check: The Triumphs and Pitfalls of 'Living History.'" Paper presented at the World Congress of History Producers, Boston, October 19–22.

Tamdgidi, M. H. 2006. "Proceedings of the Third Annual Social Theory Forum, March 27–28, University of Massachusetts, Boston." In "Re-membering Anzaldúa." Special issue, *Human Architecture* 4 (Summer).

Taylor, T. L. 2006. *Play between Worlds: Exploring Online Game Culture*. Cambridge: MIT Press.

Thompson, J. 2004. *War Games: Inside the World of 20th-Century War Reenactors*. Washington, DC: Smithsonian Institution.

Tilden, F. 1957. *Interpreting our Heritage: Principles and Practices for Visitor Services in Parks, Museums, and Historic Places*. Chapel Hill: University of North Carolina Press.

Truettner, W. H., and N. K. Anderson, ed. 1991. *The West as America: Reinterpreting Images of the Frontier, 1820–1920*. Washington, DC: Smithsonian Institution.

Turman, S. 1994. "Gaumont: The World's First Film Company Is Gearing up for Its 100th Anniversary in 1995." *Films in Review* 45, nos. 1–2: 22–25.

Turner, F. 2006. *From Counterculture to Cyberculture: Stewart Brand, the Whole Earth Network, and the Rise of Digital Utopianism*. Chicago: University of Chicago Press.

Vann, K., and G. Bowker. 2001. "Instrumentalizing the Truth of Practice." *Social Epistemology* 15, no. 3: 247–62.

Veverka, J. A. 1994. *Interpretive Master Planning: For Parks, Historic Sites, Forests, Zoos, and Related Tourism Sites*. Helena: Falcon.

Vickers, J. 1997. "'[U]framed in Open, Unmapped Fields': Teaching and the Practice of Interdisciplinarity." *Arachne* 4, no. 2: 11–42.

Vise, D. A., and M. Malseed. 2005. *The Google Story*. New York: Delacorte.

Wasko, J. 1995. *Hollywood in the Information Age: Beyond the Silver Screen*. Austin: University of Texas Press.

Weisbrot, R. 1998. *Xena, Warrior Princess: The Official Guide to the Xenaverse*. New York: Doubleday.

Wenger, E. 1998. *Communities of Practice: Learning, Meaning, and Identity*. Cambridge: Cambridge University Press.

Weston, K. 2002. *Gender in Real Time: Power and Transience in a Visual Age*. New York: Routledge.

Wheelwright, J. 1989. *Amazons and Military Maids: Women Who Dressed as Men in the Pursuit of Life, Liberty and Happiness*. London: Pandora.

Whitehead, A. N., and B. Russell. 1910. *Principia Mathematica*. Cambridge: Cambridge University Press.

Yegül, F. K. 1976. "The Marble Court of Sardis and Historical Reconstruction." *Journal of Field Archaeology* 3, no. 2: 169–94.

———. 1992. *Baths and Bathing in Classical Antiquity*. Cambridge: MIT Press.

Yegül, F. K., M. C. Bolgil, and C. Foss. 1986. *The Bath-Gymnasium Complex at Sardis*. Cambridge: Harvard University Press.

Zoidis, M. 1999. "The New History in an Old Museum." *Journal of Social History* 33, no. 1: 196–97.

Zoll, A. 2002. *Gladiatrix: The True Story of History's Unknown Woman Warrior*. New York: Berkley Boulevard.

Figures in italics.

KATIE KING is associate professor of women's studies at the University
of Maryland.

Library of Congress Cataloging-in-Publication Data

King, Katie, 1952–
Networked reenactments : stories transdisciplinary
knowledges tell / Katie King ; foreword by Donna Haraway.
p. cm.
Includes bibliographical references and index.
ISBN 978-0-8223-5054-5 (cloth : alk. paper)
ISBN 978-0-8223-5072-9 (pbk. : alk. paper)
1. Mass media and culture.
2. Mass media and globalization.
3. Popular culture and globalization.
4. Mass media—Social aspects.
5. Globalization—Social aspects.
I. Title.
P94.6.K57   2012
306.4′2—dc23   2011027457